H. V. MORTON

In the Steps
of the Master

DODD, MEAD & COMPANY, INC.
NEW YORK

First published by Rich & Cowan Ltd 1934
First published by Methuen & Co. 1937
Paperback edition first published 1984
in the United States of America by
Dodd, Mead & Company, Inc.
Copyright 1934 by Dodd, Mead & Company, Inc.
Copyright renewed 1962 by H. V. Morton

Printed in Great Britain

ISBN 0–396–08415–X

INTRODUCTION

THE story I tell in this book is a simple one. It describes the adventures of a man who went to the Holy Land to see the places associated with the life of Christ and to find out what new light the historian and the archæologist have cast upon the world of the Gospels.

Enquiring pilgrims have made the same journey from Byzantine times until to-day, and, as the pilgrimage map of the Holy Land does not alter, such a journey is much the same as it was during the Middle Ages. The thoughts also called up in the mind of the pilgrim on the Mount of Olives and in the Garden of Gethsemane, conditioned of course by the mental climate of his age, are fundamentally the same from time to time. As long as Bethlehem, Jerusalem, Nazareth and the lakeside of Galilee remain, the story told in this book will not date no matter what territorial or political changes occur between Dan and Beersheba.

Spectacular changes have indeed occurred in the Holy Land since I went there to write this book; but they call for no alteration in the text. Palestine, or more strictly a portion of it, is now the Jewish Republic of Israel, a small state that is working out its destiny in a dangerous and threatening world.

It will be interesting briefly to set down the changes, so impressive when viewed against the centuries of inertia which preceded them, that have occurred in Palestine in our time. When the Twentieth Century opened Palestine and Syria had been under Moslem rule since A.D. 634 except for a short period of eighty-eight years (A.D. 1099-1187) during the Crusades. Caliph and Sultan followed each other for centuries, culminating in five hundred years of Turkish rule. When the first world war broke out in 1914, Palestine had participated for five centuries in the picturesque lethargy of the Ottoman Empire.

In 1914 the Allies hoped that Turkey would remain neutral : indeed as the price of her neutrality Britain, France, and even her old enemy Russia, guaranteed the absolute integrity of her dominions, an offer which Sir Winston Churchill described in his book, *World Crisis*, as " the most favourable offer ever made to any government in history ". Despite this,

Turkey joined Germany and plunged into a war which ended in the disruption of her already moribund empire and the abolition of the Sultanate.

British forces invaded Palestine under Field-Marshal Lord Allenby, while that romantic character, Lawrence of Arabia, organised an Arab revolt on the flanks. The Turks were driven out of Palestine in a battle on the plain of Armageddon (Megiddo), and in December 1917, Lord Allenby, on foot and followed by his staff, walked into the Old City of Jerusalem, the first Christian conqueror since the Crusades.

The end of military rule was succeeded by twenty-five years of British rule under a Mandate from the League of Nations. This administration had been in existence for ten years when I went to Palestine to write this book, and the Palestine reflected in these pages, with its successive British High Commissioners in occupation of Government House, Jerusalem, privately comparing their lot with that of Pontius Pilate, with a British-trained police force, a British army, British law-givers and road-makers, is an important epoch in the story of the Holy Land. It was the awakening of this country from the administrative sleep of centuries and no doubt the Jewish State of Israel owes more to the administrators of that time than perhaps it is yet willing to acknowledge.

The period of the Mandate was violent and distressing. Pledged to observe the Balfour Declaration, which decreed that Britain " viewed with favour " a National Home for the Jews in Palestine, and at the same time to safeguard the territorial rights and national aspirations of the Arabs, Britain found herself in an impossible dilemma, shot at by both sides and unable to move one way or the other without causing offence to either Jews or Arabs, and with American opinion very much on the side of the Zionists.

The origin of the Balfour Declaration, by which hundreds of thousands of Jewish immigrants were admitted into Palestine, is worth recalling. Mr. Lloyd George tells in his *War Memoirs* (Vol. II, pages 584–6) that while he was Minister of Munitions in 1916 the British supply of cordite was imperilled by the difficulty of importing from the United States sufficient wood to make wood alcohol, from which at that time cordite was derived. He was advised to consult a brilliant but then unknown professor of chemistry at Manchester University, Dr. Chaim Weizmann, who later became the first President of Israel and died in 1952.

Lloyd George placed the problem before Dr. Weizmann, who promised to work day and night in an attempt to discover some new process of obtaining wood alcohol.   In a few weeks he

ISRAEL
AND NEIGHBOURING
STATES, 1952

0 10 20 30 40 50 60 70 80 90 100
Miles

returned, saying, "The problem is solved."   After a study of the micro-flora existing on maize and other cereals, also of those occurring in the soil, he had succeeded in isolating an organic substance capable of transforming the starch of cereals into a mixture of acetone butyl alcohol. Thus the British supply of cordite was assured.

"The one thing he [Weizmann] really cared about was Zionism," wrote Lloyd George. "He was convinced that in the victory of the Allies alone was there any hope for his people. . . . When our difficulties were solved through Dr. Weizmann's genius, I said to him, 'You have rendered great service to the State and I should like to ask the Prime Minister to recommend you to His Majesty for some honour.' He said, 'There is nothing I want for myself.' 'But is there nothing we can do as a recognition of your valuable assistance to the country?' I asked. He replied, 'Yes, I would like you to do something for my people.' He then explained his aspirations as to the repatriation of the Jews to the sacred land they had made famous. That was the fount and origin of the famous declaration about the National Home for the Jews in Palestine."

Dr. Weizmann remained at the head of Jewish affairs in Palestine during the troubled period of the Mandate and when this time ended at midnight on 14 May 1948, he was elected the first President of the Jewish State. The day after the new republic had been proclaimed Arab forces invaded Israel from Syria and the Lebanon in the north, from Iraq and Transjordan on the east, and from Egypt on the south. The new state was encircled by Moslem foes and for the first time since the Roman age a Jewish army fought in Palestine. The Arab–Jewish War dragged on for many months until, under the auspices of the United Nations, a truce was arranged in January 1949 under four separate armistice agreements which at the time of writing have not yet crystallised into peace.

The frontiers of Israel remain as they were at the time of the four armistices of 1949. During the war the Jordanian Arabs penetrated into Jerusalem, where they still remain, and this territory has now been officially incorporated within the Hashimite Kingdom. This means that Jerusalem itself is a frontier. The Old City belongs to the Arabs and the New to the Jews. There is at the moment no contact between the two parts of Jerusalem, except under the guidance of the United Nations officials who occupy old Government House. Similar inconvenient and illogical divisions are to be observed elsewhere. Jericho and Bethlehem are Arab, the Dead Sea is split up between Arab and Jew and the Egyptians occupy a small strip of coastal territory south of Gaza. Such are some of the anomalies of the Israeli frontiers at the moment, but he would be a bold man who would say that such an arrangement is a permanent one.

Corresponding changes have occurred in the northern territory of Syria which was until the outbreak of the second world war ruled by France under a League of Nations Mandate. With the collapse of France in 1940 this territory became two Arab republics: Syria, with its capital at Damascus, and a narrow coastal strip a hundred and twenty miles long north of Israel, the Republic of Lebanon, with its capital at Beirut.

During a recent visit to the Holy Land, I was able to compare the freedom of movement which I enjoyed when writing this book with the restrictions now imposed by the Jordan–Israel frontier. Young people accept the situation as a matter of course; others, like myself, remember with nostalgia the ease of travel, and the air of friendly co-operation which existed when this part of the world was administered by Britain and France. That was the perfect moment to have visited the Holy Land, and I hope that something of its atmosphere has found its way into the pages that follow.

I found Old Jerusalem practically unchanged, save for the fact that the Arabs have expelled the Jews and consequently the Wailing Wall is always deserted. Also, I could never see, and hear, without a smile, that the up-to-date *muezzin* does not always ascend the minaret to utter the call to prayer, but does so with the aid of a microphone and a loud speaker! In such subtle ways the elements of change storm these massive ramparts of conservatism.

As I travelled about on both sides of the frontier, I was impressed by the striking new churches which now cover nearly all the shrines in the custody of the Franciscans. This imposing architectural scheme was just beginning when I wrote this book: now it is almost complete. The churches are the work of one dedicated man, an Italian architect named Antonio Barluzzi, who died in 1960. They are remarkable for their originality and the variety of their design, which owe less to any architectural style or tradition than to the piety of their creator. All Barluzzi's shrines attempt to express an emotional response to the Gospel story. For example, one should compare the majestic gloom of his basilica in the Garden of Gethsemane with the joyful little Christmas carol of a church in the Shepherd's Fields, at Bethlehem. The same contrast may be seen

in his Church of the Visitation at Ain Karem and his basilica
on Mount Tabor; and, again, between those two churches and
the Church of the Beatitudes in Galilee.

I believe that Barluzzi will be recognised as a genius in years
to come, though, strangely enough, little has yet been written
about his work or his life. His story is a remarkable one.
Already a practised architect when the first world war ended,
he felt a call to the priesthood, but his confessor in Rome told
him to go to Palestine and rebuild the shrines. While he was
doing so, he lived as a Franciscan with the Franciscans, and
subjected himself to the discipline of the order. He was not
interested in fame or fortune, and immediately money came to
him, he gave it away. His one ambition was to complete his
act of devotion—for such his churches are—by designing the
new basilica at Nazareth for which he had prepared a plan.
In 1958 he learnt that his design had been rejected by the
authorities. During the night he suffered a heart attack which
brought on cerebral deafness and pulmonary emphysema.
Desperately ill, poor and old—he was then seventy-four—he
sought refuge with the Franciscans in Rome, and was given a
cell in the Terra Sancta Delegation, near the Lateran. There
I saw him a few weeks before his death in 1960. I found it a
painful ordeal. He was a magnificent old man, tall, gaunt and
grey-haired, but suffering had transformed him into a dying
saint by El Greco or Ribera. His memory had gone and he
was blind. Conversation was not possible; and all I could
do was to stand at the foot of his bed and, remembering the
beauty he had brought to the Holy Land, to wonder why the
life of this devout Christian should end in such martyrdom.
Soon after my visit, the Franciscan who had taken me to see
Barluzzi wrote to tell me of his death on December 14, 1960.

Every visitor to the Holy Land should know where, and on
which side of the frontier, his churches are to be found. His
chief works are:

In Jordan: The Latin Chapel of Calvary in the Church
of the Holy Sepulchre, Jerusalem; the Basilica of Gethsemane, on the Mount of Olives; the Church of St. Lazarus,
Bethany; the Chapel of the Shepherds, Bethlehem; the
Church of the Good Shepherd, Jericho.

In Israel: The Church of the Visitation, Ain Karem;
the Basilica of Mount Tabor; the Church of the Beatitudes,
Galilee.

The modern pilgrim enjoys a privilege which was, of course, denied to me when I wrote this book. That is a sight of the Dead Sea Scrolls, which have been discovered in the mountain caves above the Dead Sea at various times since 1947, and are now to be seen (in Jordan) in the Palestine Archaeological Museum in Old Jerusalem, and (in Israel) in the Hebrew University in New Jerusalem.

H. V. M.

April 1962

CONTENTS

IN THE STEPS OF THE MASTER

ILLUSTRATIONS

*Except where otherwise acknowledged, the illustrations are from
photographs by the Author.*

PALESTINE
IN THE TIME OF
CHRIST
SHOWING ROADS

SCALE 0   10   20   30   40   50 MILES

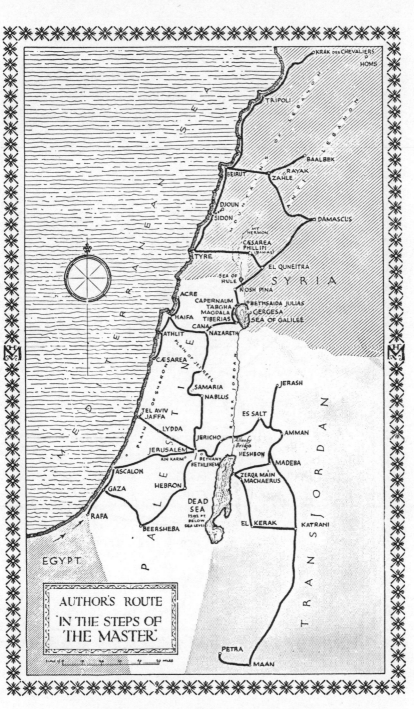

KRAK des CHEVALIERS
HOMS
TRIPOLI
BAALBEK
BEIRUT
RAYAK
ZAHLE
DJOUN
SIDON
DAMASCUS
MT HERMON
CÆSAREA PHILLIPI (BANIAS)
TYRE
EL QUNEITRA
SEA OF HULE
SYRIA
ACRE
ROSH PINA
CAPERNAUM
TABGHA
MAGDALA
TIBERIAS
BETHSAIDA JULIAS
GERGESA
SEA OF GALILEE
HAIFA
CANA
NAZARETH
ATHLIT
PLAIN OF JEZREEL
CÆSAREA
JERASH
SAMARIA
NABLUS
TEL AVIV
JAFFA
ES SALT
LYDDA
AMMAN
JERICHO
Allenby Bridge
JERUSALEM
AIN KARIM
BETHANY
BETHLEHEM
HESHBON
MADEBA
ASCALON
ZERQA MAIN
MACHAERUS
GAZA
HEBRON
DEAD SEA
1292 FT BELOW SEA LEVEL
RAFA
EL KERAK
KATRANI
BEERSHEBA
EGYPT
PETRA
MAAN
TRANSJORDAN

AUTHOR'S ROUTE
IN THE STEPS OF
THE MASTER

SCALE 10   20   30   40   50 MILES

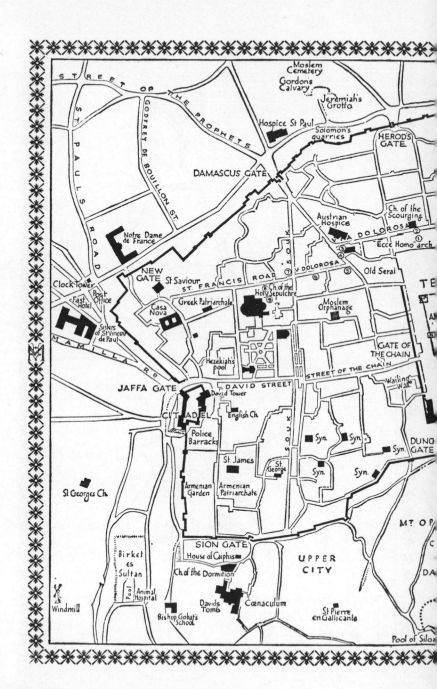

STREET OF THE PROPHETS

Moslem Cemetery
Gordon's Calvary
Jeremiah's Grotto

ST PAULS ROAD

GODFREY DE BOUILLON ST

Hospice St Paul
Solomon's quarries

HEROD'S GATE

DAMASCUS GATE

Ch. of the Scourging

Austrian Hospice

VIA DOLOROSA

Ecce Homo arch

Notre Dame de France

Old Serai

NEW GATE

St Saviour

ST FRANCIS ROAD

V. DOLOROSA

Clock Tower

Casa Nova

Greek Patriarchate

Ch. of the Holy Sepulchre

Moslem Orphanage

TE

Post Office

East Hotel

Sisters of St Vincent de Paul

MAMILLA RD

Hezekiah's pool

GATE OF THE CHAIN

STREET OF THE CHAIN

Wailing Wall

JAFFA GATE

DAVID STREET

David Tower

CITADEL

English Ch.

Police Barracks

Syn.

Syn.

DUNG GATE

St James

St George

Syn.

Syn.

St Georges Ch.

Armenian Garden

Armenian Patriarchate

Syn.

MT OF

SION GATE

House of Caiphas

UPPER CITY

DA

Birket es Sultan Pool

Ch. of the Dormition

Windmill

Animal Hospital

Bishop Gobat's School

Davids Tomb

Cœnaculum

St Pierre en Gallicante

Pool of Siloam

xviii

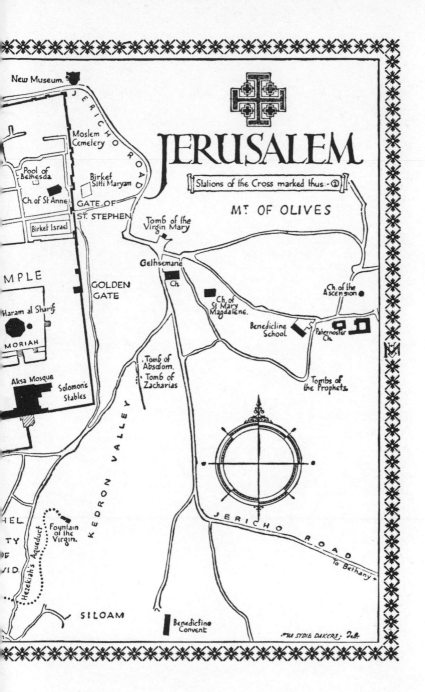

New Museum.

JERICHO ROAD

Moslem Cemetery

Pool of Bethesda

Birket Sitti Maryam

Ch. of St Anne

GATE OF ST. STEPHEN

Birket Israel

Tomb of the Virgin Mary

JERUSALEM

Stations of the Cross marked thus :- ②

MT. OF OLIVES

Gethsemane Ch.

MPLE

GOLDEN GATE

Haram al Sharif

MORIAH

Aksa Mosque

Solomon's Stables

Ch. of St Mary Magdalene.

Ch. of the Ascension

Benedictine School.

Paternoster Ch.

Tomb of Absalom.

Tomb of Zacharias

Tombs of the Prophets.

KEDRON VALLEY

HEL

TY

E

ID.

Fountain of the Virgin.

Hezekiah's Aqueduct

JERICHO ROAD

to Bethany

SILOAM

Benedictine Convent

THE SYDIE DAKERS; Jult.

CHAPTER ONE

Describes a journey to the Holy Land and an impression of Jeru-
salem. I visit the Holy Sepulchre, the Mount of Olives and the
Garden of Gethsemane.

§ I

AS the sun goes down, a stillness falls over Egypt.
Water channels that cross the fields turn to the colour
of blood, then to bright yellow that fades into silver.
The palm trees might be cut from black paper and pasted
against the incandescence of the sky. Brown hawks that
hang all day above the sugar-cane and the growing wheat
are seen no more and, one by one, the stars burn over the
sandhills and lie caught in the stiff fronds of the date
palms.

It is this moment which remains for ever as a memory of
Egypt, a moment when day is over and night has not yet
unfolded her wings, a strange between-time in whose tremendous hush the earth seems listening for a message from
the sky. The fierce day dies and the sand loses its heat and
all things are for a brief space without shadow.

During this hush I stepped into a little boat on the Suez
Canal. The water that fell from the oars was red, but
before we had crossed the narrow canal to El Kantara
it was silver, and the moon was shining. The little station
was silent and deserted among the sandhills. Moonlight
silvered the rails that ran north across the Sinai Desert
into Palestine, and all around was a green stillness stretching
out into far spaces under the stars. Kantara means " bridge "
in Arabic. Long before man left any record of his wanderings, it was the crossing place between Egypt and Palestine,
a sandy strip over which the caravans could pass dry-shod
between Lake Menzaleh and Lake Timsah. Joseph passed
this way when he was carried into Egypt. It was the way
the Holy Family fled from the wrath of Herod.

The minutes slipped into hours as I waited for the train to Jerusalem. But I liked waiting there, listening to the queer sounds of the night, the distant barking of dogs in the desert, the harsh grumbling of camels crouched in the moonlight of the station yard. The seven days at sea were all forgotten now. It seemed that in some magic way I had been carried straight from the coldness of an English February into this strange green light on the desert's edge. It was wonderful to be standing at El Kantara waiting for the train to Judæa, and I thought that when this feeling of surprise is no longer possible the time has come to give up wandering.

The train, when it arrived, lay for a long time in the station, as if working up enough courage for its nightly plunge into the sand. Then it slipped away from El Kantara and went out into the moonlight.

§ 2

The sun had not yet risen. The train pounded over a flat green plain that reminded me vaguely of the Lincolnshire Fens. I was weary, and my eyes and clothes were full of sand that had blown in as we crossed the desert during the night. Some little way off to the left I could make out the rise and fall of sandhills and, beyond them, a sullen line of steel that was the Mediterranean Sea.

There is a nightmare quality about a train journey through a strange country in the half light before the dawn. You want to stop in order to discover the reality of some half-discerned object, to make sure that a stone was not a man, or a man a stone; but you are swept on relentlessly as in a dream, inert, interested, but unsatisfied.

The land, drained of colour, seemed sinister and dead. There was nothing of the " gorgeous East " about it. The few Arabs who stood beside the road, with their heads tied up in white cloths, might have been the survivors of some disaster. They gazed dully at the train, grasping ropes to which were attached shabby and reluctant camels who preserve for ever on their faces a sententiousness that must always remind the traveller of a misunderstood and acidulated Victorian aunt. But there were strange exciting moments. Once, moving high on an embankment and out-lined against the sky, I saw a file of burdened camels plodding slowly into the dawn. And I knew that in this brief flash, before the train went past, I had seen the spirit of this road: for the railway to Jerusalem, which was made by Allenby's troops during the War, follows an ancient route. It runs over the ageless caravan road to and from Egypt, and it was along this road that Joseph was led into captivity. It was the road over which the first great Jewish financier, Solomon, sent his sandalwood and his spices to the markets at Memphis. It was a road that led everywhere: to Damascus in the north, to the desert city of Petra in the east, to Egypt in the south.

On the same embankment I saw some Arabs muffled and shrouded in the cold air. First came a donkey with a woman and a child upon its back and behind them strode a man. And I remembered again that this was the way Joseph and Mary fled with a Child into Egypt.

We came to a station where I read, with a thrill of interest, the word " Gaza." And now, as we went onward, I saw a gathering tumult in the east. A white, palpitating light was filling the sky. It was like something approaching at great speed, a mighty army with its chariots and its horsemen. Swords of light thrust their way upward, catching stray clouds and turning them to banners of pink and gold. Then, like an orange flung into the air, the sun leapt up, fully armed, into the sky; it was warm, and the dead earth was instantly, vividly, and rather violently, alive. Donkeys stand-ing in stony fields stretched forth their necks and bared their teeth in salute to the new day, cocks mounted on the roofs of mud houses crowed their welcome, women with brown faces and bare feet crouched over little fires, children, their smooth little chests bare in the sunlight, stood in the shadows of the olive trees, and from villages hedged about with prickly pear the shepherds led their flocks to pasture.

A few miles to the left I saw a blinding glare of sandhills topped by a blue line of sea. I stood up and craned my neck, but I could see nothing, although I knew that some-where in those hills lay all that is left of Ascalon. " Tell it not in Gath, publish it not in the streets of Ascalon." " There is a sound of trade, a clinking of shekels, about the city's very name," said George Adam Smith, and no doubt the streets of Ascalon were dark bazaars in which the merest whisper became a fact.

And as I looked towards the now barren sandhills of Ascalon, where no whisper is handed on to-day but that of the wind blowing from the sea, something of the sadness of this country came to me, the sadness of a land that has known too much and is not permitted to forget the things that happened long ago.

We stopped at Lydda, where St. George, who presides over the destiny of England, Portugal and Aragon, was buried after his martyrdom in the year 303. Then one half of the train went on to Jaffa and the other half went for a little while to the south before, turning eastward, it climbed into the mountains of Judæa.

The train climbs so slowly that Arab boys run beside it, holding bunches of red anemones which they offer to the passengers. The mountains are scorched and brown. The roads are white ribbons that slip in and out of the hills. Camels, absurdly large, draw diminutive ploughs sullenly and, it seems, reluctantly, over the meagre fields. Families who might be on a journey from Deuteronomy to the Book of Kings walk behind laden donkeys; here and there a fine old patriarch, who reminds one of Abraham, leans on his staff to watch the daily train go past.

As the train climbs and winds into the hills towards the mountain capital of Jerusalem, you are aware of something fierce and cruel in the air. You have the same feeling in Spain when the train crosses the Sierra de Guadarrama towards the mountain capital of Madrid. But Judæa is fiercer than anything in Europe. It is a striped, tigerish country, crouched in the sun, tense with a terrific vitality and sullen and dispassionate with age.

The fierceness of the parched gullies, the harshness of the barren hill-tops, the passion of the caked earth where lizards dart and flash, and the burning cruelty of waterless valleys, are concentrated and made visible upon the highest of the hills. And the name of this materialisation is Jerusalem.

The train came wearily to rest. I stepped out on a platform that bore the word " Jerusalem " in three languages: English, Arabic and Hebrew. Article 23 of the Mandate for Palestine decrees that " English, Arabic and Hebrew shall be the official languages of Palestine. Any statement or inscription in Arabic on stamps or money in Palestine shall be repeated in Hebrew, and any statement or inscription in Hebrew shall be repeated in Arabic."

As soon as you go out of the station you notice that signposts, proclamations, motor signals and such-like are trilingual, and you realise that history is repeating itself in the strangest way. In the imperial archives of ancient Rome there must have been a clause very like Article 23 of our Palestine Mandate. In the time of Christ the three official languages were Latin, Greek and Hebrew. And as you go into Jerusalem, glancing at the trilingualism everywhere, the words of St. John come into the mind:

" And Pilate wrote a title, and put it on the cross. And the writing was, Jesus of Nazareth the King of the Jews. This title then read many of the Jews: for the place where Jesus was crucified was nigh to the city: and it was written in Hebrew, and Greek, and Latin."

§ 3

I went to an hotel not far from the Jaffa Gate where an Arab, who was dressed like a Turk in a musical comedy, carried up my bags. An Armenian registered me. A German chambermaid unlocked my bedroom door.

It was an attractive room with a writing-table and a good light over the bed, and it had a little balcony overlooking a narrow street and the walls of a convent school. Through the windows I could see the nuns moving about a large, bare dormitory, making two rows of little beds.

I went straight out to find my way to the Church of the Holy Sepulchre. I had been studying a street plan of Jerusalem for weeks, and wondered whether I could find my way alone through the twisting lanes of the old city. As soon as I appeared in the Jaffa Road I was surrounded by eager, whispering men, wearing European suits and the red tarbush which used to be the sign of Turkish citizenship.

" You come with me to the Holy Sepulchre! " they whispered. " I show you everything! "

There seemed to me to be a definite blasphemy in their invitations, so I shook them off and went on alone. They followed me like figures in a nightmare, whispering, and once even daring to pull me by the sleeve. I had to make it very clear that I disliked them before they disappeared from sight. I was distressed to find that the real Jerusalem, full of donkeys and camels and men selling oranges, was very different from the clear street plan that I knew by heart! I came to the Jaffa Gate and saw a great sweep of the city wall running to the south. I passed in and entered the old city. I saw to my right the huge, square tower, known as David's Tower, which is in reality all that is left of Herod's great tower, Phasael. I saw it with the emotion which any relic of the time of Christ must inspire, whether the observer be a devout Christian or merely a devout historian. Those huge yellow stones at the base of the tower existed in the Jerusalem of the Crucifixion. Perhaps His eyes saw them.

Round this tower and near the Gate surged an extraordinary crowd, which seemed to me, so newly from the West, to be a perfect microcosm of the East, and I looked at it with the delight of a child at a Christmas circus.

I could distinguish peasants from the villages, the *fellahin*, born farmers and ploughmen, who are a queer mixture of cunning, simplicity and violence. I remembered a story someone once told me about the Palestinian *fellah*. It was that God, at the making of the world, sent out His angel with the gift of Intellect, and gave to each man his share. There were no complaints. He then sent out the angel with the gift of Fortune. And every man grumbled. He followed this with the world's allowance of Stupidity, and the angel, carrying this gigantic burden, encountered the *fellah*, to whom he had already given his dole of intellect and fortune.

"O angel," said the *fellah*, "what is it you bring this time?"

"O *fellah*, it is Stupidity!" said the angel.

"O angel," cried the *fellah*, assuming an avaricious expression, "give me the lot, because I am a poor man with a large family!"

So the angel gave him the world's stupidity.

It is an unkind story, but I feel that it could not have been composed about anyone who was not, in spite of everything, rather decent. I am sure that there must have been a proportion of Simplicity mixed with the angel's burden.

Then, quite distinct from the *fellah*, was the Bedouin Arab. Although he walked in rags, he moved like a king of the earth. He despises the *fellah* and his spade. The Bedouin is a man of ancestry and freedom, of flocks and herds, and tents which he calls "houses of hair." In him Abraham lives on into the modern world.

There were the town Arabs in European clothes and tarbushes. There were Armenians, Franciscan friars, and white Dominicans. There were Greek priests, who are square-bearded like Assyrian kings and stride through the crowd wearing rusty cassocks and high round black hats. Strangest of all were the queer old Jews with their long, straggling beards, and curls of hair tapping against their temples. These Ashkenezim Jews, wearing velvet gabardines and large, fur-rimmed hats, moved through the crowd, in it but not of it, silently, and, it seemed, timidly, unreadable men locked away in the mysterious depths of their own spiritual history. There were the Sephardic Jews, also Orthodox, who wore low, wide-rimmed black felt hats, and many of them were pale, spectacled and peering, with thin, fair beards.

The Oriental possesses the gift of intense passion and of an equally intense lassitude. Arabs sat dreamily under the awning of a café, sucking at hookahs; others, strung up to a high pitch of excitement, expended in the purchase of a handful of dates, or a lettuce, more passion than a Westerner expends in a month.

I dived into David Street, which leads down towards the

Church of the Holy Sepulchre. This street is typical of the lanes of old Jerusalem, which no motor traffic can ever invade. It descends in a series of steps, with a line of booths on each side. It is so narrow, and so packed with people of all kinds, of all ages and of all sizes, that you often stand helplessly with a donkey's head over your shoulder and a sack of millet against your face. There is nothing to do but to wait cheerfully and hope that those who are holding up the procession will move on. David Street is dark and cool. Sometimes the sun, slanting down into its depths, falls in a dazzling pool on a pile of oranges, melons, cucumbers and artichokes, or on a pile of the least edible looking fish you can imagine, or, more pleasantly, upon a rotund collarless person who, sitting behind a chromatic barricade of Syrian silk, every now and then lifts to his mouth a brown, ringed hand holding a gold-tipped cigarette.

In spite of all my maps and plans I confessed myself hopelessly lost in this bright chaos, but I walked on with resolution, knowing that if I appeared to hesitate for one instant a pack of guides would be on my heels. But it was not a pleasant feeling because, when I had left the crowd behind, I found myself in dark, narrow lanes faced with scabrous walls, broken only by dark openings to cellars or to dank little courtyards into which cats darted with the speed and terror of wild animals. The thought crossed my mind that anyone who ventures alone into these lanes without a knowledge of Arabic deserves a knife in the back. But, miraculously it seemed to me, I came to a cross-road where donkeys were plodding along with sacks of wheat for the grindstone. I looked up and read on a blue plate let into the wall, *Via Dolorosa*.

" If I follow this," I thought, " it is bound to lead me to Calvary, which is inside the Holy Sepulchre."

And no sooner had I thought it than I felt ashamed of my thought. I had blundered on the Way of the Cross and I had treated it as if it were any ordinary street. I felt ill at ease. I set this down because it is so typical of one's first thoughts in Jerusalem. The mind, accustomed to the divine Christ of Western churches, encounters in Jerusalem the memory of Jesus the Man, the

Jesus who ate and slept and became weary, who drove the hucksters from the Temple, who drank the cup of death on Golgotha. At home one always thinks of Jesus in heaven, on the right hand of God the Father, but in Jerusalem one thinks of Him walking the dusty white roads, and one's intelligence is perpetually rejecting or accepting certain places that tradition associates with His manhood. As God, He is everywhere, but in Jerusalem centuries of piety have competed to place His footsteps on this stone and that road. It was almost with a shock that I realised that the *Via Dolorosa* could be a real road with men and women and animals upon it.

I do not know for certain whether the *Via Dolorosa* is really the road on which Jesus carried the Cross, and neither, I think, does anyone else. Its route depends on the situation of Pilate's judgment hall and the unknown position of the Gate Genath. But it does not seem to me to matter very much whether it is the actual road or a memorial to the actual road. What is important is that men and women who have walked upon it have met there the vision of Christ.

The *Via Dolorosa* led to a gate in a wall. On the other side was a large courtyard steeped in the morning sun. It was quiet and peaceful after the crowded lanes outside. At the far end rose up the fine façade of the Church of the Holy Sepulchre, which is to-day almost as the Crusaders left it. A stone seat runs along one side of the courtyard. I sat there for a moment and watched the people going in and coming out of the church.

In the middle of the courtyard was a little stall hung with rosaries and brightly coloured pictures of the life of Christ. A Copt in a blue robe bought many of these, which he carefully handed round to his family: a woman in black, two small, brown boys, a little girl, and an infant of about three, who looked wonderingly at the pictures and dropped them on the pavement.

The strangest people went into the gloom of the church and came from it into the sharp sunshine of the courtyard. There were many monks wearing white habits and khaki sun hats. There were Arab women. There were incongruous parties from cruising steamers, shepherded by hustling, irreverent guides, and there were several old shepherds in sheepskin jackets and patched-up rags, who reverently removed their slippers in the courtyard and walked into the church barefoot. This was strange. The Jews used to go barefoot into Solomon's Temple and the Moslems remove their slippers in the mosque, and here were native Christians observing the same custom.

On the pavement just outside the door of the Holy Sepulchre is the gravestone of an Englishman, Philip d'Aubigny, who was one of the *nobiles homines* mentioned in the Magna Charta as a member of the council whose advice was taken by King John. Afterwards d'Aubigny became tutor of King Henry III and Governor of the Channel Isles. There is, I believe, an Act of Assize in existence in Jersey signed by him with the same coat of arms—four fusils in fess—as that on the gravestone in the courtyard of the Holy Sepulchre. It seems that this English knight came to the Holy Land in the train of the excommunicated Emperor Frederick II in 1229, and saw what must have been one of the most remarkable sights in the history of Jerusalem. Frederick II captured the city without striking a blow and, marching into the Holy Sepulchre, took the crown from the altar and placed it on his head with the remark, " I said I would come; and here I am."

D'Aubigny died in Jerusalem in 1236, and his grave has been preserved by the lucky accident that for years the divan of the Moslem gatekeepers was set over his gravestone.

I thought that d'Aubigny's grave and the two young British police in blue uniforms who stood a few yards from it were extraordinarily eloquent of the strange fortunes of Jerusalem.

I noticed that just inside the porch of the church, to the left hand as you go in, was a wooden divan spread with carpets and cushions. On this reclined a calm, aristocratic-looking man with a neatly-trimmed beard, a turban, and a long back robe. He was one of the Moslem doorkeepers to whose family the task of locking up the Holy Sepulchre had been entrusted by Saladin.

The Tomb of Jesus Christ is a small cell lined with marble, six and a half feet long, and six feet wide. Only two or, at the most, three people can enter at one time. On the right hand is a cracked slab of white marble, three feet in height, covering the rock on which He was placed after the Crucifixion.

From the marble roof of this tiny cell hang lamps which belong in various proportions to the Greek, Latin, Armenian and Coptic Churches. The Roman Catholics are known in Palestine as the Latins. Standing at the head of the marble slab was an impassive Greek monk with a soft, spade-shaped black beard. He wore a black cassock and a high, black, rimless hat, beneath which his hair was pinned at the back in a round bun. He held a bunch of candles in his hand and, as the pilgrims entered, gave one to them, which they lit from others burning in the tomb.

I could see a pilgrim kneeling at the sepulchre, so I waited in the small, dark ante-chamber outside.

Becoming impatient, I bent down and, peeping through the low entrance, saw that the man inside was an old, bent peasant in ragged clothes, his feet in a pair of huge shoes made of felt. He was a Bulgarian who had come over in a pilgrim ship, as the Russians used to come, and he had probably been saving up all his life for that moment.

He was kneeling at the marble slab and kissing it repeatedly, while tears ran down the deep wrinkles of his face and fell on the stone. His large, rough hands, the nails split and black with labour, touched the marble gently with a smoothing motion; then he would clasp them in prayer and cross himself.

He prayed aloud in a trembling voice, but I could not understand what he was saying. Then, taking from his pocket various pieces of dirty paper and a length of ribbon, he rubbed them gently on the Tomb and put them back in his pocket.

I thought there might perhaps be room for me, so I bent my head and entered the Sepulchre. The Greek monk, the kneeling peasant and myself quite filled the small space. And it would have been all right if the old man had continued to kneel, but, disturbed perhaps by my entrance, he rose up, the tears still falling, and whispered something to me. We were now standing, our chests touching, and, looking into his eyes, I realised that I was looking at real happiness.

This was his life's dream. I had never seen such happiness before. Never in all my life have I beheld peace and contentment written so clearly on a human face. I would have given the world to have been able to speak to him, but we stood there in the Tomb of Christ, he whispering something to me which I did not understand, and I shaking my head.

He then turned from me towards the Greek monk and said the same thing to him. But the monk could not understand, and he also shook his head. The old man became frantic with anxiety. He raised his voice slightly and then, casting a swift glance towards the marble slab, lowered it, and pointed to his forehead and to the lamps that hang over Christ's Tomb. Then the monk understood. Nodding gravely, he lowered one of the lamps on a chain and taking a piece of cotton wool, he dipped it lightly in the oil of the lamp, and with this made the sign of the Cross upon the peasant's face.

The old man sank down on his knees and turned again to the Tomb, unwilling to leave, incoherent with faith and devotion, his big, scarred hands touching the marble lovingly as if stroking the hair of a child. Presently he backed out of the candle-light into the dim Chapel of the Angel.

I sat for some time on a stone seat facing the low doorway of the Tomb. I promised myself that I would sit there every day while I was in Jerusalem. All round me was a silent, sighing crowd, a crowd that knelt in a trance-like hush, a crowd that tip-toed from shadow to shadow or sat in the twilight of the church, telling its rosaries. Matilde Serao has drawn this crowd very accurately in her book, *In the Country of Jesus.*

" The silent ghost-like throng never looks to left or right,"

SUNRISE OVER GALILEE

she says, "lost in earnest prayer, meditation, and sad memories, it seems oblivious of all else but its intense desire to plead in this Holy of Holies for pardon to the great Consoler of all the afflicted. In the gloom of the inner chapel, the thoughts of the worshipper become absorbed in such an acute sense of intense apprehension and of supreme expectancy that even identity is lost, and all material things appear shadowy and unreal.

"In that inner chamber, where, wrapped in a winding sheet, the Body of our Lord was laid to rest, and where His Mother and the holy women bathed it with their tears and wiped it with their hair, the light pours in through the perforated roof, rendering everything extremely vivid, so that the pious gathering is seen very distinctly, and you can even distinguish the nationality of each pilgrim as he passes through the low arched doorway, to fall prostrate before the august Tomb. . . .

"You may easily distinguish the Russian pilgrim by his poverty and humility, by the curious way in which he makes the Sign of the Cross, widely and slowly; and, above all, by the force with which he casts his big, heavy form prone upon the ground. His cloak is torn and his patched trousers discoloured; his bent head displays his fair curling hair, and his eyes are veiled by silent tears that trickle down his cheeks on to the pavement. His hands tremble as he grasps his old fur cap. You may easily distinguish the Maltese priest by his dark complexion, the strongly marked furrows on his brow, his tired look, his tattered garments, and the long continuance of his prostration. He has begged his way from his island home, has travelled third class, and said Mass daily in every town and village all along the mainland coast. You may recognise the poor Polish woman by her eyes bright with an inward happiness, who has been on the tramp for three long months, traversing Syria on foot, living on the charity received in convents and shelters and from passers-by, kissing everyone's hand, and speaking no other language but her own. For all her sickness and fatigue, she lives on, burning with an intense longing to see, to touch the Tomb; and when at last she beholds it, she is so overwhelmed that she faints for very joy. Again you will know the poor Greek peasant by his sunburnt hands with which he tilled the soil so long that they have absorbed its colour. How those poor hands tremble as they touch the white stone, thought of in mystic dreams and reached with so much difficulty! Thus all these believers, these Christians of every nation come from so far with such exalted, unwavering faith, each bringing that special character of adoration which is peculiar to his own land, soul, race and temperament. In all of them you discover, as they approach the Sepulchre, the same strange expression of overpowering emotion. Each seems to think that, having worshipped before the Tomb of Christ, he may return to die in peace in his distant home, the wish of his life fulfilled. He has reached the acme of his earthly desire. . . ."

There are no Russian pilgrims to-day, for Matilde Serao wrote her book long ago. But the emotion of the crowd is the same. It is a crowd which stirs one's tenderness. It is a crowd inspired by a Faith as naked as a new-born child. As I watched the silent ghost-like gathering and departure, I realised that one figure remained in an attitude of supplication. He was the old Bulgarian peasant who had spoken to me in the Tomb. He knelt before the low entrance, his hands held out on each side of his body, his head slightly on one side, the tears running down the furrows of his face. I thought that he looked like an elderly martyr who might have been painted by Giovanni Bellini. Then it seemed to me that the simple, contrite creature kneeling there in the half-light at the doorway of Christ's Tomb was a symbol not only of the questioning ache at the heart of Humanity, but also of the answer.

§ 4

The lanes of Jerusalem are striped like a tiger. You pass perpetually from strips of sunlight into bands of shadow. Some of the bazaars are vaulted. They exist in a stealthy twilight, the sun spirting down through cracks and holes in the roof as water spirts from a punctured water-skin. But most of them are open to the sky, the shadow of minaret, dome and tower flinging darkness over the cobbles and the walls.

One could write a book about walls. There are walls in Andalusia, in the south of Spain, which seem built as a barrier against lovers. There are walls in Tuscany which have been erected to keep out the assassin: and there are walls in England, like the walls of Hampton Court Palace, which seem made to hide from common eyes the pleasures of the privileged. But the walls in the old city of Jerusalem are unlike any walls I know. They have a furtiveness born of fear and uncertainty. They are high and mildewed and sunk in age. The doors in them seem built for dwarfs, and if you ring a bell, or bang one of the rusty iron hammers, it is almost certain that a grid will shoot open and an aged eye will look out at you before the bolt is shot.

Centuries of suspicion and persecution, during which Christians, their armies disbanded and scattered, held their own by the feminine qualities of guile and diplomacy, have cast a virginal terror over the walls of Jerusalem, almost as though every ringer of the bell, or every knocker at the gate, might be a ravisher of altars. All the beauty is carefully hidden behind these walls. They seem, in fact, deliberately ugly, as if to deceive the plunderer and, looking at them, one thinks of those holy nuns who mutilated their faces and cut off their noses in order to preserve their virtue when the barbarians thundered down on the last of the Roman Empire.

Sometimes, when a postern gate is open, you see beyond the stained wall to a cool paved courtyard lined with the stumps and pediments of old Roman columns. In the centre of the courtyard there may be a lemon tree, and beneath it an old monk reading a book. Then the door closes; and you wonder whether the brief glimpse of the peace on the other side was true, or merely the vision of a sun-stricken brain.

As one plods over these narrow lanes in Jerusalem, the confusion of centuries presses on the mind. There is an overpowering solemnity in the memory of all the Jerusalems that lie underfoot. The Jerusalem of the Gospels was itself rooted in old bones. And the Jerusalems that have grown up

and have vanished since the time of Christ—the Roman
city of Hadrian, the early Christian city of Constantine, the
Jerusalem of Omar, the Jerusalem of the Crusades, the Jerusalem of Saladin, the Jerusalem of Sulieman and the many
Turkish Jerusalems—these, lying one upon another and thrusting their relics through the soil, almost strike terror into
the mind. To walk through Jerusalem is to walk through
history. Beneath one's feet and scattered around in every
direction lie the bones of the Past.

As I went on through the old city, I was conscious also of
a feeling of imprisonment. All the dark little lanes, the high,
blank walls, and the jumbled buildings erected to the glory
of God, are bound tightly together by a high city wall. The
wall of Jerusalem, her armour and shield in time of trouble,
still exerts a powerful influence on the mind and you are
subconsciously aware of it every minute of the day. You
are either inside the wall, acutely aware of its encircling
embrace, or you are outside it, looking back at it, thinking
that it clasps the city in its brown stone arms as if trying to
shield it from the modern world.

I came by way of narrow street and blank wall, by sunlight
and by shadow, to the ancient Gate of St. Stephen. I saw,
framed in the graceful Saracenic arch of its stones, a brilliant
little picture of the world beyond the wall. I sighed with
relief at the sight of so much air and openness, so much sky,
and mountains with the sun over them. And the hill-side
that rose up opposite was the Mount of Olives.

All my life I have had a picture of the Mount of Olives in
my mind, a picture composed by my own imagination and
influenced by illustrations in books and by canvases in art
galleries; but it was a very different picture from the reality.
I had always thought of the Mount of Olives as an improbable
hill, perhaps something like a Kentish hop field on a Derbyshire moor, with plenty of tall cypress trees among belts of
woodland and little gardens with wells and fountains in them.
But the real Mount of Olives is a bare ridge sloping up from
the stricken-looking Kedron Valley; a ridge of rock on which
the sun beats down all day long. There are white tracks
twisting here and there among the rocks, and a few ploughed
fields terraced in the rock and upheld on the hill by breast-

high walls of limestone. In these fields are a few stumpy olive trees.

In any other place the Mount of Olives would seem bare and inhospitable, but, in contrast to Jerusalem and the mountains by which it is surrounded, it is peaceful and gracious; the only place in which to-day, as in the time of our Lord, you could go to sit under a tree and forget the nervous tension of the city.

Low down, just where the Jericho Road sends a branch road right up over the crest of the Mount of Olives, is a small patch of trees within a wall. I looked at it with the emotion it must always inspire. It was the Garden of Gethsemane.

When I came out of St. Stephen's Gate, I saw that the whole length of the eastern wall of Jerusalem overhangs a rocky gorge. The sloping ground outside the wall is covered with countless thousands of Moslem tombs; opposite on the slopes of the Mount of Olives are the Jewish tombs. Their white stones shine like bones. Both Jews and Moslems believe that the Last Judgment will be held in the arid Valley of the Kedron, between Jerusalem and the Mount of Olives. As I looked at the tombs, and then at the grim city wall, it seemed to me that Jerusalem, so cruel in appearance, so uncompromising, had, like an ogre, devoured these thousands of dead and had cast their bones over the ramparts to rot and bleach in the sun.

The road leads down into the Kedron Valley. It is white and dusty and low stone walls hem it in. It runs straight through the valley and down to Jericho and the Dead Sea. But the branch road to the left leads over the Mount of Olives to Bethphage and Bethany. And this is the road I walked, with the sun beating on it and the heat quivering like white fire on the rocks.

§ 5

I looked back from the depths of the Kedron Valley, but I could see only the tawny wall of Jerusalem towering above me on its rocky platform. As I began to climb the Mount of Olives, first a minaret, then a dome or two, appeared above the wall. Near the top of the Mount the whole city

lay before me, slightly tilted in the direction of the Mount of
Olives like an immense relief map that was slowly sliding into
the abyss of the valley.

My first thought was amazement that Jerusalem should
ever have been built. A more unlikely place for a famous
city cannot be imagined. The arid mountains lie about it,
rolling in long brown ridges against the sky, and in the valley
below is only one spring of water—the Fountain of the Virgin.
Jerusalem's water comes to-day, as it did in Old Testament
times, from Solomon's Pools near Hebron. Water is also
pumped from Ain Fara, the traditional " still waters " of the
twenty-third Psalm. To-day, as in olden times, every drop
of rain that falls on this high mountain ridge is saved in
deep rock cisterns. There is a splendid defiance about the
situation of Jerusalem, or perhaps it would be more correct
to say that no people who did not believe themselves to be
in the special care of God would have dared to have built
a city in defiance of all the laws of prudence.

And my second thought was that never had I seen a more
intolerant looking city. All the hardness of the rock and the
smouldering fires within the rock seemed to have boiled up
out of the bowels of the earth and cooled into the city of
Jerusalem. It was a perfect expression, so it seemed to me,
of the cruelty and the fierceness of the Judæan highlands.
This high city, perched above ravines and lying among the
débris of centuries, might, it seemed, be the abode not of
men and women and children, but the dwelling-place of
ruthless emotions such as Pride and Arrogance and Hate.
And as I sat for a long while looking down on Jerusalem,
I thought to myself: " That is undoubtedly the place that
crucified Jesus Christ." Like an echo to my thought came
a terrible reply: " And it would probably do so again."

The longer I looked at Jerusalem, the more I felt convinced that my first impression was not over-drawn or extravagant. If Jerusalem has not been born out of volcanic
lava, she has at least been born from the fire of men's minds.
Splendid and terrible things have happened behind her walls.
The modern world was born in their shadow. Strange that
the greatest event in the history of Mankind should have
occurred on this bare plateau; stranger still, perhaps, that

Jerusalem should still wear her historic air of intolerance. I seemed to hear a Voice in the pulse of the heat and the Voice said:

" O Jerusalem, Jerusalem, thou that killest the prophets, and stonest them which are sent unto thee, how often would I have gathered thy children together, even as a hen gathereth her chickens under her wings, and ye would not! "

The words beat against my brain like an echo of the heat that quivered above the Mount of Olives. I listened again, but there was no sound but the thrusting of a plough through the dry soil and the click of a mule's hoof against a flint.

Climbing to the top of the hill I mounted to a dome near the Chapel of the Ascension, which now belongs to the Moslems. On the paved space round the dome an elderly little guide, wearing sun spectacles, a European suit and a scarlet tarbush, was explaining Jerusalem to a crowd of English tourists, pointing here and there with an unrolled umbrella. I noticed that he talked to them about Jesus Christ as if he were a missionary explaining the rudimentary facts of Christianity to a crowd of rather feeble-minded Patagonians.

" You remember, please," he said, " that our Lord ascended into heaven."

Two or three of the tourists, who appeared to be worn-out with Scripture, turned away, while an elderly man, exactly like the caricature of a colonel in *Punch*, cleared his throat in an embarrassed way, as if it were not quite good form to mention such things in public.

" Well, please," continued the little guide, pointing with his umbrella, " the site of the Ascension is just there by the little round building, which we can enter in a moment. You will remember, please, that it was here that our Lord said good-bye to His disciples."

The group nodded. The little guide's high voice ploughed on through his deliberate recital:

" And He said, ' Go ye therefore, and teach all nations,

baptising them in the name of the Father, and of the Son, and of the Holy Ghost, teaching them to observe all things whatsoever I have commanded you: and lo, I am with you alway, even unto the end of the world.' "

There was silence for a few seconds. I like to think that all those people, who were touring Jerusalem as they would tour Cairo or Athens, felt, as I did, that a ridiculous situation had been lifted by these lovely, shining words into another world. "And lo, I am with you alway, even unto the end of the world." Even the little guide's high voice with its odd accent could not hurt these words. It seemed to me that something supremely beautiful had shone for a moment on all of us, and had gone. Then the colonel cleared his throat and asked his wife if she had remembered his sun glasses.

When they had gone and I was alone on the roof, I turned my back on Jerusalem and, looking to the east, saw something I shall never forget.

The Mount of Olives is slightly higher than Jerusalem, and stands up therefore like a screen between the city and the desert land that falls to the Dead Sea.

Jerusalem is 2,500 feet above sea level; the Dead Sea is 1,290 feet below sea level. So that in the course of about twenty-five miles the land falls nearly 4,000 feet into the hot, tropical world of the Jordan Valley. While it is frosty at night on the Jerusalem hills, it is hot and stuffy twenty-five miles away in Jericho, for the Jordan Valley is a phenomenal crack in the earth's surface which is filled with fierce heat all the year round.

From the top of the Mount of Olives the view into this tropical trench looked like a photograph of the mountains of the moon. I gazed down into an apparently sterile world, a world of brown, domed hills piled together, bare of vege- tation, and falling rapidly into the hot distance where a streak of blue marked the waters of the Dead Sea. Beyond the blueness rose a barrier of brown hills streaked with violet shadows. They were the Mountains of Moab.

This was a view that Jesus knew well, and it has not altered since His eyes gazed upon it. He saw it when He came over the hill from Bethany or Bethphage and, no doubt, He

turned, as every traveller turns, to look once more upon its
superb indifference before, breasting the ridge, the view was
hidden and Jerusalem came into sight.

How could Jerusalem fail to be the Holy City with this
terrifying breeding-place of prophets before its eyes? The
Golden Age of Israel was in the desert, when God took His
people by the hand and led them safely into the Promised
Land. It is this breath from the pure, sterilised desert
that blows through the denunciation of Elijah and, in fact,
through the denunciations by all those holy men who tried
to lead Israel away from foreign cults and luxuries back
to the old austerity. And I wondered, as I looked down on
the silent, dead hills, whether Jesus loved to sleep in Bethany
because, after the wrangling in the Temple court, He could
catch a glimpse, as He crossed the Mount of Olives on His
way back in the evening, of the calm " desert place " dedicated
for ever to God.

I came down from the Mount of Olives. The noonday sun
burned above Jerusalem. I saw the city lying compactly
within its wall, modern Jerusalem scattered round it in
clumps of white stone buildings. And the colour of old
Jerusalem is the colour of a lion-skin. There are tawny
yellows and dark browns and pale golds. It must have looked
very like this when Jesus saw it in the time of Herod Antipas:
a city like a lion crouched in the sun, watchful, vindictive,
and ready to kill.

§ 6

I went into one of the antique shops near the Jaffa Gate.
I do not know why one buys bits of gangrened bronze, coins,
fragments of iridescent glass, bone pins, old mirrors, and all
the odd scraps which someone flung on a rubbish-heap
centuries ago, unless, perhaps, one feels that they possess, or
should possess, the power of association. I have been collect-
ing such trifles since I was a boy at school, because I like to
hold them and to think " When this was new Cleopatra had
not yet met Antony and the Battle of Actium was still far off,"
or, " When this green wire was a brooch St. Paul was just
setting off on his first missionary journey." It is the most

B

harmless form of speculation in the world. It is, however, sometimes haunted by the laughter of the dead, for what could seem more ludicrous to the shade of a Roman matron than the sight of someone mounting her old saucepan handle against a background of black velvet?

The merchant had a fine selection of Roman glass, bronze pots, copper and bronze daggers, and some exquisite bronze incense shovels found, so I was told, on the mounds near a Roman city in the desert. I bought two incense shovels and, while poking about in a drawer full of scraps, discovered a Roman tile embossed with a circular stamp and the letters " Leg. X.F." On the top of the stamp was a rough impression of a galley and beneath the letters was an animal that looked like a pig or a boar. I could hardly believe my eyes.

" Do you know what this is? " I asked the merchant.

" Yes," he replied, " it is a tile with the stamp of the Tenth Legion on it. They are often found in Jerusalem. You can have it for five shillings."

I gave him the trifle and went away more pleased with the tile than with my expensive incense shovels, for I had in my pocket a relic of the legion that, in destroying Jerusalem under Titus in 70 A.D., fulfilled the prophesy of Christ that there should not be one stone of the Temple left upon another.

I took the tile to my bathroom, where I sponged it. It was covered with a hard incrustation of brown soil, which yielded eventually to moisture and came off leaving the " Leg. X.F." slightly clearer and exposing the legionary badge of the galley and the boar. I must admit, however, that neither of these symbols would have been recognisable to anyone who did not know what to look for. The Tenth Legion, which had made this tile about forty years after the Crucifixion, was known as the " Fretensis "—the legion from " fretum Siciliense," the Straits of Sicily—and the letter F. was the initial of the word " Fretensis." As I dried the legionary tile, and felt it hard under my hands, I longed to be able by some process of clairvoyance to see the world of which it was so provoking a fragment. . . .

Scholars who have studied the date of the Crucifixion believe that Jesus died either in the year 29 or 30 A.D. If, therefore, we accept these dates, we know that our Lord's prophesy about the destruction of Jerusalem was delivered during Passion Week, not later than the spring of 30 A.D., when, leaving the Temple courts, He said, to the bewilderment of His disciples, that " there shall not be left here one stone upon another, which shall not be thrown down." Such a statement must have astonished the Jews, to whom the Temple and its ritual were the very core of the national existence. The Temple was Jehovah's and, as such, indestructible and immortal.

As the disciples followed the road over the viaduct to the Mount of Olives, they pondered Christ's saying and, unable to contain their curiosity or to conceal their bewilderment, came to Him one after the other, " privately," to ask the meaning of His vision. Then Jesus, in the plainest terms, described the fall of Jerusalem and warned His disciples to fly to the mountains when the time of tribulation should come.

Forty years passed : forty years during which the prophesy of " wars and rumours of wars," " false prophets " and " tumults," was fulfilled to the letter, until all the land was on fire with hate, despair and rebellion. There is an echo of this age of anarchy in the *Acts of the Apostles.* When Paul was in trouble with the Roman authorities, he was at first confused with one of the many Messianic impostors typical of that age of false hopes along whose tempestuous paths the Jewish nation rushed towards destruction.

We see this space of forty years in a series of bloody episodes : Roman governors ordering soldiers to clear a street, zealots and fanatics murdering a Roman garrison, assassins whipping out their knives, even in the Temple courts, and Greek cities rising with drawn sword to slay every Jew within their gates. So " the days of vengeance," foretold by Jesus, approached. The general revolt broke out when the zealots, after driving the Roman garrison from Jerusalem and visiting a shameful defeat on a legion, began to organise a national insurrection. Nero was advised to teach this unruly and fanatical nation a lesson, and was forced to take action. A great army was fitted out; and the Jewish War began in the year 66 A.D.

It is, strangely enough, at this time that Britain links her name with the country of Jesus. Vespasian, the son of a Sabine tax-collector, was a soldier who had distinguished

himself during the invasion of Britain under Claudius in
43 A.D.—thirteen years after the Crucifixion. He commanded
the Second Legion, the Augusta, and fought principally in the
West Country, subduing the Isle of Wight and carrying the
Roman arms from the Solent to the Exe. Therefore the men
destined to fulfil the prophesy of Christ that " Jerusalem shall
be trodden down by the Gentiles " were trained in Britain.
It was to Vespasian and his twenty-eight-year-old son, Titus,
that Nero, in the year 66 A.D., entrusted the command of the
Roman Army in Palestine.

It is strange to think of the association. At this period the
Romans in Britain were straightening out the old Celtic track-
ways and laying the foundations of Watling Street and the
Fosse Way. London, recovering from Boadicea's revolt, was
rebuilding itself as a little, red-tiled Roman port on the
marshy banks of the Thames, and in the north the map of
Britain was emerging from the mist of antiquity. Eboracum,
which is York, and Deva, which is Chester, echoed to the
sound of the *bucina* and to the tramp of the legions. And
right across the world two men who had helped to plant this
new civilisation in the west were fated to perform the task of
bringing down the civilisation of the Old Testament and, in a
sense, opening the doors of the world to the New.

Vespasian swooped down on Palestine with one of the finest
Roman armies that had ever gone into action. His first
campaign was in Galilee, where he saw the lakeside with its
ring of busy towns more or less as Christ had seen it forty years
before. But he reddened its blue waters with the blood of the
Jews. The hills on which Jesus had preached the gospel of
love and compassion now echoed to the screams of the tortured
and the slain. Josephus, the historian on whose works we
are so dependent for details of this age, was captured and
put in chains. Six thousand of the fittest young Jews were
sent as slaves to Corinth, where Nero had just begun to cut the
Corinth Canal.

While Vespasian was scourging the Jews, an event occurred
that shook the Roman world. A plump young man of thirty
galloped away from Rome one night, arriving at daybreak at
a villa set in a lonely spot between the Nomentane and the
Salarian roads. He waited there in terror, fingering two

daggers that he had brought away with him; then, hearing the approaching beat of hoofs, he bared his breast and bade his slave, Epaphroditus, drive home the knife. The news spread over the world that Nero was dead.

In the civil war that followed, Vespasian, striding over the corpses of three stop-gap emperors, gained the purple. He was actually proclaimed emperor at Cæsarea, on the sea-coast of Palestine. Leaving the last act of the Jewish War—the destruction of Jerusalem—to his son, Titus, Vespasian made his way back to Rome.

Titus was thirty years of age when, in 70 A.D., he appeared before the walls of Jerusalem with a mighty army consisting of the Fifth Legion, the Tenth, the Twelfth, and the Fifteenth, accompanied by the usual cavalry and auxiliary troops—a total force of between 60,000 and 80,000 men. The city, now faced with the horrors of siege, was already steeped in the horror of faction fights, for one of the most terrible civil wars in history was raging within the walls. Fanatics, extreme nationalists, and bandits held various quarters of Jerusalem and waged war upon each other until the streets ran with blood. When Titus planted the Tenth Legion, the " Fretensis," on the Mount of Olives, and looked down upon Jerusalem, he saw the city that Jesus had seen forty years previously. Herod's splendid Temple was now completed, but nothing had changed very much, though various buildings, and the north suburb, had suffered in riot and siege.

Forty years is not a very long time. There were men of fifty-two in Jerusalem at this time who, as lads of twelve, had possibly witnessed the Crucifixion. Perhaps in the Passover crowds who thronged the blood-stained streets, for it was April, were many elderly peasants who remembered that as small children they had been led to a Man who blessed them, saying, " Suffer little children, and forbid them not, to come unto me: for of such is the kingdom of Heaven."

There must have been some also in Jerusalem, old men of sixty or seventy, who remembered the command of Christ that, when the time of vengeance should arrive, they were not even to take their household goods, and the man in the field was not even to return to pick up his cloak, but all were to fly into the safety of the hills. And this the first Christians had done.

They had fled secretly from the doomed city and found their way to Pella, south of the Lake of Galilee; a place that is now called Kherbet-el-Fahil.

Titus placed his main forces on the north and the north-west, leaving the Tenth, " the Fretensis," to watch the impregnable east wall from the Mount of Olives. The sound of the battering-rams shook the air day and night. Prodigies of almost maniacal valour were witnessed every day as Jews, rushing out to certain death, flung fire on the war engines and grasped the white-hot metal until their hands were destroyed. Early in May Titus entered the suburb of the New Town and ordered Josephus, the historian, to bid his countrymen to surrender. The reply was defiance. Titus then built an enormous wall right round Jerusalem, each legion being responsible for a section of it, and famine sat upon the walls of Jerusalem and mocked the grotesque sufferings of the people. Weary of flinging thousands of dead bodies over the walls into the valleys, the inhabitants began to stack corpses in the cellars and in the rooms of large houses. Five hundred deserters and captives were crucified each day until the hills bristled with this ghastly forest of crosses, and wood grew scarce.

Pitiful bands of deserters began to crawl out towards the enemy lines. Josephus, who saw them, says that they were " puffed up by the famine and swelled like men in a dropsy." Here a ghastly fate awaited them. The rumour spread among the cut-throats and the bandits, who hung like jackals on the fringe of the Roman army, that the deserters had swallowed their gold before leaving the city. In one night two thousand of these miserable wretches were slit open. Titus was so furious when he heard of it that he called his commanders together and issued an army order that any soldier found guilty of slitting open a deserter, in the hope of finding gold, should be executed. But even this did not stop the practice.

As the siege went on, the country round about Jerusalem changed in appearance. Every tree was cut down to make engines of war, scaling-ladders, and such-like. When Titus first stood on the Mount of Olives he saw the gracious, culti-vated hill with the vines, olives and fig-trees that Jesus had known and loved. But in the opening months of the siege Josephus, who had been well acquainted with the country in the old days, wrote:

" Nor could any foreigner who had formerly seen Judæa and the most beautiful suburbs of the city, but lament and mourn sadly at so great a change; for the war had laid all the signs of beauty quite waste; nor if anyone that had known the place before had come on a sudden to it now would he have known it again; but though he were at the city itself, yet would he have inquired for it notwithstanding."

In the city itself men who looked plump and well-fed were tortured with hideous cruelty to give away the secret of their store. Parents tore the food from their children's mouths. Martha, the daughter of the rich Nikdimon ben Gorion, whose marriage portion had been a million gold denarii, was seen trying to pick grains of corn from the dung in the streets.

"Now of those that perished by famine in the city the number was prodigious," says Josephus, " and the miseries they underwent were unspeakable; for if so much as the shadow of any kind of food did anywhere appear, a war was commenced presently, and the dearest friends fell a-fighting one with another about it, snatching from each other the most miserable supports of life. Nor would men believe that those who were dying had no food, but the robbers would search them when they were expiring lest any one should have concealed food in their bosoms and counterfeited dying: nay, these robbers gaped for want, and ran about stumbling and staggering along like mad dogs, and reeling against the doors of the houses like drunken men: they would also, in the great distress they were in, rush into the very same houses two or three times in one and the same day. Moreover their hunger was so intolerable that it obliged them to chew every-thing, while they gathered such things as the most sordid animals would not touch and endured to eat them; nor did they at length abstain from girdles and shoes, and the very leather which belonged to their shields they pulled off and gnawed: the very wisps of old hay became food to some, and some gathered up fibres, and sold a very small weight of them for four Attic drachmæ. But why do I describe the shameless impudence that the famine brought on men in their eating inanimate things? while I am going to relate a matter of fact, the like of which no history relates, either among the Greeks or the Barbarians. It is horrible to speak of, and incredible when heard. I had indeed willingly omitted this calamity of ours, that I might not seem to deliver what is so portentous to posterity, but that I have innumerable witnesses to it in my own age; and, besides, my country would have had little reason to thank me for suppressing the miseries that she underwent at this time.

"There was a certain woman that dwelt beyond Jordan, her name was Mary; her father was Eleazer, of the village Bethezub, which signifies the House of Hyssop. She was eminent for her family and her wealth and had fled to Jerusalem with the rest of the multitude and was with them besieged therein at this time. The other effects of this woman had been already seized upon, such I mean as she had brought with her out of Perea and removed to the city. What she had treasured up besides, as also what food she had contrived to save, had been also carried off by the rapacious guards, who came every day running into her house for that purpose. This put the poor woman into a very great passion, and by the frequent reproaches and imprecations she cast at these rapacious villains, she had provoked them to anger against her; but none of them, either out of the indignation she had raised against herself, or out of commiseration of her case, would take away her life; and if she found any food, while the famine pierced through her very bowels and marrow, when also her passion was fired to a degree beyond the famine itself: nor did she consult with anything but with her passion and the necessity she was in. She then attempted a most unnatural thing, and, snatching up her son, who was a child sucking at her breast, she said ' O thou miserable infant! for whom shall I preserve thee in this war, this famine, and this sedition? As to the war with the Romans, if they preserve our lives we must be slaves. This famine also will destroy us even before that slavery comes upon us. Yet are these seditious rogues more terrible than both the other.

Come on; be thou my food, and be thou a fury to these seditious varlets and a by-word to the world, which is all that is now wanting to complete the calamities of us Jews.'

"As soon as she had said that, she slew her son and then roasted him, and ate the one half of him and kept the other half by her concealed. Upon this the seditious came in presently and, smelling the horrid scent of this food, they threatened her that they would cut her throat immediately if she did not show them what food she had gotten ready. She replied that ' she had saved a very fine portion of it for them '; and withal uncovered what was left of her son. Whereupon they were seized with a horror and amazement of mind, and stood astonished at the sight, when she said to them, ' This is mine own son, and what hath been done was my own doing. Come, eat of this food; for I have eaten of it myself. Do you not pretend to be more tender than a woman or more compassionate than a mother: but if you be so scrupulous and do abominate this my sacrifice, as I have eaten the one half, let the rest be preserved for me also.' After which those men went out trembling, being never so much affrighted at anything as they were at this, and with some difficulty they left the rest of that meat to the mother. . . . So those that were thus distressed by the famine were very desirous to die, and those already dead were esteemed happy, because they had not lived long enough either to hear or to see such miseries."

Meanwhile the siege went on. The battering-rams and *ballistæ* were at work day and night. Heralds summoned the starving city to surrender, receiving for reply taunts and defiance. Large stores of grain and food were stacked in the Roman lines, within sight of those on the walls, in order, if possible, to torture the starving Jews into submission by the sight of plenty. This ruse also failed. Titus, again to drive home the inevitability of their fate, ordered a full-dress pay parade of the Roman army before the walls of Jerusalem. The service kit was put aside and the burnished breast-plates, helmets and parade trappings were taken from their cases, and the whole army, in full view of Jerusalem, defiled past to the sound of trumpets. The parade lasted for four days. The walls were black with people. But the sight, though it struck terror into the heart of Jerusalem, did not serve its purpose; and the war was resumed.

At the beginning of July the Castle of Antonia, near the hall in which Pilate had condemned Christ to death, was captured by the Romans. This castle rose on the north wall of the Temple. Titus himself wished to take part in the first attack on the Temple, but his commanders persuaded him to watch the assault from one of the high towers of Antonia, with the excuse that from such a high place he would be better able to award medals for bravery and to decide on promotions. For nearly a month a frightful battle for the Temple went on, the Jews insanely convinced that at the last moment Jehovah would come to deliver His ancient sanctuary, and Titus calling repeatedly for surrender and placing the blame for the sacrilege on the Jews. He wished to preserve the Temple, which was one of the world's wonders.

Titus and his soldiers looked down upon it, watching the arrows drive across those courts from whose shade Jesus, forty years previously, had expelled the money-changers. The Romans watched the fire spread among the colonnades and observed the fight sway even round the sacred walls of the Holy of Holies. They were the last men to see the Temple of Herod as Christ knew it. Early in August a successful sortie carried the Romans to the Holy of Holies. A soldier, inspired, as Josephus puts it, " by a certain divine fury," snatched a burning brand and lifting himself on the shoulders of a comrade thrust the fire through a golden window. And the flames ran through the sanctuary of the Lord.

Josephus says:

" Then did Cæsar, both by calling to the soldiers that were fighting with a loud voice, and by giving a signal to them with his right hand, order them to quench the fire. But they did not hear what he said, though he spake so loud, having their ears already dinned by a greater noise another way; nor did they attend to the signal he made with his hand neither, as still some of them were distracted with fighting and others with passion. . . . And now since Cæsar was in no way able to restrain the enthusiastic fury of the soldiers, and the fire

proceeded on more and more, he went into the holy place
of the Temple, with his commanders, and saw it, with what
was in it, which he found to be far superior to what the
relations of foreigners contained, and not inferior to what we
ourselves boasted of and believed about it.   But as the flame
had not as yet reached to its inmost parts, but was still con-
suming the rooms that were about the holy house, and Titus,
supposing what the fact was, that the house itself might yet
be saved, he came in haste and endeavoured to persuade the
soldiers to quench the fire, and gave order to Liberalius, the
centurion, and one of those spearmen that were about him,
to beat the soldiers that were refractory with their staves and
to restrain them: yet were their passions too hard for the
regard they had for Cæsar, and the dread they had of him
who forbade them, as was their hatred of the Jews and a
certain vehement inclination to fight them, too hard for them
also.

" Moreover the hope of plunder induced many to go on, as
having this opinion, that all the places within were full of
money, and as seeing that all round about it was made of
gold.   And besides one of those that went into the place
prevented Cæsar when he ran so hastily out to restrain the
soldiers, and threw the fire on the hinges of the gate in the
dark; whereby the flame burst out from within the holy
house itself immediately when the commanders retired, and
Cæsar with them, and when nobody any longer forbade those
that were without to set fire to it.   And thus was the holy
house burnt down without Cæsar's approbation."

But even then, with half Jerusalem in the hands of Titus
and the Temple a smoking ruin, the zealots refused to give
in.   They retreated to the Upper Town, where they carried
on the war.   Titus yet again begged them to surrender.
Standing on the bridge over the Tyropœan Valley, a bridge
that had known the footsteps of Jesus and whose ruins were
discovered some years ago, eighty feet beneath the ground,
he mentioned the name of Britain to them:

" Pray, what greater obstacle is there than the wall of the
ocean, with which the Britons are encompassed? " he cried,
" and yet they do adore the arms of the Romans. . . . O

miserable creatures! what is it you depend on? Are not your
people dead? is not your holy house gone? is not your city
in my power? and are not your own very lives in my hands?
And do you still deem it a part of valour to die? if you will
throw down your arms, and deliver up your bodies to me, I will
grant you your lives; and I will act like a mild master of a
family."

But the beaten Jews attempted to drive a bargain with him
of so preposterous a character than even Titus lost his temper,
and, turning angrily away, ordered the army to burn and
plunder the city.

Once more the battering-rams were pushed to the walls.
Once more the ramps were built up. Once more the *ballistæ*
flung their stones and the bows their burning brands upon the
gallant defenders. Then eventually the Romans poured over
the wall and grew sick of slaughter. They ran about the
city in search of plunder, but, breaking into houses, they
retreated horror-stricken, for every house was piled with
rotting corpses.

So Jerusalem, after a siege of nearly six months, was beaten
to the dust. The prophecy that Jesus had delivered in the
Temple forty years before had come true. " For there shall
be great distress upon the land, and wrath unto this people,"
He had said. " And they shall fall by the edge of the sword,
and shall be led captive into all nations: and Jerusalem shall
be trodden down of the Gentiles until the times of the Gentiles
be fulfilled."

Titus held a parade to congratulate his army and to distri-
bute decorations. He stood on a tribune surrounded by his
staff while the list of honours and promotions was read out to
him. He distributed gold crowns, ornaments, spears and
ensigns. Then, ordering walls and everything to be levelled
to the ground, save a portion of the western wall and the three
towers of Herod's palace, he broke up the camp and departed
with a great multitude of captives and the golden table of the
shewbread, the seven-branched candlestick, and other sacred
vessels from the Temple.

The Legion left in occupation of the smoking ruin was the
Tenth, " Fretensis." Their camp was the only sign of life
on the brown hills that had once been Jerusalem. Everything

that Christ had known, and every site that the disciples and
the first Christians had associated with the Passion, the Trial
and the Crucifixion, had been levelled to the ground, with
the exception, of course, of the rise of ground known as
Golgotha. Attached to the Tenth Legion were the usual
auxiliary troops, and these, we learn, were " of foreign origin,
drawn in part from the farthest lands of the west." Is it,
I wonder, too extravagant to imagine that among those who
witnessed the destruction of Jerusalem, who wandered among
the ruins and dug for treasure in basements and cellars,
who visited the shattered remains of Pilate's judgment hall
and who stood, without realising it, upon the mound of
Calvary, were some men from our own land? In time—no
one knows at what time—a band of Jews returned to Jerusalem
from Pella. These were the Christians who had obeyed the
last command of the Master to save themselves when the time
of danger approached. They came back and elected Simeon
as their bishop. We can imagine them gazing with tearful
eyes at the ruins everywhere around them. The oldest among
them might well have known Christ and might have seen Him
on the Cross. They must have roamed the ruins looking for
sacred landmarks, saying, " It was here He said such a thing,"
or " It was there He healed the blind man." It seems certain
that, among the ruins of Jerusalem, they looked for, and
found, the house of Mary, mother of Mark, in which it is
believed Jesus held the Last Supper. With their minds full
of holy memories, they rebuilt this house and kept it as a place
of worship.

So for sixty years there was nothing on the hills but the
camp of Legio X. Fretensis, and the hutments of the merchants
and others who always followed a legion. There would be
brickyards and tile works in which the soldiers laboured,
making flat baked tiles with the stamp on them, " Leg. X. F."
and the badge of the galley and the boar.

Of all the relics a man can buy in Jerusalem, surely none
could be more eloquent than the tile which I bought for five
shillings. The hands that made it helped to bring Jerusalem
to the dust. By some freak of chance it has survived where

so much has perished, and it remains to provoke curiosity and
to inspire imagination.

§ 7

If you arrive in Jerusalem and discover that all the hotels
are full up with cruising parties from Haifa, someone is sure
to suggest that you try to find a bed in a hospice.

A sense of fear and panic assails the European traveller
who, unaware of an earlier tradition, feels safe only in an
hotel. The word " hospice " has for him a chilly and unfamiliar ring. It suggests possibly a St. Bernard dog, or a
bed on the floor. But how little he has to fear! He pulls a
bell in a small postern gate, set in a high wall somewhere
within the Old City, and his ring is answered by a monk, who
stands aside automatically, for this sort of thing has been
happening in Jerusalem for over a thousand years.

The monk leads him to a frugal room with a bed in it, and a
crucifix above the bed, a wash-basin and a chest of drawers.
And the traveller, glancing with approval round the little
room, feels, if he has any sense in him, that he is seeing Jerusalem from the right angle.

Since Charlemagne founded a hospice, with a library and
vineyard, sometime during the eighth century—it was swept
away by the storms of Islam—Jerusalem has specialised in
hospices. It was to the hospice of the Knights Hospitallers
that pilgrims found their way during the Crusades: it was
also a hospital in the modern sense of the word, for in those days
many a pilgrim arrived stripped, wounded, and robbed.
Hospices maintained by the various churches, often under the
most appalling difficulties and dangers, have ever since wel-
comed the Christian to the Holy City.

At the present day there is the Casa Nuova, the hospice of
the kindly and charming Franciscan Fathers, the Hospice of
Notre-Dame de France, the Hospice of the Fathers of the
Assumption, the German Catholic Hospice, the Austrian
Hospice, the Russian Hospice, and the Anglican Hostel of
St. George's Cathedral. There are Maronite, Greek, and
Armenian hospices, the American Colony's house (which is
really a hospice), and the huge, new and rather incredible
American Y.M.C.A., the pious gift of a millionaire.

The latest country to build a hospice in Jerusalem is Scotland. It is a beautiful white building that stands on a rise of ground facing the old city walls and Mount Zion.

The Scots Hospice contains also the only Scottish kirk in Jerusalem, the Church of St. Andrew. Both church and hospice are a war memorial fit to stand beside that supreme expression of a nation's strength and sorrow: the Scottish National War Shrine in Edinburgh Castle.

The idea of building a Scottish church, and a hospice that would welcome all Scottish visitors and pilgrims to the Holy Land, was originated by an elder of the Presbytery of Edinburgh. It was warmly seconded by Judge James Harry Scott, the President of the Court of Appeal in Jerusalem, who pointed out that every nation in Christendom was represented in Jerusalem by a church or a hospice with the exception of Scotland.

What finer, or more fitting, memorial to those Scots " who died in the waterless deserts, in the battlefields of Gaza, among the mountains of Judæa, in the stifling plains of Jericho and the Jordan Valley . . . all twice-holy ground " than a church in which Scottish exiles could worship, and a hospice ready always to welcome the Scottish traveller and student? The idea was approved by the General Assemblies, and the foundation stone was laid in 1927.

One morning I walked down the dusty road from the Jaffa Gate to have a look at the Scots Hospice. Its site was chosen with real genius, for the white building shines from afar. There is nothing Scottish about its appearance, which is a tactful blend of Eastern and Western architecture.

I rang the bell and found myself in a circular hall, very modern in design, yet very homely. I soon encountered a charming Highland voice and was told all about the hospice. Since it was opened over 1,000 Scotsmen and Scotswomen have stayed there: tourists, students, and missionaries.

It is, in my opinion, one of the most charming and comfortable places in Jerusalem. The bedrooms have hot and cold running water in them and lights near the bed so that you can read yourself to sleep. There is a fine theological library for the use of students, a dining-room (in which I am sure they give you bannocks at breakfast-time) and a large drawing-room, or lounge, whose tall windows lead to a paved garden and a view straight ahead of the walls of the Old City.

One of the curiosities of the Scots Hospice is the dead man near the front door! While the place was being built the workmen blundered on the usual rock-hewn tomb, with an early Christian skeleton inside it. He was photographed and reverently replaced under one of the ground-floor windows.

The Church of St. Andrew is, however, the unforgettable feature of the building. It is a lesson in simplicity and purity of line and colour. The white stone walls, the gentle curve of arches, the softness of pale colours and the complete absence of decoration, are a marvellous rest cure after the dark, confused old churches of Jerusalem. To come from these places into the beauty and the peace of St. Andrew's kirk is like coming from the noise and confusion of a street bazaar into the silence of the birch woods that grow round the Lake of Menteith.

The Scots have a genius for suddenly making you want to burst into tears, the trick that Sir James Barrie knows so well— and it is a trick, when done on purpose on the stage, that can sometimes infuriate. Now and then, however, this habit, when inspired by genuine sorrow and expressed as in the National Shrine in Edinburgh, places a hand right on your heart. It happens in this church in Jerusalem.

The Communion Table stands on green-veined marble from Iona, so that, as I was told, " the minister, in giving communion, stands all the time in Scotland." And written on a brass plate sunk in the floor are these words:

" *In Remembrance of the Pious Wish of King Robert Bruce that his heart should be buried in Jerusalem. Given by Citizens of Dunfermline and Melrose in celebration of the 6th Centenary of his death.*"

I have no way of telling how this strikes you when you read it in print, but, when I read it in this chaste little church so far from Scotland, I thought that it was one of the most beautiful memorials I had ever seen. And I thought of the King's dying command to Douglas to take his heart from his body after death and carry it into battle against the enemies of Christ.

I remembered the story of the death of Douglas in Spain, when he rode against the Moors with the King's heart in a silver box round his neck. And I remembered the broken arches of Melrose Abbey, beneath which the heart of Bruce is supposed eventually to have been buried.

If the Scotsmen who built this church could have sent Bruce's heart to Jerusalem, I am sure they would have done so, and it would be lying now on the little hill below Mount Zion. They have done the next best thing. They have remembered his last wish.

The stalls in the church were given by Scottish regiments, by Scottish Freemasons all over the world, and by parishes from the Mull of Galloway to John o' Groats. The names are carved on the back. I went down the lines reading: " Maxwelltown, Methlic, Linton (Teviotdale), Linlithgow," and so on, with the feeling that all Scotland was somehow gathered in this little building in Jerusalem.

But always I shall remember the green Iona marble and the associations that cling to it. One feels that a splendid promise has been kept. One feels somehow that round the communion table of St. Andrew's Church the trumpets of Don Alfonso's army, which sounded the charge in Spain so long ago, echo faintly and die away for ever.

§ 8

A young Zionist called on me one day, and gave me an armful of propagandist literature. In retaliation, I pressed him to take me to the Wailing Wall, which he did with some reluctance, because the politically-minded young Zionists have little in common with the Orthodox Jews who wail, with renewed vigour on Fridays, for the departed glories of Israel.

We found our way to the Wailing Wall down narrow winding lanes in the old city. Turning a corner suddenly, we came upon an enormous tawny stretch of wall from whose cracks grow tufts of grass and wild caper plants. The wall is about fifty yards long and sixty feet high, and the lower courses are of enormous blocks of brownish stone—one of sixteen and a half feet long and thirteen feet wide. This is believed to be

the only fragment of the Temple wall which the soldiers of
Titus did not destroy after the siege.

The Jews who wail here are, in theory, mourning for the
departed splendour of Israel. This may seem rather strange
to those who know that there is a Jewish National Home in
Palestine sponsored by Great Britain, to which thousands of
Jews from all over the world have emigrated. But the Jew
who wails at the Wailing Wall is not a modern Jew, or Zionist;
in fact, he deplores the material character of modern Zionism.
He is an old-fashioned, Orthodox Jew, whose life is bound up
with his religion.

The custom of wailing, or mourning, is one that occurs
frequently in the Old Testament.

"Therefore I will wail and howl," cried Micah the Moras-
thite. "I will go stripped and naked: I will make a wailing
like the dragons and mourning as the owls."

"We grope for the wall like the blind," says Isaiah, "and we
grope as if we had no eyes: we stumble at noonday as in the
night; we are in desolate places as dead men. We roar all
like bears, and mourn sore like doves. . . ."

The custom of wailing at the wall of Herod's Temple goes
back to remote times. After the destruction of Jerusalem,
Hadrian forbade Jews even to come within sight of the city,
on pain of death. Under Constantine, however, they were
allowed to weep on the site of the Temple once a year. In
the twelfth century the exterior wall—the present Wailing
Wall—was allotted to the Jews as a place for prayer.

About fifty Jews, men and women, were standing against
the wall, some with books, and all of them muttering swiftly
as they rocked their bodies to and fro, as Jews always do when
they pray. Round the corner is a police box, where a British
policeman is on duty to prevent trouble, for the Wailing Wall
is one of the danger spots of Jerusalem.

"Oh, anything may happen here," said the policeman. "A
Jew may have a row with an Arab, or an Arab may insult a
Jew, and before you know where you are, there's a riot. I'm
on the telephone, and there's a police station round the corner.
Excuse me. . . . You can't use that camera, madam."

" But why ever not? " asked an Englishwoman.

" It isn't allowed.   They don't like it."

I admired the way this policeman handled the most tender spot in Jerusalem—for the wall itself is Moslem property, and on the other side of it rises the great Dome of the Rock and the Mosque of el Aksar, which occupy the site of the Temple. The frightful riots and the massacre of 1929 began at this wall with a Moslem protest against some matting and a canvas screen which the Jews had erected, and had failed to withdraw when ordered to do so by the British authorities.

The result was that a policeman, waiting for a silent moment in the prayers, removed the offending articles, but found, by the frenzy his act created, that he had accidentally picked on the most sacred moment.   The Jews complained to the League of Nations.   The dispute wore on for months, and eventually blazed up in a fury of fanaticism and race hatred, in which many Arabs and Jews lost their lives.

Many types of Jew come down to the Wailing Wall.   I saw the Polish Jew in his velvet gabardine and his fur-rimmed hat, young Jews with long, sandy hair and side-curls, dark Eastern Jews, Yemenites from Arabia, who look exactly like Arabs, Spanish Jews, and, here and there, a modern Jew in a lounge suit and a cap.

Little prayers, written on scraps of paper, were stuck in the cracks of the stones.   One girl wept bitterly as she rocked herself beside the wall, praying perhaps for the recovery of someone from illness, for the Jews believe that Jehovah has never deserted or withdrawn His compassion from those stones.   Prayers from Jews all over the world were, and probably are still, offered up at the Wailing Wall in order to gain the privilege of the special sanctity which attaches itself to the wall.

Many of the " wailers " joined in regular litanies.   This is one of them, which the young Zionist translated for me:

Leader : For the palace that lies desolate.
Response : We sit in solitude and mourn.
Leader : For the Temple that is destroyed.
Response : We sit in solitude and mourn.
Leader : For the walls that are overthrown.

Response : We sit in solitude and mourn.
Leader : For our majesty that is departed.
Response : We sit in solitude and mourn.

This, I suppose, is the lamentation that has been in the heart
of the Orthodox Jew since Titus destroyed the Temple of Herod
and scattered the race to the four corners of the world.

"Very morbid," I heard an Englishwoman whisper, after
gazing intently at the Wailing Wall for some moments. "What
is the good of crying over spilt milk ? "

And, indignantly, she departed.

Only a woman, and an Englishwoman, could, I think, refer
to the destruction of the Temple and the Dispersion as " spilt
milk "! But I understand what she meant.

The Jew feels so keenly the sacredness of the Temple area
on the other side of the Wailing Wall that he will never
enter it.

" There is an idea," explained the young Zionist with the
shamefaced expression of one retailing unworthy superstitions,
" that perhaps the Ark of the Covenant is buried somewhere
under the pavements of the mosque, or that perhaps the visitor
might, without knowing it, walk on the site of the Holy of
Holies. When one of the Rothschilds visited the mosque years
ago, he was carried in a chair in case he unwittingly trod on
a sacred place."

I turned again to watch the swaying crowd of Jews nodding
and bowing to the tremendous fragment of wall, and I thought
that never had I seen anything more determined or more
pitiful. It was much more impressive to me than the armful
of Zionist literature I had received. I seemed to see a chain
of swaying, bearded figures stretching back to Roman times,
praying, weeping, pushing their little messages into clefts in
the stone and knocking in nails, begging Jehovah to look once
again with love and compassion upon the place where His
Temple once shone like a mountain of snow.

The tenaciousness of the queer, furtive old Jews who creep
about Jerusalem, living spiritually in Old Testament times,
ruling their lives by the intricate ordinances that even Titus
and his legions could not efface, calls forth respect and also a
sense of awe. They still wait and pray for the coming of the

Messiah, and they believe that some day Jehovah, pardoning their sins, will lift from their bent backs the burden of oppression which they have carried down the ages.

Yet not ten minutes' walk from the Wailing Wall is the Jewish Agency, which is settling Zionists on the land. The place is full of typewriters and politicians. They will talk to you in English, in German or in Russian. They never mention Moses, but they can talk, earnestly, vividly and at great length, of electricity. There is in the world no stranger contrast than the Wailing Wall and the Jewish Agency, both intensely Jewish, both burning with a desire to rebuild the Jewish State; but one with the help of God and the other with the assistance of motor tractors.

" The Wailing Wall is, no doubt, a very interesting sight," said the young Zionist as we walked away.

§ 9

The sun has not yet risen. Sleepy donkeys are being led through the streets of Jerusalem. Camels in long files are plodding in from the villages with greenstuff. Bundles of rags, lying on the ledges and under the arches of the Damascus Gate, stir and stretch out lean, brown arms.

In the steep streets of the old city the fruiterers are setting out their bright stalls, cloth merchants are busy with their bales, pastry-cooks are already making their small sugary cakes; and fish merchants are putting out the queer, misshapen corpses which are sold and eaten in this mountain capital, huge pike from the Tigris and the Euphrates, which come overland in four days packed in ice, flat fish from Egypt and Jaffa, and the *musht*, a grayling known as St. Peter's fish, which is caught only in the Lake of Galilee.

As I go down the terraced streets, beautifully cool in the morning air, ancient, gloomy walls rise up on each side, and I come upon a crusaders' arch, now built into the wall of a mosque, or a blue-tiled fountain built in the time of Saladin. Suddenly the dark little street is filled with a tawny brilliance, and, glancing up, I know that the sun has risen. I can already feel the warmth in the air, for the sun in Palestine leaps up into the sky like a ball of fire and is warm to the skin from the first second of his arrival.

I hear the call to prayer from the nearest minaret. As I turn the corner, I see the muezzin standing in his little railed-in balcony, lit by the first light of the sun, an old blind man who cries in a loud chanting voice: " Allâhu akbar, Allâhu akbar. Allâhu akbar; ashadu an lâ ilâha illa-llâh, ashadu anna Muhammedarrasûlullâh . . . hayya   'alas-salâ . . . Allah is great; testify that there is no God but Allah and Mohammed is his Prophet . . . Come to prayer! "

And as he calls he does not cup his hands to his mouth, as artists always paint him, but he holds them behind his ears, the palms to the front and the fingers up.

I go on over the rough cobbles and, passing through the Gate of St. Stephen, I see ahead of me a blinding sandy road and the Mount of Olives with the sun above it.

In mountain country there is nothing older than a road. Cities may come and go, the most splendid buildings may live and die, but the little road that runs between the rocks lives for ever.   One is shown all kinds of sites in Jerusalem which may be open to doubt—such as the very spot on which the cock crowed when St. Peter denied his Lord—but one looks at them with respect for the piety which created them, and with distaste for the principle which profits from them. On the Mount of Olives, however, one *knows* that these little stony tracks that twist and turn over the rocks are the very paths that He must have taken and that they are marked more truly with the imprint of His feet than any rock within a golden shrine.

The road runs downhill from St. Stephen's Gate into the Kedron Valley.   It bends to the right, leading down to the stony place, and, when I look up, the walls of Jerusalem, with their crenellated sentry-walks, stand like a challenge, golden in the morning sun.   At the bottom of the valley the road rises over the lower slopes of the Mount of Olives, and a little to the right stands a clump of cypress trees with a wall round them.   This is the Garden of Gethsemane.

The Franciscan friars, who touch everything with beauty, grace and reverence, own the little Garden and, while they

have built a church near by, they have not touched the
Garden except to make flower-beds among the ancient olive
trees.

In a land where the footsteps of Christ, real or imaginary,
can be traced by huge churches built over stones and caves
and legends, this quiet little Garden on the Mount of Olives
stands out as an imperishable memory. Time has not altered
this Garden. City has followed city on the hill opposite, but the
Garden, so near that in the evening the shadow of Jerusalem's
wall falls across it, has remained to-day as it must have been
in the time of Jesus. There would have been a wall round it
and probably an oil press to which the people on the Mount
would have carried their olives to be crushed. Dotted about
the garden are eight aged olive trees of tremendous girth.
They are more like rocks than trees. Slim new shoots spring
out of apparently dead wood, and the old trunks, vast as ancient
oaks, are propped up with ramparts of stones and stout wooden
poles. These trees still bear fruit from which the monks
press oil.

An old monk, who is working in the Garden, unlocks the
gate for me and turns again to his weeding basket and his rake.

He is a French monk who has spent many years in the Holy
Land, and when I talk to him he straightens himself from the
hedge of rosemary and stands, politely anxious to get on with
his work, his brown gardener's hands folded across his brown
habit, the fingers locked together.

He points out to me a rock which marks the place where
Peter, James and John slept, and not far off is a column in the
wall which is the traditional spot on which Judas betrayed
Jesus with a kiss.

" And is it true," I ask him, " as so many believe, that these
are the actual trees that were growing in the time of Our
Lord? "

" They may well be the trees," he replies, " for their age is
lost in antiquity. I will tell you a very interesting thing about
them. They have never paid the tax which, since the Moslem
conquest, was imposed on newly planted trees. That means
that they were not young trees many centuries ago. That,
my son, is an historic fact, but whether they sheltered our
Lord I cannot say; but, for myself," and here the old man

smiled gently and bent towards his rake and basket, " I believe they did."

There is no sound in the Garden of Gethsemane but the click of the Franciscan's rake among the sharp flints and the drone of bees among the flowers and, intermittently, that hot sound like a whip-lash that will always remind me of the blazing sun of Palestine—the noise of grasshoppers.

And, as I stand in the shade of the olive trees, I look up and see, through a screen of leaves, the great yellow wall of Jerusalem on the ascending slope opposite, and the walled-up Golden Gate, the site of the triumphal entry into the city. In this quiet garden, striped with cool shadow, that wall seems cruel and terrible.

It occurs to me that there could be no greater contrast than the proud, hard, yellow wall and this little garden among trees, where the lizards come out of holes in the stones to stare in the sunlight with their small frogs' heads lifted, listening and watching; where every leaf and every flower achieves an added beauty by reason of the barren harshness and the cruel heat beyond the garden.

" Then cometh Jesus with them unto a place called Gethsemane, and saith unto the disciples, Sit ye here, while I go and pray yonder. . . ."

I finish the chapter of St. Matthew and close the Book. The monk has weeded to the end of his row. He stoops down, picks a stone from his sandal and bends again to his work. And above us the gaunt, cavernous trunks of the eight olive trees that will not die rise up like the columns of a crypt.

As the Franciscan lets me out of the garden he gives me a little slip of paper, which I place in my pocket as I walk back up the hot road to Jerusalem. Remembering it, as I pass in under the gate of St. Stephen, I open it and find pressed inside a spear-shaped olive leaf and a blue flower from the Garden of Gethsemane.

THE HOLY SEPULCHRE

OUTSIDE THE CITY WALLS, JERUSALEM

CHAPTER TWO

How Golgotha was discovered by Constantine under a pagan temple, how the Church of the Holy Sepulchre grew up on the site, and how this church to-day is divided between different Christian communities. I visit the underground quarries which provided the stone for Solomon's Temple, go through the Jewish Quarter on a Sabbath morning, and by night wade through the tunnel which Hezekiah cut in the rock when the Assyrian threatened to come down " like a wolf on the fold."

§ 1

WHEN Jesus says good-bye to Galilee and turns His steps towards Jerusalem, a tenseness creeps into the Gospel narrative. The lovely idyll of Galilee is over. Never again do we hear the waves falling on the lakeside, or watch a great crowd settling on the grass, or see the little fishing-boats come swinging home against the sunset. Jerusalem, high and cold on its hill, terrifying in its formalism and self-conceit, its arrogance and its supreme blindness, lies like a storm-cloud in the path of Christ.

With a wonderful economy of words the Gospels succeed in suggesting the atmosphere of the city, like the first roll of thunder on the wings of an approaching storm. Jerusalem stretches out tentacles to trap Him. Spies waylay Him to ensnare Him in rabbinical argument. He waves them off with cold, icy logic, and passes on His way out of the hot valley of the Jordan to the high, brown mountains and the storm. Never before have violence, great crowds, rings of heated faces, accusing fingers, lying enemies and the feeling of a city in the grip of fanatical hatred been suggested in fewer words. Classical literature contains nothing so vivid as the Gospel account of the events that led to the Crucifixion, and, as we read them, the background, never described but always suggested, is the tense, nervous atmosphere of Jerusalem.

45

It is an extraordinary thing that this atmosphere is characteristic of Jerusalem to-day. The city has been destroyed many times, but each time it has risen from the dead the same nervous, tense Jerusalem. The tightness in the air is a strange impalpable thing, but so real that it is a relief to escape beyond the walls of the city, if it is only as far as the Mount of Olives. No sooner do you return and pass in under one of the old gates, than you fall again under the influence of this strange power.

In the old days the electricity in the air of Jerusalem was due to the Temple and everything that the rigid Temple worship stood for in the life of Judaism; to-day it is due to the fact that the Holy City has become a thrice-holy city, and that within its walls three great faiths are always in danger of conflict. The Christian, who naturally regards Jerusalem only as the scene of the Crucifixion and the Resurrection, is apt to forget that to the Jew it is still the city of Jehovah, and to the Moslem it is the most sacred spot on earth outside Mecca. The threshing-floor of Ornan the Jebusite, which became the altar of burnt offerings in the Temple of Solomon, is to-day a Moslem shrine and from this rock, so the Moslems believe, the Prophet ascended into heaven on the back of his winged steed, el-Barûk.

It is therefore not difficult to understand why Jerusalem is filled with a violence of mind instead of the violence of physical action which characterises all modern cities. It would be unwise for a Jew to enter the Holy Sepulchre, and the great mosque is often closed to Christians. The air is full of a feeling of spiritual barriers and frontiers. Nothing matters in Jerusalem but religion. Although it is one of the most polyglot cities on earth, there are no nationalities. A man is seldom referred to as a Swiss, a German, an Armenian, a Persian, a Copt, or a Greek: he is either a Christian, a Moslem, or a Jew. These three faiths are to Jerusalem what nationality is to other cities.

It is not, perhaps, surprising that three conflicting ideas about Eternity should result in a general disagreement about time. Christian, Moslem and Jew live in different years. With us it is 1934 A.D. The Jews, however, counting from the creation of the world, estimate the date as 5694. The

Moslems, counting from the birth of Mahomet, make it 1352. But there is even a fourth time-table, that of the Greeks and Russians, who employ the obsolete Julian Calendar, which was devised by Julius Cæsar in 46 B.C. and corrected by Pope Gregory XIII in 1582.

Then Jerusalem has three holy days every week. The Moslems revere Friday, the Jews keep Saturday sacred, and the Christians follow on with their Sunday. A delightfully bizarre touch is given to Jerusalem by the Abyssinian Christians, who celebrate Christmas once a month; but that, fortunately, is purely a private affair, and does not close the banks. In this chaos of sacred observance the life of a bank clerk in Jerusalem must be at least half-way to heaven, because at Easter time Mr. Barclay almost ceases to function. Holy days succeed one another for nearly a week, and Mr. Barclay draws his blinds reverently for the Passover, for Nebi Musa, and for Easter.

So Jerusalem expresses in her daily life the complexity of all great junctions. Three main lines of faith meet there in apparent confusion before spreading out to the ends of the earth.

§ 2

The afternoon sun was filling the courtyard of the Holy Sepulchre when I made a second visit to that puzzling collection of churches.

It is, at first, difficult to understand its confusing topography. It is, in essentials, a round church, with the tomb of Christ in the centre of it. A large crusading choir leads from it, round which cluster a series of chapels. Some distance away, and fourteen feet higher than the rest of the church, is a chapel built over the holy hill of Golgotha. There is another church connected with, and behind, the choir, known as Saint Helena's Chapel, from which steps lead down into a rock cistern where the mother of Constantine discovered the Cross. But the two main sites on which the Church of the Holy Sepulchre have been built are the hill of Golgotha, or Calvary, and the garden tomb of St. Joseph of Arimathæa which was " in the place where he was crucified."

The church gives one an overwhelming impression of darkness and decay. There were passages so dark that I had to strike matches to find my way. And the decay everywhere of stone, of wood and of iron was fantastic. I saw pictures that were rotting on their canvases and I even saw canvases, still framed, that were bleached white: the last fragments of paint had peeled off, but they were still in position. There were ominous cracks and fissures in stone and marble. I thought how odd it is that extreme devotion can have exactly the same effect as extreme neglect. The Church of the Holy Sepulchre wears its air of shabby decay for the simple reason that the re-hanging of a picture, the repair of a stone, and even the mending of a window, assume such gigantic importance in the eyes of the communities that they provoke a situation capable of indefinite postponement.

What an incredible confusion of pillars and passages, of underground caves and semi-underground tunnels, has descended to us over sixteen centuries of battle and burning! It is an extraordinary muddle, and no one can understand this church in one or two visits. It is a labyrinth of passages and chapels embracing the three main shrines.

I ascended and descended steps and, led on by the light of glimmering tapers, explored dark galleries and pitch-black corridors. Once I was brought to a halt by kneeling Franciscans who were visiting the stations of the Cross, the light from their tapers shining on devout bearded faces which might have come from the walls of El Greco's house in Toledo. The first impression of the church is of a series of treasure caves. It is unlike the most ornate Roman Catholic church in Italy or Spain. Its richness and flamboyance are those of the Orient. It is as though the spoils of Asia Minor, of Russia and of Greece, accumulating for centuries, have been heaped in candle-light on the over-burdened altars. Art and vulgarity stand side by side. A priceless chalice, the gift of an emperor, stands next to something tawdry and tinsely that might have been pulled from a Christmas tree. And hundreds of ikons, glimmering in old gold, receive candle drippings on the stiff Byzantine figures of saint and king.

The Greek monks swing their censers towards the blaze of candle-light and the blue clouds of their incense spurt out to hang about the ikons and the gilded screens. The worshippers, kneeling on the marble floors, seem to be prostrate before a series of exotic jewellers' shops. Only in the chapel of the Franciscans is there that chastity of decoration which one associates with a Western church. It is plain and rather chilly. It strikes at once the note that divides the Western from the Eastern Church in the Holy Land. Those who associate the Church of Rome with outward gorgeousness of vestment and ritual find in Jerusalem that the Latins are the staid and dowdy "Protestants," in brown robes girded with a rope, while the Greeks and the Armenians go garmented in scarlet and gold, with crosses of crystal and precious stones carried before them and incense in clouds about them.

Ascending a dim flight of steps, I found myself kneeling on a marble floor with a crowd of hushed people, each one of whom carried a lit candle. The person next to me sighed as though his, or her, heart were breaking. I stole a look and saw a black Nubian face, the white eyeballs shining in the candle-light, but whether the person was man or woman I could not tell because of the voluminous folds of drapery in which he, or she, was concealed.

We knelt before an altar that shivered in yellow candle-light and glittered with golden lamps and ikons. Divided from this chapel by two pillars, was a similar chapel before which the Franciscans were kneeling, the candle-light moving over their devout, uncomplicated faces. We formed two congregations, kneeling together and facing the same way, but worshipping before separate chapels.

This was the hill of the Crucifixion: Calvary, the holiest place on earth. I looked round, hoping to be able to detect some sign of its former aspect, but that has been obliterated for ever beneath the suffocating trappings of piety. The chapel before which I was kneeling was the Chapel of the Raising of the Cross; the chapel next to it was the Chapel of the Nailing to the Cross.

When the crowd thinned, I approached nearer to the altar. There was a Greek priest there, watching the candles, snuffing some and lighting others. He beckoned me to come near the altar and pointed out a silver disc edged with candle grease and, below it, a hole in the rock in which, he whispered to me, the Cross of our Lord was fixed. The pilgrims came up, weeping and praying, to touch the rock with trembling fingers; and I went away wishing that we might have known this place only in our hearts.

I followed a band of pilgrims down a flight of steps into the Church of the Holy Cross, which is also called the Church of St. Helena. More steps lead down to the grotto in which St. Helena, in the fourth century, is believed to have discovered the true Cross. This is the Chapel of the Finding of the Holy Cross, and its roof and sides are formed of the black unsmoothed rock.

I found myself, as every pilgrim does, drawn irresistibly back to the marble shrine in the centre of the round church. I sat in front of it for a long time, thinking how unworthy a shrine it is for the Tomb of Jesus. It was built by the Greeks in 1810 after the fire in the Church of the Holy Sepulchre, so that it is not even redeemed by antiquity.

And while I sat there the services of three different churches were in progress, all within earshot of each other. The Franciscans were holding a service in their chapel, and the Greeks, next door, so to speak, were intoning their long and unmusical prayers. Immediately behind the Tomb of Christ, where the Coptic Church has an altar, rose up a weird, raucous chanting. The sound of these three services, one in Latin, one in Greek, and the third in the ancient tongue of Egypt, mingled together round the Tomb of Christ.

One of the most difficult things for the average visitor from the West to appreciate, and some never attempt to do so, is the divided ownership of the Holy Sepulchre. The shrines within the church are split up between six churches : the Eastern Orthodox Church, the Armenian Church, the Coptic Church, the Syrian Church, and the Abyssinian Church.

The Western Church is represented by the Latins, who have entrusted the custody of the Holy Places to the Franciscans since the Crusades. The head of the Franciscans in the Holy Land is known as the " Custos "—the Father Custodian.

The divided ownership began to take shape after Saladin broke up the Christian Kingdom of Jerusalem in 1187. The Crusades were Western Christianity's bid for the ownership of the holy sites in Palestine, and, during the eighty-eight years of the Christian rule which was established by the swords of the Crusaders, the Western Church controlled the Holy Sepulchre. After the Moslem conquest, however, the Eastern Churches found it possible to enter into possession by payment of rent to the infidel; and so they took over as tenants what the Crusaders had won at the point of the sword.

The fluctuating fortunes of the various communities within the Church of the Holy Sepulchre would make a large and fascinating book. Every inch of the holy space is engraved on a map of tradition. The frontier between the property of the Franciscans and the Greeks is as real as the frontier between Austria and Italy, and the space on which the Copts, the Syrians and the Armenians may tread in the course of their daily offices has been laid down by centuries of tradition.

The Tomb of our Lord and the rotunda in which it stands are the common property of all the churches. They have certain established rights to hold processions there, or to celebrate mass on stated occasions. The choir of the Crusaders, leading from the Rotunda, belongs to the Greeks, while in the corresponding sanctuary to the north, the Chapel of the Apparition of Jesus to His Mother, the Franciscans have their choir. The Copts, as I have said, have a little chapel built on to the end of the holy Tomb itself. The Syrians have a pitch-dark chapel devoid of all decoration, which leads off from the central Rotunda and is entered by a low stone door like the entrance to a dungeon. The Church of St. Helena and the Chapel of the Parting of the Raiment belong to the Armenians. Golgotha is divided between Latins and Greeks; one chapel, that of the Raising of the Cross, is Greek, and the adjacent chapel, that of the Nailing to the Cross, and also the altar of the Stabat Mater—the place on which the Blessed Virgin received into her arms the lifeless body of Jesus— belong to the Latins.

One could go on enumerating many other chapel.

and holy places, but I have named the most sacred. The Abyssinian Church, which in the sixteenth century possessed a valuable foothold within the church, has been gradually dislodged, until to-day the colony of dark-skinned monks has taken refuge on the roof, where, round the dome of St. Helena's Chapel, they have built their huts.

Other sects and churches have in the course of their history been obliged to give up their hold on sites within the Holy Sepulchre, such as the Georgians, who were forced to retire in 1644 because, owing to national misfortunes, they were unable to pay the exorbitant dues of the Turkish Government.

When people hold up to scorn the occasional squabbles that break out between the various communities in the Holy Sepulchre, they forget, or are unaware of, the extreme delicacy of the position. Such squabbles are undignified and regrettable, but human nature being as it is, they are understandable.

For instance, every inch of the territory is, as I have said, clearly marked out, and the boundaries, although invisible to the eye, are as clear in the eye of tradition as though they were outlined in electric light. But certain territories contain shrines that are common property, and the various sects have the right to light a lamp over them on specified occasions. In order to do this it is necessary for them to make a privileged invasion of neighbouring church property. This is the time of danger. When the Copts have the right to make a procession through Greek or Armenian territory, or vice versa, the weakness of the flesh is sometimes too strong to be endured !

The late Bishop Gore was once shown round Jerusalem by a friend of mine, who asked what he thought Jesus would say about the sectarian disputes round His tomb.

"I believe He would say, with that wonderful smile of His," said the bishop, "'My children must have toys. Do not all children sometimes quarrel about their toys?'"

§ 3

No building in the world has a stranger history than the Church of the Holy Sepulchre.

After the siege of Jerusalem in 70 A.D. the first Christians, who had fled to Pella, returned to the ruins of their homes. They formed a living link with Jesus Christ. The oldest among them had seen Him, and had possibly spoken to Him; and the youngest of them must have been familiar with the site of Calvary, the House of the Last Supper, the Garden of Gethsemane, and all the other places associated with the earthly life of our Lord. Any of them who were over fifty may have had vivid memories of the Trial and Crucifixion.

I remember, in the spring of 1919, walking through the ruins of Ypres and other towns in the sector which had been literally shelled from the map, or so one would have thought. I saw the pitiful sight of peasants returning to look for the places where their homes had once stood, pulling down the bricks and the stones that cumbered them and digging a way down to the cellar, where they established themselves beneath a roof of corrugated iron, or anything that would keep out the rain. The tenacity with which people return to their shattered homes after wars and earthquakes is proof that this desire to link up with the old life is one of the most powerful of instincts.

The Christians from Pella must have wandered about the mounds and ruins of Jerusalem exactly like the peasants of Ypres and Cambrai, but they had even more to assist them on their way through the desolation, because, while land-marks like the Cloth Hall of Ypres had been shelled to bits, Titus had purposely spared the mighty towers of Herod's stronghold. It must have been far easier for these early Christians to discover their old homes than it was for the people of, say, Cambrai. Also, Jerusalem is hard rock, and Titus did not destroy the buildings with high explosives. Therefore, it is certain that they began to build on sites which were doubly sacred to them, places hallowed by association with the Master as well as by their own domestic history. We do not know their attitude towards Calvary.

c

It would seem, in fact, that they held in greater sanctity the House of the Last Supper—the house of Mary, mother of Mark, the house in which Jesus appeared after the Crucifixion, in which the miracle of Pentecost occurred, and in which, tradition says, the Blessed Virgin spent the remainder of her life. A church soon grew up on the site of this house and became known as the Cœnaculum, a word that suggests *cœna*, the " dining-hall." It would surely be more natural for these people, only forty years away from the Crucifixion, to hold sacred the place associated with Christ's last teaching, His appearance after the Resurrection and the visitation of the Holy Ghost, rather than the tragic hill of Golgotha. But although they did not, so far as we know, build any church above the tomb of Christ, we can be quite certain that every one of them knew where it was. The Eastern mind never forgets any site associated with holy things.

For about sixty years Jerusalem was nothing more than the camp of the Tenth Legion, " the Fretensis." Round the camp of the legion clustered a few huts, those of merchants and camp followers, and among the ruins there rose, no doubt, a few houses, the property of time-expired men and others: and on Mount Zion was the little Christian settlement grouped about the Cœnaculum. This must have been the total population, because the old inhabitants had either been slain in the siege of Titus or carried into captivity.

At this time two men, whose names are once again linked with that of Britain, took a hand in Jerusalem's destiny. The first was the Emperor Hadrian. He had made a series of empire tours. In the course of one of them, in the year 122 A.D., he had visited Britain and had ordered the building of the great wall from the Tyne to the Solway that still bears his name. In the course of another, eight years later, he visited Palestine. It has been said, I think by Renan, that the sight of ruins always inspired Hadrian with a desire to rebuild. It is certain that the superb site of Jerusalem, lying neglected on its hills, touched his imagination. He ordered the site to be cleared for the construction of a new city, one that should be Roman down to the smallest detail; and the name of this city was to be Ælia Capitolina, a blending of his own name, Ælius, with that of the god Jupiter Capitolinus.

The news of this decision fanned the fires of Zealotry. A Jewish generation that had forgotten Titus had grown up between 70 A.D. and 130 A.D.; and once more the flame of rebellion swept over Judæa. Hadrian was forced to send to Britain for his best general, Julius Severus, who began a merciless war in which, says Dio Cassius, 580,000 persons were slain in the sieges and capture of nearly 600 fortified towns and villages. At the end of this war there was no Jewish problem. The leader of the revolt was torn to pieces with a white-hot rake. And the hills round Jerusalem echoed to the peaceful sound of the stonemason's chisel.

Ælia Capitolina, the new name for Jerusalem, was a dignified city of white columns and colonnades, with a forum and temples, surrounded by a wall built, more or less, on the lines of the old Jewish ramparts. It was dedicated to Jupiter Capitolinus on the *vincennalia* of Hadrian in 136 A.D., the anniversary of the twentieth year of his reign. Among the buildings of this new Roman city was a Temple to Venus. It was built on a slight hill that had once been just outside the walls of Herodian Jerusalem. It was the hill of Golgotha, or Calvary. It has often been suggested that Hadrian built this temple because the Christians held this hill to be holy ground and, in his desire to stamp out Jewish, or what he regarded as semi-Jewish, rites, built the Venus Temple to desecrate the memory of Christ. Paulinus of Nola, writing to the Emperor Severus in the fourth century, says that Hadrian, "imagining that he could kill the Christian faith by defacing the place, consecrated an image of Jupiter on the site of the Passion."

The method of building this pagan temple on Calvary is very interesting. They first built a twenty-foot wall round the hill and filled in the intervening space with rubble and concrete. They thus made a high level place about three hundred feet in length and one hundred and sixty feet in width, which formed the *podia*, or platform, for the temple, a stage very similar to that on which the Temple of Castor was erected in the Roman Forum, or the great Temple of Roma Æterna and Venus Felix on the Via Sacra. The platform which covered Calvary was planted with a grove of trees, and immediately above the Holy Sepulchre stood a statue of Jupiter and above Calvary a marble statue of Venus and a small temple.

If Hadrian hoped to stamp out for ever the memory of Calvary and the Sepulchre, his act had the opposite effect. It preserved and, as it were, sealed the holy places for future generations. And the evidence that this was Hadrian's object seems to be overwhelming, especially when he went to the trouble of perpetrating a similar profanation over the grotto of the Nativity at Bethlehem, above which he built a grove and temple to Adonis.

Now the site of Calvary and the Tomb of Jesus were lost beneath the platform of a pagan temple for exactly two hundred years. But they were not forgotten. During that time Christianity gained ground all over the world. Constantine the Great established it as the official faith of the Roman Empire. Among those churchmen who attended the famous Council of Nicea in the year 325 A.D. was Macarius, Bishop of Jerusalem, a man whose saintly virtues were such that St. Athanasius numbered him among apostolic men. It is believed by some that Macarius mentioned to Constantine, who presided over the Council, the frightful sacrilege created by the existence of Hadrian's Temple of Venus, and that Constantine, moved by the bishop's eloquence, instructed him to pull down the temple and uncover our Lord's Sepulchre. The only contemporary authority for these events is Eusebius, who seems to have been present as a boy when the Holy Sepulchre was discovered. His account of this discovery is given in his rather fulsome *Life of Constantine*. The historic fact remains that under the direction of Macarius, about the year 336 A.D., the Roman temple of Venus was pulled down, the rubble torn up, and below in the rock was discovered what contemporary observers believed was the Tomb of Jesus Christ. Later writers connect the discovery with the pilgrimage of St. Helena, the mother of Constantine, who, at the same time that these excavations were in progress, discovered the Cross in a deep rock cistern near Calvary.

As soon as the Tomb was discovered Constantine ordered that a house of prayer should be built round " the sacred cave." It was, as he wrote to Macarius, " to be worthy of the most wonderful place in the world." The Roman engineers thereupon set to work to cut away the rock round the Tomb until only the Tomb itself was left standing in the centre of a levelled space. This was enclosed by a splendid rotunda with an exterior diameter of more than 109 feet. Slightly to the east of the rotunda was an outer court open to the sky and surrounded by fine porches. In this rose up the rock of Calvary, which had been trimmed by the engineers to form a cube about eighteen by fifteen feet. It was a platform approached by a flight of stairs, was covered with rich mosaics, and furnished with a silver balustrade. On the top was planted a large jewelled cross. Beyond this atrium of Calvary stretched a magnificent basilica called the Martyrion. It was a severe classical building, with four aisles formed by marble columns and a crypt formed by the rock cistern of the Finding of the Holy Cross. Such was the first Church of the Holy Sepulchre.

From that time in the year 336 A.D until to-day the site has never been forgotten. There have been times in the stormy history of Jerusalem when the church was burned, and even once destroyed so that it remained a ruin for years. But another church rose from the ashes. When the Crusaders captured Jerusalem in 1099 they considered that the church was not sufficiently grand or beautiful. They rebuilt it, and in general design and partly in actual structure the present Church of the Holy Sepulchre is the church they built.

There are, of course, many who do not believe that the Tomb of Christ lay beneath the Temple of Venus, and they therefore deny the authenticity of the Church of the Holy Sepulchre. Their arguments are based on the belief that this site (now right in the centre of the walled city) was also inside the walls of Herod's Jerusalem. Among the few things we know about Golgotha is that it was " without the wall." Many alternative sites have, from time to time, been put forward, but all of them seem now to have been forgotten except that of Gordon's Calvary near the Damascus Gate.

I cannot help feeling that over sixteen hundred years of firm tradition are more reliable than any theory, no matter how plausible. When Bishop Macarius found the Tomb

of Christ in 336 A.D., he knew as well as we do that
Jesus suffered outside the walls of Jerusalem. He was also
in a better position than we to judge where those walls lay.
Why, then, should he have picked upon so contentious a site
if it were not the right one?

I have shown in this brief sketch that eye-witnesses of the
Crucifixion returned to Jerusalem within forty years of
Christ's death, and that their descendants remained there
from shortly after the siege of 70 A.D. until the discovery of
the Tomb in 336 A.D. To abandon the site of the Holy
Sepulchre is to admit that the Christians who remembered
the Crucifixion did not look for Golgotha among the ruins
of Jerusalem, did not discuss its story with their sons and
daughters and did not point it out to those fellow Christians who were not acquainted with it. When we think of
the numbers of personal dramas connected with Golgotha :
how Mary Magdalene, Mary, the mother of James, and
Joanna, went there with spices on the morning of the Resurrection; how they ran back to tell the disciples that the
Lord had risen from the dead; how Peter, and " the disciple
whom Jesus loved," went with beating hearts to learn the
truth for themselves, it would seem impossible that those
actually in touch with these wonders should not have engraved the memory of this place upon the minds of their
descendants.

It is easier to believe that Herod's Wall ran an unexpected
course than that a people, to whom the handing down of
traditional things was second nature, should have forgotten
a place of such superlative significance to them and to all
those who came after

§ 4

Among the many mysteries of Jerusalem is the roof of the
Church of the Holy Sepulchre. Hundreds of books have
been written about the inside of the church, but nothing, so
far as I know, has been written about the outside, which is
almost as interesting.

I might never have known this were I not afflicted by a
bad, and even dangerous, habit of mounting mysterious and

sinister flights of steps. Such steps are to be found somewhere at the back of the church, in a narrow lane which
leads off David Street.

I climbed up and found myself gazing at a supreme view
of Jerusalem and the Mount of Olives from the roof of
the Holy Sepulchre. Then, within a few yards, I saw a
camel sitting gracefully on the top of the Chapel of the
Apparition!

If you climbed to the roof of Winchester Cathedral, or
Westminster Abbey, and saw there a camel, or even a cow, you
would begin to worry, but it is part of the prevailing fantasy
of Jerusalem that the sight of a camel on the roof of the Holy
Sepulchre does not seem at all remarkable—except in retro-
spect. The animal had been brought up with a load of
stones for the repair of the roof.

It is perhaps only from the roof of the church that you
realise clearly that it is built on the varying depths of rock
that formed Golgotha, for you are always descending little
iron ladders of thirty steps, and mounting others of ten or
twenty, in order to explore the strange territory that lies
among the sprouting domes and the crosses of iron and
copper.

On one part of the roof I saw a line with clothes drying,
including a pair of socks that could have belonged only to a
Coptic monk. Near this was a little low outhouse with
windows, a door and a chimney of tin. As I passed, I caught
sight of the dusky anchorite within, busy, not with his prayers,
but with his washing. The knowledge that anchorites wash
their clothes was even more surprising than the sight of a
roof-bound camel.

When I climbed up to the roof of St. Helena's Chapel I
discovered what I consider to be one of the most extraordinary
sights in Jerusalem—a monastery of black monks.

Some of the monks sat about in the hot sunlight. Several
were crouched on their heels in true African style. Near
them were their huts, rough and primitive structures, with
mud roofs. It reminded me of an African village in an
exhibition. On the roof near the "monastery" is the
chapel, a building so small that it can hold only the priests
and their assistants, while members of the brotherhood, and

those members of the public who wish to attend an Abyssinian service, are obliged to sit on the steps.

The Abyssinians are the strangest, and in some ways the most interesting, of all the exotic communities who worship Christ in the Holy Land. Superior people who smile at their peculiarities should be chastened to know that these people were converted by Frumentius in 330 A.D.

They are a devout people and hold a number of strange beliefs. They trace the origin of their royal family to a supposed union between Solomon and the Queen of Sheba, and they believe that the Ark of the Covenant is hidden somewhere in their country and that with its arrival in Africa Jehovah deserted Israel and adopted the Abyssinians.

In the Middle Ages the black monks held many imposing portions of the Holy Sepulchre, including the Chapel of the Derision, but, as I have already said, they were not strong enough to retain them and were forced to seek refuge on the roof. There are about twenty monks, ruled by a dusky abbot.

I spoke to several monks, but found no one who knew any European language. They were polite and gentle. An old man led me to the little chapel and, bowing and smiling, invited me to go inside. I climbed over several rolled-up carpets and, when my eyes were used to the gloom, discovered that I was attending an Abyssinian Mass.

The little cellar on the roof—if one can use such a term— was full of black monks who leaned on long, crook-like staves and chanted monotonously in a wild, barbaric, and entirely toneless manner. The dark chapel was lit by scores of candles. Witch balls of coloured glass hung from the roof. A crude picture of St. Jerome sitting on the back of his lion decorated one wall, and the altar was separated from the tiny cell by a gaudy gilt screen and a scarlet curtain.

During pauses in the chanting, this curtain was drawn to reveal the celebrant and his assistants officiating at the altar before an ark-shaped box in which reposed the chalice. They prayed in a dense fog of incense. It rolled out of the sanctuary in acrid clouds.

The priests were robed in vivid red, blue, and green vestments of silk and brocade. Once, during the Mass, when the curtain was drawn, I saw through an opening in it that the priests were changing their vestments for even more brilliant ones, and the officiating priest placed on his head something between a crown and a mitre.

While this was going on to the sound of weird chanting, a monk entered and, after prostrating himself, stood up and opened a green umbrella with gold fringe all round it.   Then the priest came out, bearing the Host; and the umbrella— the Abyssinian symbol of royalty—was with difficulty lifted in the confined space above priest and chalice.   What would have been a procession round a normally sized church be- came a sort of rotary movement, with the black monks and myself moving round to give room to the celebrant.   Then, after closing the green umbrella to get it through the door, and opening it again in the sunlight outside, the Host was carried in procession round the roof of St. Helena's Chapel.

I watched them go and saw, framed in the little doorway, three or four Abyssinians prostrate on their faces in the blinding sunlight as the green umbrella went past.

Discussing these monks afterwards with a man who has studied the liturgical history of the Eastern communities, I was told that their services contain customs and symbols that go back to the very dawn of Christianity.   In general ritual, however, they resemble the Egyptian, or Coptic, Church.   No one knows very much about them, and the community, which is the poorest and the smallest in the Holy Sepulchre, keeps much to itself.

The black abbot is called the Abouna, a Syriac word that means " Our Father."   It is a similar word to that used by our Lord, who spoke Aramaic.   St. Mark tells us that Christ prayed during the agony in the Garden of Gethsemane, using the word " Abba," or Father.

The Abyssinians have also many strange Jewish rites mixed with their Christianity, and they keep holy both Saturday and Sunday.   As I have said, they hold Christmas once a month, except in March, and are also the only Christians who have made a saint of Pontius Pilate.

I imagine that if anyone took up the study of Abyssinian theology he would discover himself in a wonderful museum of heresies and queer odds and ends of Judaism and paganism.   The liturgical language is Gheez, the classical and long-dead tongue of Ethiopia.

There is something rather pathetic about these simple, devout black men, dislodged from the church but established on the roof, clinging to the odour of sanctity with the tenacity that has, through centuries of isolation in a world of Islam, held them faithful to Jesus Christ.   And I believe that if our Lord came back in earthly form He would visit the roof of St. Helena's Chapel, where poverty and simplicity live under the stars.

§5

About eighty-five years ago a man named Barclay was walking round the walls of Jerusalem with his dog and a gun.   When he came to the Damascus Gate he discovered that the dog was missing.   He whistled, but the animal did not appear.   Turning back he saw the dog crawling out apparently from beneath the city walls, where he had evidently made a find.   He stood barking, asking his master to come and look at his discovery.   When Barclay went over, he found that bushes, shrubs, and the débris of centuries concealed the opening to a cavern which ran under the walls and beneath the city.

Such a discovery in Jerusalem fires the imagination and encourages the wildest rumours.   The Arabs believe to this day that in such a cavern the gold and silver treasures of Solomon, the Ark of the Covenant, and the vessels used in the Temple sacrifices, lie waiting to be found.   This dream is not confined to the Arabs.   I have heard several men, whose opinions claim respect and attention, say that they believe the Ark of the Covenant is hidden somewhere in the mysterious and quite unknown underworld of the Temple area.

So Barclay wisely said nothing and, returning on the following day with a search-party, widened the small hole into which his dog had jumped and entered the cavern.

The torches of the search-party lit up a weird and terrifying scene.   The explorers stood in a snow-white cavern, so large that its extremity was hidden in the darkness.   One glance at the stone walls told them that it had been artificially made. The torchlight was not powerful enough to penetrate to the end of the cavern. It was an immense excavation that ran on and on beneath the streets of the Old City.

It was soon realised that they had discovered Solomon's Quarries—called by Josephus the "Royal Quarries"—the quarries which, lost for nearly two centuries, had provided the stone for Solomon's Temple about nine hundred years before Christ.

I think these quarries are one of the most interesting sights in Jerusalem. They are neglected by the average sightseer, although every Freemason who visits Jerusalem is aware of them. Masons from all parts of the world hold lodge meetings there at night, when they will not be disturbed or observed, because they hold the theory that the builders of the Temple were the first Freemasons.

When I visited the quarries, an old Arab who sits at the entrance gave me a lantern and warned me not to fall down any of the frightful precipices, for Solomon's quarries are no place for the short-sighted or the stumbler.

Another Arab, working in the patch of daylight that penetrates the cave, was shaping paper-weights and small hammers such as chairmen use at meetings. These objects, when decorated with appropriate triangles and compasses, are eagerly bought by masonic visitors and find their way all over the world. Stones from the quarries are also exported to become foundation stones for masonic buildings.

I went into the darkness, swinging my lantern, and the path led steeply down into an enormous entrance cave like a buried cathedral. From this excavation wide, high passages led off in many directions. I pulled up sharply on the edge of chasms and, waving my lantern in the darkness, saw that the rock fell away to lower workings, to more distant and deeper caverns.

It has been estimated that in ancient times sufficient stone had been removed from these quarries to build the modern city of Jerusalem twice over. It is a peculiar and unusual pure white stone, soft to work but hardening rapidly when exposed to the atmosphere. The Arabs call these caverns the "cotton caves" because they are so white. Here and there, however, when I flashed my lantern towards the lower portions of the roof, I saw a number of black patches. In one place I was near enough to see that they were large bats, hanging to the roof and waiting for the night.

On every hand I noticed the sign of workmen. With a feeling of awe and bewilderment, a feeling that I was dropping down through the very floor of Time, I knew that these workmen had been dead for nearly three thousand years. Yet the marks made by the Phœnician stone-cutters when Solomon was king of Jerusalem were as clean, as sharp and, apparently, as recent, as the marks a man sees in the Portland quarries to-day.

The workmen had cut niches in the walls for their lamps. And it all seemed so new, so modern, that I had the odd feeling that it was lunch hour during the building of the Temple and that at any moment I might hear the returning feet of Solomon's quarrymen, kicking aside the chips and stones as they poured back to work.

I propped the lantern on a ledge of rock, and by the light of its candle I read the extraordinarily detailed account of the building of the Temple which you will find in the Second Book of Chronicles, chapter two, and the First Book of Kings, chapter five.

I suppose a modern architect could not, given the same number of words, create for us a more accurate and vivid picture of the plans, design, engagement of workmen, rates of pay, building, and furnishing of a great building, than is to be found in these chapters of the Bible.

Down in the darkness of Solomon's quarries, with the white dust of the stone on my clothes, the building of the Temple took on a reality that surprised me. It frequently happens in Palestine that some verse of the Bible, hitherto meaningless, suddenly unlocks itself, and one is left amazed by its minute accuracy. I realised the real meaning of a verse which must have puzzled many people. Verse seven, in the sixth chapter of the First Book of Kings, describing the building of the House of the Lord, says:

" And the house, when it was in building, was built of stone made ready before it was brought thither: so that there was neither hammer nor ax nor any tool of iron heard in the house, while it was in building."

I have always imagined that this verse meant that the Temple stone was quarried far away out of earshot of Jerusalem. What else could it have meant? But why should the writer of Kings have stressed the obvious fact that distant quarrying could not be heard on Mount Moriah? Obviously the point of this verse is that the stone with which Solomon built his Temple came almost from beneath the Temple, yet *not a soul heard the cutting of the stones !*

In these quarries you can see how the stone was broken from the bed, how it was passed at once to the masons, who shaped and smoothed it—the floor is in places many feet deep in tons of chips—and how it went straight into the daylight ready to take its place in the building of the Temple.

No matter how earnestly those in the streets of the city above might have listened for the sound of hammers, they could have heard nothing.

Many stories are, of course, told of a mysterious underground passage which linked the quarries with the Temple. There is a widespread belief that the priests hurriedly hid the Temple treasure in these caverns when the Roman armies under Titus razed Jerusalem and the Temple to the ground. I do not know why treasure hunters should still think it possible to find these precious objects, for it is quite clear that many of them were carried through the streets of Rome when Titus celebrated his triumph. However, one earnest explorer some years ago probed for a secret passage—and found one! In order to reach it you have to bend down and crawl for a few yards into a narrow tunnel about three feet in height, and then you find yourself in another passage of the rock. You are at the extremity of the quarries now and moving under Jerusalem in the direction of the Temple Mount. Suddenly you come up against an ancient fortified wall. What it was for, who built it and when it was built, no one knows.

I left the quarries and went out into the blinding light of afternoon with the feeling that yesterday and to-day are one in the empty caverns where, it seems, the workmen of Hiram, King of Tyre, have just "knocked off" for a ten-minute break.

§ 6

As the sun sets behind Jerusalem on a Friday night, a hush falls over the Jewish quarter. The Sabbath has begun.

The warren of small houses in the network of narrow streets has been washed clean. You look through archways into small yards scrubbed white. Pots and pans have been scoured. Sabbath lamps are lit. And through the streets of the old city pass some of the strangest and most picturesque figures in the world to-day: patriarchs in velvet gabardines and round, fur-rimmed hats; pallid, sandy-haired young Jews with fanatical eyes and long hair, two corkscrew curls falling from their temples on each side and tapping against their cheeks; and little boys in their Sabbath garments, leading by the hand some tottering, bent Shylock, grown old and kind.

These are the old-fashioned Orthodox Jews, who live according to the Law of Moses, who weep at the Wailing Wall for the lost glories of Israel, and whose lives are rigidly bound by the minute prohibitions of the Mosaic law.

Their settlement in Jerusalem is recent, as dates go in the ancient city. The Crusaders massacred every Jew and Jewess when they captured Jerusalem. It was not until the Arab conquest and the European persecution of the Jews during the Middle Ages that small groups began to trickle back.

This strange community contains to-day a number of interesting sects. There are Sephardi Jews, who came originally from Spain, Morocco and Algeria, in 1492. They speak Ladino, a kind of broken Castilian. There are the Ashkenazim, from Central and Eastern Europe. There are picturesque Bokhara Jews from Persia, and Jews from Samarkand, who speak a Persian Yiddish.

An extraordinary people are the Yemenites, who arrived during the last century from the wilds of Arabia, claiming to be the tribe of Gad, and speaking both Hebrew and Arabic.

There are the Qaarites, who live under a curse, and the Hassidic Jews, who dance like dervishes in their synagogue. There are also the fanatical fur-hatted Jews with ear-curls, known as Agudath Israel. They talk Yiddish and refuse to speak Hebrew because they believe that its use in ordinary life is a blasphemy. They spend their time poring over the sacred books. When the Sabbath begins on Friday night, they turn out to see that all the Jewish shops are shut. If any are open, they picket the doors.

Early one Sabbath morning a young Jew took me round the synagogues in the old city. It was extraordinarily interesting. We plunged straight into the Old Testament. The narrow streets and the labyrinth of houses are full of synagogues, often merely a small room containing a few books on shelves or cupboards, a tribune, and a reading-desk containing the Torah, or Pentateuch, written on parchment and fixed to rollers.

Ancient Jews, with spectacles on the tips of their noses, rocked themselves backwards and forwards as they recited prayers; little boys and young men kept up a perpetual swaying and muttering as they repeated the sacred words.

In a synagogue of Moroccan Jews the congregation sat on the floor like Moors and the women were hidden, like wives in a harem, behind an open-work screen.

In nearly all these synagogues I saw something that illuminated a passage in St. Luke: the story of Jesus as a child of twelve disputing with the rabbis in the Temple. There were small boys in their Sabbath clothes, prayer-rugs over their shoulders, sitting beside their fathers or their grandfathers, and carefully applying themselves to the Law, repeating the words in monotonous voices and rocking their small bodies.

In one obscure synagogue, I think of Ashkenazim Jews, the morning service had just ended. A lad of about twelve years of age was standing before three bearded elders, talking to them in a precocious and animated manner. Sometimes he pleased them, and they smiled and patted him on the shoulder; but sometimes he annoyed them, and the three old men shook their beards in disagreement and frowned at the lad over their spectacles. But the little fellow stood his ground, waiting respectfully to be spoken to; then, his questions over, he gave a little bob to the old men and walked slowly away.

This, I thought, must have been something like the sight that met the eyes of Joseph and Mary when, seeking Jesus, " they found Him in the Temple, sitting in the midst of the doctors, both hearing them and asking them questions."

We came to a door in a high wall. A woman peered out through a little grid, but refused to open the door. The young Jew begged to be admitted, but she was adamant. This was the carefully guarded underground synagogue of the Qaarites, whose community was once numerous. These Jews have a peculiar story.

In 1762 the Turkish Government demanded a huge sum of money from the Jews and, in order to discuss the demand in secret, the Chief Rabbi ordered a meeting in the synagogue of the Qaarites. On the way down the Chief Rabbi felt ill and stumbled. Some of his followers, suspecting black magic, began to tear up the stairs, and found copies of the works of the Rabbi Moses Ben Maimon, which the Qaarites had buried so that they could show their contempt by walking over them. The horrified Chief Rabbi then and there pronounced a curse on the sacrilegious Qaarite community. The curse was that they would never be able to form the quorum of ten grown males necessary for public worship.

" They still live under the curse," said the young Jew. " About a hundred years ago there was great joy among them when several Qaarite families came to Jerusalem from the Crimea. At last, they thought, they would be able to worship together. But the emigrants caught the plague. Some of the men died in the streets of Jerusalem and the others died when they reached their lodgings. To-day there are only five or six Qaarite men left, so that the Chief Rabbi's curse is still on them and they can never bring a ' Minyan ' together. . . ."

While he was talking, the grid in the door was softly withdrawn and an old, very dark, very sad eye gazed out at us. Then the grid was softly shut. The young Jew knocked again. But there was no answer.

§ 7

I am sure that Hezekiah's Tunnel will never become a popular sight with visitors to Palestine. It is wet, messy and dangerous, and you have to explore it at night in order not to stir up the water of the Virgin's Fountain in which the women of Siloam wash their clothes during the day-time.

I was determined to explore this tunnel, but I could find no one in Jerusalem who had been through it or who would offer to go through it with me. One man said that he would take me to the Siloam end of the tunnel and then go over to the Virgin's Fountain and wait for my body; but I did not like the idea of going through it alone.

Eventually I encountered someone who has explored most places round Jerusalem, and he agreed to accompany me.

So one night, just before moonrise, we went down to the Zion Gate and took those dark, mysterious roads that lie beyond the walls of Jerusalem and lead steeply down into the Valley of Hinnom, which is Ge Hinnom or Gehenna—otherwise hell. It was in this valley that the abominable rites of Baal were observed, and somewhere in it once stood the fires of Moloch in which children were sacrificed.

We went down into a stony wilderness bleached white by the thousands of grave-stones which rise on both slopes of the valley, marking the graves of Jews and Moslems who wish to be first on the Resurrection morning. A few lights on a hill marked the squalid little village of Siloam. Somewhere in the darkness to our right was the Field of Blood, which the Chief Priests bought with the silver of Judas.

We had to pick our way carefully, flashing electric torches on the stony track. Behind us came an Arab carrying lanterns and thigh boots.

While we stumbled downward in single file, sometimes straying from the path and tripping over stones, I thought how astonishing it is that, while so much of old Jerusalem has perished, this tunnel of Hezekiah, one of its earliest relics, should exist to-day almost as it was seven hundred years before Christ

Hezekiah was king in Jerusalem when the Assyrian was

preparing to come down " like a wolf on the fold." If you wish to feel the terror that seized Jerusalem at a time when men lived in fear of hearing the Assyrian battering-rams against the walls, read the denunciatory thunder of Isaiah. He lived through this dangerous reign and his writings rebuke Jerusalem for her sins and promise God's vengeance on the enemy.

King Hezekiah, forced to contemplate a siege, was troubled by the fact that the only spring of water in these barren hills —now called the Virgin's Fountain—lay just outside the walls of the old City of David.

Jerusalem could not exist long if her water supply fell into the hands of the Assyrians. So, by cutting a long underground tunnel, the king brought the spring water into the city. He then decided to seal up the spring and hide it from the advancing army of Sennacherib, so that the Assyrians would not be able to cut off Jerusalem's water supply. This scheme, which must have been carried out in frantic haste, is mentioned three times in the Bible: in Second Chronicles, Second Kings, and Isaiah. In Chronicles, it is recorded:

" And when Hezekiah saw that Sennacherib was come, and that he was purposed to fight against Jerusalem, he took counsel with his princes and his mighty men to stop the waters of the fountains which were without the city: and they did help him. So there was gathered much people together; who stopped all the fountains, and the brook that ran through the midst of the land, saying, ' Why should the kings of Assyria come, and find much water? ' "

The historical accuracy of these verses was not realised until, some years ago, two boys playing in the valley dis-covered the tunnel and managed to crawl through it.

We came down to the Pool of Siloam, where we put on our waders by the light of a torch held by the Arab. The tunnel was a black hole in the side of the hill, from which water about two feet in depth was flowing. There was a weird echo in it, as if people were whispering in the darkness.

" There's nobody there," said my friend. " No Arab

would go through the tunnel at night. We are hearing echoes from a mosque on the hill."

As we waded into the tunnel our electric torches lit up the flow of brownish water and the clammy walls. The cutting was perhaps fourteen feet high and only two feet wide, but the height was never the same for very long. The marks made by the axes of the workmen of King Hezekiah were sharp and clear on the stone.

The first three hundred feet were simple, but then the tunnel became low and we had to walk bent double. There were also pot holes in which we suddenly sank well over the knees. The total length of the tunnel is over a quarter of a mile, so that I had plenty of time to regret my decision to explore it and to admire the common sense of all those people who refused to go with me!

What a weird experience it was, this slow splash through a tunnel which Isaiah must have seen in the making, a tunnel cut seven hundred years before the birth of Christ in the shadow of a hill on which Solomon's Temple was still standing.

It was clear that the tunnel had been made by two parties of men working towards each other from both ends. They worked in great haste and paid no attention to uniformity of workmanship. The main factor was time and the only thing that mattered was to bring the water within the walls of Jerusalem as quickly as possible.

I was interested to see that, here and there, the working-parties had apparently lost their sense of direction. The tunnel would go in the wrong direction for a foot or so, and then, as if the men had stopped to listen for the picks of the other party working towards them, resume in the right direction. In the centre we came to the place where the two parties met.

A mystery about Hezekiah's Tunnel which no one has yet solved is why, at a time when every moment was precious, did the workmen cut a winding tunnel 1,749 feet in length, when the direct measurement from the two points is only 1,098 feet? Why should they have cut through an unnecessary 651 feet of rock?

A once popular explanation was that they bent the tunnel to avoid the rock tombs of David and Solomon. This theory has fired the imagination of archæologists and treasure-hunters and has led several men to dig for these tombs; but nothing has ever been discovered.

As we splashed onward the roof of the tunnel became higher and the water cleaner. I knew that we were coming out towards the Virgin's Fountain. Suddenly we heard the sound of running water and, wading through a large rock pool, waist-high in parts, we came out into a clear, moonlit night. We were at the bottom of the flight of steps that goes down to the Virgin's Fountain. There we peeled off our waders and put on our shoes.

We climbed out into the Kedron Valley. I looked up and saw, high above me to the left, the walls of Jerusalem with the moonlight over them. As we went on through the lonely valley with its crowded tombs, we came to the foot of the Mount of Olives and saw the little walled Garden of Gethsemane, with the light of the moon falling between its cypress trees and lying across its quiet paths.

CHAPTER THREE

I watch sunrise from the Mount of Olives. I enter the shrine of the Dome of the Rock, which was once the Altar of Burnt Offerings, and I see in a great mosque the ghost of Herod's Temple. I go to Bethany, to Jericho, enter the Inn of the Good Samaritan, walk beside the Dead Sea, visit the Place of Baptism on the banks of the Jordan and climb the Mount of Temptation.

§ 1

I ROSE before sunrise and walked up to the Mount of Olives. It was grey and rather cold and there was no one about. One or two stars were still burning and the clear sky waited for the sun.

There was a large boulder in a barley field. I sat on it and listened to the chorus of cock-crowing that surrounds Jerusalem in the dawn. The cockerels of Siloam were challenging the cockerels of Zion. Far off came fainter crowing as the birds of Mount Scopus answered the throaty greeting from the Valley of Jehoshaphat.

" Verily I say unto thee, That this night before the cock crow, thou shalt deny me thrice," said Jesus to Peter. This remark and its touching sequel is one that must rest on Peter's own record. It is, however, characteristic of a certain school of scriptural criticism that a curious dispute has been waged on these words. There is a type of critic who, coming across the word " white," will attempt to prove with a wealth of learning that the writer really meant to say " black." It has even been suggested that when Jesus mentioned the crowing of the cock He did not mean the common barnyard sound but the time signal, *the gallicinium*, or cock-crowing, made at intervals by the Roman guard from the ramparts of the castle of Antonia. I cannot, and I do not think that anyone reading the Gospels in a normal manner could, credit such a theory. It is true that the

Midrash and the Mishna tell us that as long as the Temple stood the breeding and keeping of fowls in Jerusalem were forbidden because, by scratching up the ground, they spread Levitical uncleanliness. Therefore, argue some critics, Jesus could not have meant cock-crow when He said cock-crow. I think it is much easier to believe that the law was not observed and that, in spite of the priests, cocks crowed in the dawn round Jerusalem as they do to-day. It is rather curious, too, if there were no cock-crowing in the time of Christ, that, when mourning over Jerusalem, Jesus should have said: "How often would I have gathered thy children together, even as a hen gathereth her chickens under her wings."

I am confident that the sound I heard in the greyness of the dawn was the same that Peter heard; and "he went out and wept bitterly."

As I sat on the stone thinking of these things, a light began to fill the sky. The sun rises over Jerusalem from behind the Mount of Olives. I turned my back on the city and, looking up over the Mount, saw a great fan of light pulsing up from the east. The fire filled the sky and turned the little clouds in its path to pink and gold, but the high ridge of the Mount, almost black against the palpitating light, hid the sun from view. Swifts flew screaming through the air. The noise they made as they darted over the Mount of Olives made me think of summer evenings at home in England. These birds, I believe, migrate to Europe from Africa and fill the air of Palestine with their high, bright screaming throughout the early months of the year. Hundreds of them cut the air like darts, swooping suddenly into the Valley of the Kedron and flying up again to dart and scream above the ochre-brown walls of Jerusalem.

The sun topped the crest of the Mount of Olives and, looking again towards Jerusalem, I saw the highest buildings gilded with light though the wall was yet unlit. In a few seconds a flood of light fell over the city, ran down the wall and into the Valley of the Kedron. It swept up the stony flanks of the opposite valley, and I felt my face and my hands warm in its light.

How often Jesus and the disciples must have watched this

splendid sight from the Mount of Olives. They must have seen
the city ramparts light up with the first rays of the sun. They
must have seen, just above the Garden of Gethsemane, the
towering white and gold mass of the Temple. They must
have seen a priest come out on a pinnacle, as he came every
morning, to look towards the east and report, before the first
sacrifice of the day, " The sun shineth already! " They
might even have heard in the still air of dawn the daily cry
from the assembled priests: " Is the sky lit up as far as
Hebron? ", and the daily response of the watcher from the
pinnacle: " It is lit up as far as Hebron! " Then, before
the sun was warm among the olive trees, there would sound a
shrilling of silver trumpets announcing that the first sacrifice
of the day had been offered on the altar of burnt offerings.
Up the slopes of the Mount of Olives would steal the smell of
incense. . . .

I went down into the valley, past the tomb of Absalom, and,
climbing the narrow white track that runs up over the mounds
and ruins of Zion, walked back beneath the walls. And
from a minaret just above my head the muezzin came out,
lifting his voice in the first call to prayer.

§ 2

The Dome of the Rock, which is wrongly called the Mosque
of Omar, is one of the most startling places I have ever seen.
It is startling because, shining like a spectre through this
great shrine of Islam, is a reflection of the Temple of
Herod. I cannot understand how it is that the hundreds
of books and guide-books about Jerusalem have neglected
what I consider to be the most significant thing about this
place. When you visit the Dome of the Rock you are visiting
the ghost of the Temple in whose courtyards Jesus preached,
and from whose gates He drove the hucksters.

When Titus destroyed Herod's Temple, the enormous
space left desolate seems to have embarrassed even the
Romans. They made no good use of it and when the
Moslems came in 635 A.D. the area was a dunghill. Owing
to a dispute in the Moslem world of that time the pilgrimage

to Mecca was interrupted and it was hoped to make the old Temple area of the Jews into a rival place of pilgrimage. This explains the colossal courtyard round the small shrine which contains the rock of the altar of burnt offerings. The rock, Es-Sakhra, was intended to be a rival of the Kaba, and the space round about it was designed to hold such crowds as those which flock to Mecca. This, however, did not happen, and Jerusalem was accordingly forced to take second place among the holy spots of Islam.

In the days of Turkish control it was rather difficult to get into this mosque, but now it is merely necessary to buy a four-shilling ticket and go there between 7.30 and 11.30 a.m.

I went down through the streets of the old city and entered by the Bab-al-Silsileh, one of the seven great gates that pierce the wall of the Temple area. In contrast to the crowded, noisy streets through which I had passed, I found myself in silence and in spaciousness. The Temple area is like a gigantic stone-paved park in the centre of a congested city. My first impression was that of acres of stone flags edged with grass, stretching on to higher levels and bounded by shady colonnades. In the centre of the open space was the shrine of the Dome of the Rock, erected over the rock which is believed to have stood beneath the Jewish altar of burnt-offerings. Far off at the southern extremity of the area was the church-like Mosque of el-Aksa.

Before I entered any of the buildings I sat down and tried to get a general idea of the place, but all the time I found myself looking not at the present-day Moslem sanctuary but at the older Jewish Temple which it has replaced. The resemblance is astonishing. For instance, the sheikhs of the mosque, who trim the lamps and sweep and tidy up the place, lock the doors and perform all kinds of services, live in quarters under the colonnades of the mosque just as the priests of Solomon's Temple used to do. Like them, they have regular terms of office, on the completion of which they return home to wait until their time of ministration arrives again. This is exactly what used to happen in the Temple of the Jews. We learn in St. Luke how Zacharias, the aged father of John the Baptist, received a vision in the Temple " while he executed the priest's office before God in the order

A Bethlehem Mother

Tribal Court Judges at Beersheba

of his course." The "course" was a week's continuous
service reckoned from Sabbath to Sabbath. "When the
days of his ministration were fulfilled," says St. Luke of
Zacharias, "he departed unto his house."

Not ten yards from me, in the shade of one of the porches,
an old man sat talking to two or three boys. He was a
teacher. He was teaching and disputing and going over
points of Moslem observance and belief in the same place
where Jesus disputed with a similar "elder" in the cloisters
of Herod's Temple. When I turned to the north I saw that
the view was blocked by a tall wall and a building. It is
known as the old Turkish Barracks and was so used by the
Turks up to the British occupation. This stands on the site
of the Castle of Antonia, the Roman stronghold which over-
looked Herod's Temple and in which Jesus was charged before
Pontius Pilate. The ghost of Antonia frowned down on
the ghost of Herod's Temple as it used to do in the days
of Christ. In a city where all relics of Roman days are
buried thirty, forty, and sixty feet below the appalling débris
of the centuries, the Dome of the Rock seems to bring one
out into the daylight. It is easier to reconstruct the past in
this Moslem sanctuary than it is in the Church of the Holy
Sepulchre. It is easy to imagine Jesus preaching in an open
space like that of the Temple area, and afterwards leaving
by one of the gates and going down towards the Mount of
Olives on the other side of the wall. The reason why the
Temple area is less confusing than other sites in Jerusalem
is because it is the only spot that has not been built on
again and again: it has descended to us essentially unchanged since the time of Christ. In His day it was a
central shrine with a cluster of sacred buildings surrounded
by wide paved courts; and that description is still true
of it.

I climbed up on a kind of sentry walk on the eastern wall
and looked across the Kedron Valley to the Mount of Olives.
Not far away in this wall is the blocked-up Golden Gate,
standing, it is said, on the site of the gate through which Jesus
entered Jerusalem in triumph. Among the numbers of small
domed buildings that are grouped about the enclosure is one
known as Solomon's Throne. The story—and every inch of

the mosque area is embroidered with legend—is that Solomon was found dead on this spot.   He did not wish the demons, over whose kingdom he held authority, to know when he was dead: so, when he realised he was dying, he propped himself up on his throne and sat there as if he were still living, his staff in his hand.   And, say the Arabs, the demons thought that he was alive until the day came when worms gnawed through the staff and the dead body of Solomon crashed to the floor.

There is another legend, or rather belief, attached to a slender arcade in the north-west corner of the court.   The Moslems say that when the Day of Judgment is held in the Kedron Valley the souls of men will be forced to walk a single horse-hair that will stretch from the top of the Mount to the arcade in the courtyard of the mosque.   At one end Jesus, and at the other Mahomet, will judge the souls who successfully cross the bridge and weigh them in scales set up from the arches of the arcade.

The Holy of Holies of the Jewish Temple stood uplifted above the general level of the surrounding courts, and in the same manner the domed shrine of the Rock is to-day elevated on a platform twelve feet high, which you approach by flights of steps.   When I reached the entrance three or four small boys flung themselves on my feet and attempted to tear off my shoes.   I have always found it an excellent plan to resist on principle the impetuous ministrations of the Arab until one discovers them to be inevitable.   One generally discovers that they are not inevitable.   And so it happened at the entrance to the Dome of the Rock.   An elderly man in a brown robe approached me, holding two enormous barge-like slippers, worn down at the heels and furnished with long tapes.   These he fitted over my shoes, and I shuffled into the Dome of the Rock.

This shrine is unquestionably the most exquisite building in Jerusalem and you will find ecstatic accounts of it in every book written about the city.   It is a dim, eight-sided building whose dome is erected on columns of magnificent porphyry, breccia and other tinted stones, all of them picked up by the Moslems from the ruins of Roman Jerusalem. Most of the columns are still fitted with their Byzantine capitals, and a few of them are still marked with the sign of the cross.

An English guide who was taking a few visitors round was explaining the beauty of the windows, and telling his hushed, worried-looking audience that he could go there every day and find some new beauty in the stained glass. I have no doubt he could. They are, of their kind, perfect. I suffer, however, and have done so since I was a boy, from a deep dislike for all forms of mathematics. I was never any good at them and was always getting into trouble. And I am still no good at them. Arabic art always reminds me of mathematics. It is like algebra set to music, or, if you prefer, recurring decimals with wings on them. I experience the same unhappy feeling, when faced with Arabic art, that I would experience if you asked me to add up a long account. I feel that possibly only a senior wrangler could do justice to the exquisiteness of the Dome of the Rock.

In the centre of the sublimated multiplication table, that rises all round in arches and stained glass and peacock-tail mosaic, is something so primitive and so brutally frank in the rigid formality of that place that you hold your breath. Lying behind an intricate screen of metal-work is a huge, unsmoothed slab of the living rock. It is black in colour and polished in surface; and it lies there as out of place and as improbable as a ton of coals in the middle of a drawing-room floor. All this finnicky beauty has been built round this huge, sloping slice of Mount Moriah. But the more you think about it, the more improbable it looks, until at last it becomes terrifying. It is as if the sharp top of a mountain were pushing its way through the floor of a house. There is something uncanny and unnatural about it. The rock, as it lies there streaked with a few bars of red or blue light from the windows, seems to take on a powerful and sinister life of its own. One feels that it might move a little in its sleep and shake down the building above it as a sleeping giant might brush away the leaves that have fallen on him.

This is the rock that formed part of the threshing-floor of Araunah the Jebusite. You remember, perhaps, how David, tempted by Satan, forced on Israel a thing that nomad people hate more than anything: a census. And how David's heart smote him after he had numbered the people, and how he admitted his sorrow to the Lord and confessed that he had " done very foolishly." The Lord, however, in order to punish him visited a great pestilence upon his people:

" And when the angel stretched out his hand upon Jerusalem to destroy it, the Lord repented him of the evil, and said to the angel that destroyed the people, It is enough: stay now thine hand. And the angel of the Lord was by the threshingplace of Araunah the Jebusite."

So David, in token of thankfulness that the plague should have been stayed, decided to build an altar to the Lord on the rock where the angel had stood. He went up from the little town of David, which in those days clung to the southern hill opposite Siloam, and he climbed the uninhabited mountain that frowned above his town to the spot where the Jebusite used to thresh his wheat; and there he bought the threshing-floor for fifty shekels of silver.

And this rock, that now gleams so strangely above the painted arabesques, was part of the floor that David bought a thousand years before Christ to honour and glorify the Lord. From that moment Mount Moriah was destined to bear the Temple that was fated to form the character of the Jews, that was to bind them together in remote lands even after it had become dust and ashes. What the Tabernacle had been to the Israelites when they were wandering in the wilderness, so the Temple of Solomon was to be to them during their dangerous and tragic history as settled townsmen. When Solomon ascended his father's throne, he sent to Hiram, King of Tyre, for architects and stonemasons:

" And it came to pass, when Hiram heard the words of Solomon, that he rejoiced greatly, and said, Blessed be the Lord this day, which hath given unto David a wise son over this great people. And Hiram sent to Solomon, saying, I have considered the things which thou sentest to me for: and I will do all thy desires concerning timber of cedar, and concerning timber of fir. My servants shall bring them down from Lebanon unto the sea: and I will convey them by sea in floats unto the place that thou shalt appoint me, and will cause them to be discharged there, and thou shalt receive them: and thou shalt accomplish my desire, in giving food for my household. So Hiram gave Solomon cedar trees and fir trees according to all his desire."

The work of building Solomon's Temple was begun in the year 966 B.C., and the Temple was dedicated seven and a half years afterwards. In Solomon's letter to Hiram, King of Tyre, how clearly we see the character of the Israelites, newly from the desert, warriors fresh from their conquests just settling down to the life of cities, innocent of the arts and graces of civilisation, barren of architects and craftsmen. " For thou knowest that there is not among us any that can skill to hew timber like unto the Sidonians "! It is the sort of admission that to-day any Bedouin chief in Trans-Jordan might make to any contractor in Jerusalem.

So around this rock Solomon built his Temple. The magnificent sound of it, and the mighty memories that hedge it about, quite obscure the plain fact that it was only a temple a hundred feet long by about thirty feet wide. It was probably nothing more than the chapel royal to the palace, the armoury, the law court and the harem that rose up round about it. But never had Israel seen any building to compare with it. As Israel grew, the Temple became greater and more splendid. It was cast to the flames by Nebuchadnezzar in 586 B.C., and when it rose again fifty years later those who remembered the original could not withhold their tears. Even had the splendour of the new Temple been as great as that of Solomon, there were differences that no architect could mend. The Ark of the Covenant with the cherubim was no longer there. What happened to it no man can say. Did it perish in the war with Nebuchadnezzar? Its fate is one of the mysteries of history. There were five things missing from the second Temple, so the rabbis used to say, and they were: the Ark, the holy fire, the Schechinah, the spirit of prophesy, and the Urim and the Thummim.

It was Herod the Great, the father of Herod Antipas, under whom Christ suffered, who conceived the ambitious plan of restoring the Temple to its former architectural glory. He

was a great builder, and the shining white marble and limestone structures which he had showered on Jerusalem made
the old Temple of Zerubbabel appear shabby and unworthy.
He won over the Jews with great difficulty and cunning. He
promised not to touch a stone of the old Temple until he was
ready to build the new and, in order that the holy place
should not be defiled by unconsecrated persons, he put a
thousand priests into training as stonemasons and carpenters.
The work was started in the winter of 20 B.C. The Holy of
Holies was rebuilt in eighteen months, but eight years were
occupied in rebuilding the cloisters and the outer enclosures.
The work went on long after Herod's death and was continued throughout the reign of Antipas.

Every time Jesus visited Jerusalem He must have seen the
workmen busy on some part of the enormous sanctuary.
There is one reflection of this in the Gospels. St. John tells
us that, during one of our Lord's Passover pilgrimages to
Jerusalem, the Jews asked Him: " What sign showeth thou
unto us? "

" Jesus answered and said unto them, Destroy this Temple,
and in three days I will raise it up.
" Then said the Jews, Forty and six years was this Temple
in building, and wilt thou rear it up in three days?
" But he spake of the temple of his body."

This interesting reference to the reconstruction of the
Temple places this pilgrimage to Jerusalem at about the
year 27 or 28 A.D. Herod's Temple was not finally completed
until thirty-four years after the Crucifixion. And eight years
after that date it disappeared in flames for ever.

These are a few of the thoughts that crowd on the mind
in the Moslem shrine of the Dome of the Rock. But the
ideas of another age and of another faith break into one's
reverie. The guardian of the shrine shows you with great
reverence a gold casket in which are preserved two hairs of
Mahomet's beard. He tells you that from the black rock
the Prophet rose to heaven on the back of his winged steed

el-Barûk—" Lightning." And he says that beneath the rock can sometimes be heard an awful sound which is the roaring of all the waters of the flood.

At one side of the rock a flight of steps goes down into a cavern. From this place it is possible to trace a channel cut in the rock which drained the blood of the sacrifices made on the Jewish altar of burnt offering and carried it into the Valley of the Kedron. In this cave there is a flag-stone that gives a hollow ring when you strike it. There are all kinds of queer stories about it. What lies underneath no one knows, and I believe that no bribe has ever succeeded in gaining permission for an investigation. One cannot help wondering what lies beneath the Temple area and what marvels the spade might reveal. It is a provoking speculation. It is known that immense rock cisterns exist there, and also the remains of the bathrooms in which priests who suffered ceremonial defilement in Herod's time might wash themselves and leave the Temple secretly. But what else lies hidden there?

Many people believe that if this problem could be investigated something wonderful would be discovered, perhaps the Ark of the Covenant or those vessels of the Temple worship which were not carried to Rome for the triumph of Titus. But the Moslems refuse to allow excavation and the Temple area remains one of the most tantalising mysteries in the world.

§ 3

I went out into a blaze of sunlight, rid myself of the mosque slippers, and walked southward over the immense pavement towards the Mosque of el-Aksa. I noticed several Moslems washing their hands in the waters of a fountain that is fed, as the Temple water supply used to be in the time of Solomon, from a spring twenty-four miles away in the hills between Bethlehem and Hebron.

El-Aksa looks like a Christian church because the Arabs used in its construction the building material from the ruined Crusading church of St. Mary-the-New. It is an enormous building on the Roman pattern, its naves divided by thick-set

Byzantine columns. The floor was covered with rugs, and an ancient sheikh was slowly and lovingly sweeping the dust from one place to another.

A guide appeared from somewhere and led me to a stone in a central aisle which bore a defaced inscription. He told me that beneath it lie two of the murderers of Thomas à Becket.

We then descended a flight of stone stairs near the mosque of el-Aksa and found ourselves in an enormous series of vaults erected on massive square pillars. Eighty-eight of these pillars, ranged in fifteen rows, supported a heavy vaulted roof, and it is obvious from the bases of the pillars that much of this huge crypt is still many feet deep in ancient débris. These are the famous underground Stables of Solomon.

" Solomon had four thousand stalls for horses and chariots," says the Bible, " and twelve thousand horsemen; whom he bestowed in the chariot cities, and with the King at Jerusalem."

Although the present vaults, which uphold part of the Temple platform, appear to be Roman work of the time of Justinian, with certain later Arab reconstructions, I believe that archæologists have come to the conclusion that they occupy the site of the earlier stables of Solomon. Josephus explains very clearly that the horses and chariots left the palace at this side and descended into the Kedron Valley. This also must have been the way Queen Athalia, the daughter of Ahab and Jezebel, was thrust out to be murdered in order that the sanctuary should not be stained with her blood. " They laid hands on her; and she went by the way by the which the horses came into the king's house. . . ."

The vaults are to-day just as they were when the Crusaders entered Jerusalem. They, like Solomon before them, used the vaults as stables. Small holes drilled in the angles of the pillars still show where the Crusaders chained their chargers.

On my way out of the mosque I saw a holy man surrounded by his pupils. They sat in the shade listening eagerly to his discourse. He was teaching on the very spot where the greatest Teacher in history sat amid the vanished splendour of Herod's Temple.

§ 4

One morning I decided to " run down to Jericho," as they say in Jerusalem. They talk about Jericho as a Londoner might talk about Brighton. " Have you run down to Jericho yet? " is one of the first questions they ask the stranger, and at every dinner-party someone is sure to offer to " run you down " for a moonlight bathe in the Dead Sea.

That enigmatic emptiness to the east of the Mount of Olives, which drops into an unearthly wilderness where a strip of intensely blue water receives the shadow of mauve mountains, has powerfully influenced the mentality of Jerusalem. Like a lighthouse on a hill, she has always watched the Dead Sea country with respect and fear, for who could say what might not come up out of the wilderness, like a ship out of the ocean, to recall her to God?

To the Jewish theologian Jericho and the Jordan Valley were a portent, but to the modern geologist they are a freak. There is in all the world nothing quite like the contrast between the mountain city of Jerusalem, over 2,300 feet above the sea, and the Jordan Valley, only twenty-three miles away, sunk in a hot trench 1,300 feet below the sea. It is a climatic curiosity as fantastic as a strip of Brazilian jungle would be at the foot of Ben Nevis.

When I told a friend that I intended to " run down " to the Dead Sea for a day, he said:—

" Well, be careful to get back before dark."

" Why? " I asked.

" You might meet Abu Jildah . . ."

" Who is Abu Jildah? "

" He is a brigand who has shot several policemen. There is a price of £250 on his head, and he has a habit of building a wall of stones across the Jericho road, stopping cars, robbing you, and, if you resist, shooting you. He once held up fourteen cars in a row on this road, robbed everyone, threatened to cut off a woman's finger because her rings were tight, and was off and away to the hills by the time the police heard about it. So take my tip and get back before dusk. . . ."

As my friend was giving me this advice I remembered the Parable of the Good Samaritan : " a certain man went down

D

from Jerusalem to Jericho, and fell among thieves, who stripped him of his raiment, and wounded him, and departed, leaving him half dead."

"Do you think," I asked, "that the man who fell among thieves was attacked by someone like Abu Jildah?"

"There is no doubt about it," my friend replied. "The road from Jerusalem to Jericho has been notorious throughout history for its robberies and its hold-ups. It is, as you will see, perfect brigand country. It has been suggested that Jesus, in the Parable of the Good Samaritan, was weaving a parable round an actual happening. He told the story on His way up from Jericho to Bethany on the Mount of Olives, which rather supports this theory. Halfway down to Jericho you will see an old khan on the side of the road—in fact it is the only building, apart from a police post, that you will meet after Bethany. This khan is believed to be the inn mentioned by Jesus in the parable. No doubt it is so, because its rock cisterns prove that an inn has stood on this spot since Bible times. You should stop and go inside. . . . But don't forget to be back before dark!"

I set off at ten o'clock. I passed the Damascus Gate and went along the road through the Kedron Valley. It runs to the left, and round this corner Jerusalem was hidden from view. My attention became fixed on a downward road and a succession of nasty corners.

About three miles from Jerusalem a superb panorama of the Dead Sea country lay before me. I could see the white road twisting and turning into a sterile wilderness of parched rock, dropping ever downward into bleakness and solitude. I stopped the car and got out.

I thought that I had never seen anything that looked more like the primitive conception of hell. It was the sort of place that an early Italian painter would have peopled with hairy little devils with horns and forked tails. The hillsides were either littered with millions of limestone chips or else they were bare and volcanic. Some of the hills were domed or cone-shaped like young volcanoes and others were queerly twisted, tortured and deformed as if chewed up by fire like the clinkers that come out of a furnace.

While I was looking at the terrifying panorama of the Dead

Sea, a plump and smiling Arab came up to me holding several slings. He selected a pebble and, whirling the sling round his head, suddenly shot the stone into the air. We watched it drop into a valley half a mile below. He then pointed to a sling and to me, suggesting that I should buy one. To my astonishment I did buy one! Why, I shall never know. I have so far always resisted improbable salesmen, such as those mournful orientals who try to sell one a carpet in Cannes or Monte Carlo, but after buying a sling on the Jericho Road I shall never again consider myself immune. The Arab then pointed and said, " Bethany," and, looking in the direction of his arm, I saw that, half hidden round a left-hand bend of the road, was a little Arab village on a slight hill.

It was a huddle of houses that looked like ruins, and ruins that looked like houses. Like nearly all Arab villages, it seemed to have endured a recent artillery bombardment. On the crest of the hill was the relic of a great wall that looked to me like crusader's masonry. The ruin stood up against the sky like an old tooth.

The Arab, who turned out to be the sheikh of Bethany, led me in silence over a narrow path between the haphazard walls of piled boulders. We came to a little door in a wall which he unlocked, then, groping in his robes, he found the end of a candle which he lighted and gave to me and, pointing down into the darkness, said in English, " The Tomb of Lazarus."

This used to be a Christian church and one of the most hallowed and ancient of the holy places in Palestine, but at some later period the Moslems seized it and turned it into a mosque, which still stands above the tomb. Entrance to the tomb was forbidden to Christians for centuries and the old entrance was blocked up. In the seventeenth century the Father Custos of the Holy Land, Angelo of Messina, managed, by paying a fat bribe, to open this new door.

We descended about twenty steps into a dark and dusty cave. The flame of the candle lit up a little vestibule and the ruins of a Christian altar. Two steps lower than this vestibule was a small tomb chamber which is the traditional spot from which Christ recalled Lazarus to life. It is an interesting thing that the modern Arabic name for Bethany is el Azareyh, a form of Lazarus or Eleazar. I stumbled up into the sunlight and, getting rid of the sheikh, went up the hill and sat under one of the many olive trees that grow round it.

There is no doubt at all that this is Bethany, although the House of Mary and Martha and the House of Simon the Leper, which the sheikh is only too happy to show you for a coin, cannot possibly be authentic. This huddle of old stones, however, now inhabited by a few Moslem families, stands on the spot which Jesus knew as Bethany—"the Home of Dates." All one can say is that somewhere on the hill was the house in which Martha, Mary, and their brother, Lazarus, lived.

I think that the character study of Martha and Mary is, as a piece of writing, one of the marvels of literature. There is not one word we could do without, yet the picture is complete, and framed, as it were, by a kitchen door. St. Luke tells it in ninety-eight words:

" . . . a certain woman named Martha received him into her house. And she had a sister called Mary, which also sat at Jesus' feet, and heard his word. But Martha was cumbered about much serving, and came to him, and said, Lord, dost thou not care that my sister hath left me to serve alone? bid her therefore that she help me. And Jesus answered and said unto her, Martha, Martha, thou art careful and troubled about many things: but one thing is needful: and Mary hath chosen that good part, which shall not be taken away from her."

Sitting on the little hill above Bethany I could visualise the scene: the house with the smell of cooking around it, for the Feast of Tabernacles, at which this incident occurred, was a busy time for Jewish women, and the little arbour of green leaves—the Tabernacle of the feast—beneath which Jesus would be sitting in the courtyard with Mary at His feet. They would both be able to see and hear Martha busy with her pots and pans, and she would see Jesus and Mary, so cool and idle while she was so busy. How well her irritation is conveyed by the fact that she includes Jesus in her rebuke! . . . " Lord, dost thou not care that my

sister hath left me to serve alone?" She might have
said, "Lord, see how my sister doth leave me to serve
alone." But she is too angry. If they had been invisible
from her kitchen she might not have been so angry. She
would not have seen her sister so cool and tidy, so calm and
so intelligent. But Jesus and Mary were sitting in the courtyard in a leafy summer-house of fresh boughs, the peace
that surrounded them and the shade in which they sat throwing
into relief her own labours, quickening her self-pity and her
sense of injustice. As Martha stands before Jesus we know
her so well. She is immortal and international. In every
language under the sun, and in every age, Martha has broken
into a discussion with an indignant: "You sit there doing
nothing while I am working my fingers to the bone!"

And the reply she receives from the arbour is enough to
bring tears to her eyes. "Martha, Martha," says Jesus,
mentioning her name twice, and thus putting great affection
into what followed, "thou art careful and troubled about
many things: but one thing is needful: and Mary hath chosen
that good part, which shall not be taken away from her."
What a play of ideas is here. We might interpret these words
as: "Martha, Martha, you are busy with many courses
when one dish would be quite sufficient. Mary has chosen
the best dish, which shall not be taken away from her."

And how marvellously St. John takes up the brush and fills
in little details of this character study! When Jesus came
up from Jericho to raise Lazarus, it was the energetic and
practical Martha, who "as soon as she heard that Jesus was
coming, went and met him: but Mary sat still in the house."
This is a superbly life-like touch. The mystical Mary is still
mourning her brother, but the practical Martha has dried
her tears. "Lord," began Martha, in her usual blunt way,
"if thou hadst been here, my brother had not died." Then,
revealing the real depths of her soul, she says, "But I know,
that even now, whatsoever thou wilt ask of God, God will give
it thee." And it was to this depth of faith in Martha that
Jesus spoke those words that have brought comfort and hope
wherever a man, or a woman, has stood above an open
grave:

"I am the resurrection, and the life," He said to Martha.

" He that believeth in me, though he were dead, yet shall he live."

Once again there is a flash of portraiture. Jesus calls for Mary. Martha goes " secretly " to her sister, saying, " The Master is come, and calleth for thee." Unlike Martha, who went dry-eyed, Mary runs weeping to fall down in passionate sorrow at the Master's feet.

Not only are the opposite temperaments of these two women drawn with a touch that surely the most obdurate critic must recognise as a painting from life, but also the fact is indicated in the most subtle way that Jesus, while He recognises that their temperaments are poles apart, loves and understands both of them and thinks no less of one than of the other.

The last scene in which the women of Bethany play a part is just before the Crucifixion. This time it is Mary whose sensitiveness sees what even the disciples do not see, and once again St. John draws a scene that, one feels, he must have witnessed, no matter what some learned commentators may say.

" There they made him a supper; and Martha served. . . . Then took Mary a pound of ointment of spikenard, very costly, and anointed the feet of Jesus, and wiped his feet with her hair: and the house was filled with the odour of the ointment."

How truly drawn again are the characters of the women: Martha busily supervising the meal, Mary forgetful of the material things, anxious only to pay a tribute to the spiritual.

And how clearly we see the mean, hard face of Judas: " Why was not this ointment sold for three hundred pence, and given to the poor? " he asked.

Dr. Edersheim has estimated that a Roman pound of spikenard such as that used by Mary would have cost nine pounds in modern money. It roused the cupidity of Judas, who made his protest, we learn in a biting aside, " not that he cared for the poor; but because he was a thief, and had the bag, and bare what was put therein."

Then Jesus, rounding off the perfect story of Martha and Mary, spoke over her adoring head what has been called the loveliest sentence in literature:

" Let her alone," He said. " Against the day of my burying hath she kept this."

§ 5

I rose from the hill above Bethany and went back to the road.

The heat became insufferable and the wilderness seemed to close in on me. The air was hot and still. The khaki rocks flung back the sun like the sides of a furnace. Soon there was but little green to be seen. Black goats were grazing on tufts of coarse grass which grew in the cracks of the rock. Turning a corner, I almost ran into a herd of them. They scattered and leaping to the rocks, their long ears flapping, turned to watch me go by like angry, bearded old men.

Once I met a shepherd painfully climbing the hill, leading his sheep, talking to them all the time, and on his shoulder he carried a lamb, holding it by the four legs as in pictures of the Good Shepherd.

The road now had a sharp cliff on one side and on the other a deep drop into a ravine. It was never straight for very long.

I ran downward to the first sign of life, a well known as the Fountain of the Apostles, from which an old man was filling a pitcher. On my right, a narrow footpath ran back through the hills to Jerusalem. This was the ancient short cut to Bethany, and the road that Jesus and His Disciples would have taken when they went up to the Passover and the Last Supper.

It was not difficult to understand why the road from Jerusalem to Jericho has always been the haunt of bandits. It is a road whose serpentine bends and overhanging cliffs might have been designed for highway robbery. At hundreds of points along the road are stretches lying between two acute corners and backed by towering cliffs and projecting boulders, where two or three armed men could hold up anything that came along. The robbery once committed, nothing could be easier than an escape into the barren trackless wilderness, where thousands of caves offer secure hiding-places and where a search-party might wander without success for ever.

The road, after diving steadily downward, began to rise.

On the crest of the ridge stood the Inn of the Good Samaritan, called by the Arabs Khan Hathrur.   As I stopped outside it a man with three laden donkeys came up and halted them in the shadow of the inn.

The building is the usual Turkish khan made to provide safety for men and beasts during the night, and generally placed within an easy journey of a city.   The foundations of the khan, and the ancient rock cisterns below it in which water is stored, prove that an inn has been on this site from Roman times and possibly even earlier.   There can be no doubt that this is the inn our Lord was thinking of when He told the Parable of the Good Samaritan, because there has never been any other inn between Jerusalem and Jericho.

The building is an oblong one-storey house of indeterminate date, entered by a high arched door placed in the centre.   A large courtyard surrounded by a high wall occupies a space of level ground at the back.   In the middle of this courtyard is a well from which water is drawn by letting down a bucket on a rope.

The courtyard presented a scene of dreary desolation.   The inn had been bombarded during the war and had not yet recovered from it.   The courtyard was pitted with holes and littered with stones.   In one corner of it, surrounded by a broken-down fence, was an old mosaic floor, proving that centuries ago a church stood on the site.   The mosaics, which are mostly black and white in colour, were loose, and any curious traveller could fill his pocket with them.

While I sat on a boulder in the yard, I watched an Arab boy drawing water.   This was poured into battered petrol tins which another man loaded on the back of a donkey. A tall, masterful woman, whom I had noticed in the hall of the inn, instructed a little girl to try her charm on the stranger, and the child accordingly came running on her bare feet holding two enormous Jaffa oranges which she shyly offered to me.   I gave her a coin and took one of the oranges. The two or three Arabic words of thanks which I had learnt induced in the child feelings of the utmost panic, for she picked up her dirty little skirts and scuttled out of sight.

I read the Parable of the Good Samaritan as I sat in the shadow of the wall. It is a parable that has gone round the world, but I wonder how many people really understand why Jesus told it. He had said farewell to Galilee and was journeying towards Jerusalem and His Crucifixion. His custom was to visit the synagogues, to preach and afterwards to invite discussion. It was probably at Jericho that, after He had preached, a lawyer in the congregation, anxious to display his learning and attempting to provoke Jesus, asked: " Master, what shall I do to inherit eternal life? " The questioner was a dialectician whose business it was to interpret the Jewish Law. His question was obviously a trap, as Jesus realised, for he countered with the question: " What is written in the Law? how readest thou? ", which, turning the question back on the questioner, meant: " You are a lawyer. You have studied these things. Let us have your expert opinion."

The man replied quoting Deuteronomy and Leviticus, as Jesus knew he must reply: " Thou shalt love the Lord thy God with all thy heart, and with all thy soul, and with all thy strength, and with all thy mind; and thy neighbour as thy self."

" Thou hast answered right," said Jesus, capping the other's quotation with a paraphrase from Leviticus: " this do and thou shalt live."

But the lawyer, furious at being so swiftly worsted, thought he still saw a chance to win the battle of wits, and asked at once: " And who is my neighbour? " It was a new argument! A Jew's neighbour, according to rabbinical law, was only a fellow Israelite. The lawyer felt certain that Jesus would depart from this narrow limitation and would lay Himself open to a charge of heresy. Jesus, seeing this trap as clearly as He had seen the other, replied with a parable. He said:

" A certain man went down from Jerusalem to Jericho, and fell among thieves, which stripped him of his raiment, and wounded him, and departed, leaving him half dead. And by chance there came down a certain priest that way: and when he saw him, he passed by on the other side. And likewise a Levite, when he was at the place, came and looked on him, and passed by on the other side. But a certain Samaritan, as he journeyed, came where he was: and when he saw him, he had compassion on him, and went to him, and bound up his wounds, pouring in oil and wine, and set him on his own beast, and brought him to an inn, and took care of him. And on the morrow when he departed, he took out two pence, and gave them to the host, and said unto him, Take care of him; and whatsoever thou spendest more, when I come again, I will repay thee."

One can imagine the lawyer writhing unhappily in his seat. He had been trapped as neatly as he had hoped to trap Jesus! He was being forced to admit that one of the loathed race of Samaritans, one of the detested people with whom the Jews had no dealings, was his " neighbour." And the relentless question was put:

" Which now of these three, thinkest thou, was neighbour unto him that fell among the thieves? "

We can sense the lawyer's discomfiture in his reply. He cannot bring himself to utter the detested word, Samaritan. It would stick in his throat. Instead he has to admit:

" He that showed mercy on him."

" Go, and do thou likewise," says Jesus.

Thus a masterpiece of dialectics is concluded with a story, apparently so simple, but floating like a leaf on deeper currents.

§ 6

When I left the Inn of the Good Samaritan I plunged down into a land of fire. There was no shade anywhere. The sun beat in my eyes and quivered over the barren earth. In a little over half an hour I had left a temperate climate for the heat of the tropics.

Coming to a convenient place, I stopped the car and removed my coat, for I was suffocating. I looked into the abyss, where far below, cut in the side of a sand-coloured mountain, was a monastery built like a swallow's nest on the wall of a house. The cliffs round about this monastery were pitted with caves in which hermits still live, mortifying the flesh as they did in the Thebaid.

Onward I went down the blinding white road. There was a post with " Sea Level " printed on it; and the road still plunged downward, the heat growing even fiercer. A lizard streaked across the path leaving a twisted trail in the fine white dust. A movement on a hill revealed a group of camels, queer prehistoric-looking creatures the very colour of the sandy rocks, grazing with their calves upon the spiky bushes and the unwholesome-looking thorns. Turning a corner, I saw below me a view of the Jordan Valley and of Jericho among its trees and, to the right, the sparkling blue waters of the Dead Sea with the Mountains of Moab, streaked and slashed with shadows, rising from its eastern shores.

Some writers have described this hot gash in the earth's crust as the most horrible place in the world, while others have found it strangely beautiful. It is, I suppose, a matter of temperament or, perhaps, liver. If you are not feeling too well, I can imagine that the Jordan Valley with its overwhelming heat and its airlessness, and Jericho with its flamboyant vegetation, its reptiles and its insects, could be a terrible nightmare. Here, strangely enough, is the same awful sterility which is encountered only on the summit of great mountains. Just as a man venturing alone above the vegetation belt on a high mountain is sometimes seized with a chill of terror, feeling that he is trespassing in the workshop of God, so in this uncanny trench he feels that he is walking where no man was meant to walk. All round are piled dead rocks twisted in the agony of some prehistoric convulsion, unlike the good clean rocks from which men can build their homes: obscene rocks stained with yellow slime and covered with a ghastly shroud of salt.

The plain over which I was looking is about fourteen miles wide at Jericho. On one side of it rise the terrific mountains of Judæa and, fourteen miles away, facing them, are the mountains of Moab. The Jordan Valley is a trench between them: a parched wilderness of brown hills that lies sweltering in the burning sunlight, and streaked round the Dead Sea with patches of unhealthy white and dirty grey. In the centre meanders a serpentine streak of green. It is formed

by the tamarisks, the willows and the green bushes that follow
the Jordan's two-hundred-mile windings from the Sea of
Galilee, which is, as the crow flies, only sixty-five miles
away. And this strange dead-looking world of sandy rock,
twisted into weird shapes by ancient disturbances of the earth
and stained and streaked with chemicals, is as far below the
sea as many a British coal-mine.

" There may be something on the surface of another planet
to match the Jordan Valley: there is nothing on this," wrote
George Adam Smith in his great book *The Historical Geography of the Holy Land.* " No other part of the earth, uncovered with water, sinks to 300 feet below the level of the
ocean. But here we have a rift more than one hundred and
sixty miles long, and from two to fifteen broad, which falls
from the sea level to as deep as 1,292 feet below it at the coast
of the Dead Sea, while the bottom of the latter is 1,300 deeper
still. In this trench there are the Jordan, a river nearly one
hundred miles long; two great lakes, respectively twelve and
fifty-two miles in length; large tracts of arable country,
especially about Genesaret, Bethshan and Jericho, regions
which were once very populous, like the coasts of the Lake
of Galilee; and the sites of some famous towns—Tiberias,
Jericho, and ' Cities of the Plain.' Is it not true that on
the earth there is nothing else like this deep, this colossal
ditch? "

The greenness of Jericho rose up, an oasis in the dreadful
desolation. From the height of the road it looked much
nearer to the Dead Sea than it actually is, but I was soon to
learn that nothing in the strange air of the Jordan Valley is
more deceptive than one's idea of distance.

§ 7

In the street of mud huts, Arab houses, and banana
groves which is modern Jericho, there was only an old Arab
asleep in the shade of a wall. A herd of black goats stood in
the hot dust and a number of camels sitting in the full blaze

of the sun protruded their lower lips as they remembered
the hundredth name of God. God, says the Arab, has a
hundred names, but man knows only ninety-nine. The
camel knows the hundredth and that is why his expression is
always one of ineffable superiority.

I said there was nothing else but the sleeping Arab and the
goats and the camels; but I was wrong. In a moment
which I shall never forget, an English pointer, queerly
divorced from the sporting aquatint to which such dogs
belong, walked round the angle of a mud wall and stood
regarding me with the detached superiority of the English
dog in the East. To meet a pointer in Jericho was, to me,
as odd as it would have been to see a bunch of bananas
growing over a wall in Oxford. In fact, I wondered for a
moment whether the sun had not perhaps affected my
eyesight.

The animal, like anything English in a foreign setting
(particularly middle-aged ladies from Tunbridge Wells), was
surrounded by an aura of intense Englishness, so that I
remembered how the stubble fields of Kent lean against the
sky near Baddlesmere, and how silver-grey and still the Exe
can be on an October morning. Among the huge tropical
leaves and the heat of Jericho this pointer could not have
surprised me more than the discovery of Apperley's *Life of
John Mytton* in one of those ornate niches reserved for the
Koran in the great mosque of El Aksa.

The dog vanished round the wall, to return immediately
with his explanation: an Englishman in breeches, golf
stockings, and a tweed coat.

" Good morning," he said pleasantly. " Looking round? "

" Yes," I said. " Do you think we could raise a drink in
the hotel? "

" We could try. Hot, isn't it? I've been in the Jordan
marshes looking for quail. They come over in thousands
just about this time."

I had the queer feeling, as we threaded our way between
recumbent camels, that we were walking up the main street
of King's Lynn. We found the hotel and a more or less cool
drink. I could not place my companion. He was evidently
not a resident business man. He might be an officer in

mufti, but the battalion in Jerusalem was the Seaforths and he was no Scotsman. I put him down as Norfolk or, possibly, Suffolk.

" Do you live here? " I asked.

" I've been here since 1921. I came over with the ' Black and Tans ' to join the police. I'm still in the police. It's a good country—at least, it suits me! I get plenty of shooting."

" On the Jericho road? "

" No! " he smiled. " That's pretty quiet now. You couldn't have come down here without an armed escort in the time of the Turk. You still need an escort on some roads over there."

He nodded towards the mauve-streaked hills of Trans-Jordan.

" The shooting I like is game—anything. I spend all my leave with a pal, camping in places like the Jordan Valley, studying the wild life and—shooting. We bagged a wolf not so long ago a few miles from Jericho. I didn't know there were any left. He was a big brute too."

He pulled out from the pocket of his tweed coat a notebook in which he kept a kind of map of the available game. He brought out a pencil and entered up the current quail migration.

" The quail," he explained, " always fly by night and do the Mediterranean in one stage, choosing the narrowest part. They arrive dead beat, so exhausted that the Arabs used to put up huge screens into which the birds fell in thousands. I believe it was once suggested that the quail was the manna of the Old Testament."

" I think manna was a deposit like cuckoo-spit."

" You're interested in that sort of thing? You ought to go and see the ruins of old Jericho. I believe they're very interesting."

He looked at his watch.

" I shall have to be going."

" Before you go you might mark the traditional place of the Baptism on my map. I want to try and find it."

He took the map and marked it.

" I must go," he said, glancing towards the road from Jericho. " The High Commissioner is taking an afternoon off and I'm going to show him where the quail are. He's just about due."

He went out, followed by the pointer. An Arab carrying guns and bags joined him outside, and together they went down the road in the sun. A few minutes afterwards, as I was on my way to the ruins of old Jericho, I saw a Daimler with a Union Jack flying from tne bonnet come gliding over the Jericho road. It pulled up, and there was a moment of regal suspension before the doors were opened. Out leapt an A.D.C. and a secretary or two. Then followed His Majesty's High Commissioner for Palestine. There was nothing about him, except the extreme rigidity of his attendants and their slightly over-eager desire to anticipate his actions and desires, which would have indicated to the casual observer that there walked the lineal successor in office of Pontius Pilate. Yet so it was. Lord Balfour's Declaration, by which Great Britain is pledged to an uninterpreted phrase " a national home for the Jews," has created for the first time since the Roman occupation a Jewish political atmosphere in Palestine. Rome drove out the Jews; Britain is bringing them back. Already certain of these Jews are expressing a hatred for the policy of Great Britain, just as the zealots directed their intrigues and rebellions against Rome. It is an interesting historical parallel. However. . . .

The successor of Pontius Pilate strode in the sunlight over the parched hills of the Jordan Valley, and beside him walked an eager sportsman talking about the migration of quail. In front of them, like a watchful streak of England, went a black-and-white pointer.

§ 8

I discovered the Jericho of the Old Testament about two miles from the modern town. It stands on a level plain, and behind rises the mountain Jebel-Quarantal, on which Joshua's spies sought refuge. There is nothing to-day but a huge mound of sun-caked earth and stone from which the point of a stick will turn up fragments of ancient pottery. This mound rises to a height of about twenty or thirty feet and from the top you get a good idea of the ruins of houses and the line, here and there, of a narrow, twisting street. The town was evidently a small one, covering about ten acres, and surrounded by a wall perhaps twenty-six feet high and seven feet thick, made of mud bricks on a foundation of stone.

When Moses looked down upon the Promised Land from the heights of Mount Nebo beyond the Dead Sea, he saw this walled town standing in an enormous palm grove surrounded by its gardens. It must have looked to the hungry Israelites the very symbol of luxury and richness. Jericho has been called the " key " and the " guardhouse " of Judæa, but George Adam Smith preferred to call it the pantry! It was the first city in the path of the invading Israelites when, after crossing the Jordan under Joshua's leadership, they carried out their famous manœuvre with the rams' horns and the Ark of the Covenant.

The excavations which Professor Garstang conducted recently on the site of ancient Jericho seem to prove two very interesting things: that the Biblical computation of the date of the Exodus is more accurate than that of modern Egyptologists, and that the walls of Jericho actually did fall down. It is considered that they were destroyed by an earthquake, or some similar disturbance, which overthrew them with great violence. Wandering over the ruins, I came on a section of the wall that bore obvious traces of this.

After Joshua's destruction of Jericho it seems to have remained a ruin for several centuries. In time another city grew up there, a city rich in the vegetation which springs up wherever water is poured on the Jordan Valley, a city of dates and balsam and corn and fruit. In perfect tune with the exotic character of Jericho is the fact that it once belonged to Cleopatra. When the East fell to Antony, he tried to please her with gifts which included Greece, Cyprus, Phœnicia, and parts of Cicilia and Crete. Then she cherished the ambition to drive Herod the Great from his throne and to become Queen of Judæa. I think the meeting, and the intrigue surrounding the meeting, of two such time-servers and conspirators as Herod and Cleopatra must have been one of the most perfect human comedies of the time. One cannot withhold admiration for Antony's skill in side-tracking Cleopatra from

Judæa to the balsam gardens of Jericho. One wonders how he did it.

The gift, however, was one that must have pleased her, because Jericho was a great farm for the raw materials of perfumes, sweet-scented oils and other aromatic substances. And she arrived in Jericho somewhere about 35 B.C. to visit her plantations. Josephus says that she even made an attempt on what one must humorously term the virtue of Herod, and that he, considering her a danger to lesser princes, took counsel on the advisability of killing her, probably on the bandit-haunted road from Jericho to Jerusalem. But she departed safely out of Judæa, taking with her a shoot of balsam from Jericho, which she planted in Heliopolis.

How rich Jericho was at this time can be estimated from the fact that Cleopatra rented her balsam groves to Herod for a yearly sum of two hundred talents. Josephus does not say whether the rent was in gold or silver talents, but, at the lowest estimate, she must have wrung from the reluctant Herod something like £48,000 a year.

Soon after renting Jericho from Cleopatra, Herod decided to build a town worthy of the rent he was paying. He settled on a site some distance from the ancient town and about two miles south of modern Jericho. I found what I believe to be the site of this Jericho on slightly higher ground nearer to, and overlooking, the Dead Sea. This was the Jericho that grew into a splendid Romanised town. It held Herod's winter palace. There was an amphitheatre and a hippodrome. The pleasure-gardens of Herod's palace must have been something like the Gardens of the Alhambra. It was in this lovely spot, soothed on even the coldest winter day by a warm breeze, that Herod, eaten by disease, died broken-hearted and remorseful.

The Jericho built by Herod the Great is the town mentioned in the Gospels. During the annual Passover pilgrimage to the Temple at Jerusalem the Jews of Galilee were in the habit of travelling down the Jordan Valley to Jericho, and approaching Jerusalem by the mountain road in order to avoid the often dangerous consequences of traversing the hated Samaritan country. It was at Jericho that these pilgrims linked up with Jews from Perea (which is now Trans-Jordan) and went up in crowds to Jerusalem.

That is why we find Jesus and the disciples at Jericho before Passion Week. And in St. Luke we see an interesting reflection of the commercial importance of Jericho. Is not Zacchæus, the little man who climbed into the branches of the sycamore tree in order to see Jesus pass by, the chief publican, or tax-gatherer of Jericho? We do not know whether he was chief customs officer of the whole valley, or whether he had something to do with the Herodian balsam groves, but in this life-like, almost humorous, incident we have a memory of the day when Jericho was rich and prosperous.

To-day you can stand, as I did, upon the brown, uneasy mounds, and by an effort of the imagination try to build up a vision of the town that Christ saw when " he went on before, going up to Jerusalem."

§ 9

I dipped my hand in the Dead Sea and held my wet fingers in the sun. In a few seconds a fine white powder formed on my hand which I found bitter and salt to the taste.

The Dead Sea is beautiful to look at on a sunny day. The report spread by mediæval pilgrims of its gloom is entirely false and reflects, perhaps, not the Dead Sea but the minds of those gallant voyagers. The story that no birds can fly across it because of poison in the air is also untrue. There are not many birds because there are no fish in the sea. The few Jordan fish that do get carried into the salt lake are soon cast up mummified on the shores. But the Dead Sea itself is as blue and as sparkling as Loch Lomond or Killarney on a summer's day.

The waters lap the beach of pebbles in oily little waves. There are no shells on the beach, no evidence of any life, no growth of weeds or water plants, for the waters are sterile and dead. The reason why the Dead Sea is a huge cauldron of chemicals is because there is no outlet. It is a vast hole in the earth into which the Jordan and tributary streams pour every day nearly seven million tons of water mixed with sulphurous and nitrous matter.

Unable to escape, and subjected to the tremendous heat of the Jordan Valley, this water evaporates, leaving behind enormous deposits of salts and other chemicals in the sea. In the sea-bed there are also hot springs about which little is known. Ordinary sea-water holds from four to six per cent. of solids in solution; Dead Sea water holds five times as much. It is impossible for a bather to sink in it and a non-swimmer out of his depth cannot drown as long as he keeps his head. When Titus came to the Jordan Valley in 70 A.D. he caused several slaves to be chained together and flung into the Dead Sea. But they evidently kept their heads, for they emerged alive.

Any horror inspired by the Dead Sea is due to its appalling setting: the obscene banks of chemical slime, the grey land-slides of salt, the smell of sulphur, the weird, twisted foothills stained and tortured like the deposit at the bottom of a crucible. The hills are not shaped like ordinary hills: they are more like the fantastic outlines of cooled metal. As one wanders along the desolate shores the fate of Sodom and Gomorrah, which one may, possibly, have thought of as a tragic allegory, becomes terrifyingly real. It is as though this frightful judgment on human sin has for ever blasted and unhallowed the shores of the Dead Sea.

It was believed at one time that the ruins of those cities lie below the salt waters, but I understand that archæologists are looking for them round the shores. It is all part of the macabre setting that a mountain of salt, which the Arabs have mined for centuries, should exist far to the south, a strange place where twisted white pillars were recognised by the Jews in the time of Josephus as the remains of Lot's wife.

" Then the Lord rained upon Sodom and Gomorrah brimstone and fire. . . ."

The words of Genesis take on a horrible significance as one explores the Dead Sea. Fire has smitten the land, piled up the hills in tangled confusion and ripped great rents in the earth's body; and even to-day the smell of brimstone has not faded from the land.

There is, however, a stirring of life at the north end of the Dead Sea, where an ugly factory surrounded by salt pans is extracting all kinds of chemicals from the water. I am told that illimitable wealth lies in the Dead Sea. I was told how much, but I can never believe anything over a million. At the present moment they are separating magnesium chloride, potash, calcium chloride, bromide and common salt from the Dead Sea water. Certain of these products are being exported to all parts of the world.

Not far from the potash works is an attempt to turn the Dead Sea into a health resort. There is a timid-looking bathing beach, a café with a dance floor and a powerful wireless amplifier. It deforms such a minute fraction of the desolation that its intrusion is unnoticed.

§ 10

I took a road straight across the hills and hummocks towards the place of Christ's baptism. It was not really a road: it was an ill-defined cart-track that lost itself in thorn bushes, found itself in holes and swamps and went on twisting and winding towards the thin belt of green that marks the course of the Jordan.

No one knows where the place of the Baptism was, neither do we know where " Bethany beyond Jordan " was. But the place I discovered among the tamarisk and the willows is that which has been hallowed by centuries of pious pilgrimage. In the old days before the War, when Russia was " Holy Russia," thousands of pilgrims used to come down to this place to plunge into the Jordan, wearing white gowns which they took home to keep as their shrouds. To-day there are few pilgrims. The custom of bathing at this spot, or somewhere near it, goes back to the most remote times. It was known to the Pilgrim of Bordeaux, who visited the Holy Land in the Roman era—about the year 333 A.D., and one evening in the year 1172 Theodoric saw sixty thousand persons plunge into the river at this spot.

I was not prepared for the strange sight at the end of the road. On the river bank is an odd café, or rest-house, mounted on stilts. The roof is made of Jordan reeds, and everything about it suggests that at any moment the narrow, inoffensive river might overflow and drive the few inhabitants to their boats. Under this frail shelter are set a number of home-made tables and chairs. Hens, chickens, turkeys and goats roam carelessly round the tables. A stuffed crane and a stuffed flamingo, both much the worse for wear, hang with dreary reluctance from the roof. There is a kind of counter, or bar, with a licence which states that this collection of poles and reeds is owned by Mr. N. Stomation. I discovered that the only visible inhabitant was someone, whom I took to be Mr. Stomation, sitting with his back to the Jordan gloomily whittling a stick with a pen-knife. He was in his shirt sleeves, with an ancient khaki tunic flung across his shoulders. He paid no attention to me as I prowled about his strange retreat. The Jordan is apparently always trying to dislodge Mr. Stomation. His dwelling quarters, and also a large dome-shaped oven, are mounted on twelve-foot-high stilts. Even the chickens and the turkeys and the goats must sometimes be forced to run for it, as little pile dwellings to the side of the main quarters testify.

The Jordan, flowing a few yards from this tattered, pre-historic-looking encampment, surprised me. I felt that I was standing on the bank of some English stream, perhaps the Avon in Warwickshire high up beyond the mill in flood-time. I cannot say why I should have felt this, because the banks of the Jordan are thick with exotic, foreign trees and shrubs such as tamarisk and a thin reed, like bamboo. I think it was the way a group of willows dropped their leaves in the water exactly as they do when the Avon floods the meadows round Stratford-on-Avon in March. And as I looked at the Jordan touching the willow leaves and moving them the way of the current, I seemed to be back again in the great happi-ness of my youth, sitting upon an old green wall near Holy Trinity. There is something slow and gentle and small about the Jordan as it swings round the bend beside the place of the Baptism, something, as I say, very home-like that made me think of those devout paintings on the walls of Venice and Florence in which men have painted Bethlehem and Nazareth like their own towns. It seemed to me that there should be a lesson in this, but a better moralist than myself would have to make it: that a man should travel across the world to see the holy Jordan, and discover it to be just like the little stream at home that runs at the bottom of his garden.

I thought how true this vision of mine was, and how it would probably be contradicted by every tourist who has seen the milky-blue and sandy whirlpools of this river. For the Jordan does flow in every part of the Christian world. Some little drop finds its way into every font at every baptism.

On the way back I came to a deserted place near the river where a new church was standing among trees. It was the only building in the wilderness. While I was looking at it, a black monk came out of a side door and stood watching me; and I remembered that someone had told me the Abyssinians had dedicated a church to St. John not far from the river. Before the church was built, the monks used to live in odd little dwellings perched in the trees, more or less like Mr. Stomation's restaurant on stilts.

I went up and, by signs, made the monk understand that I would like to see the church. He beamed with pleasure and his teeth shone like snow in the night of his countenance. Leading the way, he unlocked a door and took me into a beautifully designed church, the high altar hidden, as is the custom with the Abyssinians, behind closed doors, and a great space all round the church for the processions which are a great feature of the mysterious African devotions. He took me into the vestry and showed with great pride a series of brilliant vestments, reds and blues and purples, some of them roughly sewn with bits of tinsel and gold braid. We never spoke a word, but we made many signs, smiled, nodded and bowed. When I went, anxious to give something to the church, for the Abyssinians are very poor, I brought out some silver, but a look of pain shot into the eyes of the monk and he gently pushed away my hand and shook his head. His eyes were like those of some big, gentle animal.

There is something very touching about these black men who worship Christ with such primitive but, I am told, heretical devotion. I have never encountered any people who seem so gentle and so meek.

§ 11

I got back to Jericho as the afternoon sun was sinking. I was anxious to be on the mountain road before dark, but I was also determined to climb the Mount of Temptation which rises at the back of Jericho.

It was a long but easy ascent, and with every step upward the Jordan Valley looked more terrible in its hot bleached bareness. When I reached the top of this mountain I was still two hundred feet below sea level.

Half-way up, built partly in the rock, I discovered a monastery where ten old Greek monks endure the poverty that has descended on the Eastern Church. Few pilgrims come now to pray in the little grotto where Jesus fasted in the wilderness.

One old man, who could speak two or three words of English, took me over the chapel, with its dust, its dim, gaudy ikons, its unlit candles, and its air of decay and neglect.

He pointed to a cavity beneath an altar, telling me in a solemn low voice that it was the cave in which Jesus slept before He was tempted by the devil. Then he tip-toed off to some other dusty shrine. The air of death about the place, and the old men who tottered about in their black robes, were rather depressing. Then the setting was so improbable and fantastic. A monastery carved out of a mountain side, bits of it built out here and there over ghastly chasms, while other parts of it were cut into the face of the mountain so that the walls and roof were of the rock. I wondered what happened when one of these old men died. I imagined them cutting a grave in the rock and placing their companion to rest like some ancient Moses on Nebo.

There was something pathetic in their childish pleasure in my visit. The old monk, having shown me the church, led me to a room whose balcony was built out over a sheer drop of more than a thousand feet. The little wooden erection shook so ominously under me that I stepped back into the room. It was a strange little room, furnished according to some dimly remembered standards of the distant earth. A little table with a green cloth occupied the centre, and round the walls were set old horse-hair padded chairs. The only pictures in the room were of the Tzar and the Tzarina, King Tino of Greece and, strangely enough, old-fashioned coloured lithographs of King George and Queen Mary.

The old monk sat with folded hands, smiling affably at me and speaking the most atrocious English.

" Ah ! " he said, or rather meant to say, glancing up at the lithograph of the Tzar, " poor, poor Russia ! "

He told me that in the old days the mountain path was black with ascending pilgrims from Holy Russia. But now . . . he spread his hands in a gesture of despair. At this point a young monk, the only young one I had seen, entered bearing a tray containing small cups of coffee, little plates of jam and a white liqueur that tasted like absinthe. I drank the coffee and the liqueur and ate the jam, ceremoniously bowing to the old monk from time to time and receiving in return his smiles and bows. The young monk, a rather scared-looking youth in spectacles and with side-whiskers of brown fluff, stood holding the tray and bowing stiffly every time I put back a glass or a plate.

It was the habit in ancient times to treat any stranger as if he might be a wandering Christ, and this beautiful courtesy still exists in out-of-the-way parts of the earth. We have lost it, and with it something fine and beautiful has gone from our lives. When the old monk led me to the main gate and, lifting the latch for me, said good-bye, adding a blessing in Greek, his eyes still held that antique wonder in them. I was a stranger going down and away into mystery. I turned and waved back to him, and went on down the stony path.

Never shall I forget the sunset flung back upon the hills of Moab, turning them to pink and mauve, filling the gashes in their flanks with dark blue shadows. The brown humped hills lay to the north like a map of the moon, and in the centre of the wilderness I saw the green thread that marks the river whose waters flow to the four corners of Christendom.

AIN KAREM

A Doorway in Nazareth

There were shadows over the mountain pass as I went up to Jerusalem. The sun had gone when I passed Bethany. In Jerusalem they were lighting the lamps.

§ 12

It is an extraordinary commentary on the smallness of Palestine that Jesus in the course of His missionary journeys was never more than a hundred and thirty miles distant from Jerusalem. This was on the occasion of His departure to the borders of Tyre and Sidon. The smallness of the country is such that from many of the high ridges of Judæa all the boundaries are clearly visible: snow-capped Hermon to the north, the sandy desert to the south, the Mediterranean Sea to the west, and the high ridge of the Trans-Jordan mountains to the east.

When the Bible says that Moses was shown all the Promised Land from the top of Mount Nebo, it is literally true. From this height, four thousand feet above the Dead Sea, he could see the outline of the entire country. And there are many other mountains from which the same tremendous panorama is visible.

The Life which has meant more to humanity than any other life was, therefore, lived within an astonishingly small compass, and the faith that has created the modern world was born in a country about the size of Wales, and cradled in a part of it—Galilee—that is far smaller than Devonshire.

Jesus, in the words of *Acts*, " went about doing good." But when we examine the details of these journeys in the Gospels we realise, perhaps with surprise, that the towns and villages which He visited number only eighteen. It is obvious that during the thirty odd years of His earthly life, Christ must have known this small country of Palestine from end to end. The Gospels, apart from the flight into Egypt mentioned only by St. Matthew, and the disputation with the elders mentioned only by St. Luke, deal with a brief period in the life of Christ which scholars have estimated to be from eighteen months to three and a half years. These are the years of the Baptism, the Galilean Ministry, and the

Crucifixion. How Jesus spent the greater part of His life is a mystery. Not one word has been recorded about it. Some scholars regard this as the most provoking problem in history, while others believe it to be an intentional mystery.

But to the traveller who, like myself, wishes to visit all the places associated with Jesus Christ, the fragmentary nature of the Gospel narratives presents a rather perplexing problem. It is impossible to make a tour based on any detailed chronological sequence. All one can do is to take Bethlehem as the starting place of one's journey, Nazareth as the place in which Christ's boyhood was spent (where, as St. Luke says, " the child grew and waxed strong in spirit "), the lakeside of Galilee as the central point of one's travels, and then back to Jerusalem to reconstruct the vivid and well-documented evidence of the Crucifixion.

This, then, is what I propose to do. The journey will take me into many places which are not specifically mentioned in the Gospels as having been visited by Christ, but who can doubt that, if the full story of His journeying were known, His steps would lead one over the length and the breadth of the land, following a thousand paths unknown to us?

CHAPTER FOUR

On the way to Bethlehem I discover a relic of Pontius Pilate. I visit Bethlehem, enter the Grotto of the Nativity, meet descendants of the Crusaders, travel to Hebron and to Beersheba, where I attend a sitting of the Tribal Court. I sleep at Gaza, explore the sandy ruins of Ascalon, and watch camels bathing in the sea in accordance with the ancient ritual of Job's Feast.

§ 1

THE road was like any other road in Palestine. The sky was a hot lid above it. The snapping of grasshoppers in the olive groves was a steady rhythm in the heat.

The road was white with the dust of powdered limestone, a floury dust which the heels of the donkeys kicked up in clouds; but the soft feet of the camels hardly moved it, as they passed silent as shadows. White stone walls lay on either side, and behind them the stony terraces, planted with olive trees, lifted themselves in sharp white ridges against the darkness of the sky. Little brown lizards with the watchful heads of frogs lived in the chinks of the stones. They would come out to lie in the sun, still as the stones, except for a quick beating in their throats. Sometimes I could go to within a yard of them, and would be just about to touch them with an olive twig, when, swift as a whiplash flicked out of the dust, they would be gone.

The heat was a nervous tension enclosing the world. All sounds were an invasion, except that of the grasshoppers, which was the palpitating voice of the heat. A shepherd boy piped somewhere on the hill, playing a maddening little tune without beginning or end, a little stumbling progress up and down a scale, like the ghost of a waterfall. And the white road led on under the sun.

It was, as I have said, just like any other road in Palestine. But there was one thing that marked it out from all other roads in the world. It was the road to Bethlehem.

As I walked on, I thought that travel in Palestine is different from travel in any other part of the world because Palestine exists already in our imagination before we start out. From our earliest years it begins to form in our minds side by side with fairyland, so that it is often difficult to tell where one begins and the other ends. Therefore the Palestine of reality is always in conflict with the imaginary Palestine, so violently at times that many people cannot relinquish this Palestine of the imagination without a feeling of bereavement. That is why some people go away disillusioned from the Holy Land. They are unable, or unwilling, to reconcile the real with the ideal.

Any truthful account of travel in Palestine must mention this conflict. Every day you hear travellers say, as they visit some place: " I never imagined it quite like that," or " I always thought of it in a different way."

And as I went on to Bethlehem I remembered a place hushed in snow where shepherds wrapped in thick cloaks watched their flocks under the frosty stars. There was a little shelter in this place in which beasts stamped in their stalls and blew the fog of their breath into the cold air. On the straw near the mangers, sitting in exquisite detachment, was a Mother with a gold circle about her head and a little Child. The stars shone coldly, and through the air came a sound of far-off bells.

I know perfectly well that this picture was edged with gilt. It was my own private little vision of Bethlehem, something that has been with me all my life, something made up in my mind from Christmas cards sent to me when I was a child, from pictures that I loved before I could read, something formed by the piety and reverence which a cold northern land has cast round the story of the Nativity. Every Christian nation has translated the story of Christ into its own idiom and cradled Him in its own barns. The great mediæval painters have, each man in his own way, painted in the national background of his own country and his own time. And we who come from Europe to Palestine come from an enchanted country to the bare rocks and crags of reality.

I walked along in the airless heat, sorry to say farewell to this little picture of mine; and the heat of the white road to Bethlehem quivered like fire over the limestone walls and beat like the breath of a furnace upon the grey little olive trees and shone through the greenness of the uncurling fig leaves.

I came to a place where a few trees made a pool of shade on the dust of the road. And under the trees was an old well with a stone basin beside it, so that shepherds and camel-men could pour out water for their beasts.

This well, like so many things in this land, has several names. Some call it Mary's Well, because of an old story that the Holy Family, travelling the five and a half miles between Bethlehem and Jerusalem, once rested there and drank its waters. It is also called the Well of the Star. The legend is that the Wise Men on their way to Bethlehem lost the Star and, coming to this well to slake their thirst, found it again shining in the water.

I went on past the Well of the Star. On the left the earth suddenly fell into space. The terrific landslide fell away into the heat, and down below, far off, like land seen from an aeroplane, lay a brown-and-blue map of the Dead Sea and the Mountains of Moab. Ahead of me was Bethlehem, with slender cypress trees rising above the flat roofs, white buildings shining among the olive trees, and terraces falling away into a wall of heat. Beside the road, facing the view of Moab, was a stone seat. There was no shade above it and the stone was hot. A lizard streaked away into hiding as I rested there. There were words carved on the stone: " Thou shalt love the Lord with all thy heart, and with all thy soul, and thy neighbour as thyself." Beneath this summary of Christ's teaching was an inscription which stated that the seat was placed there in memory of William Holman Hunt by his wife, Edith.

Holman Hunt's picture *The Light of the World* was the most famous religious painting of the nineteenth century. It must be known to everyone. Holman Hunt painted it when he was twenty-seven years of age and at a time when, discouraged by the difficulty of selling his pictures, he was trying to make up his mind to forsake art and take up farming in the Colonies. This painting decided his life. The recognition it brought enabled him to realise his dearest ambition: to live in Palestine and paint biblical subjects in the country of Christ's birth. Of all the famous pictures painted by Holman Hunt in Palestine, perhaps the best known is *The Scapegoat*, a pitiful study of a poor, starving creature wandering in dreary solitude among the salt hills of the Dead Sea, bearing the sins of humanity upon its head.

I remember reading somewhere that Holman Hunt's favourite view was that from the road near Bethlehem, and I suppose this seat marks the place. No doubt the hot, forbidding vista of the Jordan Valley from this point first suggested to his mind the idea of *The Scapegoat*.

The sight of the parched valley and the barren, waterless Mountains of Moab made the hot road seem cooler. Down there, I thought, the Dead Sea would be warm to the touch. The palms would be standing in a burning stillness and the water would have dried in the baked mud trenches that run between the banana trees.

It is not difficult to know why mystics have always gone into those terrible hills to find Truth. Such indifference to Mankind seems to promise a revelation of God; their unwillingness to quench the thirst of the body suggests that they might be willing to slake the thirst of the soul.

I went on, past the white domed Tomb of Rachel, which is venerated by Christian, Jew and Moslem, and, just where the road branches off to Hebron, I looked over a stone wall and saw something which an archæologist in Jerusalem had told me not to miss; the only surviving relic of Pontius Pilate. It is the ruin of an aqueduct which ran from the Pools of Solomon to the Temple Area. It was an engineering work which involved Pilate in a financial scandal.

Pilate was appointed procurator of Judæa in 26 A.D. and remained in office for ten years. The custom of long-term governors was approved by Tiberius, who used to say with bitter cynicism that an enriched governor was better for a country than a new and still rapacious one. Much more is known of Pilate's career in Palestine than is to be found in the Gospels.   Josephus and Philo give long, but biased, accounts of his record.

He expressed an active dislike for the Jews and a bewildered contempt for their religious taboos.   He regarded them as dangerous maniacs and instigators of every kind of sedition. He had the plain, blunt soldier's loathing for the political intrigue by which he was surrounded, and he possessed the worldly man's dislike for the fanaticism which he met at every step.   He lost his temper quickly and frequently ordered his troops to attack the Jews; but, reading the history of his time, one wonders what else he could have done.   Roman tolerance was always interpreted as weakness.

His first act did not endear him to the Judæans.   It was a custom with the Romans, who always observed the greatest respect for the religious beliefs of their subject peoples, never to permit troops to march into Jerusalem with the image of the Emperor on the legionary standards.   These were always unscrewed and put away out of deference to the Mosaic injunction against graven images.   Pilate, however, when moving troops up to Jerusalem, marched them into the city under cover of darkness with the eagle and the imperial image on the tops of the standards.

When the Jews awakened in the morning and saw this, the city was in an uproar.   Deputations surrounded his palace for five days, begging him to remove the images.   He threatened that unless the agitators went away he would order a massacre.   On the sixth day he was forced to meet the deputations, who cried that they would willingly die rather than suffer the violation of their laws.   Pilate was beaten and had to order the removal of the eagles.

Another and an even more serious conflict was that of the aqueduct whose remains still lie beside the Bethlehem road.   In order to bring water from Solomon's Pools to the Temple (although his enemies said that the water was really intended for military purposes in the event of an insurrection), Pilate raided the enormous funds known as the Corban, lying in the Temple treasury.   The appropriation of this money created violent opposition.   The storm broke when Pilate came up to Jerusalem from his headquarters at Cæsarea, probably during the annual Passover pilgrimage, when he was always present with extra troops in case of trouble. This time Pilate sent troops disguised as Jewish pilgrims among the crowds. These troops, at a signal, attacked the Jews and quelled the disturbance. If this episode occurred at Passover time, there seems to be an echo of it in St. Luke, who mentions the " Galileans whose blood Pilate mingled with their sacrifices." Should this supposition be correct, a remarkable possibility is dependent on it. The Galileans whom Pilate slew were not subject to him: they were the subjects of Herod Antipas. Now, when Pilate handed Jesus, the Galilean, over to Herod, we learn from St. Luke " and the same day Herod and Pilate were made friends together: for before they were at enmity between themselves."

If it is possible that Pilate sent Jesus as a peace-offering to the ruler of Galilee in return for the Galileans he had attacked on a previous occasion, then the strange thought occurs that the building of this aqueduct—the cause of the original enmity between Pilate and Herod—was a contributory factor in the crucifixion of Jesus. . . .

I climbed over the wall and inspected this extraordinary relic. Few people know that it exists and, unless someone takes care of it, the remaining water pipes, or rather stones, will be carried away and used for building material. In fact the head of the Magi's well further back along the Jerusalem road is one of these stones.

The aqueduct runs at the edge of the boundary wall and disappears from sight beneath a house. It is formed of huge blocks of stone with a central hole drilled in them, and so arranged that each stone fitted with a neck firmly into the next, making a solid rock channel for the water.

If the theory I have advanced is reasonable, this line of stones is one of the strangest and most significant relics in the world. In any case, a few of them deserve a place in Jerusalem's magnificent new museum.

I went on towards Bethlehem thinking of Pilate and of the odium that has been cast on his name. The trial of Jesus gives us a full-length portrait of the Roman: haughty, blunt, weak enough to be blackmailed, but distinguished from the Jews by a sense of justice. He did try to save Jesus. He tried again and again with a growing sense of exasperation and hopelessness. The Jews, with that brilliant insight into the weak spot in human nature, a gift that has never deserted them, suddenly ceased from attacking Christ and attacked Pilate. The cry went up: " If thou release this man, thou art not Cæsar's friend!" It was blackmail. And it sealed the fate of Jesus.

Pilate's attitude changed when that cry went up. He had good reason to visualise an influential embassy visiting Rome behind his back and plotting against him. " The Governor of Judæa," they would say, " has set free a man who calls himself King. He is not Cæsar's friend."

Pilate owed everything to Tiberius. One word from the Emperor and he fell from power, perhaps into exile and disgrace. Pilate knew, and the Jews knew, that there is nothing easier to poison than the mind of an autocrat.

So Pilate, too weak and too worldly to challenge the voice of the blackmailer, was once more beaten by the Jews. As a last gesture of disapproval he called for water and washed his hands.

He survived in office for another six years: until, in fact, he made a serious error in judgment which those who lay in wait for him used in order to procure his recall. A certain impostor appeared in Samaria and summoned the Samaritans to the top of Mount Gerizim, promising to reveal to them the sacred vessels which he said Moses had buried there. An armed crowd gathered at a village called Tirabatha. Pilate, who was always on the look-out for armed rebellion, misjudged the seriousness of the assembly and sent troops to disperse it, which they did with great slaughter. The Samaritans appealed to Vitellius, the Legate of Syria and Pilate's superior, who, finding that Pilate was in error, had no other choice than to send him to Rome to answer the charges made against him. While he was on his way to Rome Tiberius died, and the inquiry into Pilate's conduct was apparently forgotten in the confusion of the new reign. So Pilate disappears from history to emerge again in legend. It was related in very early times that, falling into disgrace under Caligula, Pilate committed suicide. But there is no historical justification for this story.

In the apocryphal gospels, *The Acts of Pilate* and the *Gospel*

E

of Peter, which were written centuries after Pilate's death, he is shown in a favourable light and is assured of divine forgiveness.

Legend, however, shows him, like Judas, pursued by demons of remorse and despair. It was said that his body was flung into the Tiber, but evil spirits so terrified the neighbourhood that it was taken up and conveyed to Vienne, in the south of France, where it was flung into the Rhone. There the same thing happened. The body was therefore taken up a third time and carried to Lausanne, in Switzerland, where it was walled up in a deep pit surrounded by mountains. Another story says that Pilate's corpse was eventually flung into a dark lake on the mountain still known as Pilatus, and it is recorded that people travelling by night in those desolate parts have been horrified to see a white figure walk from the lake and go through the motion of washing its hands.

§ 2

The white houses cluster on the hill like a group of startled nuns. They stand on the edge of the road and gaze down into a pit of heat. Where the striped terraces end and the bare rock begins, the last olive trees seem to be struggling desperately to run back up the stony terraces away from the heat and the sterility of the rock. The white houses watch them with open mouths that are doors, and startled eyes that are windows. And the hot sunlight beats down from the blue sky.

Above the flat, white roofs rise the bell-towers of convents and orphanages and monasteries. There is always a bell ringing in the heat. If it is not the bell of the Salesian Fathers, it may be the bell of the Sisters of St. Vincent de Paul. At the bottom of the road that leads up to this white hill-town is a notice-board which absurdly pins this region to reality: "Bethlehem Municipal Boundary," it says. "Drive slowly."

The traveller, approaching Bethlehem with his mind on St. Luke and Botticelli, pauses in surprise before this board because it has never before occurred to him that Bethlehem could be confined by municipal boundaries. It seems to him, at first, almost sacrilege that Bethlehem should possess a mayor and a municipality. Then, when he ceases to feel and begins to think, it occurs to him that the Mayor of Bethlehem is a wonderful symbol. He is a sign of an almost terrifying continuity of human life. His predecessors in office extend back before the time of Christ into the days of the Old Testament, and probably into dim, distant regions of legend. Bethlehem is typical of the strange immutability of these Palestinian towns. Wave after wave of conquest has swept over them without, apparently, making much difference to them. Bethlehem has known the Jews, the Romans, the Arabs, the Crusaders, the Saracens and the Turks. They have all erected their notice-boards on her boundaries. And now there is one in English at the bottom of the hill asking you to " drive slowly."

As you walk up the hill into Bethlehem, wishing only to be left alone, young Arabs in European clothes, red tarbushes above their eager faces, greet you and lead you against your will into strange little shops. There you are offered pious objects carved in mother of pearl, in olive wood, and in a black stone that comes from the Dead Sea. If these fail, they try to sell you the wedding dress of a Bethlehem woman. When you ask what on earth you would do with such an embarrassing possession, they smile and thrust the garments towards you:

" You have no wife? Ah, young English ladies much like! Very pretty . . . Look, sir . . ."

But they seem quite pleased if you buy only a post-card.

The British passion for justice, which to the Arab is one of the many perplexing problems about his new master, is stamped clearly on the ancient face of Bethlehem in the form of a new building: the Bethlehem Police Station.

" Justice ! " an Arab is reported to have said. " In the old days of the Turk we paid money to the judge and knew the result beforehand, but now we pay much more money to the solicitor and know nothing till the case is over. And you call that Justice ! "

But the police station is like a new bookplate in a very old book. It is a sign of the latest owner. Its very newness accentuates the illusionary nature of possession. A few paces beyond it the narrow main street of Bethlehem begins, running now up and now down through the clustered warren of white houses. Even in Rhodes and Malta and Cyprus, where, so I believe, the Crusades have lingered in bastion and outwork, there could be nothing so vividly crusading as the main street of Bethlehem. Here the Crusaders are still alive! They look at you with their blue European eyes. Although they call themselves Christian Arabs, their faces are Flemish and French, and, perhaps, English. Old women sit in the shade of white walls and lift towards you the lined face of an authentic Memling.

The dress of the Bethlehem woman, which is unique, is also a memory of the Crusades. The married women wear a high headdress covered with a flowing veil which is pinned under the chin and falls down the back and over the shoulders. This is believed to be the fashion that in Europe developed into the tall foolscap with its pendant veil, the headdress worn by nearly all princesses in fairy tales. Whether the fashion was brought to Palestine by European women during the Crusades, or whether it was developed by them in the East—a version of the silver horn headdress that has only recently died out in Syria—and carried back to Europe, I am not able to say. But those who have studied this question, and that of Bethlehem's crusading blood, agree that both the fashion and the face beneath it are a relic of the Latin Kingdom of Jerusalem.

Why should this not be so? Bethlehem is an entirely Christian town. In punishment for an insurrection the Moslems were driven out about a century ago by the terrible Ibrahim Pasha, whose memory lingers in Bethlehem much as that of Judge Jeffreys lingers in Wiltshire. It is true that recently some Moslems have come back, but there are very few of them.

Throughout the centuries the Christian community, descendants, if you like, of the Crusaders, have lived in Bethlehem, keeping very much to themselves, marrying and intermarrying and thus preserving the marked European strain. The women are very shy. They expend great ingenuity in avoiding the cameras of tourists. They fly from a camera as from the devil.

The town itself is small and unspoilt. Shops and workshops line a part of the main street. They are merely arches open to the road, which is so narrow that the cobbler can sit at his last and talk to his friend, the grocer, on the opposite side of the road without raising his voice.

The impression I received in Bethlehem was one of peace and graciousness. Jerusalem is taut with mental conflict Bethlehem is quiet and, I think, happy. For once the prevailing Mohammedanism is keyed down and almost inaudible. There is only one muezzin in Bethlehem, but there are many bells.

I thought at times that if the white houses had been bowered in trees, or if bougainvillea had spilt itself from white walls, I might have imagined myself in some little town of Andalusia But one is never quite permitted to imagine this. The hot highlands of Judæa are always visible through an archway or at the end of a street.

I once read a story, I think it was written by H. G. Wells, in which someone discovered a door in a very ordinary wall which led into the Garden of the Hesperides. The memory of it came to me in Bethlehem when I encountered a door in a massive wall. It was so low that even a dwarf would have to bend his head in order to pass through it. On the other side of it was the Church of the Nativity. They say in Bethlehem that all the doors into this church were walled up long ago, except this one, which was made low in order to prevent the infidel from riding into the building on horseback and slaying the worshippers.

But no sooner had I bent my head and stepped across than I straightened up—in Rome! It was the Rome of Constantine the Great, or, perhaps I should say, New Rome. It was the biggest surprise I had had in Palestine. I expected the usual ornate church, the dark, burdened altars, the confused stairs and passages of a reconstructed building, and here I was in a cold, austere Roman basilica. Massive Corinthian pillars made of some dull red stone upheld the roof and divided the church into a nave and aisles. I was in the church that Constantine the Great built long ago as a sign that he had become a Christian. Surely one of the marvels of Palestine is the fact that this church should have

survived the dangers that have swept the other buildings of
its time to dust? Here it is, the earliest Christian church in
use to-day, and more or less as it left the hands of its builders.
On the walls are the remains of dim gold mosaics.

I looked up to the roof. Is there, I wondered, anything
left of the English oaks with which Edward IV reconstructed
the roof of the Church of the Nativity? He cut down oaks
and sent tons of lead for this purpose, which the Republic
of Venice transported to Jaffa. There the Franciscans took
charge of the pious gift and conveyed it to Bethlehem. I
believe the lead was melted down by the Turks in the seventeenth century and used as bullets against the very Republic
that had conveyed it to Palestine; but somewhere, perhaps,
high up above the Roman nave, may linger a fragment of oak
from the forests of fifteenth-century England.

The church is built above a cave which was recognised as
the birthplace of Jesus Christ two centuries before Rome
became a Christian state. The grotto must have been sacred
to Christians in the time of Hadrian. In order to defame
it, as he tried to defame Golgotha, he built over it a temple
to Adonis. Constantine pulled down this temple and built
this present church in its place. There seems to me something so touchingly formal about it, as if the Roman Empire
did not yet quite understand this new faith, but was making
a first, puzzled genuflection in its direction. One feels
that these pillars are really the pillars of a temple to
Jupiter.

A service was in progress. I thought the choir was filled
with nuns, but they were ordinary Bethlehem women wearing
the tall veiled headdress of the town. Beneath the high
altar is the cave which tradition claims as the spot where
Christ was born. It is entered by flights of steps set on each
side of the choir. On the way down I had to press myself
against the dark little staircase as two Greek monks, black of
eye and beard, came up in a cloud of incense.

Fifty-three silver lamps hardly lighten the gloom of the
underground cavern. It is a small cave about fourteen
yards long and four yards wide. Its walls are covered with
tapestry that reeks of stale incense. If you draw this
tapestry aside, you see that the walls are the rough, smoke-

blackened walls of a cave. Gold, silver and tinsel ornaments gleam in the pale glow of the fifty-three lamps.

I thought I was alone in the cavern until someone moved in the darkness, and I noticed the policeman who is always on duty to prevent disputes between the Greek and the Armenian priests. This church, like the Church of the Holy Sepulchre, suffers from divided ownership. It is in the hands of the Latins, the Greeks, and the Armenians.

So jealous are the various churches of their rights that even the sweeping of the dust is sometimes a dangerous task, and there is a column in which are three nails, one on which the Latins may hang a picture, one on which the Greeks may do so, and a neutral nail on which no sect may hang anything.

In the floor there is a star, and round it a Latin inscription which says: "Here Jesus Christ was born of the Virgin Mary." The removal of this star years ago led to a quarrel between France and Russia which blazed into the Crimean War.

Such truths may seem terrible; but this, alas, is an imperfect world. It is therefore necessary, as you stand in the Church of the Nativity, or in the Holy Sepulchre, to try and forget the frailties of men and to look beyond them to the truth and the beauty which they seem to obscure.

As I stood in this dark, pungent cavern I forgot, I am afraid, all the clever and learned things written about the Navitity by German professors, and I seemed to hear English voices singing under a frosty sky:—

> O come, all ye faithful,
> Joyful and triumphant,
> O come ye, O come ye to Bethlehem.

How different is this dark little cave under a church from the manger and the stable of one's imagination! As a child, I thought of it as a thatched English barn with wooden troughs for oats and hay, and a great pile of fodder on which the Wise Men knelt to adore " the new-born Child." Down the long avenues of memory I seemed to hear the waits singing in the white hush of Christmas night:—

> While shepherds watched their flocks by night,
> All seated on the ground,
> The Angel of the Lord came down,
> And glory shone around.

There was a rhythmic chinking sound on the dark stairs. A Greek priest, with a black beard curled like that of an Assyrian king, came slowly into the cavern swinging a censer. The incense rolled out in clouds and hung about in the candle flames. He censed the altar and the Star. Then, in the most matter-of-fact way, he genuflected and went up into the light of the church.

Beneath the church is a warren of underground passages. In one of them, a dark rock chamber, St. Jerome conducted a number of his keen controversies and translated the Vulgate.

But I found my way back to the cavern where the incense drifts in the lamp flames. The grotto was full of little children, silently standing two by two on the stairs. They came forward, knelt down and quickly kissed the stone near the star. Their little faces were very grave in the candle-light. Some of them closed their eyes tightly and whispered a prayer.

No sooner had the last of them gone, than I heard the chink-chink of the censer; and into the gloom of the Grotto of the Nativity came again a Greek priest like an Assyrian king.

§ 3

There are a number of old houses in Bethlehem built over caves in the limestone rock. These caves are exactly the same as the sacred grotto under the high altar of the Church of the Nativity, and they are probably as ancient. No one who has seen these houses can doubt that Jesus was born in one of them, and not in the stable of European tradition.

I suppose the idea that Christ was born in a stable was suggested by St. Luke's use of the word " manger." To the Western mind this word presupposes a stable or a barn, or some outbuilding separate from the house and used as a shelter for animals. But there is nothing in St. Luke to justify this.

These primitive houses in Bethlehem gave me an entirely new idea of the scene of the Nativity. They are one-room houses built over caves. Whether these caves are natural or artificial I do not know : they are level with the road, but the room above them is reached by a flight of stone steps, perhaps fifteen or twenty. The caves are used to this day as stables for the animals, which enter from the road level. There are, in most of them, a stone trough, or manger, cut from the rock, and iron rings to which the animals are tied during the night.

The family occupy the upper chamber, separated only by the thickness of the rock floor from the cave in which the animals sleep.

Now, if Joseph and Mary had visited the " inn " at Bethlehem and found it full, there would have been no stable for them to go to, because the " inns," or khans, in the time of Christ were merely open spaces surrounded by a high wall and a colonnade under whose arches were rooms for the travellers. The animals were not stabled in the European sense, but were gathered together in the centre of the enclosure. The Greek word *katalyma* used by St. Luke, and translated as " inn," would be more exactly rendered as " guest-chamber."

Therefore I believe we must imagine the Nativity to have taken place in one of these old cave-houses of Bethlehem. The guest-chamber, or upper room, which it was the Jewish custom to offer to travelling Jews, was evidently already occupied, and therefore the host did his best by offering to the Holy Family shelter of the downstairs room, or cave.

It is interesting in this connection to remember that the earliest tradition in the Church was that Jesus was born not in a stable or an inn, but in a cave. Justin Martyr, who was born about 100 A.D., repeats a tradition current in his time that, as Joseph had no place in which to lodge in Bethlehem, he discovered a cave near by. But even before Justin's time it seems that the cave below the Church of the Nativity was venerated as the scene of Christ's birth. It is not unreasonable to assume that the caverns below this church were once above ground and formed the bottom storeys, or basements, of inhabited houses.

St. Matthew, describing the birth of Jesus, says:

" And when they were come into the *house*, they saw the

young Child with Mary his mother ; and fell down, and worshipped him."

One of the houses which I visited might have remained unchanged since the time of Christ.   The man was attending to the animals, two donkeys and a foal, which were tied up to the rock in the cave.   In the room above the woman was sifting some small grain, like millet, through a sieve. From time to time she talked to her husband as he busied himself in the room beneath.

The living-room was, like most rooms in the East, bare of furniture.   In a corner of it were the matting beds rolled up and tucked away out of sight.

The thought came to me that the nearest approach to the kind of building in which Christ was born is probably a Connemara cabin.   I remember once going to a wake in a little white cabin rather like these Bethlehem houses, except that it was all on one floor.   The living-room was separated from the animals' quarters by a pole and a curtain of sacking. The noise of beasts stamping came clearly to us as we sat round the turf fire.   I remember thinking at the time that perhaps the Nativity took place in the same humble surroundings.

§ 4

A friend who has lived most of his life in Jerusalem, and speaks Arabic perfectly, met me in Bethlehem, and together we explored the alley-ways and the courtyards.   While we were looking at a Roman mill in a dark stone crypt, a girl came out on a flight of stairs to one side of the courtyard and began talking to us.   My friend suddenly turned into an Arab and began pinching the air with his fingers, putting his head on one side and making graceful gestures with his hands.

The girl laughed and he laughed.

" What are you talking about? " I asked.

" I am asking her to let us enter the house," he said.   " She has gone to ask her father."

She came out again and leaned over the balcony. She was the loveliest girl I had seen in Palestine. I think she was about eighteen. I was delighted to discover that women do still exist in Palestine who justify the rhapsodies of Solomon.

"She says," explained my friend, "that we must wait until the cobbler has gone, because he is a great gossip and it would be all over Bethlehem in five minutes that strange men were received in the house. But we are invited to enter."

So we poked about the yard, pretending to be interested in the old stones, until we saw the cobbler come down the steps holding a pair of old shoes. Then we went up the stairs and entered the house.

There was an outer room, or hall, with a room on each side of it. They were quite bare of furniture. The family was poor and humble. They worked in the fields. The father was a grey-bearded old Arab in a brown *galabieh*, and the mother was resting on a mat covered with a blanket.

The girl brought in an elder sister and a beautiful little child with yellow hair. We all sat on the floor and my friend talked as if he had known these people for years. The place rocked with laughter.

"I am," he said, "going to show you what the Bethlehem women wear under their veils. I am asking the elder girl, who is a widow, to put on her wedding dress."

By what process of bare-faced flattery, or by what charm of manner, he was able to do this, I cannot say. But the surprising fact is that the girl, blushing charmingly, disappeared to put on her bridal garments.

"How on earth can you come into a strange house and order people about like this?" I asked.

"Oh," he said, "the Arabs are extraordinarily nice people and so easy to handle if you know how to tackle them."

The younger sister, who, I thought, would make a perfect model for Ruth, entertained us with a bright flow of talk until her sister arrived in her heavily embroidered wedding garments, with her *znekb*, or chain, and the high Bethlehem

head-dress with its flowing white veil. She readily removed
the veil and showed me that the little tower from which it
hangs is a small red fez held upright on the head by two cords
which tie beneath the chin. All round this little fez are sewn
row upon row of coins. The *znekb* hangs from the head-dress
and contains ten coins with a central pendant.

" Those coins represent a bride's dowry," explained my
friend, " and it is possible that they illustrate our Lord's
parable of the Lost Coin. You remember how it goes:
' What woman having ten pieces of silver, if she lose one
piece, doth not light a candle, and sweep the house, and seek
diligently until she find it? ' And so on. Now, why should
she be so anxious to find one piece out of ten? "

" I have always considered it a tribute to the carefulness
of women."

" So have most people. But there is more to it than that.
In Jewish times ten drachmæ, or ten pieces of silver, were
sewn on the headdress of the married woman, and to lose
one of them was a terrible reflection on her carefulness and,
possibly on her wifely respect for her husband. It may
also have flung her into the superstitious fear into which the loss
of a wedding ring will fling a modern wife. That was why
the woman in the parable took a lamp and swept the house
with such anxiety. . . ."

The family were too poor to offer the usual coffee, but
they made up for it by the charm of their manners and their
air of fine breeding. The old man talked to us of the
approaching harvest and the poverty of the times. His
wife, tired out after a day in the barley fields, talked to us
from her bed on the floor.

" I can point out the explanation of another parable to
you," said my friend. " You see the matting bed. When
an Arab family is young, father, mother, and all the children
unroll a large mat and retire to sleep on it, lying together in
a row. You remember the Parable of the Stranger. Jesus
drew a picture of a man who is knocked up, after he has retired
to rest, by a friend who asks for three loaves. The man
replies that he cannot oblige the stranger for ' the door is
now shut and my children are with me in bed; I cannot
rise and give thee.' You can see that, like the *fellah* in

Palestine to-day, the man in the parable could not get up, once he had gone to bed, without awakening the entire family."

We said our good-byes and descended the steps. The two girls hung over the balcony, the young one like Ruth and the other in her crusading veil; and their laughter followed us into the little narrow street where the donkeys passed with their loads.

§ 5

In Jerusalem I engaged a car driven by a silent Armenian. He knew every part of the country and was, I was told, an excellent man to engage for a journey of many weeks.

One morning he called for me and we slipped out of Bethlehem just after sunrise, the time when the shepherds lead their flocks to pasture.

The road to Hebron goes to the south out of Bethlehem into a wilderness of brown hills. A few miles along this road you come to a valley in which a high square building like an old castle stands beside the road.

It is one of the many inns, or khans, erected centuries ago on the lonely roads of Palestine in order to protect travellers from the Bedouins.

This one, the Kalat el-Burak, or " Castle by the Pools," was built at this place so that grape merchants and others, on their way from Hebron to the markets at Jerusalem, could reach it before sunset, spend the night there in safety, and, starting out before sunrise, arrive in Jerusalem in time for the morning market. So, also, on the way home they would reach the safety of its walls before dusk.

Behind the khan are the famous Pools of Solomon. I walked down to them and on the way watched a group of girls, who might have stepped straight out of the Old Testament, draw water from a spring near the khan. Unfortunately the petrol tin has largely replaced the graceful water-pots which Arab girls used to carry on their heads.

The Pools of Solomon are three large reservoirs which stand in a valley where lusciousness and fertility form a remarkable contrast to the barren hills which rise all round. No doubt Solomon was thinking of this place when he sang:

" I made me great works; I built me houses, and planted vineyards; I made gardens and orchards, and set them with trees of all kinds; and I made me ponds of water to water therewith the wood of the young trees."

It was to this district that he used to come at dawn, wrapped in a white cloak and escorted by guards in chariots.

The Pools are still used, and one of the first things the British administration did when it took over Palestine after the War was to clean out the old reservoirs—one of them was a flourishing tomato nursery—and bring them into use again.

I was interested in an underground spring called Ain Salih. It is covered with masonry, but you can descend a flight of about twenty-six stairs into the cool darkness, where the water of several springs wells up out of the rock.   In this ancient covered well one realises why Solomon, in his superb love-song, likens his spouse to a sealed fountain. Perhaps this is the very fountain he had in mind when he wrote:

" A garden enclosed is my sister, my spouse—a spring shut up—a fountain sealed.
" Thy plants are an orchard of pomegranates—with pleasant fruits;
" Camphire with spikenard—spikenard with saffron;
" Calamus and cinnamon—with all trees of frankincense.
" Myrrh and aloes—with all the chief spices:
" A fountain of gardens—a well of living waters—and streams from Lebanon."

The garden enclosed, or the fountain sealed, to prevent the soiling or the theft of the precious liquid, was a perfect image of purity.

The road then goes for twelve or fourteen miles into a wild land of hills and tawny wadis. Gorges lead off here and there, and tracks go up into a bleak wilderness. Shepherds lead their flocks over the roads. Herds of black goats graze on the grass that grows in chinks of the rock.

Suddenly the road bends down into a fertile valley, a valley where the lush green of cultivation is striped by the barrenness of harsh rock, a valley whose hills are frilled to the tops with terraces of vines, of olives and of figs. And in this hollow lies Hebron, one of the oldest towns in the world, a small, grey, stone-built place with white domes shining in the sun.

Hebron comes into history when Abraham, wishing to bury his wife Sarah, buys, after a delightful piece of bargaining, the cave of Machpelah. This became the family vault to which in time were gathered Abraham himself, Isaac, Rebecca, Leah and, finally, Jacob, whose body was brought from Egypt.

This cave still exists under a mosque which is, to the Moslems, one of the holiest places in the world. The walls of the mosque are of the mighty proportions of the Wailing Wall in Jerusalem and, like that wall, is a spot at which Jews have been mourning for at least five centuries.

Until the War no Christian was allowed to set foot in the mosque, and even a few years ago permission to enter had to be signed by the Grand Mufti. However, the doors now open, though not very willingly, for five shillings.

There is an open courtyard and a church-like building from which two passages go down to the Cave of Machpelah. In the mosque above are six huge cenotaphs which are said to stand directly above the graves of the patriarchs. Those of Abraham, Isaac and Jacob are covered with green and gold cloths; those of Sarah, Rebecca and Leah with crimson. Two scribes sit before an opening, which is said to descend into the sacred cave, and for a shilling write out prayers which they drop down, presumably on the grave of the patriarch.

I believe it to be a fact that no one has entered the cave since the Crusaders went down and saw the amazing sight of the mouldering bones of the Old Testament chieftains lying in the darkness. They bathed the bones in wine and, reverently replacing them, sealed up the tomb with heavy iron clamps which are still in position.

Shaking off a band of the most persistent guides I had encountered in Palestine, I set off to perform the rash act of walking through Hebron by myself. I was engulfed by a sinister street, dark and arched, which seemed to have been designed in remote times for a series of swift murders. Ominous doors were open, giving a glimpse of clammy stone stairs. There were also smells, some soft and low, others like cornet solos.

Just as I was feeling lost, and rather suspicious of the beggar who was following me, the most determined of the guides whom I had a few moments before rebuked with dignity, appeared round a corner, touched his forehead and his breast, and said:

"Naharic saide," which means: "May your day be blessed."

This was too much for me, so I engaged him to take me round. While I was doing this I discovered that he could speak only a few words of English. His favourite was the word " shilling."

However, we got on very well with signs and face-makings and head-shakings.

Hebron is full of industry, and it is the same industry that has been going on there since the time of David. We came to an open archway in which three men squatted before a furnace. They wore Phrygian caps and looked like Phœnicians from an ancient tomb relief. In the furnace was molten glass. The three gnome-like men thrust long rods into the furnace and, with two or three swift movements, blended several coloured glasses into the small round camel's-eye beads which are worn as charms all over Palestine.

These glass-makers blow vivid red, blue and green bottles and make all kinds of glass cups. The place in which they have worked for centuries looks like the crypt of an old church. They were not apparently interested in selling anything and, after one glance at me, continued with rhythmic movements to make their little blue charms.

In another gloomy cellar we saw a blind man spinning goats' hair. Hebron is a great tanning centre, and the hair from the pelts is spun into thread and woven into a coarse sacking. All the spinners and most of the weavers are blind.

In a third archway I watched a potter at his wheel. As the wet pot went flying round, his magic hands shaped it, drew up the spout, flattened it or elongated it at will. An assistant waited until each pot was shaped, then added it to an enormous pile that stood ready for the furnace.

Then we came into a shopping street where the produce was piled on stalls, each man sitting by his small collection of food. Hebron is a great fruit-growing district. It is well watered and its soil is rich. It is an extraordinarily interesting fact that the best grapes grown round Hebron come from a place called Ain Eskali, the modern Arabic for the Vale of Eshcol, from which the spies of Moses returned with great clusters of grapes carried between them on poles.

" And they came unto the brook of Eshcol, and cut down from thence a branch with one cluster of grapes, and they bare it between two upon a staff and they brought of the pomegranates and of the figs."

This might very well be written of Hebron to-day.

" Well, good-bye," I said to the persistent guide.

" You leef London? " he asked.

" Yes, I live there.   What do you know about London? "

" I know all-ting.   Me scholar.   Learn in school.   London big, big, big," and here a look of great reverence came over his face as he added, " and plenty rain."

This sounds like a joke to us, but to the Palestinian, whose crops are so often burnt up and ruined by the sun, whose vines wilt for rain, whose cisterns empty and whose beasts die of thirst, rain is never a joke; it is always a blessing.

As I drove off from Hebron I had a vision of some teacher trying to explain the wonders of London to a class of Arab boys, drumming into their heads the marvellous fact that somewhere was a paradise-city in which there was always " plenty rain."

§ 6

As mile succeeded mile I saw nothing but hard brown earth with the sun burning over it.   There were low ridges of hills,

hot and brown, and cone-shaped " tels " under which lie
buried the towns that knew Abraham. Boys in sheepskin
coats chased goats across the barren land as my car reeled
towards them over a road made for camels.

Here and there the desolation was broken by the black
goat-hair tents of the Bedouin, a few tethered horses, a few
she-camels and their long-legged infants, and perhaps a flock
of sheep nosing the burning earth for stray grass.

It is the wild tribal country, with its precious wells, its
flocks, its herds and its family feuds, that we know so well
from the pages of *Genesis*. It is extraordinary to discover a
tract of the earth that has not changed in any essential way
since the days of Abraham.

Sheikhs like Abraham, with wives like Sarah and sons like
Isaac, are still moving from well to well across this hot,
parched land. Sons like Esau are jealous of brothers like
Jacob, and sometimes even carry into effect the threat in
Genesis: " Some day I will slay my brother Jacob."

And the road leads on over the wilderness to the little
oasis of Beersheba.

There is nothing at Beersheba but a few scattered trees, a
mosque, some small shacks, the wells that Abraham knew, a
Government house, and a memory of the War in a cemetery
of British dead : and, in a parched little group of trees, a bust
of Lord Allenby.

The Bedouin who drift into Beersheba to seek tribal justice,
or to buy things on credit until the barley harvest is over,
admire Lord Allenby, as they admire all warriors ; but
they hate the bust.

" There has been no good luck," they say, " since the
graven image came to Bir es Seba . . ."

For the Allah of the desert Bedouin is in many ways very
like the Jehovah of the Old Testament, and the sheikh
believes firmly and literally in " Thou shalt not make unto
thee any graven image, or any likeness of any thing that is in
heaven above, or that is in the earth beneath, or that is in the
water under the earth."

So if the barley fields are burnt up and the rains fail, if
the lambs die, if disease smites the goats or the camels, and
if death visits the goat-hair tents, the brown men who walk

like kings over the parched sands of Beersheba avert their eyes superstitiously as they pass the bust of Lord Allenby.

I went up to the court-house in Beersheba with a letter of introduction to one of the most romantic men in Palestine, Arif el Arif, Governor of the Beersheba District, which is half as large as Wales. During the War Arif fought with the Turks against us and was captured by the Russians : he escaped to China, where, after a series of extraordinary adventures, he linked up with the British and eventually found himself editing a newspaper in Jerusalem. He said, wrote, or did something which led to his arrest by the British authorities. He escaped and made his way on foot over the desert to Jericho, where he forded the Jordan and took to the Moab Hills. The Bedouin tribes hid him and befriended him.

He became an Arabian Bonnie Prince Charlie and the most exhaustive Government inquiries failed to discover his hiding-places. He just disappeared. Sir Herbert Samuel, then High Commissioner, took a trip into the desert with a small force of yeomanry. The desert sheikhs were by no means friendly, and it was at Es Salt, in the wild hills of Trans-Jordan, that the rumour went round that Arif el Arif was near.

Some of the officials present wished to search the country and arrest him, but a moment's thought told them that to do so would cause trouble. A handful of troops would have been helpless against thousands of armed Arabs. However, the local sheikhs presented a petition to the High Commissioner. They advanced in a line with their arms linked and begged him to pardon Arif. This, to their unbounded joy, was granted, and in a second Arif—who had been hiding in the crowd all the time—was hoisted on the shoulders of his Arab friends and brought to the tribune to make peace with the King's representative.

From that moment Arif el Arif has been one of the most valued and trusted members of the Palestine administration. His government of the desert tribes of the Beersheba district is a triumph of personality, for no man could rule these people unless he was both trusted and admired by them.

His most remarkable achievement has been the carrying out of a census of the Bedouin. This is the first time in history that the desert tribes have been numbered because, like the Israelites of old, they have a strong prejudice against a census. " Allah knows our numbers," they argue, " so why should we be counted? " Exactly the same attitude was adopted by the Israelites, who blamed the plague that afflicted them under David to the king's attempt to count them.

But Arif has conquered centuries of prejudice and, although he does not pretend that his census is exact, it is the first time that the Bedouin population has been even approximately estimated. Those who know the Bedouin and their prejudices regard this as an astonishing achievement.

The court-house was a fairly large stone building standing by itself on the parched sand. Ferocious-looking desert Bedouin sat all over the steps. Grey-bearded sheikhs, curved scimitars slung across their bodies, walked about like dignified assassins.

As I went in, two Bedouin came out hand in hand, talking in the most affectionate manner. I was told that the weekly tribal court was in session and that these two were litigants whose case had just been settled. Although violent enemies a moment before, they became friends as soon as judgment was delivered and were going off to drink coffee together.

The hall, stairway and upper rooms were packed with Bedouin crouching on their heels and waiting for their cases to come before the judges.

Arif, who was dressed as a Bedouin sheikh, received me in a room shuttered against the sun. A map of " his " desert was on the wall. He spoke to me in the very good English which he had learnt during one of his captivities.

" What I want to know is how you managed to count the Bedouin," I said.

" It was not easy! " smiled Arif. " As soon as my intention was made known, five thousand of them packed up and escaped to Sinai. Whole tribes went into hiding. It took me eight months to persuade them. I had to go out and live with them, sleep with them and eat with them. But what won them over in the end was the idea that if their numbers were known to the Government, it would be clear that there could be no room for Zionists in the Beersheba district."

While we were talking a magnificent old sheikh came in with an ivory-handled sword swinging against his robes. He went into solemn conference with the Governor.

" Excuse me," said Arif, " but I must take my seat on the bench. Perhaps it would interest you to come and sit beside me? This law court is like no other in the world. We hold it once a week to settle the quarrels and the disputes of the desert. We cannot apply British law to these disputes, because the problems of European people do not arise in the desert. This court lays down the traditional desert law, the law of the patriarchs, the law that, before this central court-house was built, was delivered by the sheikhs in their tents. But come! I will translate some of the cases for you and you shall see how we deal with them."

We entered an upper room in which about forty Bedouin were talking together. They sat in five main groups at tables. The hot, blinding light of the desert was excluded by green wooden blinds. There was a magistrates' bench at one end of the room, and to this the Governor led me. We took our seats together and surveyed the extraordinary scene.

The group on the floor below us represented a fraction of the week's litigation. Outside in ante-rooms, all the way down the stairs, in the basement, on the porch outside, and squatting picturesquely near their tethered camels and horses, were the waiting defendants and plaintiffs: for there is nothing the Bedouin loves more than a lawsuit. Law with him is not so much a matter of justice as revenge.

Every week, out of an apparently empty desert, rides this same savage-looking horde of litigants. They come in the best of friends, fight each other with words and impute the most disgraceful motives to each other, but, once the case is settled, go off together in perfect amity.

The law administered in this court is older than many of the books of the Old Testament: it is the old tribal law that was observed in the desert centuries before the children of Israel fled from Egypt.

There are fifteen judges. They are all sheikhs of the various local tribes, and are chiefly old men who wear huge, old-fashioned ivory-handled scimitars as a badge of office. Three sheikhs judge each case. One judge is chosen by the plaintiff, another by the defendant, and the third represents the majesty of the British Government. Five cases are usually being argued at once round the little tables in the court-house, and it is generally possible to polish off about eighty in one day. Now and then, however, they strike a difficult one that, with adjournments, lasts for years.

The fundamental difference between desert law and the law as we know it is that the tribe, and not the individual offender, is held responsible for a crime. And the reason for this is fairly obvious. In the deserts of Sinai and Trans-Jordan the criminal can nearly always escape. If you had to punish the individual, you would have to mobilise an army and comb the desert for years in order to put him in the dock! Therefore a criminal brings trouble—for crime is not a disgrace among the Bedouin—first to his tribe and, secondly, to his family.

The commonest offences are raids on animals, blood feuds or murder, breaches of desert etiquette and disputes about land, money, and so forth. Women rarely enter the desert courts and crimes against them are practically non-existent. The fine for molesting Bedouin women is half that of the fine for murder, about twenty riding camels, unless the offence occurs at night, when the fine is only ten camels.

" And the reason for that is," explained the Governor, " that in day-time the girl would be alone, drawing water or at work in the desert, while at night it is her own fault if she is not safe in the family tent."

The disputes that were being argued below us were varied. One man was suing a friend for having borrowed—not stolen —a sheep. It is the recognised law of the desert that, if a stranger appears at your tent door and your sheep are grazing far away, you are entitled, in order to fulfil the ancient laws of hospitality, to borrow a neighbour's sheep and to slay it in honour of your guest.

Now, a guest is allowed to stay for three days with the Bedouin without question. During that time his life is sacred, and the man whose sheep has been borrowed must not ask for a sheep to replace it. But instantly the guest departs, the man who has borrowed the sheep must, according to desert etiquette, present himself at his friend's tent and say:

" Here is a sheep which I return to you in place of the sheep I took."

If not, he is allowed fourteen days to replace the sheep. Should he fail to do so, he may be obliged to return four sheep.

Another case was one of etiquette. A man had entered another man's tent without permission and gazed upon his neighbour's wife. This was regarded as a serious offence, and everyone was very excited about it. Even the judges seemed angry.

A third case had something to do with a blood feud. These blood feuds exist throughout the desert and nearly every family has one in running order or in temporary suspension. If blood feuds get out of hand they spread like an epidemic of influenza and end in whole tribes having a pitched fight and driving off each other's camels.

A good, sporting blood feud in the desert is more or less as cricket and football are to us. The murder of one Bedouin by another is punished—if the game can be stopped without a return match—by a fine of camels inflicted on the tribe. The murderer is hanged only if he kills an outsider and can be caught, which rarely happens.

The individual murderer often hides with an enemy tribe and is never seen again. Sometimes a member of the murdered man's family leaves home, wife and everything and devotes his whole life to tracking down the offender. Quite often a horribly gashed body is found in some desolate *wadi* and, after a few months, the hunter slips quietly home looking lean but satisfied. And no questions are asked.

" An eye for an eye and a tooth for a tooth."

Suddenly the arguments round the little tables were interrupted by a violent old Bedouin with a lean face and scanty beard, who rose up and shrieked in fury at the judges. The Governor hit the bench with a mallet, but the old man rushed forward foaming at the mouth with rage.

It appeared that this old man charged a young Bedouin of the same tribe with the theft of £400, which the old man said had been kept in a pot. The defence was that the old man had never had £4, let alone £400. Whereupon the old fellow started to scream with rage.

" He is demanding the trial by fire," said Arif el Arif.
" I do not think we shall allow it in this case."

" You don't mean to say that you permit trial by fire? "

" It is the most respected verdict of all. The whole desert
respects the trial by fire," he replied. " The men who
administer it are known as *Mobishaa*, and the ordeal itself as
Bishaa. There are only two such men in all Arabia, one in
Sinai and one in the Hedjaz. We employ the man from
Sinai.

" The method is this. The *Mobishaa* first asks for a confession. If this is not made, he takes fire and heats an iron
in it until it is white hot and covered with white sparks. He
then collects his fee! This is £10. Defendant and plaintiff
each give him £5, and at the end of the ordeal he returns
half the fee to the innocent party.

" The accused steps forward, is given water to wash out his
mouth, and is then asked to lick the red-hot iron three times.
At the end of this ordeal the *Mobishaa* examines his tongue
and gives judgment. It is an extraordinary thing—and you
will think I am romancing—but I have seen men pass
unscathed through the ordeal."

" But that can have nothing to do with their guilt or
innocence ! "

" On the contrary, I believe it has. The guilty man is so
terrified that his mouth goes dry and he gets terribly burned.
But the innocent man's saliva continues to flow and he does
not show anything on his tongue after the ordeal but a red-
ness. Anyhow, the *Mobishaa's* verdict is never questioned.
It is the verdict of Allah. . . ."

We went outside and sat in the shade. Two or three of the
leading sheikhs came round and stood in a dignified, statuesque
manner, their hands on the hilts of their swords. Father
Abraham, who dug the wells of Beersheba a few yards from
where we were sitting, was, I felt, a man just like these tribal
chiefs, with the same shrewd but uncomplicated eyes, the
same ideas of life and the conduct of life.

While we were talking, two Bedouin came from the court-
house. They walked across the blinding patch of sun to the
trees at the side of the building. Here a horse was tethered
to a fence and a camel was sitting in the sand. One man

got up on the camel, the other on the horse. They were apparently great friends. I recognised them as the two violent enemies of the court-house: the one the man who had charged his friend with having entered his tent and gazed on his wife without permission, and the other the defendant.

They rode off together in the most amiable manner and were lost to sight behind a cactus hedge.

" Game and set," I said.

The Governor asked what I meant.

" It means that somebody's won the contest," I explained, " but will cheerfully get his own back some day."

This was translated to the sheikhs, who bowed gravely, their hands on their ivory hilts.

§ 7

I motored across the desert from Beersheba and spent the night in Sir Flinders Petrie's camp on the outskirts of Gaza. The veteran archæologist had, with his usual wizardry, found a hill near the sand dunes and the sea in which are the ruins of many cities that were old in the time of Abraham.

His discoveries are bewildering to anyone who thinks that 1000 B.C. is a long time ago. Professor Petrie, on his hill at Gaza, was like a man directing a powerful searchlight at a past which has been considered dark and unfathomable. But, wherever he turns his light on the dark ages of pre-history, there are seen men and armies and ships, and women putting gold rings in their ears. Vigorous civilisations had already developed and fallen into decay on this hill when the Children of Israel fled from Egypt.

We went out on the hill and looked at the ruins of three palaces, built one on top of the other. The first was built in 3100 B.C., the second in 2500 B.C., and the third—with a horse's skeleton marking a foundation sacrifice—in 2200 B.C. What astonished me even more than a bathroom built in 3100 B.C., and perfectly preserved mud doorways through which Abraham might have walked, were Celtic ear-rings of Irish gold exactly like the prehistoric gold ornaments in the Dublin Museum.

How did they get to Gaza? What adventurous galley brought them to this spot in the days before Saul or David?

In the morning I set off on the road to Ascalon. It ran for fourteen or fifteen miles through flat, green country. I met the usual strings of camels roped together, slouching along on the edge of the road, and the usual overburdened donkeys. The green fields, with their growing oats and barley, were a welcome sight after the bare, bleached desert to the south. Near El Mejdel I came to a perfect paradise of cultivation and saw, with more attention than one usually gives to such a sight, fields of onions.

Onions have been grown round Ascalon for thousands of years. The Romans liked them and called them Ascalonium, from which we get the word *echalote* or, in English, shallot. I had no idea that this historic bulb was still grown there.

When I left the main road and made for the coast, I encountered hundreds of Arabs in brilliant holiday clothes. Every road was thick with them, and they were all making for the sea coast.

There were families mounted on camels and donkeys, the women wearing brilliant blues and reds. I had never before seen so many beautiful girls in Palestine, marred only by the unfortunate fact that they were nearly all cross-eyed. Reaching a slight hill that commands the plain, I saw that for miles around the population, literally in thousands, was making for the seashore at Ascalon. It is an unusual sight to see women and children riding on camels in Palestine, because these animals are always reserved for hard work. But there were thousands of camels, each one with its cargo of little brown children. It was a delightful sight, for the *fellahin* on their frequent feast days let themselves go, put on their gayest clothes, and dance and sing and behave as if they had not one care in the world. Only the camels preserved their impassive superciliousness. Most of them had been shaved and oiled and smeared with mud. This barbering of camels takes place before the great heat sets in.

My first thought that some village feast day was being celebrated was soon banished when I drew nearer to Ascalon. The population of an entire district was streaming down the narrow roads to the sand dunes.

" It is the feast of Nebi Ayub," I learnt, after asking perhaps thirty Arabs who could not understand a word of English.

Ayub, I was told, was an ancient prophet who had cured himself of boils by bathing in the sea and, therefore, once a year on his feast day everybody goes to the water. It occurred to me that this Ayub was none other than Job.

The city that was once Ascalon is lost under the sand dunes. The Mediterranean waves break in white foam on miles of magnificent hard sand. Here and there, sticking out of the dunes, are massive old walls of black stone built by English hands, for these are the walls that were rebuilt in 1191 when Richard the Lion Heart captured Ascalon.

There are other memorials of Ascalon's past. The ground everywhere is thick with Roman pottery and bits of broken green glass. Among the dunes, near a water-wheel turned by a camel who plods round and round in an endless circle, are broken statues that were dug up from the Ascalon that Herod built. What treasures still lie under these gold sand mountains one can only imagine.

I took a narrow path over the dunes and came out on the sea shore. One of the most astonishing sights I have ever seen was spread out for miles on the edge of the Mediterranean.

Hundreds of camels were being given their annual bath. On the sand dunes at the back sat the crowds of women and children who had trekked down from every village in the district: the men and the boys were engaged in the serious process of washing the camels. There was not, of course, one bathing costume among the camel washers, and they looked magnificent as their wet brown bodies caught the sun.

Groups of five or six pulled, prodded and pushed their camels into the breaking waves. Some camels resisted. Some started to kick. Some even broke loose and stampeded back to the women, pursued by wild and angry boys.

On the other hand many of the animals, once they had been persuaded to sit down in the sea, appeared to enjoy themselves. They refused to move! It was as difficult to get them out as it had been to get them in. They sat on the very edge of the sea, with their absurd supercilious heads lifted high above the advancing waves.

As soon as the beasts were settled in the water, naked men

rushed at them with knives, with which they scraped off the caked mud.   It was a delightful sight, because the camel, like the donkey, does not receive much attention in this life.

I learnt afterwards that the feast of Nebi Ayub is the only occasion on which the Arab indulges in mixed bathing.   In the evening, I was told, thousands of men and women would enter the sea.   The women would form little groups apart and run unclothed into the sea.   The men would dash in at other parts of the shore.

The Feast of Nebi Ayub seems to be a ceremonial cleansing whose origin is lost in the very mists of time.

I travelled over a fertile plain dotted with Arab villages hedged about with cactus.   The people, so it seemed to me, might have walked out in a body from the pages of the Old Testament.   One of the most interesting things about Palestine is that in some districts, notably that south of a line drawn from Jerusalem to Jaffa, the *fellahin* are the descendants of the Canaanites.   In feature and habit they bear the signs of their ancient origin.   Conquerors have thundered over the land without dislodging them.

I made a slight détour to see the graceful village of Ain Karem, which lies not far from Jerusalem among brown hills planted with vines and olives.   Nebi Samwîl, the traditional tomb of Samuel, crowns the neighbouring ridge, one of the highest mountains in Judæa.   It was known to the mediæval pilgrim as the Mount of Joy because from its heights he caught his first glimpse of the Holy City.

An ancient tradition claims Ain Karem as the birthplace of the Forerunner, and the Franciscans point out the grotto of his nativity in their church.

While I was climbing the steep hill to the Russian church, I stopped to watch a gardener at work.   His land was watered by a series of little channels cut in the soil and dammed by a stopping of earth at various strategical points.   Whenever he wanted to irrigate a new portion of garden, he simply lifted his bare foot and kicked away the earth at some point so that the water rushed forward into new places.   In this act I recognised the description in *Deuteronomy* of Egypt as a land " where thou sowedst thy seed, and *wateredst it with thy foot*, as a garden of herbs."

The poverty of the Russian Church is to-day one of the most pitiful things in the Holy Land.   There is at Ain Karem a community of Russian nuns who are each living on an allowance of ten shillings a month.   Their diet is tea and brown bread.   They are devout women whose misfortunes have, so it seems, made the flame of their piety burn even more brightly. Their church, in contrast to some of the dusty, dark places in the hands of monks, is spotlessly clean.   The poor half-starving women lavish on it a passionate love and tenderness. The abbess, her pale face bound in a black veil and crowned by the high round headdress of the Russian Church, might have sat for a portrait of the Madonna, and when an old peasant woman knelt to kiss her hand, her angelic smile, and the gentle way she lifted the old woman from her knees, made a picture I shall never forget . . .

I reached Jerusalem as the dusk was falling.   In the morning, sharp at five a.m., the bell in the convent opposite began to ring.   I rose up and dressed and went through the horrible ritual of packing, for I had a long day before me. In a few hours I was setting off on the main road to the north.

CHAPTER FIVE

*I travel through Samaria, see Jacob's Well and meet the last
Samaritans. I stop for a while in Nazareth and watch the village
carpenter at work, go on to Haifa, where I see Mount Carmel, explore
a crusading castle and stand among the ruins of Cæsarea.*

§ 1

I ONCE believed that the phrase " from Dan to Beer-
sheeba " indicated the extremes of distance. Nothing,
it seemed to me, could be farther apart than these two
places. In actual fact, a man in a good car can breakfast on
the ruined hill of Dan under the Lebanons and eat his evening
meal beside the wells of Abraham on the desert plain round
Beersheba in the south.

Distances are surprisingly short. Jerusalem is only about
seventy-five miles from Nazareth and about one hundred
miles from Tiberias and the Lake of Galilee. Bethlehem, as
I have said, is only a five-mile walk from Jerusalem, and
Jericho is under twenty miles from the capital.

That the smallness of Palestine should be a perpetual surprise to me is probably because the Bible is pervaded by an
atmosphere of spaciousness. When Jesus turned His back on
Nazareth and went to Capernaum, I used to think that
He had made a long journey; but He had only walked
to a place about twenty-five miles away. The wanderings
of the patriarchs suggest tremendous journeys, whereas, in
reality, they could probably be packed into two or three
English counties. When David stood on the hills round
Jerusalem he could actually see the country of his enemies,
the Philistines, about twenty miles off to the west. All the
dynastic dramas and the inter-tribal strife of the Old Testament occurred in a region not much larger than the Highlands
of Scotland.

In the old days, it is true, the illusion of size was present

146

because of the mountains and the difficulty of transport. Old-fashioned guide books, printed before the War when travellers went through Palestine on horseback, allow five or six days for a journey that can now be accomplished comfortably by car, and over excellent modern roads, in a day.

The motor-car has, of course, revolutionised transport in Palestine. It has unfortunately killed the picturesque, long-distance camel caravans and caused the romantic desert khans, or inns, to fall into ruin and decay. Only a few years ago the pace of Palestine was that of a string of baggage camels doing an average of twenty to twenty-five miles a day. Goods, once carried by camels from Bagdad to Damascus, and on to Jerusalem, are now borne by powerful motor lorries driven at top speed by Arabs who have no fear of death.

The road from Jerusalem to Nazareth descends from the mountains on which Jerusalem is enthroned into a blinding, burning valley where every hill is marked with the ghosts of ancient terraces.

In the time of Christ these Judæan hills must have been covered with fig, olive and vine. You can see signs of ancient cultivation running in bands round the hills, just as under the grass of English meadows you can sometimes trace the line of old furrows.

Now up and now down, and always rising or falling in a series of double hairpins, the road goes on through the yellow hills into the country of the Tribe of Benjamin. Where the road bent sharply to the right, I saw a straight track leading away over a narrow plain and another, crossing it, leading in the opposite direction. The first was the road over which St. Paul was led by night to Cæsarea, and the other was the old Roman road to Damascus.

Every little hill carried on its crest a village whose name is known to millions of people, the little villages of the Old Testament. They looked like rows of mud boxes ranged in lines round a hill-top. Girls with water-pots on their shoulders walked through fields of growing barley, and beside the road stood little boys like young David, fitting smooth pebbles into the bag of their slings. I have never until now felt sorry for Goliath! But, with all his size and strength, he must have had about as much chance against David and his sling as a man with a spear would have against a modern gunman. The sling, when wielded by a practised hand, can be a deadly weapon.

One has to visit Palestine to understand how meticulously accurate is the Bible. It has become the fashion to say that the Old Testament is a collection of Jewish fables, and I am sure some young people to-day imagine that men like Saul and David never existed. Not only did they exist, but to-day there are men whose lives and outlook are exactly the same. You meet them on every road. The Bible is a most accurate guide to the life of modern Palestine. Let me give an instance.

I stopped at a humble little village. I do not know the name of it. There were some few fields round about it, a well near it, and a baked mud road leading through to the flat-roofed houses and the little mosque. In a clearing near the village several women sat beside a black pot beneath which blazed the thorn bushes that grow all over Palestine. As the thorns burned they made a crackling, splitting sound, and I realised the descriptive power of that famous line in *Ecclesiastes*: "As the crackling of thorns under a pot, so is the laughter of the fool."

To me, one of the fantastic things about Palestine is that people, so obviously ancient Canaanites should be called Arabs and should worship Allah!

In the fields round the villages men were unconsciously illustrating the Bible. One man was guiding a plough drawn by an ox and a camel. This is very unfair on the smaller animal. The wooden yoke sinks from the high camel to the low ox so that he bears more than his share of the weight, and this clumsy arrangement chafes the necks of both animals.

Is not this exactly what St. Paul meant in his Second Epistle to the Corinthians: "Be ye not unequally yoked together with unbelievers: for what fellowship hath righteousness with unrighteousness, and what communion hath light with darkness?"

There was another ploughman. He drove a restless, difficult ox. The beast was not broken in to the plough. He lowered his head and tried to back. The ploughman carried in his hand a pointed stick used for scraping the earth from the ploughshare. Whenever the ox grew difficult he prodded him with the spike, and I knew that I was seeing something that Jesus had seen and noticed as He walked the roads of Palestine.

" Saul, Saul," cried Jesus, " why persecutest thou me? It is hard for thee to kick against the pricks."

I came to a little village called El-Bireh, which, it is said, was the place where Joseph and Mary missed Jesus on their return from Jerusalem to Nazareth. They retraced their steps and found their Son disputing with the elders in the Temple. This incident, which is given only by St. Luke, has often been questioned by the higher critics. Some writers have considered it inconceivable that parents would not have missed a child during " a day's march." On the spot, however, the explanation is very simple. A " day's march " in the East is generally the distance covered in seven hours of slow travel. But the first day's march by caravan was always a short distance, because these large and confused assemblies were often late in starting. On the main roads round Jerusalem are ruined khans, only a few miles from the city, which mark the first short " day's march." El-Bireh has such a ruin. It was here that the Nazareth caravans rested and spent the night before setting off in earnest on the following morning.

What could be easier than that Joseph and Mary should have missed Jesus in the confusion of an Eastern departure? He was then twelve years of age and would probably have been in the habit of travelling with other boys of His own size. How natural that, as the caravan wound its way out of Jerusalem, His parents should have assumed that He was with them.

Jesus was, I feel sure, not the only boy who has been left behind in Jerusalem during the hectic departure from a festival.

The road went on dipping into green valleys and climbing into dead hills. There was a little village called Sinjil, a

F

name which carries with it the memory of a crusader, Ray-mound de Saint Giles, Count of Toulouse.

I went on and entered Samaria, where, it seemed to me, the fields were greener and the hills less fierce. On the side of the road were a few trees, and among them Jacob's Well, where Jesus met the Woman of Samaria.

§ 2

All travellers in Palestine repeat with monotonous regularity the true statement that the history of the country is " writ in water." Roads, villages, and even cities have disappeared from the map, but the spring that gushes out of the rock remains a constant factor in the life of the country and a true landmark to the historian.

To-day, as in Bible times, the well is the resting-place on a journey and the meeting-place of all the village maidens and matrons in the morning and the evening. The task of draw-ing water in pitchers, or, alas, in empty petrol tins (for who can arrest progress!) is a purely feminine duty. It is true that men do draw water from the wells and springs, but they are members of the water-carrying trade and bear their burdens not in pitchers but in goat-skins which they carry on their backs. The ordinary male Arab would no more be seen drawing water in a pitcher than the average Westerner would care to walk up and down his suburban road pushing a perambulator. It is true that men do occasionally push perambulators; also Arabs do now and then break the rule I have just set down and draw water in pitchers. But I have never seen an Arab man drawing water, and I have been on the look out for a long time.

It was the rarity of this sight which gave point to Christ's command, before the Last Supper, that two of His disciples should go into Jerusalem, " and there shall meet you a *man* bearing a pitcher of water: follow him. And wheresoever he shall go in, say ye to the goodman of the house, The Master saith, Where is the guest chamber, where I shall eat the passover with my disciples? "

Until I came to Palestine I pondered the apparent vagueness of such a direction. Surely, I thought, the disciples would have seen many such men. How then could they be certain which one to follow? I now realise that Jesus was giving them explicit instructions which they could not mistake, for the sight of a *man* with a pitcher on his shoulder would be so unusual that everybody would notice him

Round the wells in the country districts gather groups of women, Arabs in name but Canaanite by blood, the descendants of the hewers of wood and the drawers of water who have performed this duty for untold centuries. Jacob's Well at Sychar must have been one of the most famous wells in the country, although there is no authority in the Old Testament for the belief that Jacob made it " near to the parcel of ground " that he gave to his son Joseph. But even the Jews and the Samaritans were agreed on the truth of this tradition.

The well to-day is enclosed behind a wall and covered by a little Greek church. All round it lie the pillars of other churches that once stood on the site. The Crusaders had once built a church so constructed that the well was immediately below the high altar. While the Greek priest went in search of the key, I stood under a fig tree in the peaceful little garden and looked up to the stony flanks of Mount Gerizim which lie opposite, and on the top of the mountain I could see something like a ruined tower, all that remains of the Samaritan Temple which was erected in rivalry to Jerusalem.

The priest led the way down a flight of stairs into the crypt of the church. The well, he explained, was about seventy feet in depth and still contained water at certain times of the year. He held a dripping candle over it and the grease dropped down and cooled in grey spots on the stone.

Most authorities agree that this is the well where Jesus met the Samaritan woman. When I came up into the sunlight I sat under the fig tree in the garden and read the fourth chapter of St. John. St. John must have been an eye-witness of this exquisite episode. There are little touches in the narrative, especially when you read it on the spot, which suggest that it could not possibly have been written by anyone who had not been there.

The long tiring road over the hills of Judæa had wearied

the Master, who paused by the well to rest. It has been suggested that St. John reckoned time not by the Jewish code, but according to the Roman civil day, from midnight to midnight. Therefore it would be six in the evening. Jesus rests there with the stony heights of Mount Gerizim rising before Him and, some distance away, the little village of Sychar, which is now called Askar. A woman with a water-pot on her head comes along the path from the village to draw water.

Why, ask those critics who argue about St. John's Gospel, should the woman have come all the way to Jacob's Well when there was a well nearer her village at Sychar? Perhaps the answer is that she wanted rain water instead of the hard limestone water of the 'Ain Askar. In Greek the word she uses to describe Jacob's Well is " cistern " or " pit," which is exactly what it is, a place where the soft rain-water accumulates. There may have been another reason. The woman had had five husbands and was living in sin with a man. She was therefore, we cannot doubt, an object of gossip. Perhaps this explains why she took a long walk to get water at a well where she would not encounter the scorn of good women. Either of these explanations seems to me easier to believe than that the writer of the episode was not present on the occasion.

" Jesus saith unto her, Give me to drink.

" Then saith the woman of Samaria unto him, How is it that thou, being a Jew, askest drink of me, which am a woman of Samaria? for the Jews have no dealings with the Samaritans."

Jesus, gently and step by step, leads her into a spiritual discussion, comparing the water in the well to living water of faith.

" ' Sir, give me this water, that I thirst not, neither come hither to draw,' " says the woman.

Some commentators have detected irony in her request; and this may explain why Jesus, like a modern psycho-analyst breaking down repression or resistance, bids her suddenly :

" Go, call thy husband and come hither! "

" I have no husband," she replies.

" Thou hast well said," remarks Jesus. " For thou hast

had five husbands; and he whom thou now hast is not thy husband."

" Sir, I perceive that thou art a prophet," whispers the woman.

And beside the well at Sychar Jesus for the first time imparts to a human being, this sinful woman of a hated race, the divine secret of His Messiahship. The disciples return and are amazed that " he talked with the woman."

" A Jew might not greet a woman," wrote David Smith in *The Days of His Flesh*, " he might not talk with a woman on the street, even if she were his own wife or daughter or sister. In the Morning Prayer the men blessed God ' who hath not made me a Gentile, a slave, a woman.' There was a strict sort of Pharisee nicknamed the Bleeding Pharisee because he went about with closed eyes lest he should see a woman, and knocked his head against walls until it bled. It was impiety to impart the words of the Law to a woman: sooner should they be burned."

Even to-day in Jerusalem the women are not permitted to worship in the synagogues with the men. There are sometimes adjacent rooms in which they can gather, or else they are hidden away behind a screen in a gallery. We are apt to take for granted the outstanding part played by women in the Gospel story. That women were equal with men in all the relationships of life, and that they were as capable of spiritual development, was a profound revolution in thought which we cannot possibly appreciate. To a Samaritan woman Jesus spoke of His mission, to Martha He confessed His Divinity, and to Mary Magdalene He confided His victory.

Reading St. John beside Jacob's Well, one realises how the conversation grew out of the surroundings and could not have been imagined by anyone. The water, the mountain, the road to Sychar on which the Samaritans soon appear, drawn by the news which the woman has carried to the village, are all so life-like, so vivid. And Jesus bade His disciples:

" Lift up your eyes, and look on the fields; for they are white already to harvest."

Critics have written learned dissertations to prove that the fields could not have been white with the harvest: it was too early in the year. And others have provided all kinds of explanations to force this episode into Gospel chronology. But as I sat by Jacob's Well a crowd of Arabs came along the road from the direction in which Jesus was looking, and I saw their white garments shining in the sun.

Surely Jesus was speaking not of the earthly but of the heavenly harvest, and as He spoke I think it likely that He pointed along the road where the Samaritans in their white robes were assembling to hear His words.

§ 3

On the roads of Palestine, and on the hills, you see the good shepherd. He comes along at the head of his flock, generally carrying over his shoulders a lamb or an injured sheep.

He is a man burnt almost black by exposure to the sun. He wears the flowing Bedouin head-veil, the *keffiyeh*, bound with two black twisted cords known as the *agaal*. Beneath his robes he often wears a sheepskin coat with the fleece turned next to the body. He is one of the many characters who walk the roads of Palestine exactly as they must have done in the time of our Lord.

A most remarkable thing is the sympathy that exists between him and his flock. He never drives them as our own shepherds drive their sheep. He always walks at their head, leading them along the roads and over the hills to new pasture: and, as he goes, he sometimes talks to them in a loud sing-song voice, using a weird language unlike anything I have ever heard in my life. The first time I heard this sheep and goat language I was on the hills at the back of Jericho. A goatherd had descended into a valley and was mounting the slope of an opposite hill when, turning round, he saw his goats had remained behind to devour a rich patch of scrub. Lifting his voice, he spoke to the goats in a language that Pan must have spoken on the mountains of Greece. It was uncanny because there was nothing human about it. The words were animal sounds arranged in a kind of order. No sooner had he spoken than an answering bleat shivered over the herd, and one or two of the animals turned their heads in his direction. But they did not obey him. The goat-herd then called out one word and gave a laughing kind of whinny. Immediately a goat with a bell round his neck stopped eating and, leaving the herd, trotted down the hill, across the valley and up the opposite slopes. The man, accompanied by this animal, walked on and disappeared round a ledge of rock. Very soon a panic spread among the herd. They forgot to eat. They looked up for the shepherd. He was not to be seen. They became conscious that the leader with the bell at his neck was no longer with them. From the distance came the strange laughing call of the shepherd, and at the sound of it the entire herd stampeded into the hollow and leapt up the hill after him.

I would like to know what an English sheep-dog would make of the Palestine sheep, because our principle of droving is something that neither Arab shepherds nor their sheep-dogs understand. It is all done by word of mouth, and the sheep follow their shepherds like dogs. The Arab sheep-dog is used therefore not to drive sheep but to protect them against thieves and wild animals.

Early one morning I saw an extraordinary sight not far from Bethlehem. Two shepherds had evidently spent the night with their flocks in a cave. The sheep were all mixed together and the time had come for the shepherds to go in different directions. One of the shepherds stood some distance from the sheep and began to call. First one, then another, then four or five animals ran towards him; and so on until he had counted his whole flock.

More interesting than the sight of this was the knowledge that Jesus must have seen exactly the same sight and described it in His own words:

" He calleth his own sheep by name, and leadeth them out. And when he putteth forth his own sheep, he goeth before them, and the sheep follow him: for they know his voice. And a stranger they will not follow, but will flee from him: for they know not the voice of strangers. This parable spake Jesus unto them. . . . I am the good shepherd, and know my sheep and am known of mine."

It is with a feeling of delight that one realises how many things in the Gospels which one has regarded as figures of speech are literal descriptions of the things that were happening round Jesus and His disciples as they walked the roads of Palestine. The ordinary sights are so frequently mentioned by Jesus that I believe many of His sayings and parables were suggested by the things that were happening round Him. Whenever I read the Gospels now, I always imagine Him pointing out something, as He undoubtedly pointed to a field of flowers when He said, " Consider the lilies of the field," and as He may have pointed to a shepherd calling his sheep together before He expounded the parable I have just quoted from St. John.

One reason why the sheep and the shepherd are on such familiar terms in the Holy Land is that sheep are kept chiefly for wool and milk, and therefore live longer and exist together as a flock for a considerable time. Also the shepherd spends his life with them. He is with them from their birth onwards, day and night, for even when they are driven into a cave or a sheep-fold for the night, he never leaves them.

In the time of Jesus sheep must have been even more numerous than they are to-day. The Temple sacrifices demanded an incredible number of them. When Solomon dedicated the Temple he sacrificed a hundred and twenty thousand sheep. Enormous droves, destined to be offered on the altar, were always moving along the roads of ancient Palestine. The shepherds at Bethlehem during the birth of Christ were, no doubt, men keeping guard over a sacrificial flock from the well-known Migdal Eder, the " watch tower of the flock."

The species has not varied since the time of Moses. It is a peculiar type of sheep and I have never seen any other like it. Its distinctive feature is a broad, fat tail, or, more correctly, rump. This grows to such an enormous size that, I am told, it has often to be tied up along the sheep's back. I think Herodotus was the first writer to mention that sometimes the shepherds make little wheeled carts to carry these tails! I have never seen one and neither have residents in Palestine whom I have questioned.

The weight of these fat tails is, I believe, extraordinary.

I have read that some of them weigh twenty pounds and that a sheep weighing sixty pounds has been known to possess a tail weighing twenty.   The fat is something between butter and lard, and the Bedouin regard it as a great delicacy.   In this, as in their other habits, they faithfully reproduce the life of the Old Testament.   The fat tail was included in the " rump " that is mentioned in the Old Testament.   In *Exodus* it is laid down that " Thou shalt take of the ram the fat and the rump," and in *Leviticus* it is ordered that the officiating priest must take off " the whole rump . . . hard by the backbone." It was Jehovah's special delicacy.

There are two interesting references to sheep—or rather rams and lambs—in the Psalms:

" The mountains skipped like rams, and the little hills like lambs."

" The voice of the Lord breaketh the cedars: yea, the Lord breaketh the cedars of Lebanon.
" He maketh them also to skip like a calf; Lebanon and Sirion like a young unicorn."

I suppose nobody would take these references literally and imagine that these animals actually skipped, or that, if so, the skipping was anything more than the high spirits which are sometimes associated with lambs in spring-time, but rarely with the rams.   But did the Israelites, I wonder, teach their flocks to skip and dance?   If so, a new significance is given to the above verses.   I ask this because I have come across a strange account of dancing sheep in an account written in 1745 by a missionary in Palestine named Stephen Schultz.

He describes how he was entertained in a Bedouin camp on the Plain of Esdraelon and how the women set up a chorus of extemporaneous praise, as, in fact, they do to this day.   Meanwhile, in compliment to the guests, the flocks were paraded under their several shepherds.

" Besides this shouting for joy in the women's tent," wrote Schultz, " the sheep are led through the men's tent.   It was done in the following manner: the shepherd went on in front and had a shepherd's pipe or flute, upon which he played, and the sheep followed him. As the shepherd modulated the tone when piping, by raising, lowering or letting it run fast or slowly, the sheep made the same movements, and as accurately as a French dancer would do whilst following a minuet. When one shepherd had passed in such a manner with his sheep, another followed with his flock; and so one after the other, during which progress the skipping of the lambs and he-goats drew special attention. Not all the shepherds had flutes, but some of them had other musical instruments.

" The dance of the sheep, he-goats and lambs being ended, the camels came. They, however, had not to dance through the hut, but round it. While this skipping of the animals was going on, the tongue-rattling of the women was often heard."

Has this extraordinary custom died out completely or does it still linger, as so many Old Testament customs do, among the Bedouin in the remote desert? No one who has seen the authority exercised by the Arab shepherd over his flocks, or the obedience of the sheep to their shepherd, can doubt that this pretty trick could be possible.

No animal mentioned in the Bible can compare in symbolical interest with the sheep. I believe it is mentioned over five hundred times. And you cannot go very far along the roads in Palestine without encountering the figure who, staff in hand, symbolises the love and compassion of Jesus Christ.

§ 4

I travelled through a fiery land of hills to the lovely Vale of Shechem, where the ancient town of Nablus—the Shechem of *Genesis*—lies in a narrow defile between mountains.

The busy streets of Nablus are narrow dark tunnels crowded with camels, donkeys, and the vivid life of the East. The people are fanatical Moslems, and one recent guide book tells you that it is unsafe to go about without a guide. I did not find it so. I admit that my appearance was not a signal for general rejoicing and that quite a number of people looked as though they would like to knife me; but that was merely their natural expression.

When I broke the ice, I found them exceedingly kind. For instance, I entered what I thought was an old crusading church to discover myself in an Arab soap factory. They were delighted to see me. They showed me how the soap was made, and when I left they showered cakes on me so that I emerged bulging all over with the stuff which, I discovered later, was absolutely devoid of lather.

But I had come to Nablus to see the strangest and the most ancient sect in the world—the Samaritans. These people have remained absolutely pure in blood for 2,500 years. They claim that they are the only true representatives of the ancient Children of Israel, and they hate the Jews to-day almost as much as they did in the time of Christ.

The anæmic relics of this once powerful race number only about one hundred and fifty. They have nothing in common with the twenty thousand Moslems among whom they live.

The Samaritans are a race apart. They are ruled by a High Priest, whose predecessor, centuries ago, was a rival to the High Priest of the Temple in Jerusalem, and they worship in a synagogue according to their ancient and peculiar laws. The only books of the Bible which they recognise are the five books of Moses, and their most treasured possession is an ancient copy of the Pentateuch written on lambskin by, so they claim, Aaron, the brother of Moses.

Every year the Samaritans sacrifice lambs on the top of their holy mountain, Gerizim. This extraordinary festival is carried out exactly as the Passover was carried out in Old Testament times. The entire community leaves its homes and camps out on the top of the mountain. On the eve of the Passover, as the full moon rises, the High Priest intones the prayers and the slayers draw their knives across the throats of the lambs—a disgusting, but historically fascinating, ceremony, the last relic of the ritual of ancient Israel.

The tent doors are smeared with the blood. The lambs are then roasted and eaten: and the Samaritans gulp down the meat in large mouthfuls to simulate the haste with which the Israelites set out from Egypt.

It is a curious thing that, owing to Christ's parable about the Samaritan, the word " good " has become attached to their name, and the term " good Samaritan " is used every day to indicate anyone who is noble and self-sacrificing. Whereas the feeling among the Jews at the time of Christ was that a more violent and unpleasant people than the Samaritans never existed. These two peoples loathed each other and the dislike which the modern Samaritan professes for the Jew is a survival of the world's most ancient hatred.

This antipathy dates from the break-up of the Hebrew kingdoms. When Solomon died, civil war broke out, resulting in the division of the nation : ten tribes formed the Northern Kingdom of Israel, with a capital at Samaria ; Judah and Benjamin formed the Southern Kingdom, with its capital at Jerusalem. The Assyrians defeated Israel and deported the ten northern tribes in 721 B.C. ; the Babylonians sacked Jerusalem in 586 B.C. and carried Judah and Benjamin into exile. About fifty years later a proportion of Judah and Benjamin returned to Jerusalem (hence the word Jew), and began to rebuild the Temple. They found that, during the exile, Assyrian colonists had inter-married with the relics of the old northern tribes and now inhabited Samaria. The Jews rejected the friendship of this cross-bred race ; and the ancient hatred began.

I found a man who could speak English, and we went together to the house of the High Priest. This was a small, new stone villa, for a recent earthquake destroyed the old Samaritan quarter, and the sect is rehousing itself on the outskirts of Nablus.

We were asked to an upstairs room in which there was nothing but a quantity of bedding piled on a shelf and a few chairs. The High Priest was a tall, thin, hook-nosed man with a jet-black beard, who might have stepped straight from a bas-relief in the palace of Ashur-bani-pal. He motioned us with a grave and courtly gesture to be seated, and then sat down opposite with his hands on his knees, and told us that times were very bad for Samaritans. No rich Americans ever came rushing through Nablus these days. It was a great pity, because they needed a new synagogue.

He spoke of America as Francis Drake might have done,

as a region of boundless wealth, and he expressed his determination to learn English in order to go and get some of it.

Passing with difficulty to less material topics, I gathered that he was firmly convinced that his one hundred and fifty Samaritans are the only people on earth who know anything about God. Such conviction is impressive.

He referred to some rebuilding operations in Palestine which I took to have some connection with the earthquake, but I discovered to my astonishment that he was talking about the rebuilding of Solomon's Temple by Zerubbabel five hundred years before Christ.

A pale, refined young Samaritan like a delicate racehorse came in holding a tray on which stood little egg-cups of sweet Turkish coffee. He handed them round languidly, and sat in a corner of the room gazing at us with large sensitive eyes, the very picture of inbred lassitude.

The High Priest, however, although a tremendous aristocrat, was a hustler. He wanted things, particularly a synagogue and a school. He sipped his coffee and told us that he was thinking of visiting London to raise funds for the Samaritans. I told him, as tactfully as I could, that England had a number of nearer claims on her international generosity. He was very self-confident and proud. He regarded his attenuated flock as the salt of the earth. I gathered that he expected to walk straight into Buckingham Palace and ask the King for a new school.

We walked down into the old town to see the synagogue. The Samaritans have lived so long with the Arabs that all sense of racial difference has vanished—on the part of the Arab. But I think that the Samaritans consider the Arabs, who have been there only since 638 A.D., as interlopers!

We passed through ancient streets, streets that have not changed since the time of Saladin. I saw a water-seller filling his goatskin from a fountain whose stone trough was a crusader's coffin. We passed out of blazing sunlight into a narrow tunnel where men sat cross-legged, making mats and shoes, smoking hookahs, beating out ploughshares and cooking little sweet cakes, while, to shouting and the sound of a stick, donkeys came nosing through the crowd and camels with bells on their necks slouched on, aloof and supercilious.

The Samaritan synagogue was in a poor part of the town, a little dark stone building, with rugs on a dais on which we sat in state while the famous Pentateuch was produced. This extraordinary manuscript is written in the ancient Samaritan characters on the hair side of ancient sheepskin. I was told that Aaron wrote it on skins of Passover lambs. I believe, however, that scholars give it a much later date; but, even so, its antiquity is very great.

It is kept in a silver box. The manuscript is in the form of a scroll, wound on two rollers. The parchment is so old and brittle that it crinkles up, and so brown that bits of it are illegible.

The casual way in which the Samaritans handled their treasure horrified me. Messrs. Maggs or Quaritch would probably have had a fit on the spot. I was allowed to hold the precious bundle, and then it was reinterred in its silver cylinder.

The Samaritans who crowded round the door of the synagogue were mostly pale, inbred people. They are all closely related to each other. The men, I was told, outnumber the women. If a man's wife is childless he is allowed to take a second one. There is also a rather unpleasant law which decrees that when a man dies his nearest relative, other than his brother, is bound to marry the widow.

They are probably the only Eastern people who, on account of the shortage of Samaritan women, prefer girl children to boys.

An interesting story has been handed down among the Samaritans for over twenty-two centuries. They say that when Alexander the Great conferred certain privileges on the Jews, the Samaritans, hoping to receive similar concessions, met him in state on the borders of Samaria and begged his sympathy. But it seems that they angered Alexander, in what way my informant was unable to explain. However, in punishment Alexander ordered that, in violation of the strict Mosaic law against graven images, statues of himself were to be erected all over Samaria. To this the unhappy Samaritans were forced to agree.

Years afterwards Alexander, when making a progress through the country, looked for the statues but could not discover one of them. In a furious temper he visited Shechem and called for the High Priest.

"How is it," asked Alexander, "that my commands to the Samaritans are disregarded? Did I not tell you to erect statues of myself throughout Samaria? Why have you not done so?"

"But, my lord," said the High Priest of the Samaritans, "it has been done even as you commanded."

"Show me my statues!" commanded Alexander.

The High Priest raised his voice and cried "Alexander!" and there came running to him from all quarters little boys, all of the same age.

"We would not insult your fame, my lord," explained the high priest, "by making statues of dead stone in your honour. We have made you living statues."

It appears that as soon as Alexander had issued his decree the Samaritans named all their male children Alexander. I do not know whether this story is true or not. It is just the sort of story that Josephus loved to tell, though it is not to be found in his works. I heard it from the lips of a man who knows the Samaritans and has made a study of their folk-lore.

<h2 style="text-align:center">§ 5</h2>

The following description of the Samaritan sacrifice on Mount Gerizim is from Sir Harry Luke's book *Ceremonies at the Holy Places*:

"By the sunset of the eve of the Passover preparations for the sacrifice are complete. Beside the camping place is a small, oblong plot of ground marked out with a low rubble wall as a prayer enclosure; here a trench has been dug, while on a rough altar of unhewn stone water is being boiled in copper cauldrons. A few yards away, excavated in a piece of higher ground, is a round pit or kiln, some six feet in depth and lined with stones, where the sheep are to be roasted after having been slaughtered on the altar, and this is being brought to the requisite state of heat by the burning of brush-wood inside it. The animals, each one 'a lamb without blemish, a male of the first year,' which up to this time have been browsing unconcernedly about the camp, are now being collected by the young men and brought to the altar, and the worshippers proceed to the first part of the service, consisting of the 'sacrificial prayers.' Clothed, for this occasion, in robes of white linen, they face the rock on the summit of Gerizim which marks the site of the Holy of Holies of the Samaritan temple, the High Priest taking his place at the head of the congregation. It is to be noted that each man, before praying, performs ablutions similar to the ritual ablutions of Moslems, that he stands on a prayer-rug or cloth, and that he prostrates himself at certain parts of his services with his forehead touching the ground in precisely the same manner as does the Moslem. These practices, together with several Samaritan liturgical formulæ which have curiously exact counterparts in the Qoran, suggest that the Samaritans have made substantial contributions to the ceremonies and devotions of Islam.

" As the sun drops to the horizon the High Priest turns to face the congregation and begins to read the twelfth chapter of Exodus, so timing himself that the passage ' and the whole congregation of Israel shall kill it ' is reached as the sun disappears. At the word 'kill' each of the three official slaughterers, who have been standing over the lambs, cuts one throat with a sweeping movement (the knife must not be used twice on one lamb nor must the victim emit a sound), then jumps swiftly to the next animal for the same purpose. To the visitor unaccustomed to such sights this process, and the animals' ensuing death-struggles, can hardly be said to afford a pretty spectacle, but to the assembled Samaritans the cutting of each throat is the signal for an outburst of joy, the people shouting, singing and clapping their hands. A young priest now collects some of the paschal blood in a basin, stirs it with a bunch of wild thyme and daubs with it the lintel of every tent in accordance with the injunction of Exodus xii. 22, while the children dip their fingers in it and apply a few drops to their faces. Next, boiling water is poured over the lambs, so that the wool can be plucked off; for the skin is left intact in order to protect the flesh in the oven. As soon as the animals have been fleeced, they undergo a rigorous ritual inspection, and any of them found to be not absolutely flawless are rejected. Such a case, which is rare, occurred on the occasion when I saw the Passover. An animal which utters a sound while it is being slaughtered is similarly rejected from the sacrifice. Now comes the actual sacrifice to the Almighty, the ' offering made by fire, of a sweet savour unto the Lord.' The ' fat that covereth the inwards . . . and the two kidneys and the fat that is on them . . . and the caul above the liver ' are collected and placed upon the altar, beneath which the fire is kindled anew, and here the burnt offering remains until it is entirely consumed.

" Meanwhile the carcases have been prepared for the oven. From the hind quarters one particular sinew has been removed in accordance with Genesis xxxii. 32 (for the Samaritans claim to know the very tendon which was touched by the angel in the hollow of Jacob's thigh), and much salt is rubbed into the flesh in obedience to Leviticus ii. 13. The right fore-legs and portions of the heads are now cut off, to be roasted separately as a portion for the priests, for ' this shall be the priest's due from the people, from them that offer a sacrifice . . . the shoulders and the two cheeks.' The animals are then spitted and lowered into the kiln, by this time red hot, the top being sealed with a wickerwork lid covered with earth. While this is being done the worshippers shout aloud : ' There is no God but one,' a phrase significant as the possible prototype of the Moslem profession of faith : *la illaha illa 'llah*.

" More prayers and readings now occupy the time until the meat is cooked, and, in the course of these, the High Priest raises aloft before the people one of the scrolls of the Pentateuch. Then, when the lambs have been sufficiently roasted, the oven is opened, the meat is distributed and eaten ' in haste . . . with unleavened bread and with bitter herbs,' great care being taken that not a bone is broken ; and the world's oldest rite, the aim and fulfilment of the Samaritans' existence as a people, is brought to its close."

§ 6

As the road sweeps across the broad green Plain of Jezreel and climbs into the mountains on which Nazareth is enthroned, the visitor can think of nothing but the boyhood of Jesus. Every rock and every hill is important, for these things do not change and He must have known these rocks and these hills. Looking back, the great plain stretching to the sky and the outward thrust spur of Carmel to the west are intensely significant.

When the road straightens out at the top of the hill and runs towards the snow-white houses of Nazareth, towards the thousands of spear-like cypresses, the terraces of fig and olive trees, the town is exactly as one likes to imagine it. Even Bethlehem is not more satisfying to the eye. But, even while a stranger's car approaches, children hold out their hands greedily from the roadside, and the awful cry " Baksheesh " comes down the wind. On arrival, there is a rush for the unfortunate victim.

Small waspish children crowd round, shouting " Baksheesh " at the top of their voices, while various unpleasant persons thrust out postcards, murmuring " Pictures of the Virgin's Fountain, very cheap ": and among those who run towards the stranger and pull him by the sleeve are old women with trays of lace, who leave in his hand cards which read: " Dear friend! Will you kindly give this to shop or to a person who likes to deal with me in needlework, and thank you for your favour. Forget me not! "

It may be childish to be furious because one's picture of Nazareth is spoilt by a horde of noisy people, and because arrival in one of the few towns on earth which should be holy is made horrible by every kind of mean huckster trading on the sacredness of the place, and by touts who offer to take you " to the house where Jesus lived " as touts offer to take you round the sights of Cairo. I don't think so. There are some places in this world which should be grave and quiet and lovely.

It is, however, not the fault of the poor children and the street traders. If they behave badly it is the fault of the tourists who swarm into Nazareth as people swarm into Stratford-on-Avon; and in exactly the same attitude of mind.

It is a pity that some holy places in Palestine are not on the top of precipitous mountains, with nothing but dangerous mule tracks leading up to them.

One is shown all kinds of holy places in Nazareth, but perhaps the only one that really convinces is the Virgin's Fountain. This is, and ever has been, the only water supply of Nazareth. The stream gushes out of the mountain and runs through a conduit to a public fountain where women fill petrol tins with water all day long. The Greeks have built a church above the source of this spring and, when you go down into the darkness of this sanctuary, you can hear the water bubbling up from the rock. This must be the spring from which the Virgin Mary drew water.

Down in the narrow streets of the town I found a whole street of carpenters busily at work sawing wood, and using planes and chisels. These men, who work in archways open to the street, are mostly Christian Arabs, and a characteristic product of the trade is a wooden cradle on rockers which is common all over Galilee. These cradles are always painted blue, a colour which is believed to ward off evil spirits.

As one stands among the wood shavings of these little shops in Nazareth, the old question: " Did Jesus work at the carpenter's bench? " comes to one's mind. St. Mark calls Him " the carpenter," but St. Matthew, " the carpenter's son." An attempt has often been made, by an examination of the similes used by Jesus, to prove that He was a practical carpenter during the years of His life of which we know nothing. But these references are too slender for anyone, except a Biblical critic, to found an opinion.

There are His sayings " Cleave the wood and there you will find me " ; " If they do these things in a green tree, what shall be done in the dry " ; and there is the similitude of the mote and the beam. Surely to these we might add the parable of the house built upon sand?

I was interested to discover that the carpenters of modern Nazareth are of two kinds: the modern carpenter, who makes furniture and prepares wood for the builder, and the old-fashioned carpenter.

If Jesus did adopt the trade of Joseph, we must imagine Him working as the old-fashioned carpenters of Nazareth work to-day. The methods have not changed.

Their clients are the small farmers and the agricultural labourers of the district. They contract to make, and to keep in repair for a year, all the agricultural tools of a village. Payment is made in grain, so much for each yoke of oxen. At the end of the year the village carpenter goes round at threshing time to all his clients and draws his pay in barley, wheat, sesame or olives.

In the old days these carpenters had more work to do. They used to make doors and window-frames from the dwarf oaks of Bashan, a wood called by the Arabs, *Siindian*. But this branch of their work has been monopolised by the modern craftsmen, who can do much cheaper carpentry in Austrian wood.

I came to one dark little hovel in which a very old man, squatting on the floor among a pile of aromatic wood chips and shavings, was using a primitive hand drill. Round about him were various yokes and ploughs and agricultural tools. He was the real old-fashioned carpenter of Palestine, a character who has existed unchanged since the invasion of the Israelites.

While I was exploring the street of the carpenters, I recalled a rather significant remark of Justin Martyr, who wrote that Jesus, " when amongst men, worked as a carpenter, making ploughs and yokes, thus teaching the marks of righteousness and making an active life."

There is an ancient and curious legend to the effect that the Emperor Julian, the apostate who tried to crush Christianity and bring back the pagan gods, once asked a Christian: " What is the Carpenter doing now? " And the Christian answered, " He is making a coffin." The point of the anecdote is that Julian died soon afterwards.

There seem, among the early Christians, to have been some men who believed that Jesus practised the craft, and others who, piously considering that such humble work lowered His dignity, attempted to disguise the fact. But there can be little doubt that Joseph the Carpenter was exactly like the village carpenters in Galilee to-day, whose skill ministers to a whole village and whose reward comes at harvest time.

§ 7

I arrived in Haifa after dark. I had a glimpse of harbour lights and oily still water, the tall shadows of ships and a

mountain cutting out the stars. The hotel was like a stray
piece of England: comfortable chairs, old oak, and dozens
of illustrated magazines full of the most hideous of all photographs, those taken at hunt balls. I went straight to bed,
but stood for a moment on a little balcony outside my room.
I could hear the Mediterranean pounding on the sands quite
near, and I could see a sword of light sweep across the sea
from the head of Mount Carmel. . . .

Then I heard a bugle blowing reveille! Half asleep and
half awake, I began to think of all the things that reveille
brings into the mind. But the bugle became silent and a
bagpipe squealed in the still morning. I was up and out of
bed and on the balcony. The sun was up, the sea was blue,
and half-way up Mount Carmel a white mist lay like a veil.
Opposite my hotel was a parade ground surrounded by tin
huts. There were two goal posts in an immense expanse of
brown, baked earth. In the very middle of this expanse a
piper walked solemnly, playing " Hey Johnny Cope." Across
the patch of beaten earth he came, a white sporran swinging
against the dark green Seaforth tartan of his kilt, the pipes
cradled snugly and the ribbons flying.

Oh, it was a great sight, the greater because it was so far
from home.

Two Arabs driving a ragged mule stopped in fascination near
the barbed wire and watched, and from the tin huts came
the old familiar sound of soldiers tumbling and stamping out
of sleep. A crescent moon was still in the sky, escorted by
one star. The blue waves pounded on the sand. And in
the dawn Mount Carmel, on whose heights Elijah brought
down fire from heaven, looked a bit like Edinburgh Castle.

When I got down to breakfast a major of the Seaforth
Highlanders was standing in the hall. He told me that the
battalion, the second, had just come from India. Then, with
the directness of the Scot, he turned to me and touched the
top button of my coat with his little ribbed cane.

" I know who you are," he said, " because I've seen your
name in the visitor's book. And I've got a bone to pick with
you."

Then, fixing me sternly with a pair of intensely blue eyes,
he said:

" Are you sure you really did find Annie Laurie's house as you say you did in your last book on Scotland? "

" I think I did."

" Well, I'm not so sure. Annie Laurie was an ancestress of mine and I know the house fine. I've got some pictures of it in my billet. Will you look in one evening? "

An orderly came up and saluted, and the descendant of Annie Laurie walked with him across the dusty road to the baked parade-ground.

The Berberine servant in the breakfast room thought that I was smiling at the poached eggs.

§ 8

On those few occasions when I have not been dead to the world at the end of a day's journey, I have been reading in bed the three crusading chronicles of Richard of Devizes, Geoffrey de Vinsauf and of John, Lord de Joinville, High Seneschal of Champagne. Their narratives make me wonder more deeply than ever whether the Crusades should be catalogued under Religion, Commerce, or Colonisation. They seem to have been from first to last a chaos of mixed motives.

However, these three writers inspired me with a desire to visit the ruins of the great crusading castle of Athlit, or, as they called it in the old times, Castrum Peregrinorum, which stands among the Mediterranean waves about fourteen miles south of Haifa.

They told me in the hotel that they did not think I could get there because the road is generally impassable after rain, but that they would ring up the police and find out. The police said that the road had dried up: so I set out.

The road ran round the foot of Mount Carmel. The white breakers crashed on miles of firm gold sand, and the road ran on over flat green land that broadens out into the great Plain of Sharon. About three miles away from Haifa I saw the lovely sight of a camel caravan of about twenty animals padding softly along at the edge of the waves. Sometimes the white foam would come creaming over their feet and they would splash on like a vision of the early world. This was the road of the caravans in the times of Solomon. It was a caravan like this that had carried young Joseph into Egypt. The Roman legions, marching down from Antioch to Cæsarea, came this way and no doubt, like the camels, enjoyed the white foam creaming at their sore feet. The Crusaders rode along these yellow sands with their banners flying and for centuries the pilgrims to the Tomb of Jesus marched this way beside the sea, with their cockle-shells and their staves, and their sun-bitten faces turned ever towards the city of God.

The road became alarming. There were great pits in which you could have buried a horse. Here and there exasperated travellers, unable to endure it, had blazed a new way through fields of young wheat so that there were two roads, an old one and a new one, side by side, always parting at difficult moments and meeting again sooner or later.

As I went on the Carmel range retreated inland and the plain widened: a lovely green plain sown with spring crops. The ground was covered also with the most lovely wild flowers. Everyone I have met who knows Palestine has spoken in glowing terms about the spring flowers, but, exquisite as they are, I cannot honestly say that they beat an English wood in spring-time. Think of our bluebells like a blue mist above the grass, our foxgloves, our primroses, our violets, our cowslips, the wild flags in marshy places, and our humble exquisite buttercups, and the beautiful but unloved dandelion. I cannot be convinced that the wild flowers of Palestine are lovelier than ours; but I will admit that they are almost as lovely.

Now and then I came across hillsides that were blood red with the scarlet anemone, which is the biblical "lily of the valley," and again I came to stretches of the road that were sweet for yards with the scent of the white narcissus, which is the "Rose of Sharon." The translators of the Bible became rather confused by the word *habhazzeleth*, which they rendered as "rose." It should, say modern scholars, have been translated as "narcissus."

"I am the rose of Sharon, and the lily of the valleys."

So sang Solomon, according to the Authorised Version.

But this is how Dr. James Moffatt renders it in his brilliant, but less musical, new translation of the Bible:

" I am only a blossom of the plain, a mere lily of the dale."

It is strange that in the old version you can actually smell the flowers, but in the new they might be pressed in a book or, worse still, lying in a glass case in a museum.

" I am only a blossom of the plain, a mere lily of the dale " may be an accurate translation, but " I am the rose of Sharon, and the lily of the valleys " has authentic beauty.

I met nothing now on the road but wild-looking men leading flocks of black-and-tan goats, a few Arabs mounted on donkeys, and once another car containing a town Arab and his three wives. He sat in the front next to the driver and the wives sat together in the back, muffled to the eyes, swaying together with the lurching of their car like three black ghosts. A side road led down to the sands and to the ruined castle of Athlit.

This great fortress lies among the rocks on the shore like an old battleship that is being slowly broken up by the tides. Nothing has ever given me a clearer impression of the international character of the Crusades than this colossal derelict town, for it is absurd to call it a castle. Its area, including the trading town that clustered round it, must once have covered at least fifty acres. It was one of Europe's base camps for the conquest of Palestine, and even in decay it still looks like that. It was the last place held by the Crusaders.

An Arab village squats in the middle of the castle, and the inhabitants swarm through ruined Gothic halls in order to be first to show the departed glory of the place. They lead one into cavernous vaults, into tremendous chapels and armouries; they point out towering ramparts, now tottering to a fall, which were erected to last for ever.

In 1218 it was the chief seat of the Knights Templar and it remained for over seventy years one of the main bulwarks of the Christian power in the East. The departed glory of the great Crusading Orders is sadly symbolised by the massive ruins, but as I explored them I remembered that there is still one place in the Holy Land where a Crusading Order performs its original function—the care of the sick. This is

RUINS OF HEROD'S JUDGMENT HALL, SEBASTE

BOATMEN ON THE SEA OF GALILEE

the eye hospital of the Order of St. John of Jerusalem, whose
Priory in Clerkenwell is, by the way, one of the most interesting
places in London.   The revival of the Grand Priory of England
over a century ago, and the magnificent work it has done since
for the care of the sick in peace and war, justify that over-
used word " romance."

The cross of the Order flies in Jerusalem above the eye
hospital whose full name is like a fanfare of Crusading trumpets:
" The Ophthalmic Hospital of the Grand Priory in the British
Realm of the Venerable Order of the Hospital of St. John of
Jerusalem."   Inside the white modern building there are no
politics: Moslem, Christian and Jew are all received and
cared for under the authority of one of the most brilliant
ophthalmic surgeons in the world.   Some idea of the scope of
the work which the Order of St. John is doing in Palestine
may be gathered from the fact that annual attendances
number over eighty thousand, and more than three thousand
operations are performed every year.

I think the ruins of a great crusading castle like Athlit are,
perhaps, the most perfect surroundings in which a man may
salute the memory of a great religious order which still
remains true to the original purity of its motives.

I went on to the south until I came to the melancholy
desolation that was Cæsarea.   During the lifetime of Jesus
this was a port as large as the Piræus.   Its harbour, its buildings and its fine streets were famous among the world's sea-
ports.   Herod, who began to build it in 25 B.C. and took
twelve years to finish it, employed the finest architects of the
time and the most up-to-date engineers, so that Cæsarea
ranked among the ancient towns of Palestine like a small
New York.   All the streets led to the harbour and were
intersected by straight parallel avenues.   We would probably
have considered it the best type of American city !   The remains
of subways which connected various parts of the city with the
beach have also been discovered.   There were magnificent
theatres and a hippodrome, and facing the sea was the marble
temple which Herod built to the honour of his master, Cæsar.

One can imagine how readily the Romans centred their

authority in this splendid modern seaport and how glad Pilate must have been to have lived there in the great palace of Herod rather than in the old and savage city of Jerusalem. It was from Cæsarea that Pilate set out with his retinue to attend the Passover during which he condemned Jesus to the cross; it was to Cæsarea that St. Paul came many times, once under escort after his arrest in Jerusalem; and in Cæsarea the legions hailed Vespasian as their emperor.

And to-day there is nothing. The sea beats on a desolate coast. There is a rock some way out at sea which may be a relic of the once famous harbour, and the palace in which Pilate lived, the splendid forum, the great hippodrome, and the circus, are now meagre cornfields.

CHAPTER SIX

In which I go to the Sea of Galilee and stay in Tiberias. I walk the hill which once held the palace of Herod Antipas, and go out fishing with men of Galilee.

§ 1

GALILEE is one of the sweetest words I know. Even were it possible to dissociate it from the Ministry of Jesus, it would still be a lovely word whose three syllables suggest the sound of lake water lapping a shore. It is as soft as the word Judæa is hard, as gentle as Judæa is cruel. It is not necessary to visit the Holy Land to appreciate the rocky harshness of " Judæa " or to hear the water falling from the oars in " Galilee."

The meaning of the word Galilee is " Ring, or Region, of the Gentiles." The Hebrew word *Galil* means a circlet, or anything that is round. Chanctonbury Ring and the Links of Forth convey the same idea in English. The district was never entirely Jewish, even in the earliest times. Ten cities of Galilee were given by Solomon to Hiram, King of Tyre, as part payment for the building of the Temple, and the invasion of the Gentile population continued in later times. When Jesus went to live beside Galilee, the western shore of the lake was dotted with a ring of towns and fishing villages in which the non-Jewish element was very strong. The pure-blooded Orthodox Jew of Jerusalem looked down with contempt upon the Galilean and made fun of his dialect and of the way he pronounced the gutturals. Those who stood in the court of the High Priest's house after the arrest of Jesus detected that St. Peter was a follower of Christ. " Thou art a Galilean," they said, " for thy speech bewrayeth thee." Amusing errors in grammar and absurd mistakes due to mispronunciation were constantly cited by the

175

superior Judæans as proof of the stupid, yokel character of the Galileans.

It seems, however, that in freeing itself from the Rabbinic rigidity of Judæa, Galilee found room for idealism and an intense nationalism. While the Judæan had bound himself up in formalism, the Galilean had become speculative and independent. It was not chance that led Jesus to sow the seeds of His teaching on the receptive shores of Galilee. . . .

Now, when the time came for me to set out for the Sea of Galilee, I found myself almost nervously apprehensive. Would it be cheapened by competitive piety, as many parts of Palestine have been cheapened? Would there be anything left to remind a man of Christ? I did not know. I was conscious only of the fact that Galilee must be the supreme adventure in any journey to the Holy Land. Above all places on the earth, it is the one most closely associated with Jesus Christ, and whenever the lovely word is spoken it calls up a picture of Him, not yet the Christ of whom St. Paul preached, but the Jesus of our inmost hearts who called little children to His knee and preached the gospel of love and compassion to the humble, the simple and the heavy laden.

§ 2

Some instinct warned me to stop on the hill that runs up into Nazareth. I looked back to the south over a sweep of country that recalls much of the sorrows and triumphs of a nation.

I saw the great Plain of Esdraelon stretching like a smooth, green sea to the distant hills of Samaria. The shadows of the clouds moved over it as if the ghosts of old armies were crossing the haunted plain. There are over twenty battlefields down there. The level arena has known the thunder of chariots from Egypt, Assyria and Babylon. Somewhere on the plain, Barak smote the Canaanites. From its green levels Gideon drove the Midianites towards the Jordan. On the hills at the back Saul went by night to consult the Witch of Endor, and by day saw his armies scattered and his sons slain. It was down there, too, that the dead body of Josiah was hurried from the triumphant Egyptians and borne in sorrow to Jerusalem.

The brown hills to the south, the hills of Samaria, had known the denunciatory figure of Elijah. They had heard his burning words and seen the prophetic fire in his eyes. On the skyline was the hill that held Naboth's Vineyard and the hill on which Jezebel met death. To the right the long calm ridge of Carmel cut the sky, and I looked at it remembering the priests of Baal and the fire that Elijah drew down from heaven to confound them.

When I had looked my fill at this tremendous map of Old Testament history, I went on through Nazareth; and the road ran upward to the top of another hill. There I stopped, not from instinct but from amazement; for down below me to the northward lay a new world—Galilee.

I do not know the name of this hill, but I shall always think of it as the Hill of the Two Testaments. To the south lies the Old Testament; to the north lie Galilee and the New. As I looked northward to the new land, the idea came to me that this hill reproduces in nature the title-page which printers of the Bible place between the books of the prophets and the life of Christ. And I thought that although Jesus may not have visited all the places which are now called holy, there can be no doubt that He must have often stood on this hill as a boy. He must have known all His nation's ghosts, which crowd up from the south, and He must have looked with affection towards the calm and lovely north and the road that runs down over the mountains to the lake.

One pictures Him in imagination rising from the hill as the sun drops into the sea and going down through the hush of the twilight to Nazareth. Night is closing in on the Plain of Esdraelon and the hills of Samaria are already in shadow. But the last thing that fades from sight on the plain below is a white streak. It is the road that goes on through Samaria and through the wilderness of Judæa to end at last far to the south before the gates of Jerusalem.

As I went down into Galilee, I knew that I had learnt something about the Gospels that I could never have known in any other way. Nazareth is a frontier post between the north and the south. To go into Galilee is to turn one's back on the arena of the Old Testament, and there is something in the formation of the land that gives a feeling of finality to the act: one cannot possibly go into Galilee without the knowledge that one has definitely said farewell to Judæa. It is not until one crosses this Hill of the Two Testaments that one's mind shakes itself free from the powerful hypnotism of Jerusalem.

By going into Galilee Jesus performed a symbolic act. He turned His back on the world of the Old Testament, and from the moment of that turning away the New Testament begins.

Everyone must feel how different are these two worlds. In the New Testament we seem to have emerged from a dark, fierce Eastern world into a clear light that is almost European. In fact Rome is already in sight. The centre of the Old Testament world is rigid, exclusive Jerusalem; the centre of the New Testament world is international Galilee, a country crossed in the time of Christ by the great military roads from the north and by the ancient caravan routes from the east, a country in which a man seen in the distance might be an imperial messenger riding to Cæsarea with tidings of the Emperor's death, or a tax-gatherer from the main road to Damascus, or a Greek architect on his way to build a new theatre in Jerash in the Decapolis.

This busy international corridor was the place in which Jesus taught. He alone of all the prophets who had come out of Israel deliberately cut Himself off from the theological stronghold of Judæa. And the roads He chose to tread were not the roads of the priests and the rabbis but the roads of the world. So in the road that runs over a hill from Nazareth to the Sea of Galilee a man detects the first promise of Christianity.

§ 3

The road runs down towards a green valley enclosed by gentle hills. Brown hawks hang in the air, watching the

earth. Now and then one drops like a stone out of the sky
and is up and away again in a flash. Tumbled rocks, in
which thorn and cactus grow, line the road and slope down
to the valley; and in this green valley is a trickle of water.
After the thirsty Highlands of Judæa, where every drop of
rain is saved in cisterns, the sound of running water is
luxurious and extravagant. The blue iris that grows in wet
places seems almost spendthrift.

To the left is a straggling brown town on a hill with a
crusaders' castle on the top, ruined but still dominant. This
is Sepphoris, which Herod Antipas made the capital of his
tetrarchy in the time of Christ. Always slavishly flattering
the ruling power, Herod called it Diocæsarea in honour of
Augustus, just as a few years later he called his new capital
Tiberias in honour of the successor of Augustus. One
wonders if the Cæsars were really flattered by such architectural toadyism.

Half-way down the hill is a pitiful dead village called
Raineh, which has never recovered from the earthquake
of 1927. Its houses still lie in ruins and its walls have
fallen down. If anyone wants to know what a biblical
town must have looked like after it had been conquered
by warriors like Saul or David, let him go and look at
Raineh.

At the foot of the hill is a small impoverished Arab village.
Bare hills interspersed with sparse wheat fields surround it;
beyond lies a wide green plain which the pilgrims of the
Middle Ages believed to be the place where Jesus gathered
the ears of wheat on the Sabbath.

The little village is called Kefr Kenna, which scarcely
disguises the name of Cana of Galilee, where Jesus turned the
water into wine at the marriage feast.

There are two churches in Cana, one a simple Greek
church and the other an archæological Franciscan church.
In the first a fat Greek priest shows you two stone urns which
he tells you are the very water-jars of the miracle. One of
them, I believe, was a baptismal font in an eighteenth-
century church and the other, I understand, is no older than
the sixteenth century. When you express doubt about these
relics, the fat priest shrugs his shoulders. The kindest thing

one can think about him is that he probably believes in them himself.

The Franciscan church, on the other hand, is interesting. It is built on the site of an ancient church which was standing in 726 A.D., and I have no doubt that tradition says that it stands on the spot occupied by the house of the wedding feast. The Franciscans, with their keen eyes for authentic relics, suspected that the ruins of the old church lay beneath the soil and began negotiations for the purchase of the site in 1641. Two hundred and fifty years later they received permission to build a chapel! Patience is one of the Franciscan virtues in the Holy Land.

A friar leads you under the choir to a dark crypt in which there is an ancient cistern and also a Jewish pitcher of great antiquity: and in a small museum are displayed many objects of Roman date discovered in the ruins, including mosaics of the Byzantine period and coins of Constantine. There is little doubt that the Franciscans have rediscovered the Byzantine Church which, it is believed, stood on the site of the marriage feast.

The road bends round past Cana and plunges again into the hills. A strange, saddle-shaped mountain lifts itself to the left. It is known as the Horns of Hattin: in its shadow Saladin defeated the Crusaders and brought to an end the eighty-eight years old Latin Kingdom of Jerusalem.

Suddenly you see, lying a thousand feet below, a strip of bright blue. It is your first sight of the Sea of Galilee. As you sometimes look upward in a mountain gorge and see a strip of blue sky shining, so in this place you look downward through a gorge to a distant strip of water as blue as any sky. This first sight of the Sea of Galilee is one of the most sacred memories of Palestine.

The road begins to run steadily downhill. The air grows hotter. You are reminded of the heat of the Jordan Valley. You continue to descend into the hot trench and at the end of the road—seven hundred feet below sea level—you come to the palms, the greenness, the blue lake water, and the white roofs of Tiberias.

§ 4

The little hotel in Tiberias stands near the lake. From my room I could see over the flat roofs of houses and, through the branches of eucalyptus trees, a strip of blue water backed by a range of hills as barren and as pink and mauve in colour as the Mountains of Moab at Jericho. The room was hot and stuffy, but, unlike the dry, windless heat of the Dead Sea, it was tempered by a slight breeze from the lake, a breeze not strong enough to move the palm fronds but enough to shake the eucalyptus leaves.

I have discovered that whenever one arrives in an hotel in Palestine it is a good idea to follow the stairs right to the top. There is always a flat roof that gives an excellent general view of whatever town one may happen to be in. I came out on a space as large as a tennis-court, so white and dazzling that I could see nothing until I had put on sun glasses. Then I looked down on Tiberias.

I saw hundreds of flat-roofed white houses marching down a gentle hill-slope to stand in picturesque confusion on the lake-side. Little white domes varied the rectangular uniformity of the white roofs. Here and there a minaret like a Georgian pepper-pot stood up higher than domes or roofs. There was one dark, narrow main street from which hundreds of squalid little lanes radiated, and this street was congested with men, women, children, camels and donkeys. The background was a high green mountain with a few houses dotted about its slopes.

In front of me the Sea of Galilee lay ruffled by a slight wind. It was not a uniform colour. There were patches of dark and light blue and also touches of pale green. I wondered with what lake I could compare it, and explored my memory in vain. The Emperor Titus intended to call the Lake of Neuchâtel, in Switzerland, Galilæa because it reminded him so much of the Sea of Galilee, but he must have changed his mind. The lake is heart-shaped, with the narrowest part to the south. It is thirteen miles long and at its widest part about seven miles across. Loch Lomond is eleven miles longer than the Sea of Galilee, but it is nowhere as wide. Lough Neagh in Northern Ireland is five miles longer and four

G

miles wider. Mountains rise all round the lake. On the western shore they are green mountains; on the eastern shore they are the brown barren precipices of the desert, part of the rocky barrier that rises east of the Jordan and marches south with the river, past the Dead Sea down to the Gulf of Akaba. When I looked to the north I saw the sight that impresses itself upon the mind of all who live in Galilee: I saw a magnificent ridge of mountain covered with snow. It stood up like a screen to the north. The snow never melts in its deepest corries even in the height of summer. It was Mount Hermon, the Mountain of the Transfiguration.

What makes it so impossible to compare the Sea of Galilee with any European lake is the sub-tropical climate. It is a little inland sea sunk at the beginning of the tropical trench that divides Palestine from Arabia. It is seven hundred feet below sea level and, like its companion lake, the Dead Sea, many miles due south, it belongs to a different latitude from the rest of Palestine. The mountains that rise all round it have their heads in a temperate climate and their feet in a lake round whose shores banana, palm, bamboo and sugar-cane thrive. And the water of the Sea of Galilee is fresh, not salt and bitter like that of the Dead Sea.

The second thing that impresses one about the Sea of Galilee is its desolation. It is, with the exception of the white town of Tiberias, a deserted lake. Through glasses one can see, far off along the western bank towards the north, a dark clump of eucalyptus trees which are supposed to mark the site of Bethsaida, and next to them a small white building and more trees which stand where Capernaum is believed to have stood. You see uneasy mounds of black stones near the shore which are the dead bones of old cities. When you look at the pink and mauve hills opposite, you see that they are wild and desolate, slashed with brown thirsty valleys as with the slashes of knives. Dotted about them here and there are little black squares, sometimes near the shore but more often higher on the hills. They are the goat-hair tents of Bedouin tribes. It is a wild desert country over there and is part of French Syria. There are few roads. Mud villages are mounted on the tops of mountains, and the traveller who ventures among them without a knowledge of the language is advised to take an armed escort with him.

But the Sea of Galilee, even in its desolation, breathes an exquisite peace and a beauty that surpass anything in Palestine. The landscape has altered in detail since Jesus made His home in Capernaum, but the broad outline has not changed. The hills are the hills He looked upon, the lights and shadows that turn the Gergesene heights to gold and purple, the little breezes that whip the lake into whiteness, the blue water that fades to a milky green where the Jordan enters at the north; none of these has changed. These are the things that Jesus looked upon and loved when He lived in Galilee.

I went into the streets of Tiberias. It is a shabby, squalid little town and crouches like a beggar on the lakeside. It is a town of rags and dark eyes and dark cellars, of little jumbled shops and narrow streets. The ruins of a fine crusading wall of black basalt, in whose bastions families live in unspeakable poverty, rise from the water's edge.

The Herodian ruins lie a little way to the south of the modern town. Only a few rubble walls exist to speak of the town that Herod built to minister to his summer palace on the hill. Part of the three-mile wall can still be traced, but stretches of it have fallen into the lake. The hill at the back is pitted and scarred with ruins. High up on its slopes are mounds, shattered pillars and old masonry, which mark the site of the palace of Antipas. From the side of this hill I picked out all kinds of Roman pottery and small fragments of iridescent glass.

One relic of Roman times is still alive. From a hill near the lake gushes a stream of hot mineral water. This spring, which is claimed to give the same water as that of Carlsbad, and was mentioned by Pliny, was known and valued in the earliest times. No doubt Vespasian and Titus bathed in it when they carried the war into Galilee. And it is still healing the woes of humanity. I visited a large bathing house to which patients come from all parts of Syria, Palestine and Trans-Jordan.

In the time of Jesus these baths attracted the sick from every part of the country. One cannot help marvelling at the number of sick people who were brought to the lakeside to be cured by Jesus. At times they came to Him, not singly but in great companies. Now, Capernaum was only ten miles along the shore from the hot baths at Tiberias. One imagines that the presence of the most famous spa in the country, and the gathering there of many hundreds of invalids, must have been responsible for many of the crowds who sought our Lord's help in Capernaum.

I went down to the lakeside as the sun was setting. The houses and other buildings come right down to the edge of the water, but there is a small clear space occupied by a wooden jetty from which the few fishing-boats put out in the evening. This primitive jetty is probably the descendant of the splendid harbour from whose steps the barges of Herod once set sail over the blue waters. A few Arabs sat in the dust. Three boatmen were getting their craft ready for a night's fishing.

The sun sank behind Tiberias, and the last light was flung on the opposite hills. Every valley and crevice was clearly defined in the bright light. The clarity of the air made the opposite shores seem no more distant than a mile or so. The lake became a sheet of blue glass and no wind stirred the trees. Ripples widened on the still water where fish were jumping. Kingfishers flew like darts through the air. Gradually the last light of the sun grew from gold to brown on the hills. The valleys filled with blue shadows and a strange mauve colour shimmered a moment and deepened into blue. The hills held the light of the vanished sun for a long time. The east glowed with a white incandescent radiance and a pink afterglow throbbed in the west. The silence was deep. The light splash of a fish, the clapping of pigeons in flight, and the scream of swifts were the only sounds. Far to the north Mount Hermon lifted up its wall of snow. All Nature seemed listening in the important hush of the sunset; and in this deep silence the first star burned above the Sea of Galilee.

§ 5

Rising at the exquisite hour of four a.m., when the world is hushed and cool, I went up to the roof of the hotel to watch the sun rise over the Lake of Galilee.

At this time Tiberias is covered with a shroud of silence and greyness. An Arab, who picked himself from the dust where he had spent the night, stole off into the morning stillness like a ghost.

There was one star still burning in the sky. Beyond the flat roofs of the intervening houses the Sea of Galilee was lying cold and grey like an old mirror, unruffled by any wind of dawn. On the opposite bank the savage Gergesene hills halted at the water's edge like crouching beasts. Behind those hills a faint pink glow filled the sky, growing every second more powerful; it widened and spread, quenching the last star, and giving, even before the sun rose, the thinnest shadows to palm trees and houses.

Men and animals knew that a new day had come. Cocks crowed in a chorus that was echoed from hill to hill. Arabs, their heads still shrouded in their robes, for they sleep fully dressed, led camels and donkeys to water. Sparrows sent up an excited chirping, and swifts filled the air with their bright screaming.

Then suddenly the sun leapt over the hills of Gergesa and— everything was changed! It was warm. The lake was blue. I could see the snow shining on Hermon to the north. The bells of the Greek convent set up a deep ringing. There was a smell of cooking from somewhere. And the muezzin came out on the minaret of the mosque and called the faithful to prayer. So a new day came to Tiberias.

I wandered in the early morning on the hill where the palace of Herod Antipas once shone in a glory of marble and gold. I looked down on the Sea of Galilee, blue under the morning sun. Sometimes I saw a white sail leaning against the wind, moving to the north, where the best fish are caught just where the milky-green Jordan flows into the lake. But more often there are no sails. There is only blue water lying still in the

windless heat and a shore curving round to the north, with
Magdala, Bethsaida and Capernaum lying in the hollow of
the curve. Peace lies like a benediction over the Sea of
Galilee: the peace of silence, of solitude, of memory.

Always on this hill my thoughts turn to the savage, unhappy
men, the kings of the Herodian House, who ruled Palestine
in the time of Christ. They flash in and out of the Gospels—
Herod the Great, his son Antipas, and Philip the Tetrarch.
But they are only lay figures in the tragedy. The Gospels
are memoirs. They were written perhaps twenty, perhaps
forty, years after the death of Jesus to remind a new generation
of His deeds on earth. The people for whom they were written
knew the background of the time. They knew the tragedy of
the Herods. It was enough to tell them in a sentence that
when Herod the King knew that he had been tricked by the
Wise Men from the East he " was exceeding wroth " and
" sent forth and slew all the children that were in Bethlehem,"
because such an act required no explanation. They knew well
that this was in tune with Herod's life, in perfect conformity
with a hundred other deeds of savage rage. Again, when
Jesus came before Pilate and was sent by him to Herod Antipas,
we are told that Herod " was exceeding glad because he
hoped to see some miracle done by him." What a different
Herod is this son from his violent father. The Herod who slew
the infants of Bethlehem on the impulse of a moment would
never have behaved like that.

Thus, while the main characters in the Gospel narrative
are drawn with firm strokes, the background is just etched in
with fine lines, a sentence here or a word there. If one wants
to find out what this background was like, it is necessary to get
behind the Gospel story, as it were, and, by reading Josephus,
and searching historians like Livy, Tacitus, Plutarch, Diodorus
Siculus and Strabo, discover allusions which help to fill in a
background which the evangelists had no need to paint.
The misdeeds of Herod the Great, the scandal of his son's life,
the good qualities of the Tetrarch Philip, who always travelled
his domains with the divan of justice, were common gossip
in the time of Christ. Kings and common men were much
nearer together in ancient times than they are to-day. There
was no class between them. The rumours of courts were the

gossip of taverns. Every slave was a scandal-monger. And we may be sure that when Jesus stopped to talk to poor men on the lake-side of Galilee He heard many a " secret " from the palace on the hill. I sit there, where once the splendid palace of Antipas rose in shining terraces, and I try to build up a picture of Herod and his sons. . . .

In the autumn of 31 B.C. a number of light Ligurian war-ships anticipate by sixteen centuries the defeat of the Spanish Armada. They dash in among heavy battleships, out-manœuvre them and put them to flight. Those ships which fail to escape are burnt to the water. It was the Battle of Actium. Antony and Cleopatra commit suicide, and Octavius—Augustus Cæsar—is master of the world.

Among those who view with terror the new distribution of power is Herod, King of the Jews, friend of the defeated Antony. Herod is a man of thirty-five, handsome, courageous, cultivated, and a man of the world. He possesses a genius for survival; or perhaps it is merely gambler's luck. He deserted Pompey for Cæsar. When Cæsar fell, he backed Brutus. When Brutus fell, he successfully cultivated Antony. On each occasion he took his fate in his hands and risked it, as it were, on one cast of the dice; and every time he won. But the Battle of Actium is the greatest crisis in his life. Once again he decides on the bold course. He will go to Augustus and meet death or—return greater than ever. First he leaves secret orders that should he not return his beautiful wife, Mariamne, who must never belong to any man but himself, is to be slain. Then he sets sail for Rhodes, where Augustus is resting after his victory.

Herod removes his diadem before he enters the audience room. He walks boldly towards Augustus and greets him as a king greets his equal. He is no eastern potentate abased before the conqueror: he is bold, courageous, dignified. There are moments when truth is so unexpected that it carries all before it. This is one of them. Herod does not apologise for his friendship with the fallen Antony. He enlarges on it. He stresses his loyalty. He says that many a time he begged Antony to rid himself of Cleopatra, but nothing could save the man. He carried defeat in himself. Herod looks Augustus in the eyes. He has served Antony faithfully. He promises to serve Augustus as faithfully if he will accept him as the ally and friend of the Roman people. Augustus looks back into the clever, bold eyes of Herod and tells him to put on his diadem. So Herod wins again. After a triumphal progress with Augustus, he returns richer and more powerful.

Now, Herod lives two lives: one a brilliant public life, the other dark and private, a hideous nightmare of jealousy, fear and intrigue from which there is no way out at times save by the poisoned cup and the dagger. His halls are haunted by the relatives he has murdered. In public, he is an enlightened western king; in private, he is an Eastern despot.

Mariamne listens coldly to his good fortune. She has heard of the order to put her to death in the event of his failure. How else could she have been told this secret, thinks Herod, except from the man who had betrayed his confidence? This man is instantly executed. Mariamne is flung into prison. Her enemies whisper in Herod's ear. They say that she has plotted to kill him. He cannot believe it. But wretches drawn out on the rack say anything in their tortures. Herod, torn between love and jealousy, gives way to the accusers, and Mariamne is led to execution. No sooner is she dead than all the furies of remorse tear at Herod. Her ghost haunts him to the end of his life.

Thirty-five years pass, and Herod is dying. His long and spectacular reign is over. Hated and detested in Jerusalem, admired in Rome, this man, half Jew and half Gentile, sinks towards the grave, eaten by disease and a prey to remorse and fear. His land is covered by splendid new buildings and new cities. The new Temple lifts itself on Mount Moriah like the snow-fields of Hermon. His territories exceed those of Saul or David. Yet his people pray for him to die. His insane dreams have been haunted by Mariamne, by her two lovely sons, both slain by him, and by a numerous company, his own flesh and blood, some stabbed with daggers, some strangled with cords, some poisoned.

They tell him, as his bloated body is borne from the hot springs by the Dead Sea to the warm gardens of Jericho, that a king has been born in Bethlehem. There is no king but

Herod! Has he not slain his two splendid sons, Mariamne's boys, because someone said that they would be kings before their time? Let them kill all the male infants in Bethlehem. Let them do it at once! Although Herod is dying, there is no king but Herod.

And they come to him again, whispering that his son and heir Antipater, who is in Rome, is plotting his death. This time they speak the truth. The young man is brought home and cast into Herod's dungeon; and the seventy years old king sinks into a mass of disease and insanity. " The distemper seized his whole body," says Josephus, " and greatly disordered all its parts with various symptoms. . . ."

The time comes when he no longer makes and remakes his will. Death is on him. But, in a sudden spasm of energy, he asks for an apple and a knife to peel it. He lifts the knife to plunge it into his breast. His attendants spring forward and prevent him. The commotion in the palace is heard by his son Antipater, who, thinking his father is dead, tries to bribe the jailer to set him free. The jailer runs to the dying king and tells him. " Kill him at once! " shouts the king. So Herod's last murder is committed. And five days later he dies.

Such was the king in whose last year Jesus Christ was born. History calls him Herod the Great; and so he was. Savage, monstrous and cruel, he was yet a statesman of the first order. His fear and jealousy had removed the three sons who were chosen to succeed him, but he had a numerous family by his ten wives. The three sons between whom he finally divided his kingdom were:

Archelaus, the elder son of a Samaritan woman called Malthrace, who inherited the Kingdom of Judæa, Samaria and Itruria.

Antipas, the Herod of the Trial and Crucifixion, the younger son of the same mother, who inherited Galilee and Peræa.

Philip, the son of the beautiful Cleopatra of Jerusalem, who inherited the poorest part of the kingdom, the tetrarchy of

Batanæa, Trachonitis and the domain of Zenodorus, a desert region north-east of Galilee and south of Damascus, inhabited chiefly by Greek and Syrian settlers.

The last two were the only native rulers in Palestine during the life of Jesus, and both of them are mentioned in the Gospels. The first, Archelaus, was deposed before Jesus grew to manhood. He came to grief not only with the people of Judæa, but also with his relatives. The result was a bitter family dispute about Herod's will. Some said that the old man was mad, or suffering undue influence, when he made it; and the other side claimed that he was in his right mind. So bitter was the public and the private feud against Archelaus, that the matter was taken to Rome for the decision of Augustus.

Archelaus went to Rome, so did Antipas, and so did a Jewish deputation which was anxious to depose both rulers and establish home rule by the High Priest under Roman supervision.

Augustus heard the dispute and deprived Archelaus of the title of king, sending him back as Ethnarch of Judæa and promising to make him king later if he behaved himself. This must have occurred during the first years of Christ's life, because we learn from St. Matthew that when Joseph " heard that Archelaus did reign in Judæa in the room of his father Herod, he was afraid to go thither: notwithstanding, being warned of God in a dream, he turned aside into the parts of Galilee: and he came and dwelt in a city called Nazareth."

This is the first time that the splitting up of the kingdom between the sons of Herod was to influence the life of our Lord. It would have been impossible for Joseph to have felt secure in Nazareth during the previous reign, because it was all one country; but, after the partition, to live in Nazareth was to live in a different state, the Galilee of Antipas. In His later life Jesus crossed the boundary line between these little states many times, whenever He left Galilee for Jerusalem, when He went into the Phœnician territory round Tyre and Sidon, and when He journeyed to Cæsarea Philippi, under the snows of Hermon. Cæsarea Philippi was the capital city of the good and just Tetrarch Philip.

It is not, I think, generally recognised that Jesus may have introduced some of these dynastic disputes into one of His discourses. Surely in the Parable of the Pounds we may see in " a certain nobleman " who " went into a far country to receive for himself a kingdom," and the behaviour of his servants during his absence, a shadow of the embassy of Archelaus to Rome?

However, the worthless Archelaus, who exhibited all his father's vices with nothing of his strength and personality, allowed affairs in Judæa to lapse into a state of general anarchy. He made things worse for himself by falling violently in love with a twice-widowed Greek beauty whose first husband had been his half-brother, Alexander. For her sake he put away his wife and contracted one of those unlawful typically Herodian marriages which always horrified the Jews. After nine years Archelaus exhausted the patience of his people and his family. One night when he was seated at a banquet a messenger arrived and handed him a letter. It was a summons to Rome. He went again before Cæsar, but could not answer the long list of his misdeeds and was banished to Vienne in Gaul. With Archelaus went for ever the crown and sceptre of Judah.

The Romans marched down on his territory and restored order. They added Judæa, Samaria and Idumea to the Roman province of Syria. They established a kind of home rule, with the Sanhedrin as the legislative body, but in authority over this body was Cæsar's representative, the Procurator of Judæa, with headquarters at the coast city of Cæsarea. So with the banishment of Archelaus, and the arrival of the Romans, we see the formation of the administrative background of the Trial and Crucifixion with which we are so familiar. At this time Jesus was a child of ten in Nazareth.

Herod Antipas slyly watched his brother's crash from power from the neighbouring tetrarchy of Galilee, thinking, no doubt, that he would be too clever to make such a fool of himself. But Nemesis seemed to have a standing invitation to the madhouse of passion and self-indulgence in which the Herods lived; and the time of Antipas was to come.

Antipas was not a violent man like his brother: he was weak and cunning. The gift of diplomacy which enabled his father to twist Antony and Cleopatra, and even Augustus, round his finger was watered down in him into slyness. Jesus described him once and for all time as " that fox."

His public achievements were a pale shadow of his father's, but he was a good and active builder. He reconstructed the mighty fortress of Machærus, which stood on the barren heights of Moab above the Dead Sea, and he founded, among other towns, the magnificent Tiberias, named so in compliment to the successor of Augustus. When they were digging the foundations of Tiberias, however, the remains of an ancient cemetery were discovered. This, by Mosaic Law, rendered the place unclean and unfit for human habitation. No strict Jew could enter or leave the place without performing a seven days' purification. In order to secure a population, Herod was obliged to bribe slaves, beggars and all kinds of ruffians and riff-raff to take up residence there. The place stank in the nostrils of the rabbis.

Beneath the magnificent palace overlooking the Sea of Galilee there grew up a town that was entirely pagan in outlook and appearance. But its levitical uncleanliness remained; and that is probably the reason why there is no indication that Jesus ever visited the town, although it lay within the radius of His Ministry and must have been a sight He saw every day from Capernaum and from the lake.

The ruin of Antipas came, however, not through his public, but through his private, life. When he was on a visit to Rome he stayed with his half-brother, Herod Philip; not Philip the Tetrarch, but another son of Herod, who had retired from the horrid tangle of ambition and was living the life of a wealthy private citizen.

Philip, following the incestuous custom of his family, had married Herodias, a grand-daughter of Herod the Great. Antipas therefore, as another son of Herod, stood in exactly the same degree of consanguinity to Herodias as Philip, her husband. She was a woman of great beauty and strong character. She had a daughter, Salome.

Antipas and Herodias decided that they were made for each other. Herodias was an ambitious woman in whose veins ran the turbulent blood of the Maccabees, and she was living the safe, boring life of a wealthy Roman matron. Such an existence was not dangerous enough for her. In

Herod Antipas she saw possibilities of unlimited excitement. He could give her power. The blood of many evil and violent ancestors urged her to betray her husband and ally herself with the Tetrarch of Galilee and Peræa. But she made her bargain! If he would swear to divorce his wife, the daughter of Aretas, King of Petra, she would marry him. Herod promised to do this and they went off together, accompanied by Salome.

This sordid little drama of passion and ambition becomes supremely interesting because of its bearing on the Gospel story. When St. John the Baptist thundered his hatred of the union and told Herod to his face that it was not lawful for him to have his brother's wife, the sly king should have seen the writing on the wall. But he did not. Herodias never forgave the Baptist. The insult rankled in her mind and she took her revenge on the bleak heights of Machærus when she, through her daughter, demanded the Baptist's head on a charger.

The story of Herodias and Antipas worked itself out in the strangest manner. The ne'er-do-well of the Herodian family was a spendthrift called Agrippa. He was the brother of Herodias, and his life was a long wandering in the wilderness of his debts, a passage from one money-lender to another. When his sister ran off with Antipas he scented, with the sure nose of the prodigal brother, a refuge, and possibly an allowance from his new brother-in-law. Antipas gave him a yearly income and made him governor of the new town of Tiberias. But one night, when Antipas had drunk too much, he told his scapegrace brother-in-law exactly what he thought of him, with the result that Agrippa removed his intriguing personality elsewhere. Like most prodigal brothers, he was very attractive and had a wife, Cypros, who adored him.

He arrived eventually in Rome, which he knew well, having been educated there in the time of Augustus. With the good luck of the true adventurer, he won the affection of Caligula and they became inseparable. When Tiberius died and Caligula became Emperor, he loaded his Jewish friend with honours and gave him not only the estates left vacant by the death of Philip the Tetrarch, but also the right to wear the diadem and to use the title of king. Therefore

Antipas and Herodias saw with bitter chagrin the homeless wanderer, the pensioner, the man who still owed them a lot of money, come strutting back to Palestine as a crowned king! Instead of rejoicing at her brother's good fortune, Herodias was consumed by jealousy. Why should this man and his wife wear crowns while she and her husband were uncrowned? Why should Agrippa be King Agrippa while her husband was merely the Tetrarch Herod?

Her anger, her envy, and her persistence were such that Antipas permitted himself to be taken to Rome to point out the injustice of it all to the mad Emperor. Agrippa, however, seeing an opportunity of getting even with his sister and the brother-in-law who had taunted him, sent a swift messenger ahead to his friend Caligula informing him that Antipas had smuggled sufficient arms into Galilee to fit out an army of seventy thousand men. When Antipas and Herodias arrived in Italy, the Emperor questioned them about the arms and, finding their answers unsatisfactory, decided to banish them both and give their possessions to the scapegrace Agrippa. So the headstrong ambition of Herodias was the ruin of Antipas.

The place of exile was to be Lyons in Gaul. Caligula, however, exempted Herodias because she was the sister of his friend. He offered her not only liberty, but all the possessions to which she could lay claim. But Herodias, with a flash of the Maccabean pride, scornfully refused to accept the favour. With a touch of grandeur, which makes one hesitate to judge her harshly in spite of all her sins, she decided to stand by her husband. Side by side, these two, the woman who slew the Forerunner and the man who had had it in his power to save the life of Jesus Christ, depart together into the mists of history.

And Agrippa inherited all their possessions. He was a good king. The crowds loved him.

So one wanders over the hill where so much emotion has been spent, and there is nothing now to mark the place where Herod schemed and where Herodias dreamed of a crown save a broken pillar half-buried in the earth and a cave or two where the jackals hide. It is difficult to believe that in this lovely place above the blue waters of Galilee envy, hatred, ambition and jealousy deformed the lives of men. How strange it is to think that, while the scented lamps burned above Herod and Herodias in the palace on the hill, a Teacher stood beside the Sea of Galilee and said:

" Out of the heart of men proceed evil thoughts, adulteries, fornications, murders, thefts, covetousness, wickedness, deceit, lasciviousness, an evil eye, blasphemy, pride, foolishness: all these evil things come from within, and defile the man."

And again the Teacher spoke, saying:

" For what is a man profited, if he shall gain the whole world and lose his own soul? "

I wonder if His eyes were turned for a moment to the white palace on the hill above Tiberias.

§ 6

I went down to the little jetty one morning and arranged to go for a day's fishing on the Sea of Galilee.

The boat was a large, clumsy affair manned by four fishermen who took it in turns to row with oars as thick as cart-shafts. There was a sail lying in the bottom of the boat, ready to go up in the unlikely event of a breeze. So we set off in burning sunlight over a still, blue lake.

About sixty men earn their living on the Sea of Galilee by following the trade of St. Peter. They are all Arabs and are mostly Moslems. The fishing nets used on the lake are of three kinds: the hand-net, or *shabakeh*; the draw-net, or *jarf*; and the floating-net or *m'batten*. The first two are the most popular. The hand-net is used all over the lake, but the draw-net is employed chiefly in the Jordan estuary at the north end.

While two of the fishermen rowed, the other two sat in the boat preparing their nets. These were circular and of very fine mesh, weighed down on the outer edge with dozens of small leaden weights. They are flung by hand and are evidently the same kind as those mentioned in the Gospels.

The disciples, when first called by Jesus, were " casting " their nets.

The youngest of the fishermen spoke quite fair English, and from him I learnt that fishing on the Lake of Galilee is not a very profitable business.

" We go out all night and catch our fish," he said, " but in the morning we get only a few piastres for them. But the merchant, he get many, many piastres. . . ."

And my mind sped northwards, far from the sunny waters of Galilee, to the cold North Sea and to the pilchard fleet of Cornwall, where so often I have heard the same grouse against the middle man; it is the eternal lay of the fisherman.

There was not a breath of wind. The sky was blue. But Abdul, the young fisherman, sniffed the air and, looking to the south, said that a storm was coming. This is, and always has been, one of the peculiarities of the Lake of Galilee. Sudden storms swoop swiftly over this low-lying sheet of water, whipping the surface of the lake with fury and covering it with waves that frequently swamp the small rowing-boats. The reason is that winds from the west passing over the highlands come swirling down through a hundred gorges and narrow valleys into the deep pit in which the lake lies. The water is smooth one moment and the next it is a raging sea in which men battle for life. Three men had recently been drowned in such a storm, said Abdul, and their bodies had not yet been recovered.

It was one of these storms that is described so vividly in the Gospels:

" And, behold, there arose a great tempest in the sea, insomuch that the ship was covered with the waves: but He was asleep.

" And His disciples came to Him, and awoke him, saying, Lord, save us: we perish.

"And He saith unto them, Why are ye fearful, O ye of little faith? Then He arose, and rebuked the winds and the sea; and there was a great calm."

How lovely it was on this hot morning, the shores receding, no sound but the creak of the huge oars, the splash of the water and the little Arab songs that one of the men would sing, softly humming a verse that would lead to a shouted chorus.

We made for the opposite bank, where the hills of Gergesa seemed even more terrible and inhospitable as we drew nearer. They looked as they must have looked in the time of Christ: thirsty, burnt-up hills scored with thousands of thin slashes, the marks of dried-up torrents, and invaded by dark gullies in which no man would venture unarmed.

How faithfully the Gospels paint the characteristics of this country. Even to-day, after a lapse of nearly two thousand years, this country of the Gergesenes is the place in which one would expect to meet a mad-man.

It was from one of those fearful precipices that the Gadarene swine stampeded into the lake. Has it ever occurred to you to wonder why swine, an unholy beast to the Jew, should have been feeding round the Sea of Galilee? Tucked away in these hills are the ruins of Greek cities which flourished in the time of Jesus, the cities of the Greek-speaking Decapolis. And they had no prejudice against pork.

We jumped ashore and clambered over the hot rocks. There were three or four Bedouin tents pitched near by. The Bedouin were poor, hungry-looking people. The whole tribe turned to look at us, staring with the uncompromising intensity of animals.

A few minutes' walk from the encampment brought us to a wild little valley in which a few strips of barley were growing. Here we saw a Bedouin crouched on the ground, eating grass.

" He is hungry," commented Abdul, " and has nothing else to eat."

" But the lake is full of fish," I said. " Why doesn't he catch some? "

This seemed to puzzle Abdul. He shrugged his shoulders. " The Bedouin do not catch fish," he said.

The sight of the man's poverty depressed me so much that I performed the usual act of a sympathetic European and gave him a shilling. But in order to buy anything with it he would have to cross the lake to Tiberias, or walk about thirty miles into the mountains!

Poor Nebuchadnezzar! He looked at the coin in his palm and thanked me; then, with the innate politeness of the desert Arab, he bent down and swiftly plucked some long blades of grass, which he pressed into my hands. It was all he had to offer.

We rowed off again and set our course for the supposed ruins of Capernaum. This town, like all the lakeside villages which were so well known to Jesus, has disappeared from the map. Many archæologists, however, believe that its site is marked by a mound of black basalt ruins lying on the eastern bank of the lake; a fine synagogue was recently discovered here and has been as far as possible rebuilt.

There is a grove of eucalyptus trees through which the synagogue shines like a small Roman temple. Many people believe that this is the ruin of the synagogue in which Jesus preached, but I think I am right in saying that the building is of a much later date, probably of the second century.

Within ten minutes by boat from Capernaum is a little bay which is said to mark the site of Bethsaida, and next to it is a squalid huddle of Arab houses called el Mejdel, the supposed site of Magdala, the town of Mary Magdalene.

We beached the boat in a desolate little bay. One of the fishermen girded his garments to the waist and waded into the lake with his nets draped over his left arm. He stood waiting, as if watching for a movement in the water. Then, with a swift over-arm motion, he cast the hand-net. It shot through the air and descended on the water like a ballet dancer's skirt when she sinks to the ground. The dozens of little lead weights carried the bell-shaped net through the water, imprisoning any fish within its area.

But time after time the net came up empty. It was a beautiful sight to see him casting. Each time the neatly folded net belled out in the air and fell so precisely on the water that the small lead weights hit the lake at the same moment, making a thin circular splash.

While he was waiting for another cast, Abdul shouted to him from the bank to fling to the left, which he instantly did. This time he was successful. He waded out and felt round with his feet. Then he drew up the net and we could see fish

struggling in it.   I was interested in this, because the fishermen were unconsciously repeating one of the most wonderful
incidents in the Gospels.

Jesus appeared to seven disciples after the Resurrection.
He stood on the shores of the lake at dawn and cried:

" Children, have ye any meat? "

They answered Him, " No."

" Cast the net on the right side of the ship, and ye shall
find," He said.

They cast as Jesus had directed and " drew the net to
land full of great fishes, an hundred and fifty and three:
and for all there were so many, yet was not the net
broken."

No one unfamiliar with the fishermen and the fishing
customs of the Lake of Galilee could have written the twenty-
first chapter of St. John's Gospel.   It happens very often that
the man with the hand-net must rely on the advice of someone on shore, who tells him to cast either to the left or right,
because in the clear water he can often see a shoal of fish
invisible to the man in the water.

Time and again these Galilean fishers are in the habit of
casting and getting nothing; but a sudden cast may fall over
a shoal and they will be forced to " draw the net to land "—
as St. John says so exactly—and their first anxiety is always
to discover if the net has been torn.

St. John, in describing the miracle, makes the amazingly
matter-of-fact statement that " yet was not the net broken."
Who but a fisherman, or one intimately acquainted with them,
would dream of mentioning this at such a moment?

The fish we caught were *musht*, or comb-fish.   This is the
characteristic fish of the Lake of Galilee.   It is a flat fish about
six inches long, with an enormous head and a comb-like spine
that stands up along its back.   It is also called St. Peter's
Fish, for legend says that it was from the mouth of this fish
that Peter took the tribute money.

I sat with a pile of these strange fish before me and remembered the incident as described by St. Matthew.   Jesus
and Peter arrived in Capernaum together after the Transfiguration on the slopes of Mount Hermon.   One of the
gatherers of the Temple Tribute came to demand payment of

the half-shekel, levied on every male Jew of religious age, which was devoted to the enormous expenses of the daily sacrifice and other offices in the Temple at Jerusalem. Jesus and Peter were evidently without money, and Jesus said to Peter:

" Go thou to the sea, and cast an hook, and take up the fish that first cometh up; and when thou hast opened his mouth, thou shalt find a piece of money: that take and give unto them for me and thee."

Just out of curiosity I opened the mouth of a *musht* and placed a ten-piastre piece inside it. This is the same size as an English two-shilling piece. The coin went in easily, for the mouth of this fish is out of all proportion to its size. The male *musht* has the peculiar habit of carrying the spawn about in his huge mouth, and when the young fish hatch they use the parent's mouth as a nursery and a place of safety in time of danger. As the young fish grow, the mouth of the parent fish becomes so distended that it is difficult to understand how he can feed himself.

But to return to the fishermen. No sooner were the fish dead than one of the men built a little fire of twigs. Another made three slashes with a knife on the backs of the fish and roasted them on the fire. Abdul ran to the boat and brought back with him two or three " loaves," or rather flat cakes of Arab bread, thin, brittle stuff like an overdone pancake.

One of the fish was taken from the fire, placed on a cake of bread and given to me. I pulled it apart with my fingers; and it was very good.

Once again, these fishermen were re-enacting one of the most solemn and beautiful episodes in the Gospel of St. John. It was in this way—the way the Galilean fishermen always eat when out fishing—that Christ, risen from the grave, commanded the seven disciples to cook the miraculous draught of fishes.

He stood on the shore in the greyness of dawn. At first they did not know Him. When He told them to cast their nets, they obeyed, thinking that He was a fellow fisherman on the bank who had seen a sudden shoal of *musht*. But when they came nearer St. John whispered: " It is the Lord."

" Now when Simon Peter heard that it was the Lord, he girt his fisher's coat unto him (for he was naked) and did cast himself into the sea. And the other disciples came in a little ship; (for they were not far from land, but as it were two hundred cubits) dragging the net with fishes. As soon then as they were come to land, they saw a fire of coals there, and fish laid thereon, and bread. Jesus saith unto them, Bring of the fish which ye have now caught."

I have seen many things in Palestine which have not changed since Bible days, but nowhere else have I met modern men acting quite unconsciously a sacred chapter of the Gospels. The fishermen of Galilee may be Arabs and Moslems, but their habits, their method of work, and the tools of their craft are the same as in the days of Peter, of Andrew and of Philip.

§ 7

I was talking to a young Air Force officer on leave from Irak. He told me that under the British flag there is a battalion of Assyrian levies which speaks Aramaic, the language that Jesus spoke. When I asked him how one of these Assyrians would say our Lord's words from the Cross he wrote down for me: " ' Alhahi, alhahi lama swkhtni.' "

" Take the last verse of the First Epistle to the Corinthians," he said. " It ends in our English Bible with ' If any man love not the Lord Jesus Christ let him be Anathema Maran-atha.' I always used to wonder what Anathema Maran-atha could mean. There should be, of course, a full stop after the word Anathema. Maran-atha is an Aramaic phrase that would be understood by the battalion in Bagdad to-day. Mar means lord, an means our, and atha means he comes; so that this word means ' Our Lord comes.' There are many other Aramaic words in the New Testament which are more or less the same as those used to-day by the Assyrians."

Books have been written to prove that the language of Jesus was Greek, and scholars have tried to prove that He spoke Hebrew. Modern research, however, seems to have established beyond any doubt that the speech which He habitually employed in His conversation with His disciples and with the people of Palestine was Aramaic. This language derives its name from Aram, the fifth son of Shem, and it was spoken in North Syria and in Mesopotamia in the most ancient times. Hebrew was the language of the Old Testament and was spoken until 586 B.C., when Judah was carried into exile. When the two tribes returned nearly fifty years later, they discovered that the northern language had invaded the south. These returned exiles took to this language but introduced into it many Hebrew words. The *Book of Ezra* and the *Book of Daniel* are written to a great extent in this patchwork tongue. In the time of our Lord it seems that Aramaic had become the vernacular language of the whole country. Hebrew was, so far as the common people were concerned, a dead tongue. It was the language of students and rabbis. So little was Hebrew understood in the age of Christ that interpreters had to translate from Hebrew into Aramaic the Scripture read during the synagogue services.

The New Testament contains a number of Aramaic words and phrases. The cry of Jesus from the Cross is, of course, known to everyone. When Jesus had raised the daughter of Jairus He said " Talitha cumi " (translated in our Bible as " Damsel, I say unto thee, arise "), which Dr. James Moffatt in his new translation renders as " Little girl, I am telling you to rise." The word " cumi " is still regularly used by the Arabs to-day for " get up." During the Agony in the Garden of Gethsemane, Jesus prayed, saying " Abba, Father, all things are possible unto thee." In this instance the translation is given after the Aramaic word " Abba." An Aramaic word that we use every day is " mammon," which occurs four times in the New Testament and was the common Aramaic term for riches. Other Aramaic words employed in the Gospels are Gabbatha (the name for the pavement in Pilate's Judgment Hall), Raca (a term of contempt), and Golgotha, the name of the place where Jesus was crucified. The word Golgotha is a Greek transliteration of the Aramaic *Gulgŭlta*. The

Hebrew is *Gulgóleth.* This means " the place of a skull."
The Latin equivalent, *calvaria,* gives us Calvary.

When the Rabbis taught in the schools, or when they
gathered under the porches of the first court in the Temple
at Jerusalem, the language they spoke was the literary Hebrew.
No doubt Jesus was familiar with it. When He disputed with
the elders in the Temple His arguments were probably spoken
in Hebrew, but afterwards, when explaining His absence to
His parents, He would have pronounced His immortal " Wist
ye not that I must be about my Father's business " in Aramaic.

Greek and Latin were the other two languages spoken at
this time. Latin was the hated official language, the speech
of the officers, the Roman troops, and the detested tax-
collectors. The Jews never spoke it, and the very sound of it
reminded them of their bondage to Rome. Greek, on the
other hand, occupied quite a different place in their life.

Palestine is to-day surrounded by the ruins of Greek cities.
In the time of Christ these were thriving communities. Since
the time of Alexander the Great the Greek language had been
making its way, loathed by the Orthodox Jews and cultivated
by the modern, liberal-minded Jews who were susceptible to
the Hellenistic movement that at one time threatened to wreck
Orthodoxy. Outside Palestine, of course, the enormous
Jewish settlements, such as that in Alexandria, had adopted
Greek as their common speech. The Old Testament appeared
in Greek and was thus available to the cultured world nearly
three hundred years before Christ was born. Jews outside
Palestine had to speak Greek in order to exist. In Palestine,
however, one point of view was clearly expressed by a passage
in the Talmud: " he who teaches his son Greek is accursed
like him who keeps pigs "; but the cosmopolitan people,
such as the Herods and their courtiers, revelled not only in
the Greek language but in Greek art and philosophy.

Did Jesus speak Greek? It has often been argued that He
did. St. Mark tells us that a Syro-Phœnician woman came
to Him. " The woman was a Greek," says St. Mark, " a
Syrophenician by nation; and she besought him that he
would cast forth the devil out of her daughter."

But it might just as well be argued that the conversation took place in Aramaic. Again, it has been sug-

gested that Jesus and Pilate spoke in Greek. But surely it is quite as reasonable to expect that Pilate had an interpreter? Forty years later, when Titus wanted to call on Jerusalem to surrender, he used the historian Josephus as interpreter and sent him to shout out in Aramaic the Roman terms to the defenders of the wall.

It is an interesting thing that Hebrew, which has not been used as the vernacular speech in Palestine since the Israelites were carried into captivity, is to-day heard all over Palestine in the Zionist settlements. The revival of a liturgical language for every-day use is a remarkable thing and, to me, more wonderful than any of the materialistic achievements of the Zionists. To hear a couple of Jews from Roumania talking Hebrew is as remarkable as it would be to hear two Italians gossiping in Latin. I do not know enough about it to be able to say whether the language of the Old Testament is sufficiently flexible for use in the modern world : all I can say is that the Zionists I have heard appear quite fluent.

§ 8

There are only one or two places in which one can stay on the shores of Galilee. I believe it is possible to stay with the Fathers of the Holy Land, who have a small monastery and guest house at Tel Hum, the site of Capernaum. There is an Italian hospice on a hill not far off. But the most beautiful spot on the shore—I caught a glimpse of it when I was with the fishermen—is a bower of trees and flowers known as Tabgha. Trailing masses of bougainvillea, flowering shrubs, eucalyptus trees and palms grow by the water-side, and in the centre of this paradise is a little villa which belongs to the German Catholic Committee of Palestine. There Father Täpper welcomes strangers to Galilee.

I decided to go there for a few days.

Ruins of Synagogue, Capernaum

Entrance to "The Street Called Straight"

CHAPTER SEVEN

I stay in a garden by the Sea of Galilee, discover the ruined church of the Loaves and Fishes, try to reconstruct the life of the lake-side as Jesus knew it, visit all that remains of Capernaum and the desolation that is now Bethsaida.

§ 1

THERE is a state of mind for which there is, so far as I know, no name. It is not happiness, which is an active appreciation of things, neither is it contentment, which is placid and might be termed the evening of happiness. The only words I can think of are both so worn-out, debased and generally ill-used that they will probably make you smile. One is " well-being " and the other is our old friend, " love."

Everyone can, I hope, remember a time in childhood when this state of mind lasted not for seconds but for days and weeks on end. Sometimes by an effort of the imagination one attempts to project oneself back into those shining moments of life when the mind, untarnished by sin and undaunted by Eternity, lived as the butterfly lives, searching for, and finding, only sweetness everywhere.

In those days the earth and the flowers smelt more richly and the sun seemed brighter than it is to-day; the rain, the snow and the mist were enchantments, and we were unconsciously a part of the visible beauties which surrounded us. Life is to most of us a gradual growing-away from this enchantment. But amid the million trials and difficulties of life that can harden and embitter it is possible now and again to re-capture fractional seconds of this earlier world : so momentary are they that one is left wondering whether they ever happened, or whether they may be a stray memory of some other existence.

When I awakened in Tabgha on the first morning and looked at the Sea of Galilee, I felt such an unutterable sense of peace and so great a detachment from the world that I

might have been Adam gazing with wonder at the Garden
of Eden. My room was set in a tropical jungle of trees.
Huge sweet flowers, whose name I do not know, climbed over
the little iron balcony and twisted themselves round the
windows. Although the sun had only just risen, the blossoms
shook with the weight of bees; and down below the blue lake
was calm in the first light of the sun. It was so still, so silent,
so lovely.

I remembered my arrival on the previous evening. Father
Täpper, a big square-bearded Rhinelander, wearing a white
sun helmet and a priestly suit of black with an alpaca jacket,
came striding forward with a great crunching of feet over the
path of white lake pebbles. Above his head were bowers of
hibiscus blossoms; behind him shone and glowed his incredible
garden.

" Ah, you have come, my friend! " he cried, placing a great
hand on my shoulder, and I looked at his blue eyes, his apple-
pink cheeks, his square, brown beard and his broad shoulders,
and thought that the Crusaders must have looked just like
Father Täpper. " Let us talk."

We went into a room where the blinds were down against
the heat, where doors and windows were blue with mosquito
netting. As Father Täpper lit his pipe, I noticed his large,
brown gardener's hands. The garden in which the Tabgha
Hospice stands is the only patch of cultivated beauty round the
Sea of Galilee. From Tiberias it looks like a little dark spot
on the lake-side, but when you are there the palm trees, the
eucalyptus wood, the walls of purple bougainvillea, the lemon
and the orange trees, the carnations, the geraniums, the
Persian lilac, the nasturtiums and the banks of hibiscus flowers,
form a little world of their own, a sanctuary made more
precious by the bleak, bare hills and the wilderness that lie
all round. This garden overflowing with flowers, musical
with water, is the only spot round the shores of Galilee in
which it is possible to dream for a little of the once luxuriant
glory that ringed the western shore in ancient times. The
lake as Jesus knew it must have been something like Tabgha.

Father Täpper and his predecessors have, like good Rhine-
landers, tried to bring to the shores of the Sea of Galilee a little
turreted castle copied from those that stand on the headlands

from St. Goar to Mannheim. But the lake of Galilee said
" No ! " And the flowers have flung their richness over the
walls and the creepers have climbed them like a storming
party, so that it is only from a certain place in the garden that
you can still detect beneath the coloured bowers the crenellated
outline of a little toy castle.

We talked until the sun had almost set. We spoke of Jesus,
of Bethsaida (which many people think is Tabgha), of Capernaum, of Magdala, where Mary Magdalene was born, of
Peter, of Andrew and of Philip; and of the customs house
where Matthew once took toll of the lakeside traffic. Father
Täpper's pipe went out. He drew his chair a bit nearer.
Above the long square beard the blue eyes of a German boy of
about ten years of age gazed at me, wide with enthusiasm as
he described his gardening and the strange things that a
gardener finds under the soil on the shores of the Sea of
Galilee. Not long since he and his Bedouin had been digging
on the property near the lake-side and suddenly—Ach
wunderbar !—they saw in the brown earth a gleam of blue and
then a flash of gold and then a touch of green.

Then they flung down their spades and worked with their
bare hands so that nothing should be hurt, for they had
discovered the long lost mosaic pavement of the little Roman
church of the Loaves and Fishes. It had been lost since
Aetheria of Aquitaine came to pray in Galilee in the year
386, and now there it was with the sunlight shining on it once
again. And when they went on scraping and digging they
found the stone on which legend says our Lord blessed the
bread and the fish. It had been used as an altar and lay there
under the soil poised on four little Roman pillars. . . .

" I will take you there," said Father Täpper, " and you shall
see. It is covered with sand and soil to keep the sun from
hurting it, but someday I wish to build a roof over it and make
it safe for ever."

Now I stood in the stillness of the morning looking down on
the garden. The sun, rising from behind the Gergesene Hills,
was climbing into the cloudless sky, and the garden was a network of sunlight and shade and full of the little early morning

noises, the squeakings, the rustlings, the sound of wings, the
cooing of pigeons and, from a fountain buried under trailing
flowers, the falling of water.

The years fell shivering away from me and I was at that
moment a small boy again, up and awake before anyone,
looking out on the lovely world. I seemed to be a part of it
and it seemed to be a part of me. The blue kingfisher,
balancing himself on the very top of a fir tree, had come to
say good-morning to me, and the little black lizard on the path
who, seeing me move, had stopped dead in his tracks with his
head lifted, he also, sharing this moment, shared fellowship.
The same joy in life that used to send me running over the
meadows at sun-rise, that would draw me to the corner of
woods where the rabbits played, and to the edge of streams
where the trout lay, drove me now to feel and to touch the
morning, and to hold it in my arms. I flung a towel over
my shoulder and went down the garden to a path cut
through rocks at the edge of the lake. It ran south into a
dark wood of eucalyptus trees that melted into the broad
deserted Plain of Gennesaret.

There was not a soul to be seen. At the edge of the wood
a stream of fresh water flowed from a pool overhung by
precipitous crags. The pool was very still and deep. I flattened myself against a tree trunk and watched two kingfishers
diving. They flew in circles over the pool and would suddenly begin to flutter in the air, at the same time pointing
their long beaks towards the water until they looked like poised
darts. Then they would drop like stones. They would touch
the water swiftly and lightly and rise again; and, as they
wheeled, the sun would shine a moment on the little silver
fish in their beaks. The stones were covered with water
tortoises. They looked like mud puddings, some dark from
the water, others light and sun-dried. When I moved, they
slid softly from their rocks into the pool.

The edge of the wood near the lake was a narrow half-moon
of shingle. I stepped from my clothes and walked into the
Sea of Galilee. The water was painfully cold, but I liked it.
The stones underfoot were hard, but I did not mind them. I
walked on and on into the shallow water. The sun was warm
on my body but my knees were in ice. Soon it was deep

enough to swim.   I hugged myself in cowardice for a moment
and then went in.   The water was no longer cold and I
struck out towards the Gergesene hills, which rose up from the
lake with the morning shadows dark and clear on their sides.
I swam back slowly.   To the left I could see the shore curving
south to Tiberias.   I could see the little cluster of white boxes
that was the town.   In front of me was the green Plain of
Genesaret and the dark belt of the eucalyptus trees.   The
sensuous, satisfying touch of the water, the beautiful blue
water, was ecstasy on this enchanted morning.   I heard a
clapping in the air and, lying on my back, watched the flock
of white pigeons from Tabgha wheeling against the sky.   And
there was a little silver moon that I had not noticed until
then, lying on its back against the blue.

I ran back to Tabgha.   And there was honey for breakfast.

§ 2

I went with Father Täpper to see the ruins of the Church
of the Loaves and Fishes.   It is only five minutes' walk from
the hospice.

No one knows when this church was built.   It was probably
erected in late Roman times and rebuilt.   All that is left is
the pavement and the stumps of a few pillars.   The old
Bedouin who guards the precious relic took up a broom and
swept away the covering of earth, and with each sweep
exquisite little pictures flashed into the sunlight.   The floor
was formed of small, delicately tinted mosaics in which
blue and green predominated.   The artist, whoever he
was, knew and loved the bird life of the Sea of Galilee and
rendered it in his little coloured stones in a most affectionate
way.   The pavement is divided into a number of squares
about the size of an average carpet, and each square is a design
of decorative birds and animals, but so lovingly done, and with
a sly sense of humour too, that one can imagine the creator
of this pavement hiding in the lakeside reeds, smiling to himself as he watched the often absurd movements of ducks and
cranes and the self-assured twittering little birds that hung
to the rushes.

I liked his picture of an extraordinarily smug goose pulling a lotus flower. There was another spirited picture, a fight between a heron and a serpent. There were also plump quail. And I admired the astonishing skill he showed in capturing, in what one would imagine to be an intractable material, that sudden moment when a water-fowl stands up in the water and flaps its wings once or twice, like a man yawning and stretching his arms. It is just a flash, and is gone. But this man who centuries ago watched the water-fowl on the Sea of Galilee has managed to pin down this moment in his little tinted stones, for among his triumphs is a bird rather like a crane that is about to flap and stretch, chest out, tail up, and one wing just slightly higher than the other.

The only four-legged animal in the designs of this great but unknown artist is a funny little fellow rather like a rabbit. There is a red ribbon round his neck. I like to think that this was the artist's pet, for a man who observed Nature so accurately and so humorously must have loved animals. I also like to think that he put this little creature into his design in the confident hope that it would please God.

The central theme of the mosaic is a basket containing loaves of bread on each side of which is a fish.

There was something appealing about this pavement because, I suppose, unlike the usual relics of antiquity, a broken pillar or the plinth of a column, it had come out of its grave with a message that conquered time and language. If a voice had suddenly spoken to us from the earth, saying, " I think the wild duck on the lake are very amusing, don't you? Have you noticed how they turn upside down? And have you observed their expressions when they bob up again? Then the fatness of quails and the thinness of storks, how amusing they are! "—if, as I say, a voice had spoken to us in those words, we could not have felt nearer to the artist.

The Miracle of the Feeding of the Five Thousand did not, of course, take place on this side of the lake at all, but the little church must have been a memorial to it.

Standing on the shores of the Sea of Galilee, it is easy to visualise the details of this miracle. News had just been brought to Jesus that Herod Antipas had murdered John the Baptist in order to gratify the injured vanity of Herodias.

Our Lord is advised, or perhaps He considers it wise, to with-draw from the territory of Antipas. In order to do so it was necessary only to cross the lake, for the desert mountains of the eastern shore were in the tetrarchy of Philip. Accordingly, says St. Matthew, " he departed thence by ship into a desert place apart." In other words, He crossed over to the deserted eastern banks of the lake.

Now, while the little boat was crossing the six or seven miles of water, a great multitude carrying their sick with them " followed him on foot out of the cities." When you know the shape of the Sea of Galilee, this incident becomes very vivid. Evidently the crowds had converged, as usual, on Capernaum, but when they discovered that the Master had gone, they looked over the water to follow the direction of His boat. They saw with joy that He was going only to the opposite shore, probably to the little fishing port of Bethsaida Julias at the inlet of the Jordan. This meant that if they lost no time and, racing round the northern end of the lake, waded over the shallow Jordan, they would reach Bethsaida Julias almost as soon as Jesus. We can therefore place the Miracle of the Feeding of the Five Thousand more or less accurately as happening on the brown hills nearly opposite Capernaum, for if Jesus had taken a southerly course down the lake the multitudes could not have caught up with Him on foot, and in fact would not have attempted to do so.

As Jesus crossed the water He would see this great race of over five thousand round the north end of the lake, and He would know that whatever thoughts He may have had, of pray-ing in a desert place apart and of meditation on the death of the Forerunner, were fated to be given up in service to the crowds. No sooner had He landed than the crowds came to Him, and we learn that He " was moved with compassion toward them, because they were as sheep not having a shepherd."

With the approach of sunset and the swift coming of night the disciples became anxious for the multitude, hungry and in a desert place. They advised Jesus to disband them and send them home.

" Give ye them to eat," answered Jesus.

They returned to say that only five loaves and two fishes

could be found. St. John, whose account of the miracle is remarkable and detailed, says that the loaves and fishes belonged to a boy. The exact words are: " There is a lad here, which hath five barley loaves, and two small fishes: but what are they among so many? "

Commentators have imagined that this lad was one of the bread boys who are still to be seen in Arab towns, sometimes with strips of dried fish which they sell with the bread.

" And Jesus took the loaves ; and when he had given thanks, he distributed to the disciples, and the disciples to them that were set down ; and likewise of the fishes as much as they would. When they were filled, he said unto his disciples, gather up the fragments that remain, that nothing be lost."

There is one point in St. John's account of the miracle which is extremely interesting. In describing the fish eaten on this occasion he uses the Greek word *opsarion*, which our translators render as " small fish." St. John is the only evangelist to use this word, and the real meaning is not " small fish " but " a savoury dish " or, as we might say, hors d'œuvres. This is exactly what the small pickled fish of Galilee were in the time of Christ.

This is a wonderful instance of the vivid local colour which has been detected in the Fourth Gospel, because no one unacquainted with the life and speech of Galilee could have employed this word.

Again, so it seems to me, St. John conclusively proves his Galilean origin in his account of our Lord's appearance to the disciples in the dawn, when they are fishing near the shore. Who except a fisherman would have worried about the condition of his net at such a moment? The Master who had been crucified was standing in the greyness of the dawn, calling to them from the shore, but St. John says that when they drew the great haul of fish to land " yet was not the net broken."

It would never occur to a man of any other occupation, and certainly never to a student writing in a study, to note such a detail. But the Galilean fisherman who nets a heavy catch is always anxious about the net, because the bottom of the lake is covered with sharp stones for perhaps twenty or thirty feet before the sand begins. What a shouting goes up to-day as a heavy net is drawn out of the deep water towards the sharp stones, with what care the fishermen run thigh-deep into the lake to lift the precious burden clear of rocks!

In revealing details like this, and in the use of the word *opsarion*, St. John proclaims his origin. If one came across the word " smokie " or " ling " used as St. John uses the word *opsarion*, one would have very good reason to conclude that the writer was a Scot.

I have tried not to bore the reader with the learned scholastic battles that are waged round the Gospels, but I would like to suggest that, while it is perfectly simple to sit in a study and argue about Matthew, Mark and Luke, no man ought to presume to write about John until he has lived for some time in Galilee.

§ 3

I awakened at sunrise. The feathery pink clouds high in the sky above the Gergesene Hills, and the great fan of light that rayed downwards on the water, were so lovely that I flung on my dressing-gown and ran through the garden with a camera. I might with luck capture something of that beautiful dawn over Galilee before it passed away. And the photograph is included in this book.

If you look carefully at it, or take a magnifying-glass, you will see almost in the middle a little black dot that is a rowing-boat. I did not notice it at the time. However, as I sat on the stones beside the lake watching the clouds melt away before the sun, the boat drew nearer, and I began to wonder what it was doing on the lake at that early hour. It was not one of the large fishing-boats: it looked like Father Täpper's dinghy. Suddenly I heard through the still morning air a remarkable sound. It was the noise of a typewriter.

I can conceive no time and place where the sound of a type-writer is more surprising than at sunrise on the Sea of Galilee. The boat was too far from land for me to distinguish those inside it, and it went off, keeping well in the middle of the lake, towards Magdala. But there was no mistaking that

H

familiar tap, tap-tap, tap-tap-tap-tap over the stillness of the morning sea.

I went back up the stone water-steps into the garden, and through an arch heavy with hibiscus blossoms I saw Father Täpper on his way to say Mass in the little chapel.

While I was dressing I began to worry about the typewriter. It seemed too improbable. Could I have been mistaken? For a moment I wondered whether the sun had affected me. Many people are suddenly knocked out by sun-stroke in Palestine. I began to think of the sound of that tap-tapping with an almost superstitious fear. An ordinary typewriter is bad enough, but the idea of a supernatural typewriter makes the blood run cold.

I meant to ask Father Täpper at breakfast whether any of his guests had taken the dinghy out in the early morning; but he was not there, and the red-bearded Lazarite Father was almost sure that the boat had not gone out. This Father, who is a scientific archæologist and very positive, and nearly always right, filled me with the gloomiest forebodings. Perhaps the boat as well as the typewriter had been a phantom!

Later in the morning, when I was writing on the little balcony that runs round my room, I heard it again. A typewriter! It was loud and fluent. I leapt up and ran to the railings. Down below me, sitting at a little table which he had brought out from the lounge, was a tall, thin, middle-aged man. He was dressed in a grey tweed suit and, although it was blazing hot, he had made no concessions: he was wearing a stiff white collar and a buttoned-up coat. His fingers travelled rapidly over the keys and he was intent and lost in the web of his words. I began to eliminate his possibilities. He might be one of the distinguished, elderly correspondents who sometimes represent *The Times*, though I had never seen one in a sufficiently urgent state of mind to get up with the dawn and go on writing in a garden full of flies. He might be a novelist, because novelists do the strangest things. What is known as inspiration might suddenly have fallen upon him. Yet he did not look like a novelist. If this had happened in Scotland I would have said that he was a commercial traveller trying to catch the daily post with his urgent orders. But it was the Sea of Galilee.

Pausing a moment for a word, he caught sight of my fascinated face on the balcony:

" I hope I'm not disturbing you," he said, " if I am, I'll . . ."

" On the contrary, you've relieved my mind."

He gave me a shy smile.

" May I ask if you are writing a book ? " I said.

" Oh no," he replied, and gave a deprecating little laugh. " Nothing like that. I'm writing to my wife."

One learns never to be surprised when one travels, but this man did surprise me.

" Were you writing to your wife," I asked, " as the sun was rising this morning ? "

" Oh, you saw me ? "

" No, I heard you, quite clearly."

" Yes, it was all part of the same letter," he said.

" If it won't interrupt you too much, I'd like to come down and talk to you."

He gave me a friendly smile, and I ran down the stairs and went over to him. He was, as I say, tall and thin, with a white moustache and spectacles. There was a pile of typed manuscript on his little table, about five thousand words. He saw me glance at it, fascinated.

" That's my next letter," he said. " I shall post it when I get back to Jerusalem."

And they say that the age of letter-writing is dead !

" You see," he explained, " I come from Australia. All my life I have longed to travel. All my life ! And my wife has let me take a trip round the world. I shall be away nearly a year. So, you see, I feel that the least I can do is to write to her every day. But I like to write to her when I'm actually doing something, if you see what I mean, so that she can feel that she is with me. For instance, I wrote her a letter from the top of the Great Pyramid when I was in Egypt. I typed her another from the top of the Leaning Tower of Pisa. It makes it more vivid and real."

He took up a page of typescript:

" Now this morning I begin, ' I am writing to you from a boat on the Sea of Galilee, and it is nearly five A.M. The sun has just risen and we are rowing slowly along ' . . . you see the idea ? "

My first feeling of amusement melted into a warmth of friendliness for him. His disarming smile and his tremendous enthusiasm were attractive and unusual in a man of his age.

" It's hot out here," he said. " Would you like to come to my room and have a chat? I love talking to people. It gives me more to write about too."

He led the way under the hibiscus-covered archway near the little chapel. Father Täpper had made up a bed for him in a kind of ground-floor vault known as " the museum." His shaving-stick and razor were standing among fragments from the excavation of the ancient Church of the Loaves and Fishes. His suit-case was propped up on a couple of broken Roman columns, and he could not unpack because of the litter of Roman and Greek glass and pottery, coins, handles of amphoræ and fragments of Byzantine mosaic by which he was surrounded.

" Rather unique ! " he smiled.

" Tell me," I said, " are you disappointed in travel? Is the world as wonderful as you thought it would be ? "

" I know what you mean," he said, looking grave. " No; I'm not disappointed. I think the world is wonderful."

Again he gave me that charming, shy smile.

" I think you're rather wonderful," I told him, " because you have set out in middle age with all the fire of youth in you. If I might make a frightful pun, you seem to have escaped the hardening of the hearteries."

" Well, it's just the way one looks at things. . . . But I've had some wonderful experiences. Would it bore you? I have ! Wonderful ! I was received by the Pope. There were a lot of other people there, too, of course ! I don't want you to think that His Holiness saw me alone, or anything like that. I knelt there with my hand full of rosaries and as he passed he blessed them, and, although I'm a Protestant and teach in Sunday school, I said, as he passed, ' God bless you '—just like that ! And do you know why I said it ? So that I could write and tell my wife that I had spoken to the Pope."

A gleam of happiness and triumph came into his eyes.

" I make it a point," he went on, " of swimming in every famous river and lake. I have swum in the Thames, the

Seine, the Moskva at Moscow, the Tiber, the Abana at Damascus, and in the Dead Sea and the Sea of Galilee. I nearly got arrested in Rome for swimming in the Tiber. The current is very strong, but I only went in and out, just long enough to fill my bottle."

" I don't understand."

" You see, I am taking back with me to Australia little bottles containing the waters of all the famous rivers and lakes. They'll think a lot of them at home. Here they are in my suit-case. Looks like a chemist's shop, doesn't it? And those stones. Do you know where they came from? From the river-bed where David slew Goliath."

We talked on into the hot afternoon, or rather he talked and I sat admiring his zest for life. Everything was, to him, exciting and superlative. " I am always ready for adventures," he said. Genuine enthusiasm carries with it an entirely spurious atmosphere of originality. Yet is that true? The man was really blazing a trail through all the well-worn paths of the world: he was blazing it through the terrific jungle of his own enthusiasm. I admired him because he was so genuinely in love with the world. He had absolutely no shred of cynicism.

" There's one thing I would appreciate," he said. " I'd love you to take a photograph of me bathing in the Sea of Galilee."

" I'll do it with pleasure."

" Well, let me find my bathing-suit. Here we are and— here's my camera! "

He strode off into the blazing sun, bare-headed, but with his tweed coat still buttoned. He undressed behind a clump of eucalyptus trees, and when he was reclining in the Sea of Galilee, with the happy expression of a boy of ten, I waded in and snapped the shutter.

" Thank you," he said. " That will be immensely appreciated at home! Are you sure you've wound the film? "

§ 4

It surprises me that people should express astonishment, as they do, that nothing at all is left of Roman Galilee. They

have evidently never seen a touring car half an hour after it
has fallen over a cliff near a remote Arab village. I have.
There was hardly enough left of it to make an alarm clock!
There is something so savage in the lust for loot, and something
so primitive in the capacity for destruction, that in this
happily uncommon spectacle one seems to be observing the
history of the land.

In the time of Jesus the Sea of Galilee was one of the busiest
centres of life in the country, and the western shore was ringed
with towns and villages. The ruler of the province had his
palace on the hill above Tiberias. The lake was crowded
with ships.

One has always imagined that Jesus preached His Gospel
to simple country-folk in a remote part of Palestine where
no whisper of the outside world ever interrupted the immortal
current of His thought. In actual fact His Ministry was
conducted not only in the most cosmopolitan region in the
country, but also in a territory where the ancient trade routes
from Tyre and Sidon on the west, and the old caravan roads
from Damascus on the north-east, as well as the great imperial
highways, met together and branched out over the country.
Galilee was on the main road of the ancient world, a half-way
house between Damascus and the Egyptian frontier, on one
hand, and between Antioch and Jerusalem on the other.

It was also a busy agricultural and industrial district.
The hills round the lake, now so desolate, were planted with
palms, olives, figs and vines. The fruits grown round the Sea
of Galilee were famous in biblical times. The trades carried
on round the lake were boat-building, dyeing (at Magdala),
pottery works and fish curing. The large curing factory was
at Tarichæa—the " pickling place "—to the south of the lake,
where fish were salted and packed for export.

There was always a big market for salt fish in Jerusalem.
In Old Testament times the fish trade seems to have been in
the hands of the Tyrians and the Egyptians. The " Fish
Gate " of ancient Jerusalem, round which the fish market was
held, lay near the northern gate, the natural entrance from
Tyre. It seems fairly certain, however, that about fifty years
before the time of Christ the Greeks broke this monopoly by
introducing the fish-curing industry to the Sea of Galilee.

Pliny says that in his time the pickling place at Tarichæa gave its name to the whole lake, which suggests that the industry must have been at first a Greek enterprise. The trade must have expanded enormously, for we know that barrels of these cured fish were carried all over the Mediterranean world and that enormous quantities were sent to Jerusalem every spring for the Passover crowds on pilgrimage to the Temple. A Franciscan friar in Jerusalem told me a very curious legend about the Galilean fish trade. I paid little attention to it at the time, considering it to be merely one of the hundreds of ingenious theories that the traveller hears and forgets.

There is in one of the back streets of Jerusalem a dark little hovel, now, I believe, an Arab coffee-house, which contains stones and arches that were once part of an early Christian church. The Franciscan tradition is that this church was erected on the site of a house which had belonged to Zebedee, the father of St. John. This family, said the Franciscan, were fish merchants of Galilee, with a branch office in Jerusalem from which they used to supply, among others, the family of Caiaphas, the High Priest. Therefore, he said, this explains the otherwise mysterious reference in St. John's Gospel to the fact that he, St. John (who refers to himself anonymously as " that other disciple "), gained admission to the house of the High Priest after the arrest of Jesus *because he was known to the door-keeper.*

When one realises that disciples like St. John belonged, no doubt, to prosperous trading families with points of contact in the capital, this tradition does not seem so extravagant. How otherwise, in fact, could the son of Zebedee, from Galilee, be known to the door-keeper of the house of the most important man in Jerusalem? He might have been related, of course, but surely a much more likely explanation is that he was well known as a prominent local tradesman. If his father had a fish shop in Jerusalem, it is not extravagant to assume that he was known as the man who sometimes delivered the fish. If St. John worked in this way in Jerusalem, it helps to explain two of the most interesting characteristics of his Gospel: the detailed topographical knowledge both of his native Galilee and of Jerusalem.

I have already written of his intimate knowledge of fishing
habits on the lake.   But he is also quite at home in Jerusalem.
He knows that the Kedron is a torrent that can be crossed on
foot only in the dry season.   He alone of the Evangelists
mentions the name Gabbatha, the pavement in the Prætorium.   He alone tells us that the multitude, acclaiming Christ
as the Messiah, took branches of the *palm* trees that grew on
the Mount of Olives.   It is in these vivid touches that St.
John proves that he was a native of Galilee who was intimately
acquainted with Jerusalem.

In attempting to reconstruct the busy life of the Sea of
Galilee as Jesus saw it, we must also remember that the hills,
now so stark and bare, were at that time covered with trees.
An intricate system of aqueducts, whose ruins are to be seen
here and there (notably in some rocks at the back of the
hospice at Tabgha), carried streams of fresh water wherever
they were required.   The climate must have been less
fever-ridden than it is to-day.   Possibly the wooded hills
attracted a greater rainfall and also tempered the heat.
One must think of this beautiful blue lake barred by a
rampart of brown barren hills to the east, and ringed on
the western shore with an almost unbroken chain of little
towns lying at the foot of green hills thick with woods, bright
with gardens, and loud with the music of running water.
There would be the docks and harbour of Tarichæa, the
long rows of sheds, the sound of hammers as the coopers
barrelled the fish, the noise of shipbuilders—possibly at
Capernaum—the smoke and smell of the dye-works at Magdala, and the pottery kilns.   On the hill behind the regal city
of Tiberias rose the magnificent Herodian palace whose Greek
sculptures shone in the sun from afar: well-built town walls
met the lake-water and enclosed streets, villas, theatres, and
an amphitheatre where Greeks, Romans and Sadducees applauded touring companies from Antioch, or watched
gladiators whose names were famous throughout the
Decapolis.

The lake as Jesus knew it must have been one of the busiest
and most cosmopolitan districts of Palestine.   Greek, Latin,
and Aramaic were spoken in its towns.   Its people were
immersed in the affairs of the moment, and were, in fact, a

part of that vivid, variegated world balanced between the East and the West: the world of the Gospels and the Early Church.

When Jesus walked the roads of Galilee He met the long caravans working southward across the fords of Jordan; He saw the sun gleam on the spears of Roman maniples and cohorts; He met bands of Phœnician merchants travelling into Galilee; encountered the litters and chariots of the great, and saw the bands of strolling players and jugglers and gladiators bound for the gay Greek cities of the Decapolis.

The shadow of this world falls across the pages of the New Testament. Jesus, walking the roads of Galilee, is walking the modern world, with its money-changers and its tax-collectors, its market-places and its unhappy rich men. When we think of Him beside the Sea of Galilee, we must not imagine Him as retired from the world, preaching His Gospel to a few faithful, simple souls: we must realise that He had chosen to live among people of many nations and upon one of the main highways of the Roman Empire.

§ 5

I took the boat one morning and rowed among the lonely little bays to the north of Tabgha. It was a perfect day and I had not seen the lake a deeper blue. The bare hills rose from the water to lie in gentle curves against the sky. Piles of black basalt lay everywhere, on the hills and at the water's edge, and so characteristic is this volcanic stone that even the lizards have coloured themselves in imitation of it. In the curve of a small bay a white temple hides itself among hedges and eucalyptus trees. There are four columns up-holding a broken architrave, a paved court in which the grass grows, a doorway that leads nowhere, and the usual chaos of broken pillars and fallen stones. Most scholars now agree that this is all that is left of Capernaum.

I tied up the boat and, walking through the garden of the Franciscan friars, who have their dwelling near by, wandered among the tumbled stones. The temple is the ruin of Capernaum's synagogue. Some experts say that it is the very building in which Jesus preached and performed His miracles; others say that it is not actually the building, but one erected much later on the same spot. But does it matter? It was here that Jesus Christ lived during the two or three most important years in the world's history. Somewhere among the piles of black basalt that scatter the hillocks is the site of Peter's house, where our Lord lived; somewhere on the little curve of shore is the very spot where " he saw Simon and Andrew, his brother, casting a net into the sea: for they were fishers. And Jesus said unto them, ' Come ye after me and I will make you to become fishers of men.' " A little further along the shore is the place where James and John, the sons of Zebedee, left their father in the boat with the hired servants in order to follow the Master. Perhaps on this very spot, deserted now except by the little black lizards that run among the stones, Jesus expelled the unclean spirit and healed the man with a withered hand. If not from this bay, from one exactly like it, Jesus put out in a little boat and spoke to the multitudes that were gathered on the shore.

This white ruin among the eucalyptus grove is, I think, one of the most touching links with our Lord's Ministry to be seen in the Holy Land. The Franciscan friars, who guard each stone with love and reverence, have left untouched this white ruin facing the lake, so that one can sit there and know that Jesus, when He stood there, looked across the blue water to the parched hills of " the desert place " opposite, and saw, to the south, the lake stretching into a heat haze that gives an illusion of the sea.

The synagogue must have been one of the most beautiful in Galilee and the frequency with which it occurs in the Gospel story suggests that it was possibly the most important one on the lakeside. Perhaps the Bedouin strain in the Jews explains why they never developed an architecture of their own. Even their chief building, the Temple in Jerusalem, was a modification, first of Phœnician and, later, of Greek architecture. And this temple by the lake is plainly Roman. That is one reason why many learned scholars have suggested that it was built in the time of Christ by the Good Centurion of Capernaum. You remember how St. Luke tells that when the centurion's servant fell ill the elders of the

Jews went to Jesus, saying that the Centurion was worthy of
help because "he loveth our nation and hath built us a
synagogue."

It is generally assumed that the Centurion of Capernaum
was a Roman. But why should the Romans have placed
troops in the territory of Herod Antipas? Surely it is more
likely that he was a Gentile soldier in the army of Antipas,
whose headquarters were probably at Tiberias, a little lower
down the lake? But whether he were Roman or not,
surely no centurion would justify the description of "wealthy"
and "influential" which several writers apply to him. I
am afraid we have the habit of promoting centurions to a
grandeur which they did not possess. In reality, a centurion
was merely a non-commissioned officer in command of a
hundred men and he was invariably promoted from the ranks.
There were sixty centurions in a legion and, although they
were the backbone of the Roman army, they were not, by
any means, rich men, and only the *primus pilus*, or chief
centurion, was an officer of any consequence. Juvenal in one
of his satires tells us that the centurions were laughed at (in
the same good-natured way that we laugh at a policeman's
feet) on account of their stocky calves and their hob-nailed
shoes and their general air of toughness. It is surprising to
me that so many brilliant scholars should have considered for
a moment that a man of such rank could have afforded to
erect an expensive building like the synagogue of Capernaum.
What he probably did do, I humbly suggest, was to put
a room at the disposal of some of his Jewish friends out of
sympathy and interest for the Jewish faith; a room like any
of the humble one-room synagogues that are to be found in
modern Jerusalem.

One sits in the ruin of this building watching the blue lake,
trying hard to build up a picture of Jesus as He appeared to
His contemporaries. The traditional, bare-headed Jesus of
Christian art cannot be correct. Perhaps Dr. Stapfer has
drawn a more authentic portrait in his *Palestine in the Time of
Christ* :

"He had neither the fine linen nor the sumptuous raiment
of those who live in kings' houses," he wrote, "neither had

he a long flowing robe like the scribes and Pharisees. Upon His head He must have worn the turban, the national head-gear, used alike by rich and poor. Painters make a mistake when they represent Christ bare-headed. As we have said, everyone wore the head covered. The turban He wore was probably white. It was fastened under the chin by a cord, and at the side fell down to the shoulders and over the tunic. Under His turban He wore his hair rather long and His beard uncut. His tunic, and underneath vesture, was of one piece without seam; it was therefore of some value (John xix. 23) and had probably been given Him by one of those women who ' ministered to Him of their substance.' Over this He wore the *talith*, loose and flowing. The mantle was not white, for we are told it became white during the Transfiguration. It was not red, for that was only the military colour. It is possible it was blue, for blue was then very common, or it may have been simply white with brown stripes. In any case, Jesus had at the four corners of this mantle the *Ciccith*, the blue or white fringes of which we have just spoken. He wore sandals on His feet, as we learn from John the Baptist; and when He was travelling, going from place to place, He doubt-less wore a girdle round the loins and carried a stick in His hand. . . ."

I rowed back towards Tabgha and came ashore at the place where probably Capernaum ended. Here are several huge heart-shaped stones called the *Mensa Christi*, and they were in all probability the quayside stones of the ancient town.

A naval officer to whom I showed photographs of the *Mensa Christi* told me that the stones are exactly like many ancient quaysides in the ports of Asia Minor. Each stone has a worn hollow in the centre of it made, said my friend, by the grappling-irons or anchors of the fishermen. I think I am right in saying that this site, although known to the earliest pilgrims, has been lost for centuries.

If these stones are really the ancient quayside of Capernaum, they are one of the most interesting relics in Palestine. May it not have been on the quayside that St. Matthew was sitting at the receipt of custom? Until I came to Palestine I imagined that St. Matthew was stationed at a custom-house on the extreme northern limit of the lake, probably a kind of frontier between the territory of Herod Antipas and that of Philip, Tetrarch of Gaulonitis. But, reading the Gospels on the spot, one cannot help thinking that St. Matthew was not on the road but on the lakeside. " And he went forth again by the seaside: and all the multitude resorted unto him, and he taught them. And as he passed by, he saw Levi the son of Alphæus sitting at the receipt of custom, and said unto him, Follow me. And he arose and followed him." It would seem clear from St. Mark that the custom-house was near the lake. If so, it was for the purpose of taking a tax on goods landed and a percentage of fish caught by the fishermen. The only place for such a toll-house would have been on the landing-stage.

Matthew was obviously only one of many detested publicans round the Sea of Galilee. The place must have swarmed with them. It was a frontier district, and everything coming into it from the many caravan roads, from the neighbouring tetrarchy of Philip, or from the opposite side of the lake which was Greek territory, was subject to duty. Herod's income from his tetrarchy was two hundred talents (about £42,240), and we may be sure that the publicans squeezed out the last farthing.

Matthew, who is often spoken of as a Roman official, was really nothing of the kind. He was a local *douanier* in the employment of Herod Antipas. The Talmud mentions two kinds of publicans: the general tax-gatherer (*Gabbai*) and the custom-house official (*Mokhes*, or *Mokhsa*), both of whom were as heartily loathed and detested by Jews in the time of Christ as the landlord's agent was detested in nineteenth-century Ireland. In Judæa the tax-gatherer was the minion of an oppressive alien administration, in Galilee he was the agent of an equally rapacious autocrat.

One imagines that Matthew, if his post was on the quayside at Capernaum, had many an opportunity of seeing Jesus as he arrived or departed. This is the opinion of Dr. Edersheim, who paints a beautiful little picture in *The Life and Times of Jesus the Messiah*:

"We take it, long before that eventful day that for ever decided his life, Matthew had, in heart, become a disciple of Jesus. Only he dared not, could not, have hoped for personal recognition—far less for call to discipleship. But when it came, and Jesus fixed on him that look of love which searched the inmost deep of the soul, and made Him the true Fisher of men, it needed not a moment's thought or consideration. When he spake it, 'Follow Me,' the past seemed all swallowed up in the present heaven of bliss. He said not a word, for his soul was in the speechless surprise of unexpected love and grace; but he rose up, left the custom-house, and followed Him."

The most solemn and wonderful association of these strange heart-shaped stones is that of the grey dawn over the lakeside, when Jesus appeared to seven of the disciples after the Resurrection. They did not recognise Him. They saw a lonely figure standing on the shore and they heard a voice calling to them. If these stones are what tradition claims them to be, it was upon them that the Risen Christ prepared "a fire of coals" and "fish laid thereon, and bread." As the grey light brightened into sunrise, one of the most moving incidents in the Gospels took place when Peter was forgiven for his denial and was bidden, as in the first days of his discipleship, to "Follow me."

And it was from these stones that the little band of followers heard the words which sum up the whole duty of the pastoral office:

"Feed my lambs."

§ 6

Throughout the month of March the cranes fly north over the Sea of Galilee. They migrate from Central Africa and journey up through Palestine to Russia. "The stork in the heaven knoweth her appointed times; and the turtle and the crane and the swallow observe the time of their coming: but my people know not the judgement of the Lord," said Jeremiah.

I shall always think of the flight of the cranes as one of the most characteristic sights of Galilee. They fly at a great height and you might not notice them until the sun, shining on their white feathers, turns them into a snowstorm against the blue sky.   They move slowly, wheeling in the air, in great companies many thousands strong, sometimes seeming to stop and wheel above one particular spot as though contemplating a descent.   But in half an hour, if you look for them again, they have vanished against the white head of Mount Hermon.

Everywhere round Tabgha you see black and white kingfishers, generally in pairs.   They hover above the Sea of Galilee like hawks and plunge down to the water, rarely failing to rise with a small fish.   These white and black kingfishers, so plain in plumage compared with the iridescent blue-green kingfishers of English streams, remind me of a curious legend about this species.   The story goes that they were all originally grey or white and received their lovely colours when, released from the Ark, they flew straight into the light of a sunset.   How the kingfishers of Galilee escaped the Flood I am not prepared to say !

There are several other birds very like our own brilliant kingfishers, but these are the Smyrna ice-birds and the bee-eaters.

The most homely sound on the Sea of Galilee is the chirping of sparrows.   There is a tremendous colony of them in the eucalyptus wood at Tabgha and every evening they set up a shrill chirping that lasts until dusk, when they settle down and go to sleep.

This grove is the most exquisite spot on the Sea of Galilee. It is always cool under the tall trees, and the ground underfoot is soft and crackling with dead leaves, almost like a wood at home.

I can sit there for hours in the heat of the day, watching the kingfishers and the water-tortoises.   The tortoises are very timid, but the young and inexperienced sometimes lie on the edge of the stream instead of occupying stones in the centre. It is quite easy to catch them, and you are rewarded by the sight of a funny little snake's head popping back into its shell and the beady glance of two sharp slanting black eyes.   They swim with remarkable speed under water, and you can trace their journeys by the blunt noses thrust above the surface every so often as they come up for air.   I am glad that the Arabs have not discovered any commercial possibilities in their shells, or they would very soon cease to exist. Although they venture out round the edges of the Sea of Galilee, they seem to like the warm rock pool best of all.

The Arabs tell a pretty story about the tortoise. They say that once upon a time a woman was busy at her oven baking bread when another woman passed by and asked for some of it. It is a terrible thing to refuse bread to anyone, nevertheless the woman said that she had nothing to spare. Then the Lady Fatma, for she it was, put a curse on the baker of the bread, and the curse was that she should go about the world for ever with the oven on her back. The poor woman became a tortoise, and the Arabs, picking a tortoise from the water, will point out to you the brown marks of burning on the oven, or shell.

Sometimes in the evening an Arab boat will slide in near the shore and Abdul the boatman, who has never recovered from the size of the first tip I gave him, will jump into the water and leap on land. He loves English cigarettes, which he inhales with his head thrown back.

I asked him once if the Arabs on Galilee tell any stories of Jesus.

" Oh, yes," he replied. " Jesus cured the daughter of the King of Gergesa, who had devils under her nails."

I have no idea what " devils under the nails " can be, and no one has been able to explain it to me.

The Arabs know that Jesus walked on the waters of the lake, and they hold in great reverence a tree which grows on the top of a hill and stands on the place where, so the story goes, one of the miracles was performed. This tree is called the Tree of Blessing, and a branch of it burned in a fire is believed to cure all kinds of diseases.

A number of Abdul's stories seem to have no point, or possibly his English is not adequate, or perhaps my wits go wandering in the heat of Galilee. I like to sit listening to the soft drone of his voice, watching the blue water of the lake, the tortoises sunning themselves on the stones, and the slow flight of the cranes on their way to the North.

§ 7

One morning some fishermen rowed me to the mouth of the Jordan, where, leaping ashore with Abdul, I walked to the ruins of El Tell, which some learned men think is Bethsaida Julias.

We walked beside fields of growing corn and leapt over gullies and irrigation trenches. Turning a corner suddenly, we disturbed a large water buffalo who was having a splendid time in the Jordan. He snorted and stampeded away, sending a shower of mud over us.

" When God was making the cow," said Abdul, " the Horned One passed by. . . ."

The Arabs, who have a superstitious dread of calling unpleasant things by their right name, refer to the devil as the Horned One.

". . . the Horned One passed by," he continued, " and when he saw the cow that God was making he laughed loud and for a long time. He said he had never seen such a funny-looking animal. So God told him to make a better one himself. So the devil made the water-buffalo. . . ."

An Arab who was wading about on the opposite shore of the Jordan, which is here about twenty yards wide, gave us a shout and said something in Arabic.

" The gentleman over there," said Abdul, " asks us for a cigarette."

" But we can't throw a cigarette across the river."

" Oh, no," he replied, " we leave it on a stone and he will wade across for it."

So I took out a cigarette and left it under a stone.

The " gentleman over there " called down a thousand blessings on us.

When we got to the ruins of El Tell there was nothing to see but the usual confusing mound of basalt. We were surrounded by dozens of small Bedouin lads, who stood in a ring and looked at me as though I were an apparition.

Suddenly we heard an extraordinary wild chanting in the valley below. It was a monotonous song, the same verse and tune repeated. Abdul said that it was a Bedouin wedding. About thirty horsemen suddenly appeared, galloping and

wheeling their horses and uttering blood-curdling cries:
" The gentleman in front," explained Abdul, " he marry a
lady over there and he, with his friends, go to carry her off."

The " over there " meant a neighbouring encampment.
While we were watching them, a horseman detached himself
from the wedding party and rode suddenly at us, setting his
horse up the stony hill at a canter. He entered into a long
and rather angry conversation, of which I was obviously the
subject.

It appeared that by going to El Tell I had crossed the
boundary between Palestine and French Syria. I was now
in French territory and—without a passport. Was I a Jew?
No! Then was I a spy? No! The wild man on the horse,
who was a kind of policeman sheikh, inferred that unless I
left the district within four hours he would arrest me.

There was nothing to see, so we left at once. On the way
back we noticed that the man on the other side of the Jordan
was smoking a cigarette.

§ 8

The Lake of Galilee is, of all the places that I have seen, the
one in which the Spirit of Christ is still present. There are
no warring sects, no rival shrines; only lake water falling on
black stones, a slow procession of crops, the ripening of fruit,
the bright flight of kingfisher and bee-catcher, the sun by day
and the stars by night.

Time has taken no revenge on the lakeside where Christianity was born. It is even lovelier than imagination paints it.
There are no temples made by hands, no clash of creed, no
jealousy and no hate.

In the silence of night the little fishing-boats set off under
the stars as they used to do when a Voice called from the
shore: " Come ye after me, and I will make you fishers of
men."

CHAPTER EIGHT

I explore the ruins of Cæsarea Philippi, go to Sidon, visit the hill once dominated by Hester Stanhope, draw a pen for St. George, climb the ramparts of the greatest crusading castle in Syria, travel over the Lebanons to Baalbec and Damascus, stand beside the tomb of Saladin and go south to keep a promise.

§ 1

ALTHOUGH it was early March, the wheat was ready for harvest on the Plain of Gennesaret.

Father Täpper's bananas were, however, a disappointment to me. They lay concealed like small ivory tusks in a tough, tattered jungle of leaves, and the most careful search never revealed one fit to eat.

I could feel the heat increasing day by day. Stray copies of fortnight-old English newspapers, left behind by visitors, spoke strangely of snowdrifts in Scotland, and the back pages contained pictures of people tobogganing in Derbyshire. All this was difficult to believe as the hot, golden days followed one another on the Sea of Galilee.

There is no suggestion of heat in the Gospels, unless the general atmosphere of a free, open-air life conveys it. I think the only clue is the fact that St. Peter was naked and " girt his cloak about him " in the dawn after the Crucifixion. It is only in a sub-tropical climate that men can go unclothed in April.

When the time came for me to leave Tabgha I was sorry and unwilling to go. I would have taken advantage of any excuse I could have made to stay. But the morning came when, promising a hundred times to come back someday, I bade good-bye to Father Täpper and went off, past the black Bedouin tents and the ruins of the Church of the Loaves and Fishes. The road led up to the mountains below Hermon. I was going to Cæsarea Philippi.

As the car climbed into the hills, the air became cooler. I felt a new energy. There was a fresh wind. The hills blazed with colour. It was as if a giant had seized the hill-sides and in broad sweeping strokes had painted them bright red, and blue, and white. The narcissus—the " Rose of Sharon " —shone in the sunlight mile after mile. Whole hillsides were covered with the wild anemone—the " lily of the field "— and with pink flax, crowfoot, iris, broomrape and borage.

These flowers bloom suddenly on the hills of Galilee like a song of praise and die as quickly as they come. There arrives a day when they fall and wither in the sun and from that day the country grows brown and parched, the streams get thinner and die away and the heat closes down on the land.

The road to Cæsarea Philippi is one associated with a crisis in the development of the Twelve Disciples. It was along this road, just over the frontier of Galilee, that Jesus led them in order to prepare their minds for His death and Resurrection. One likes to fancy the immortal travellers crossing the hills in sunlight, pausing now and then to look back on a scene of so many wonders, for every few yards upward along this road gives a more beautiful bird's-eye view of the distant lakeside.

It was the summer of the year before the Crucifixion. The shadow of the Cross lay already across the path of Christ. Of all the memories of Him which a man with the Gospels in his hand conjures up along the roads of Galilee, this journey "into the parts of Cæsarea Philippi" is among the most solemn.

There is a small dead volcano standing by itself on the right of the road as one travels north. Its sides are scored with the tracks of lava. It is a hill made for anyone who wishes to look down upon the Sea of Galilee and to say good-bye to that lovely place. I climbed it, and, as I did so, I had the feeling that He had stood there for a moment on that summer's day, gazing back into Galilee. The distant lake lay below, blue and windless in the heat of the valley, and the tall hills enclosed it ; every road, every tree was sharply defined in the crystal atmosphere. I saw not only the lake from end to end, but beyond it to the south, where the Jordan runs out into its fiery valley.

The past and the future were in the mind of Jesus that day, as He led His followers up to the slopes of Hermon. Surely He must have looked back. Only a little while before the Pharisees and the Sadducees, burying their mutual hatreds, had come seeking a sign, " asking that He should stop the sun," suggests St. Chrysostom, " or rein in the moon, or hurl down thunder, or the like." And he sighed deeply in His spirit and said, " Why doth this generation seek a sign? Verily I say unto you, There shall no sign be given unto this generation."

The imagination draws a picture of Jesus on these hills gazing sadly down upon the country of His ministry, upon the chain of little towns whose people, deaf to the higher things of the spirit, clamoured only after wonders and miracles and signs. As He turned His back on the distant lake, the ridge of Hermon, dusted with snow, rose up before Him like a wall; and He turned to the Twelve as they walked on, and asked:

" Who do men say that I am? "

They told Him that some men, like Herod Antipas, believed Him to be John the Baptist come back to life, others thought He was Elijah or one of the ancient prophets.

" But who say ye that I am? " asked Jesus.

Peter said: " Thou art the Christ."

" And I say also unto thee," replied Christ, " that thou art Peter, and upon this rock I will build my church; and the gates of hell shall not prevail against it."

The city which Jesus and His followers approached was the great pagan city of Cæsarea Philippi that nestled in a beauty of marble columns and running water among the thick woods of the lowest slopes of Hermon. In all Palestine and Syria there was no more lovely site for a city. In the hills at the back was a dark grotto in which one of the sources of the Jordan welled up from the earth to rush sparkling in the sunlight through the city to the plain. The Greeks had called the place Paneas, because such grottos were always sacred to the god Pan. Herod the Great had adorned Paneas with a temple to the Emperor Augustus. When Philip the Tetrarch inherited this exquisite spot in the year of Christ's birth, he built there a city which he called Cæsarea in honour of the Emperor Tiberius, adding his own name to distinguish it from the city of Cæsarea on the sea-coast.

But there is no indication that Jesus ever entered this city. Like Tiberias, it was pagan and therefore unclean. Many writers, however, have liked to imagine Him there in the guise of a humble wayfarer, gazing upon the temples of the old gods and then silently passing on His way.

The dividing line between Palestine and Syria to-day is the Jordan, just as it used to be when Jesus passed from Galilee into Gaulonitis.

Perhaps somewhere on the road near our frontier station of Rosh Pinna the police of the Tetrarch Philip had their outpost. To-day the Union Jack flies over a small building on the side of the road. An official came out, glanced at my passport and waved me on into French Syria. In a mile or so I came to the French frontier post. There the tricolour was flying over a building near the Jordan, and under the shade of a eucalyptus tree the French officials were playing cards with the local sheikhs.

While I was waiting for the return of my passport, I heard some Arabs say that a sheikh was about to perform *fantasias*. This is a word the Arabs are very fond of using to describe anything exciting and out of the ordinary. How did this Greek word get imbedded in the Arabic? Surely it is a word they took over centuries ago from the Greeks of the Decapolis.

There was a wild clatter of hoofs, and round the corner of the passport building came a sheikh mounted on a small, fiery, white mare. He dashed out at full gallop, wheeled round, also at the gallop, and disappeared. Then we heard him returning, and as he came up the steep hill and the white mare slackened her pace a bit, he leapt from the saddle and leapt up again, hanging over one side as Buffalo Bill's cowboys used to do when the Deadwood Coach drove into the ring.

I left the frontier station by way of a steep hill that led into a much wilder country than Galilee: hard mountain country with sudden wide vistas into distant valleys and glimpses ahead of hills and volcanic cliffs of black basalt.

The people I met on the roads were different from the folk of Galilee: they were wild-looking Druses in shaggy coats of sheepskin. With the tireless pace of highlanders they strode along beside their camels and their donkeys.

The change from the peaceful lakeside of Galilee to the mountains of Syria reminded me of the contrast between the softness of Loch Lomond and the wildness of Glen Falloch and the road that runs to Rannoch and Glencoe. I had definitely crossed a frontier. And the dominating feature of this wild land was the tremendous ridge of Mount Hermon, its main peaks more than twice the height of Ben Nevis. This gigantic range, for you cannot call it a mountain, is over twenty miles in length. Vines and olive and mulberry trees grow half-way up its slopes, but after five thousand feet the bare rock piles itself in fantastic ridges, heaped above terrible chasms, the haunt of eagles, wolves and mountain bears.

Snow lies on this gigantic mountain nearly all the year. It is a landmark all over Syria and Palestine and so firmly does it dominate the country that, as you travel, it is impossible to keep your eyes away from the stupendous flanks with their white snowfields.

Mile after mile went by and the road was empty, running down, now into mountain gorges where stricken-looking Druse villages built of mud and stones melted into the harsh landscape, and now up into the cool mountain winds, where there was no sign of life but the slow flight of an eagle.

§ 2

A steep hill clung to the side of a mountain for several miles and then the road dropped into a green valley watered by the melted snows of Hermon. The shaggy foothills gave no hint of the awful desolation that lies above them. They are, in spite of their desolation, comfortable hills, darkened here and there by fig and vine and olive. But they are lonely hills. No houses disturb their monotonous solitude, no terraces transform their primeval untidiness.

And suddenly, below a ruin that used to be a key castle

of the Crusades, I saw the well-hidden little Arab village
of Banias, once the magnificent city of Cæsarea Philippi.
Of all the adventures this place has suffered in the course
of its long life, none is stranger than that of its name.   First
it was Paneas.   Then it was Cæsarea Philippi.   Then, in
compliment to Nero, it became Neroneas.   And now, all its
grandeur departed, the few Arabs who live in the twenty or
thirty mud hovels have gone back to the old Greek name,
Paneas, but, because there is no *p* in their alphabet, they
call it Banias.

An inhabited ruin is more pathetic than one that is
desolate.   Banias to-day is a tangle of briars and a huddle of
mud houses.   There is nothing to remind you of the beautiful
city that once stood there except a few Greek shrines to Pan
carved in the rocks and the broken pillars that encumber the
ground.   A depressing object lesson in the death of Roman
civilisation is the sheikh's house.   It is a confused mass of
stone, nearly all of it Roman.   Built into the walls, not
upright but in a parallel position, are dozens of lovely marble
columns.   At first it looks as though this place is built of
round stones.   Then one realises that these are the bases of
columns.   There is something positively sickening in the
sight of it.   One sees in imagination the onrush of barbarians,
the frightful destruction of beauty and the blind, ignorant
rebuilding by a savage race.   When the Roman Empire
fell, towns like Cæsarea Philippi became stone quarries.
One can see so clearly how a statue by Phidias could be
hacked to pieces to fit into the walls of a hovel.   We all
know that these things happened, but the sight of one building, with altars and inscriptions built into its walls and
Corinthian columns used to support floors instead of roofs,
seems to bring home more vividly than any chapter by
Gibbon the horror that attends the extinction of culture.

In Roman times the city must have been one of the finest
in the country.   The sound of running water enlivened its
streets : even on the hottest summer day the pale green
melted snow water went rushing through them into the
valley.   And to-day the tumultuous sources of the Jordan
leap out from the roots of Hermon and go singing over the
dead body of Cæsarea Philippi.

An Arab took me to the hills at the back, where he pointed out a dark grotto. It is half choked with stones and rubbish. But in the depths can be heard a queer stirring as of something alive. It is the Jordan welling up out of the earth. Above the grotto are a few Greek shrines carved in the face of the cliff. It is possible to read an inscription here and there. " Priest of Pan " is one. Above, on a slope of the hill, is a little white building with a dome, the Moslem shrine of Sheikh Kedir, who, as the guides tell travellers, is really St. George. This is not quite true. Sheikh Kedir is a mythical prophet who, when on earth, discovered the Well of Life and, drinking of its waters, became " the green one." That is the meaning of the name. The Arabs believe that his soul animated St. George, who is, therefore, worshipped all over Arabia as an incarnation of El Kedir. It is certainly curious to find a Christian saint held in veneration by Moslems, and the explanation is that St. George, who was martyred near Constantinople in 303 A.D., became so famous throughout the East nearly three centuries before Mahomet was born that even Islamism could not dislodge him from the category of holy men.

To the student of religion there can be few spots of greater interest than this grotto at Banias. Pan lives again in the name of the place, and on the spot where Herod raised a temple to the deified Augustus the Arabs have built a little domed shrine to the spirit of the patron saint of England.

I could easily understand why the people of Banias believe this eerie grotto to be haunted. The Arab told me that only the night before the whole village was awakened by a voice calling to prayer.

" It was a prophet," he said in explanation.

The Moslem believes that while the souls of ordinary men wait for the resurrection, the souls of prophets can move about and manifest themselves. He told me that someone in the village had caught sight of the spirit, and that he " was very white and not like an Arab."

An ancient tradition places the Transfiguration of our Lord on Mount Tabor near Nazareth. Many authorities believe, however, the more reasonable theory that it occurred on the slopes of Mount Hermon during the withdrawal " into the parts of Cæsarea Philippi." Tabor is not a very high mountain, neither was it a lonely one. Mount Hermon, on the other hand, with its snowfields and its miles of desolation, seems to me a far more probable scene for this revelation. And when I stood by the young Jordan at Banias, looking up at the foot-hills that mount to the bleak wilderness of the Hermon ridge, I felt that this mighty barrier between Jewish and Gentile lands must have been the "high mountain apart" into which Jesus led the three chosen disciples, Peter, James and John.

On the slopes of this mountain the three faithful disciples saw Jesus transfigured before them.

"And his raiment became shining, exceeding white as snow; so as no fuller on earth can white them. And there appeared unto them Elias with Moses: and they were talking with Jesus . . . and there was a cloud that overshadowed them: and a voice came out of the cloud, saying, This is my beloved Son: hear him. And suddenly, when they had looked round about, they saw no man any more, save Jesus only with themselves."

"The real import of this wondrous incident emerges only when it is recognised that, like the Lord's miracle of walking upon the Lake, it was an anticipation of the Resurrection," wrote David Smith in *The Days of His Flesh*. "By the power of God the body of Jesus assumed for a season the conditions of the resurrection-life. It became, in the language of St. Paul, 'a spiritual body,' and He appeared to the three even as He manifested Himself after He had risen from the dead on the road to Emmaus, in the room at Jerusalem, on the shore of the Lake. It was designed, in the first instance, to strengthen Jesus and nerve Him for the dread ordeal which awaited Him. It was like a vision of home to the exile, like a foretaste of rest to the weary traveller. . . . And the Transfiguration had a purpose also in relation to the disciples. It was designed to reconcile them to the incredible and repulsive idea of Messiah's sufferings by revealing to them the glories that should follow."

From the heights of Hermon, whence the dew comes that

descends on Zion, they would have looked down on the line
of the Jordan. They would have remembered the Baptism
and a Voice. They would know for the first time that hence-
forward the steps of the Master were to descend from Mount
Hermon and, following the Jordan to the south, ascend the
slopes of Calvary.

§ 3

I walked from the grotto into the poor little village of
Banias. I saw something lying in the road that at first I
took to be an old coat, or a garment that someone had
thrown away. Then it moved, and I saw that it was a dog.
I thought that it had been run over and went over to it.
The poor thing was a Saluki dying of hunger.

She was so weak that she could not move. She could only
lie in the hot dust of the road, too weak to shake the flies
from her sores. Her eyes were lost in a world of unutterable
pain. She was grotesque and misshapen with suffering. Her
ears had been clipped close to her head—a common habit
with the Bedouin, who believe that to clip the ears of a dog
increases its hearing.

I had never in my life seen an animal in such a ghastly
condition. She was too weak to run away from me. She
lay in the road, watching with her pitiful eyes and waiting
for me to hurt her.

When I brought sandwiches from the car and tried to feed
her with small pieces of meat, she could not realise that I
was attempting to help her. She looked frightened. Then,
very gently, she took a piece of meat in her parched, scarred
mouth, but it fell out into the dust.

I found myself blazing with anger. The utter callousness
of the Mohammedan for the suffering of animals is a terrible
thing. Two or three Arabs gathered round and watched me
as if I were a lunatic; as, indeed, they thought I was.

" She dies of hunger," they said.

" Why does nobody feed her? " I asked.

" She belongs to nobody," they replied. " The Bedouin
left her. She does not belong to this place."

That was their point of view. She belonged to no one.
Allah had given her life. Let Allah take away the life he
had given. It was not their affair. So, after stoning her
for a bit, they had permitted her to lie about and die.

She managed to eat two or three pieces of meat. She lay
in the hot dust, begging me with her terrible eyes not to
leave her.

" Has anyone got a gun? " I asked.

They looked shifty and lied. " No," they said.

" Well, a knife? "

Yes, they had knives. I offered ten shillings to any of
them who would put the poor thing out of her pain; but,
although ten shillings would have been more than three
months' income to any of them, they looked at me with horror
and flatly refused. The dog must die when Allah willed.

I found two Armenian policemen in the village, but they
refused to do anything. They knew the dog and would very
much like to shoot her, but it would cause trouble in the village.
These people were very devout Moslems. They were afraid
nothing could be done. They were sorry and sympathetic.
They brought out tins of black tobacco and, shrugging their
shoulders, rolled themselves cigarettes.

The greater the opposition the more I was determined to
help the dog, even if it meant sleeping among the fleas of
Banias for a week. There were three things to do: kill her
myself, which I dreaded because of her eyes; to take her
away in the car, but she was mangy, unable to move, and
would certainly be refused by any hotel; or to find someone
who would swear to take care of her. This I eventually did.
He was a nice, gentle Arab in an old suit of khaki. I was told
that his job was to sweep out the shrine at El Kedir.

I gave him ten shillings to buy food for the animal, and
warned him that I would return within a week to see how
she was getting on. He looked at me as though he knew
that, although quite mad, I was serious. I made him pick
up the dog and show me where he was going to keep her.
He led the way, followed now by the entire village, to his
house. This was a desperately poor little hovel enclosed by
a high mud wall. There was a yard with several one-storey
houses opening on to it.

He placed the dog tenderly in the shade and brought a few sacks for her to lie on. A woman came out of a house and watched the proceedings with a complete absence of feeling, although the animal's plight was enough to have wrung a word of sympathy from a fiend. I felt that I had done all that I could do and, warning the man that I would return, I went away.

As I travelled on I began to wonder whether I had done the right thing. It was almost cruel to attempt to revive the pale spark of life in a creature so near to death.

I travelled for hours through a smiling land of hills and valleys. I saw a crusader's castle perched like an eagle's eyrie on the crest of a mountain. And far off I saw the blue Mediterranean and the road that runs to Sidon.

§ 4

The road that runs beside the Mediterranean, through Tyre and Sidon to Beirut, is, I think, the most interesting coast road in the world. No other coast road has such memories.

On one side the waves pound on yellow sand; on the other orange and banana groves lift themselves gently towards the distant snow-dusted Lebanons. Camels roped together in files, ten at a time, their necks hung with blue beads as a charm against the Evil Eye, slouch along led by fat men on donkeys.

Optimistic children hold out fish to motorists who are doing forty miles an hour. Little girls extend bunches of oranges with the green leaves still on them, calling shrilly to every passer-by.

No one ever seems to buy anything from these children, but they never get tired of trying to sell something.

The road is dotted with trelliswork cafés on whose crazy little platforms men in baggy Turkish trousers, with red fezes on their heads, sit cross-legged and suck at their hookahs, watching the blue waves curling over in white foam, watching everything that goes by on the road and talking all day long about money and politics.

On the Palestine side of the road they suck their hookahs and curse the British because they are letting so many Jews into the country; on the French side of the road they suck their hookahs and curse the French because they say the French are the most selfish and autocratic nation in the world.

On the Palestine part of the road they say that they could not be worse off under the French, and on the French part they say that they could not be worse off under the British!

" What have we got from the War? " they ask.

" Nothing! "

And they begin to talk with affection of the good old days before the War, when the nice, kind, thoughtful, generous and entirely adorable Turk ruled these parts.

And in the fields the women are all hard at work.

Strung along this road, sharp and blinding in the sun, are little flat-roofed towns standing with their feet in blue waters, palm trees straggling on the sands, white minarets lifted against the dark, hot sky.

They look very white and bright until you dive into them, and then you find that their narrow, winding streets are all in shadow. But each little street is like a row of peep-shows.

The shops are small, windowless caves in each one of which something is happening: a carpenter sawing wood, a shoemaker cutting leather, a fishmonger skinning a fish, a blacksmith hitting red iron.

It is all very intimate and friendly. And through the cool shadows of the streets a man with lemonade in a brass urn on his back claps drinking cups together and shouts that his lemonade is not only the best in the whole world, but is ice-cold and packed in snow from the Lebanon.

" Ya balash ! " he cries, which means " O ye, for nothing ! " How strangely reminiscent is this of Isaiah: " Ho, every one that thirsteth, come ye to the waters, and he that hath no money ; come ye, buy, and eat ; yea, come, buy wine and milk without money and without price."

There are crumbling towns on this road, like Acre and Tyre and Sidon, which are sunk in the ruins of their past. The labourers in the fields around them never know what the

spade will turn up. They have found Roman goddesses
sleeping under the sands near Tyre. They have come upon
Egyptian graves near Acre. They have found beautiful little
green bottles and gold rings and silver images beside the sea at
Sidon. An old and brilliant world has crashed to ruin along
this road, and the men who live on it to-day seem like a break-
down gang camped among the relics of a noble mansion.

I shall always remember Acre as I saw it when I went
there from Haifa in the light of early morning, the sun
straying between the date palms that grow on the sand near
the sea. The little white town stood out to sea like a ship,
its old wall rotting in the blue water. It is now half-dead,
but when Richard the Lionheart laid siege to it long ago it
was the key to Jerusalem. It was in the palm grove of Acre
that the English king caught fever.

If you walk to-day through Acre there is silence and the old
rotting walls are too big, it seems, for so small and quiet a
town. The past lives in strange, dark cellars half-full of
rubbish, into which you peer fearfully, astonished to see that
the roof swings up to a Gothic arch. And the spirit of the
place is the old blind man who comes tapping down the
street, feeling his way along the great crusading wall, touching
the huge stones with fingers that take the place of eyes.

It was from towns like Acre, Tyre and Sidon that hook-
nosed men set off in the very dawn of the world to voyage
to the Tin Islands of the West. On this coast returned
mariners described to their friends a first impression of
Cornwall or the Isle of Wight.

In this hot, bright world beside the Mediterranean what
gloomy stories the Phœnicians must have told of the misty
cold island at the world's end where the small dark men
mined tin.

In Tyre I found men building a ship on the edge of the
sea. Somehow the sight seemed to blow away the centuries,
and the ancient Tyre that sent its cypress wood to Solomon
and its ships all over the world seemed to live again in the
sound of the hammers and the saws.

The shipbuilders were not making a large ship. It was a
fishing-boat for the Mediterranean. They were sawing
Gopher wood from the Taurus Mountains, which is called

quatrani by the Arabs. It is a kind of pitch-pine and is the wood, so it is said, from which the Ark was made.

Their method of sawing was very primitive. The wood was rested on two upright pillars. One man stooᴗ above it and one below, each holding the end of a long saw. One man pulled up while his companion pulled down, and the saw cut only on the downward pull.

On the beach near Tyre I saw the thin coloured sea shell from which in ancient times the famous Tyrian purple was made.

And now in the heat of the afternoon I came to Sidon, another city camped out in the ruin of its old splendour. There was a fortress in the centre of the town near the sea, and from its tumbled walls I looked westward over the Mediterranean and, inland, over a pink foam of apricot blossom to groves of olive, fig and orange.

Greater than any memory of splendour and conquest shared by the sister towns of Tyre and Sidon is the memory of the Man who " departed into the coasts of Tyre and Sidon " where He cured the girl who was " grievously vexed with a devil."

Jesus seems never actually to have entered these towns, although He visited the districts round about. The people, however, of both Tyre and Sidon were among the very first to join the great multitudes who flocked to Galilee to hear the Master's words.

In the course of His scornful reproach to His own lakeside towns of Galilee, such as Chorozain and Bethsaida, Jesus compared their faith unfavourably with that of Tyre and Sidon:

" If the mighty works which were done in you," He cried, " had been done in Tyre and Sidon they would have repented long ago in sackcloth and ashes. . . ."

§ 5

I have always wanted to visit the hill of Djoun on which Lady Hester Stanhope once held her eccentric court. When I reached Sidon I asked if anyone knew where Djoun was and at least twenty men and boys leapt all over the car, expressing themselves willing to guide me there. I picked on one of them, and we set off up a side road at the back of Sidon and began to climb steadily into the Lebanons.

Hester Stanhope's name occurs in most of the travel books and journals written about Syria a century ago. Kinglake's account in *Eothen* of her bizarre establishment at Djoun is perhaps the best known. Every traveller tried to gain an audience with " the Queen of the Desert," or " The Princess of the Lebanon," as this extraordinary woman called herself. At one time she was the most influential European in the Near East, and at all times she was the most picturesque and eccentric.

She was William Pitt's niece and had kept house for him at Downing Street in the years before his death. She was handsome, brilliant, headstrong, and had a tongue like a whip. She moved contemptuously through the most brilliant society of her time. Pitt's death in 1806 was a terrible blow to her, and when Sir John Moore died at Corunna three years later with her name, platonically, it is said, on his lips, poor Hester Stanhope retired from London.

At the age of thirty-four, accompanied by her doctor and maid, she set out on a grand tour from which she never returned. After an adventurous journey she arrived in Palestine and, driven on by an extravagant vanity and an ambition which verged on madness, began to imagine herself as a sort of female Messiah or, at least, " the Queen of Jerusalem." Her first conquests were made amongst the Arabs round Damascus, who had never in their wildest dreams seen anything like Pitt's niece. She cast aside European clothes, dressed as a sheikh, rode an Arab steed superbly, and achieved even greater fame than Colonel Lawrence has attained in our time. She was as brave as a lion and lavish with borrowed money, two traits which endeared her to the Arabs.

She settled eventually in a ruined monastery in the Lebanon, and later in a stronghold she had built for herself at Djoun. There she dispensed justice, rode abroad with a dashing Arab bodyguard, interfered in politics, and on one occasion waged war on a mountain tribe, leaving three hundred slain and a number of ruined villages behind.

I

She studied magic and was regarded as a divinity. Her stables contained a white mare with a spinal deformity which gave the effect of a saddle. This poor creature, she was convinced, was destined to bear the Messiah. Travellers have left records of her astonishing fortress at Djoun, of the regal state she observed there and of the interviews she granted, always at night, when she would sit dressed as a sheikh and sucking a hookah, talking for hours of astrology and astronomy and the magic sciences. During one of these interviews a strong man fainted away. Her discourses went on into the dawn.

One feels that Lady Hester Stanhope just missed being really great. As it was she established a tremendous, almost legendary, reputation throughout the East, but sank into old age loaded with debts. Her fall from splendour into squalor and her death, neglected, alone, robbed and forsaken, were terrible. Dr. W. M. Thomson, the missionary, made a journey over the Lebanons to bury her, and he has left an account of the gruesome scene in *The Land and the Book*:

" The British consul at Beirut requested me to perform the religious services at the funeral of Lady Hester," he wrote. " It was an intensely hot Sabbath in June 1839. We started on our melancholy errand at one o'clock, and reached this place about midnight. After a brief examination, the consul decided that the funeral must take place immediately. The vault in the garden was hastily opened, and the bones of General L—— or of his son, I forget which—a Frenchman who died here, and was buried in the vault by her ladyship—were taken out and placed at the head.

" The body, in a plain deal box, was carried by her servants to the grave, followed by a mixed company, with torches and lanterns, to enable them to thread their way through the winding alleys of the garden. I took a wrong path, and wandered some time in the mazes of these labyrinths. When at length I entered the arbour, the first thing I saw were the bones of the general, in a ghastly heap, with the head on top, having a lighted taper stuck in either eye-socket—a hideous, grinning spectacle. It was difficult to proceed with the service under circumstances so novel and bewildering. The consul subsequently remarked that there were some curious coincidences between this and the burial of Sir John Moore, her ladyship's early love. In silence, on the lone mountain at midnight, ' our lanterns dimly burning,' with the flag of her country over her, ' she lay like a warrior taking his rest;' and we left her ' *alone* in her glory.' There was but one of her own nation present, and his name was *Moore.* . . .

" The morning after the funeral the consul and I went round the premises and examined *thirty-five* rooms, which had been sealed up by the vice-consul of Sidon to prevent robbery. They were full of trash. One had forty or fifty oil jars of French manufacture, old, empty, and dusty. Another was crammed with Arab saddles, moth-eaten, tattered, and torn. They had belonged to her mounted guard. Superannuated pipe stems without bowls filled one room. Two more were devoted to medicines, and another to books and papers, mostly in boxes and ancient chests. Nothing of much value was found anywhere, and the seals were replaced to await legal action. The crowd of servants and greedy retainers had appropriated to themselves her most valuable effects."

The road clung so closely to the edge of the hill that every corner appeared to end in a wall of rock and a drop into the valley. It was wild mountain country on the grand scale: a foreground of green hills sloping into lonely valleys backed by the Lebanon range, whose peaks were powdered with snow.

We came after ten miles of acute mountaineering to a collection of square little white boxes ranged round the top of a terraced hill. They were blinding in the sunlight. The bell of the Greek monastery was ringing. The air snapped with the sound of the cicadas in the olive terraces. This was Djoun. The whole population was soon gathered round, and a murmur of interest went up when it became known that I had come all the way to visit the grave of Lady Hester Stanhope. But they do not call her by her name in Djoun. She is " es Sitt "—the Lady.

They pointed out through the branches of the olive trees a similar hill to that on which the village stands. It is called "Dier es Sitt"—the House of the Lady. The young Arab from Sidon strode off down the hill, and I followed him into one of the loveliest little valleys I have ever seen. The ground beneath the olive and the apricot trees was sheeted with millions of red anemones, with daisies and with buttercups. The grass was the greenest I had seen since I left England. Where the trees flung no shade, however, the ground was burnt-up and parched.

We climbed the hill, which was in the possession of a savage dog and two countrywomen with their families. They live in all that is left of Lady Hester's stronghold. We questioned them about her. Yes, they said, this is where the daughter of an English lord had once lived. They pointed to a series of ruined vaults. That was where she kept her prisoners, they told us.

All that is now left is a high encircling wall of white limestone, the remains of cellars and a few out-buildings, and the courtyard where Lady Hester's Albanian guards were in the habit of challenging visitors. There were also traces of what must once have been a lovely garden.

An old woman led us across a stony field to the place where an olive tree flings its shadow on the " sitt's " grave. Contrary to my expectation, the grave was as neat and well kept as if it were in Golders Green. The woman said that the monks looked after it. On a square block of stone, approached by three steps, are the words: " Lady Hester Lucy Stanhope. Born 12th March, 1776. Died 23rd June, 1839."

It is a strange resting-place for the grand-daughter of the great Earl of Chatham. One feels that there should be some kind of moral to be drawn from her life, but what it is I do not know. The thought of a hostess of No. 10 Downing Street entrenched behind her ramparts above the olive trees, whipping her negro slaves and listening to the spies who crossed the mountains to whisper to her, appeals to one's love of the extravagant in human nature. If only she could have met a man as mad and a little more imperious than herself. If Mr. Philip Guedalla ever writes a book on

imaginary marriages, perhaps he would mate Hester Stanhope
with Napoleon or—Burckhardt!

§ 6

I reached Beirut as it was growing dark.

The town is a huge, rather ramshackle place filled with
the little tinkling tram-cars which seem to flourish wherever
France sets her foot. Like all the coast towns from Haifa
northwards, the situation of Beirut is perfect: a blue sea, a
curved bay and the high snow-dusted Lebanons piled up all
round the town.

My hotel stood out to sea like a ship. From my balcony
I looked down on the blue waters of St. George's Bay, and I
sat there for a long time watching the sunset reflected over
the Lebanons in a pink light that grew to rust-red and
brown. Grey cobweb mists hung in the valleys and were
swathed across the mountains; and the first stars came out.
Lights danced on the water. The masts of ships grew black
and adventurous against the pyramid of lights that was the
town.

I began to think of St. George, that sadly libelled saint,
who was the patron of Beirut centuries before we in England
placed his cross on our banners. I think Calvin began the
belittlement of St. George, but Gibbon certainly started the
libel. It is a curious thing that thousands of Englishmen
who have not read *The Decline and Fall* will tell you that
St. George was a villainous army contractor of Cappadocia.
He was nothing of the kind. Gibbon, very strangely for a
man of such meticulous accuracy, confused two men, or
rather assumed that George of Laodicea, who was murdered
in the reign of Julian and whose body was flung into the
sea, was the Christian soldier who was martyred under
Diocletian. Gibbon's George was indeed a bad character,
a man who, as Gregory Nazianzen said, would " sell himself
for a cake." He became Arian archbishop of Alexandria
and the retribution which overtook him must have been of a
singularly brutal character, because the Emperor Julian wrote
a letter of remonstrance, in which he said " the people
actually tore a man to pieces as if they had been dogs."

The saint was, however, a Roman officer of high standing who suffered death rather than countenance a Christian persecution ordered by Diocletian. I remember discussing him with Sir E. A. Wallis Budge, whose book *St. George of Lydda* should be read by everyone interested in the saint. Sir Ernest believed that his martyrdom might have occurred as early as 200 A.D., although the accepted date is 303. The traditions of East and West agree that after St. George was martyred in Nicomedia, a town about forty miles east of Constantinople, his body was brought to Lydda—now Ludd, near Jaffa—for burial.

The veneration he inspired among the members of the early Church was so great that hundreds of extravagant legends gathered round his name, among them the story of the Dragon, which many scholars regard as a pagan myth grafted to the Christian tree. Many an agnostic points to the ridiculous stories about saints and martyrs to prove the credulity of the early Church. It is not generally realised that many of these stories were recognised as fiction and as nothing else. Pope Gelasius made war on such devout fictions at the Council of seventy-two Bishops in Rome as early as 494 A.D., when he ordered the faithful to discontinue the reading of such stories for the reason that they called down ridicule on the Christian Faith. Among the stories which he banned were those about St. George.

When the Crusaders came marching along the coast road towards which I was looking, they had already encountered St. George at the very gates of the East, for the Bosphorus was called " the Arm of St. George." Everywhere they went they heard stories of the saint's courage and holiness. In time they came to believe that he was riding beside them. Stories in no way more remarkable than that of the Angels of Mons, in which thousands of modern people believed in 1914, began to spread when the Crusaders were in trouble. A mysterious white horseman with a red cross emblazoned on his sur-coat was seen helping the cause of Christ, first at Antioch and later in many desperate battles.

The Crusaders, returning home to England, told stories of the saint and of his miraculous interventions. It was, there-fore, natural that Richard should have restored the Church of St. George at Lydda, should have used the name of St. George for the English battle-cry, and should have returned from the Holy Land with a patron saint who was recognised in the East and in the West as the perfect Christian soldier.

I was awakened that night by the voices of fishermen passing in their boats under my balcony. I saw a strange light moving over the ceiling. I got up and, walking out in the starlight on the balcony, saw a sight as old as the Syrian hills.

Four men rowed a little boat on the dark sea. One held a flaming torch which dropped sizzling pitch into the water and sent jagged spears of light dancing in the green depths. Kneeling in the prow of the boat was a man with a poised spear who gazed intently into the lit water, waiting his chance to spear a fish.

This way and that the little boat went with its burning torch, the men whispering together and sometimes crowding together to gaze into the water. It was extraordinarily dramatic and also savage. It was like a little scene from the beginning of man's history.

Swiftly and suddenly the man lunged with the spear. He withdrew it with something white and writhing on it! At first I did not know what it was, but, as it passed into the light of the torch, I saw that it was an octopus, its arms waving, clutching and sucking at the spear that transfixed it.

The fisherman shook off the horrid thing and bent again to the water. . . .

It suddenly occurred to me what the strange, sweet fish was that I had eaten at dinner and, feeling rather sick, I went back to bed.

§ 7

Few people have ever been to the Krak-des-Chevaliers because until recently it took ten days to get there and back from Beirut; and you required a troop of horses as well as an armed escort.

Now, however, thanks to the motor-car and the worst road in creation (as well as to the French habit of executing highway robbers with the greatest speed and publicity), it is possible, if you are sufficiently mad, to get there and back in a day, starting from Beirut at dawn. This I did; but I would never do it again.

The Krak-des-Chevaliers is a ruined castle about fifty miles north of Tripoli. When you see it from the plain you feel that the agony of getting there is almost worth it. It is the Camelot of your dreams—the castle of every fairy tale. It stands up on the edge of the sky, with its turrets and its walls, and it seems to you that the sound of the Crusaders' trumpets has hardly died away from its tremendous ramparts.

The Arab guide who took me there knew absolutely nothing about its history, but I was not surprised. These incredible castles, which the Crusaders dotted about the highest mountains in Palestine, are the most silent and mysterious ruins in the world.

They were Christianity's barrier against the Infidel, and they look as though their builders believed that the Latin Kingdom of Jerusalem would endure until Doomsday. It is a remarkable fact that neither Jew, Greek nor Roman has left any memory in Palestine and Syria to compare with the few centuries of the Crusades. The Crusading castle, ruined and desolate, lifts itself from the mountain; the Crusaders' church stands in Arab towns, covered with rugs on which the Moslem kneels with his face to Mecca.

This tremendous movement, the most powerful religious-political-commercial movement of the time, succeeded in bringing Europe to this eastern land for nearly a century. And little bits of the East began to take root in Europe.

We owe the apricot to the Crusades, the lemon, the melon, sugar, and maize. The colours lilac and purple were brought back from the East. Cotton, muslin and damask are some of the things which the Crusaders sent as gifts to their wives; so were glass mirrors and rosaries. Every faithful Moslem has a rosary containing thirty-three, sixty-six, or ninety-nine beads, which he uses for repeating the ninety-nine attributes of God.

These are a few of the things I thought of as I toiled up the winding road to the Krak-des-Chevaliers.

As we drew nearer, the tremendous fortress became even more impressive. Its size was stupendous. The whole of the Tower of London could have been put in a corner of it. If you could take Windsor and Edinburgh castles, knock them about and plant them on the top of Ben Nevis, you would have a faint idea of the impression created by the derelict Krak-des-Chevaliers.

Now as I approached the great gateway which, even in decay, looked like militant Christianity's front door, I noticed that the castle was alive with men. They were hiding on the ramparts and watching us as we approached. Here and there I could see a head between the machicolation of the walls. Men had probably been watching us from the moment we began to climb out of the valley.

" But I thought the castle was deserted," I said to my guide.

" Oh, no," he replied, " it is a big village."

In this mighty ruin the half-starved, savage-looking hill people have lived for centuries. They swooped down at first, no doubt, as soon as the castle was deserted to loot anything left behind. Now they live there among the falling arches and the broken ramparts.

As we approached the great gate with its bastion towers and the ruins of its portcullis and the long inclined pathway up which the knights used to ride their horses, a strange gnome-like figure came running stiffly towards us. He was a queer old man with a white beard, dressed in very old riding boots into which were tucked the ends of a pair of baggy Turkish trousers.

He laughed and pranced round us like a clown, patting us on the back and telling us that he was eighty-three years old. In proof of this he stuck his fingers in his mouth and pulled it wide to show us that he did not possess one tooth. He was very proud of this, though it detracted considerably from his charm as a conversationalist.

" Who is this frightful old ruffian? " I whispered.

" He calls himself a guide," I was told.

The old man ran ahead like a naughty little boy, chattering

away, pointing to tottering arches and falling key-stones and indicating with laughing gestures the terrible crash that would occur—probably very soon—when one of the massive, leaning bastions finally decided to fall straight down several hundreds of feet into the distant valley.

I noticed that the bastion contained several hovels in which his friends and relatives—probably his great grandchildren— were living, but this did not interfere with his relish for a good smash.

I climbed up to the highest tower over steps which looked as though they might collapse at any moment, and looked down over the great courtyard of the Krak, over the enormous halls in which the knights had feasted in victory and had held council in danger, over the high watchtowers from which the Knights of St. John of Jerusalem had long ago watched the brown, fierce hills for signs of Saladin.

Sparrow-hawks had built their nests in the chinks of the stones. A mother hawk was feeding her young in a hole above the doorway of a chapel. I could see the bare necks of the fledgelings thrust out as she darted up to them from the valley.

And below me in the dead town of the Crusaders there was silence, but not death. Arab children played in the dust. Donkeys picked their way over fallen stones as if threading the narrow streets of a town. Nothing, I think, is more depressing than the sight of uncivilised people living in squalor amid the ruins of something that has once been noble.

While I was indulging in this gloom my attention was distracted by three veiled women far below in the courtyard, walking together in high-heeled European shoes as they delicately avoided the puddles and dead cats. I asked the old man who they were.

" The three wives of the sheikh," he explained.

Poor things! If ever three fair dames were imprisoned in an ogre's fortress they are the Three Wives of the Krak-des-Chevaliers.

And they go about the desolation as closely veiled as if each stone concealed a desperate Romeo!

The sight of the ruin and decay in the halls, the magnificent

Gothic chapel, the vast stables, the guard houses and the hundreds of other rooms was terrifying. Storey had crashed down on storey, circular stone stairs ended against the sky.

A hall as long as Westminster Hall was choked with débris half way to the roof. I tripped up against several bones which I think were human, and was driven out of the place by dust, flies, and smells. Yet the arches of this hall, pure Gothic, rose to the roof like a Gregorian chant.

The gibbering old man led us into dark halls, in one of which he pointed out the remains of a Turkish bath, but whether it was made by the Crusaders or by the Beybers, to whom the Knights of St. John surrendered in 1271, I cannot say. And everywhere in the ruins were the dark, animal-like eyes of the present inhabitants. Above a squalid cave from which the smoke of a thorn fire came in clouds I saw, cut in the stone of a wall, the Rose of England.

It was irritating to have come so far and to be surrounded by the evidence of such magnificent achievement and to learn so little about it.

My guide was in terror of starting back late because of the bad road and the possibility of highwaymen, so that I was forced reluctantly to leave. The old man came chattering to the main gate. I gave him half a crown, half a roast chicken, a bag of walnuts and two oranges.

He ceased to be a nice old man and became an exceedingly nasty one. He held the half crown in his hand and reproached me. He said that a French officer had once given him ten shillings. He implored me to give him more, and even dragged in Allah to support him.

I have discovered that when this sort of thing happens you forfeit the respect of the person who is trying to impose on you unless you turn swiftly and pretend to fall into a towering passion.

When I paused for breath, a look of deep reverence dawned in his face, and, carefully putting his money away, he advanced and took my hands in both of his in an attitude of deep respect and humility. I gave him a playful smack on the back of his plus tens and we parted the best of friends.

My last memory of the tremendous Krak-des-Chevaliers was of his aged, but agile, figure waving me lovingly out of sight.

§ 8

High up in mountain snows, over six thousand feet above the sea, grow the last cedars of Lebanon. There are about four hundred veterans, some of them eighty feet in height and of enormous girth. Their ancestors provided the timber for Solomon's Temple and their majesty suggested many a splendid metaphor to the writers of the Old Testament, for the cedar was the king of trees.

" Open thy doors, O Lebanon, that the fire may devour thy cedars.

" Howl, fir tree; for the cedar is fallen: because the mighty are spoiled: howl, O ye oaks of Bashan; for the forest of the vintage is come down."

In these verses Zechariah gave voice to the poetic idea that when the king of trees fell to the earth the fir and the oak, as lesser trees, mourned the death of their monarch.

I shall always regret that I did not visit the Mountain of Cedars. I was told that a recent fall of snow had made the road impassable. I should think it quite likely that many of the famous English cedars came originally from Lebanon and I am told that the Maronite monks, who to-day guard the cedar grove, will give you seeds that are almost certain to take root in the right soil. I remember that one of the gardeners at Dryburgh Abbey in Scotland told me that the vast cedar tree in the gardens there had been planted by the Crusaders; but I have since read somewhere that the first cedars in Scotland date only from 1740, and were planted in the Marquis of Linlithgow's grounds at Hopetoun House. There are, or used to be, many older cedars in England. There is the famous Enfield cedar, which was planted between 1662 and 1670 by Dr. Robert Uvedale, there was also a magnificent cedar in Bretby Park, Derbyshire, and others at Woburn Abbey and in the grounds of Warwick Castle.

In the morning I left Beirut by the French post road to Damascus. It climbs over the Lebanons through a pass that is nearly five thousand feet above sea level.

The road mounted upward past white summer villas whose

windows gazed down through a green mist of trees to a blue arc of sea and a coast-line curving north to Tripoli and south to Sidon. Then it left such trivialities behind and plunged upward, with an almost savage intensity, into a bleak world of ravines and rock walls, of perilous bends and sudden heart-shaking curves. And as it mounted the blazing sun lost its warmth and the air became cold. Gradually the tremendous panorama of the Lebanon range unfolded itself: a hundred miles of plateaux, of canyons and of rugged mountain-tops, still and brilliant in the sun, a vast dead world lifted up towards a cloudless sky.

As the air became colder, I noticed small patches of hard snow under the rocks. The wind blew like ice. The road mounted steadily upward, leading to a white and dazzling world. At the top of the pass I came to a French customs post, and on the slopes of the mountain round about were carts, drawn by mules, into which men in sun helmets were shovelling the snow. I got out, shivering, to watch them. Each cart-load was taken to a large underground pit on the mountain-side. It was tipped out, and the men in sunhelmets shovelled it down as if they were shovelling coal into a cellar. They packed it tight. These pits, which are lined with masonry, each contained several tons of snow.

" It lasts right through the summer," explained the French customs man. " They come up for it from Beirut and Tripoli and take it back in motor lorries. What do they do with it? They cool wine in it! The man who sells lemonade in the streets packs his bottles in the snow. Have you not heard them crying in Tripoli ' cooled with the snow of Lebanon '? "

He told me of the terrible snow storms that sometimes occur round his lonely station while the world below is gasping in the heat. But he liked the mountain and the solitude. He was a *chasseur!* And were there not panther in the Lebanon, and wild boar and gazelle and wolves?

While we were talking I saw the strange sight of a file of camels tenderly picking their way through the snow as they came up over the mountain top from the Plain of el Bikaa.

I dropped down over the crest of the Lebanons and in ten minutes the snowfields, when I looked back, seemed like a dream, for I was again in the fierce heat of the sun. The Plain of el Bikaa is more like one's conception of the Land flowing with milk and honey than ever the Jordan Valley could be. Spring lay over it in a pink-and-white foam of apricot and almond blossom. There were miles of mulberry trees, for this is where much of the Damascus silk is spun, and there were miles of vineyards and orchards of orange and lemon trees.

As I went on over the flat roads that cut across the plain, I thought that the Lebanon is racially one of the most curious districts in the country. It shelters a complex population which includes Metawali, who are Moslems, Maronites, who are Christians in communion with Rome (but say Mass in Syrian and permit married clergy), and the Druses, whose religion is still a mystery.

It has often been stated that the Druse religion is a queer relic of the grossest form of paganism mixed with Christianity and further confused by misunderstood Greek philosophy. Many writers of the nineteenth century were convinced that the Druses worshipped the Golden Calf. This has never been proved, although I once talked to an ex-member of the French Foreign Legion who swore that he had seen representations of the Golden Calf in a Druse mosque. The central fact of their faith, however, is the belief that the lunatic El-Hakem bi-amr-Illah, Fatimate Caliph of Egypt, was an incarnation of the Deity. Hakem, who was assassinated in 1021 by orders of his own sister, was clearly as mad as a hatter. He once slew every dog in Cairo because a dog had barked at him. He ordered the destruction of all vineyards. He ordered that no woman should show her face out of doors or even at a window on pain of death, and he forbade the shoe-makers to make women's shoes.

His determination to stamp out Christianity within his domains led to the complete destruction of the Church of the Holy Sepulchre in the year 1012. He then made war on the Moslems and became a homicidal maniac. As the disease took a firm grip on him, he proclaimed himself to be God. In this blasphemy he was supported by a man called Ed Darazi, who, however, was forced to fly from the wrath of the Egyptians. He took refuge in the Lebanon,

where he established the Druse sect. These people believe
to this day that the mad caliph Hakem was not killed, but
taken up to heaven, whence he will return to conquer the
world.

The Druses are a fine-looking race of mountaineers, but it
is scarcely surprising that their Christian neighbours have
attributed to them dark and horrible practices.

The ruins of Baalbec on that bright spring afternoon lay
in a mist of white fruit blossom. The gigantic columns of the
Temple of Jupiter, and the great Temple of Bacchus, stood
against the tremendous screen of the Anti-Lebanons on whose
bare flanks the snow shone like silver.

As a single group of ancient buildings they can be compared
only with the Temple of Karnak at Thebes. So much has
been written about them in terms of gold light over tall
columns, dark ruined halls and dry fountains, that one hesitates to add to it. Nothing can give a true idea of their
size. A commonplace, but just, comparison occurred to
me. If you could take St. George's Hall, Liverpool, the
Birmingham Town Hall, the Madeleine in Paris, and one
or two of Barclay's more Corinthian banks, wash them gold-
brown in colour, transport them to the orchards of Hereford
and bombard them with field artillery, you would have
something like Baalbec.

These ruins are among the few left in the country which
give an idea of the massive splendour of paganism. Every
student of the Bible ought to see them. Their strength even
in decay is astonishing. Many of the columns are of Egyptian
granite, and it is said that it took three years to transport
them from the Nile to the Lebanon. Some of the stones
are more massive even than the Herodian stones in the
Wailing Wall. The pomp and pride of paganism just before
the conversion of the Roman Empire has no more revealing
memorial than these magnificent courts and buildings,
forming a great city of temples dedicated to the Baal of
Syria, the Helios of Greece and the Jupiter of Rome.

One tries to image the army of priests who ministered in
this colossal sanctuary, the numbers of consecrated women,

the sickening blood rites, the strange crowds from the east and the west who would meet there to propitiate their several deities; and one finds it almost impossible to reconcile the dark, primeval theology with the magnificence of its setting.

My memory of Baalbec is that of fruit blossom, and of a little Arab goat-herd who sat on the base of a column under an almond tree, playing a flute. While he played the white petals fell like snow on the grass around him.

§ 9

After a journey across the bleak mountains of the Anti-Lebanon, I arrived in Damascus with my eyes and my throat and my nose choked with sand.

Before I went to bed I had a brief vision of Damascus as a large flat city with plenty of white domes and mosques in it, little French tram-cars, sheikhs in white robes drinking coffee, bursts of wild music from shuttered houses and hundreds of French colonial troops walking about under the lamplight.

I was awakened in the morning by the roar of an aeroplane. I watched it zoom off to the east. It was the Bagdad air mail. Then my eyes, straying about the room, saw all sorts of things that did not belong to me. There was, for instance, a bale of silk, a red dressing-gown, an Egyptian scarab, two or three rugs, and a hideous little table inlaid with mother-of-pearl.

Oh yes, of course, I remembered! I had weakly shown a passing and purely polite interest in these things on the previous night. Earnest men had asked me fifty times the amount of money they were worth. But I had refused to play their game, which is to put on a contemptuous expression and offer fourpence. So, temporarily baffled but firm of faith, they had sent everything round to my hotel in the hope of tempting me.

I went out on the little veranda of my room and felt the lovely warm morning sunshine. The air was crystal clear. The dust storm had died away. On the platform of the minaret opposite I saw the muezzin step out, an old man with a white beard and a green band round his turban, and when he lifted his robes he exposed a pair of bright red Russian boots. Through the still air of morning came the call to prayer.

You can disbelieve everything you have heard about Damascus except the beauty of its situation and the perfection of the pink foam of apricot blossom which surrounds it. It lies on an enormous plain, with sand-coloured mountains rising up on the west. Across this plain, and through Damascus, flows a narrow, rushing river, el Barada, which is the Abana of the Old Testament.

It is wonderful in this parched land to hear the sound of running water. No wonder the Arabs drew their conception of Paradise from Damascus, which is literally an orchard enlivened by streams of flowing water. The same love which the Arabs feel for Damascus and its streams was expressed with exquisite art by the Moors when they built the Gardens of the Alhambra in Spain.

The city itself is disappointing to anyone who, like myself, has always believed it to be the very soul and essence of romance. I have always imagined Damascus as the very heart of the East of the Thousand Nights and One night.

But it is not. It is a city that is saved only by sunlight from looking like a slum. The world-famous bazaars of Damascus are dark avenues under curved corrugated iron roofs which look like some elongated and poor relation of King's Cross Station. And everything about Damascus has a faint second-hand French accent.

The walls and the gates of Damascus, unlike the walls and the gates of Jerusalem, have long since disappeared. The bazaars, instead of being full of the riches of the Orient, are full of the brass ware which one associates with Birmingham. I know nothing about rugs and carpets. Damascus carpets are probably very good and worth at least almost a twentieth or a sixtieth part of the price asked for them.

"You don't understand the merchant of Damascus," said a Frenchman who heard me saying how I loathe the process of bargaining. "The art of buying is a game with rules that we all understand and—we have all the time in the world to play it.

"You English people, when you refuse to bargain, hurt the Damascene, just as you would be hurt if someone with whom you were playing bridge suddenly threw down his hand and walked away. You must sit down and drink coffee. While the Damascene praises the goods you must run them down. It is all a flight of the imagination, a battle of wits, if you like—a contest, a game!

"He asks you £50. You show horror! You kick the rug with contempt. You offer him £2. It does not matter what you offer so long as you offer something! For it is on your offer that is built up this silly, fascinating, but never tedious game called, by us in Damascus, commerce!"

This is, of course, true, but I simply cannot play the game. Perhaps I am too impatient. Even if I do try to play, and make a few moves and drink a few cups of sweet coffee, the time comes when I throw down my cards and crying, "Oh, keep your rug!" walk straight out of the shop.

Nothing that you can do in Damascus is, I feel, worse form than this. No one would think any the less of you if you murdered a man, as long as you could get away with it, and admiration would be heaped on a successful thief. But to walk out on a man when only two days and sixteen cups of coffee from concluding a deal . . . it simply is *not* done!

It was disappointing to discover that the long-distance camel caravan traffic between Damascus and Bagdad is over. Until a few years ago these strings of camels used to come in loaded with all the merchandise of the distant Orient after weeks in the desert.

Tucked away in the narrow streets of Damascus are the old khans in which the merchants and the caravan men once lodged. They are lovely buildings with Moorish arches, fountains in the centre, and galleries from which the guest chambers are reached. These fine old buildings are now either disused or hired out as warehouses.

All the desert traffic to-day is borne by motor-vans and lorries. They come in from Bagdad covered with dust and sand, but I cannot feel the same about them as I do about the old-fashioned caravan which has used this road since the time of Abraham.

The most interesting thing to a Christian in Damascus is the Street Called Straight.

A year or two after the Crucifixion, Paul, "breathing out threatenings and slaughter against the disciples of the Lord," was on a journey to Damascus. A few miles south of the city, on a slight hill which is still pointed out, he received the vision that changed his life.

"And suddenly there shined round about him a light from heaven, and he fell to the earth and heard a voice saying unto him, Saul, Saul, why persecutest thou me? And he said, Who art thou, Lord? And the Lord said, I am Jesus whom thou persecutest. It is hard for thee to kick against the pricks. And he, trembling and astonished, said, Lord, what wilt thou have me to do? And the Lord said unto him, Arise and go into the city, and it shall be told thee what thou must do."

Saul went on into Damascus, a blind man. He went to the house of Judas in the Street Called Straight, and there Ananias, a follower of Jesus, came and healed him.

So Paul was baptised. One of the greatest enemies of Christianity had become one of the greatest of all Christians.

The Street Called Straight is nearly a quarter of a mile long and is without a bend. It has from the earliest times been called Vicus Rectus, and also Derb el Moustaqim, or Straight Street.

It is covered, like many Damascus streets, with an arched roof through whose holes the sun squirts in widening beams like little searchlights. The traditional site of the house of Judas, a site reverenced by Christians and Moslems, is now a tiny mosque. It has no minaret, so the muezzin has to call the faithful to prayer from a small green balcony just like the balcony of any other house in the Street Called Straight.

I felt that I would like to look inside the mosque, even though there is nothing there now to remind one of Judas or St. Paul. I took off my shoes in the street and was preparing to enter the building when an old man, who was smoking a hookah on the opposite side of the way, came running across and made a great show of opening doors and leading me inside.

It was a small, whitewashed building. A tank of rather green and stale-looking water was let into the floor on one side. Five or six men, kneeling towards Mecca, were performing their prayers in silence, touching the stones with their foreheads and rising again, eyes closed.

It was strange to think that this little white-washed mosque should have been the place from which the missionary appointed by Christ Himself set out to conquer the world.

§ 10

I have suggested that Damascus disappointed me. There are, however, little bits of Damascus that are superb and unforgettable. One is a mosque of the Dancing Dervishes, a cool silent place of white pillars and marble fountains. Another is the House of Asad Pasha, now turned into a kind of museum by the French authorities.

This really is a page from *The Arabian Nights*, for a very ordinary door leads to it from a crowded dusty bazaar where donkeys and camels crowd you against the wall as they pass. On the other side of the door, however, is a fairy palace of three hundred rooms. Oranges and lemons shine in the bright sun through their screen of green leaves, water splashes on marble fountains, and even the shouts in the street outside fail to penetrate this secret paradise.

Another exquisite thing in Damascus is the Grand Mosque, which was once a mighty Christian Church dedicated to St. John the Baptist. It has often been burnt and destroyed, but nothing can hide the splendour of the old church that the Emperor Theodosius the Great built in 375 A.D.

In a narrow lane near the mosque, and set in a little green garden, is, to my mind, the jewel of Damascus. It will remain in my memory long after more splendid and ambitious things have vanished. It is the modest little tomb of the great Saladin, the hero of Walter Scott's *Talisman* and the one enemy of Christendom whose name runs through all the history books as that of a brave and chivalrous foe.

The tomb chapel is no larger than an ordinary room. Over the door these words were written centuries ago in Arabic:

" O God, accept this soul, and open to him the gates of Heaven, that last victory for which he hoped."

Inside is a quiet marble room with walls of striped stone and arches covered with beautiful coloured tiles.   There is just space enough to walk round the carved marble sarcophagus in which lie the bones of the great champion of Islam.   There are framed pictures lying on the tomb which recount in Arabic the great deeds which Saladin performed for Mohammedanism, and at the head of the tomb is Saladin's turban.

An old sheikh guards this tomb, sitting outside in the sunlight near the door.   He came in and rattled away to me in Arabic, explaining the deeds and wonders of Saladin's life.

I would like to have been able to tell him that we in England remember Saladin chiefly because he came up against Richard Cœur de Lion, who, in spite of the fact that he could not speak English, never spent any time in his own country, and nearly broke us by the weight of the tax levied to ransom his romantic person from captivity, is nevertheless one of our most cherished heroes.

We might have enjoyed an interesting conversation, but I could only nod and pretend to understand what he was saying to me.

Saladin seems to have been a great and good man, even when you burrow under the legends which have grown up over him and get down to the hard facts of history.   I am afraid one must admit that he could boast more of the Christian virtues than his opponents.

Just as everyone in England knows the story of Alfred and the Cakes, and everyone in Scotland can tell you about Bruce and the Spider, so everyone in the East can tell you stories of the kindness and the compassion of Saladin, but they call him Salah ed-din, which sounds much prettier.

The historic fact remains that this man who drove the Crusaders from the Holy Land, who conquered provinces and gathered incredible wealth, gave everything away and died so poor that, wrote one of his friends, " We were obliged to borrow money to purchase everything necessary for the funeral, even down to the things that cost him but a half-penny, such as the straw to be mixed with the clay (for the bricks of the tomb)."

Saladin seems to have cared nothing for money and would make enormous gifts to the poor when his war chest badly needed gold. When he was dying he called his standard bearer to him and said:

" You who have carried my banner in the wars will now carry the banner of my death. Let it be a vile rag set upon a lance, and as you carry it through Damascus cry to the people: ' Lo, at his death the King of the East could take nothing with him save this cloth only.' "

It is recorded by those who were present that, as Saladin's simple funeral cortège moved through the narrow streets of Damascus in the year 1193, men broke down in tears, crying that a saint had left the earth. Perhaps the most solid tribute to Saladin's memory is the fact that all the doors were shut and " no one thought to pillage the city."

Curiously enough, the only apparently shabby trick performed by this paragon of chivalry was one directed against our own Richard the Lionheart. During the battle of Jaffa, Richard's favourite horse Fanuelle, " the yellow-coloured," who was almost as famous as his master, was killed under him. Richard was forced to carry on the fight dismounted. Saladin saw this from the enemy lines and was shocked that so noble a warrior should fight on foot. He therefore sent as a present to his rival a magnificent Arab charger.

Richard was apparently in a more than usually cunning mood that day. He ordered one of his knights to mount the horse and try him out. No sooner had he done this, than the animal, taking the bit between his teeth, galloped straight back to Saladin.

Possibly only the evil-minded would attribute such deception to Saladin! We learn on the authority of one who was present—Bernard de Tresorier—that Saladin was so ashamed to think that Richard might believe his present to have been a trap that he could not look up when he apologised to the runaway English knight.

However, he sent him back mounted on a charger of less obvious homeward instincts; and on this steed Richard fought until the inglorious end of the Crusade.

As I left Saladin's tomb, I thought how satisfactory it is to stand at the grave of a hero whose life bears the test of time. He was one of the greatest enemies that Christianity has ever known, yet so fine were his qualities of mind and heart that we cannot think of him without affection. His life seems to have been ruled by Justice, Truth and Compassion.

In fact, a student of the Crusades is bound, perhaps reluctantly, to confess that Saladin was at heart the best " Christian " of them all. It is one of Time's little ironies!

§ 11

The memory of the starving Saluki of Banias returned to me every day. Sometimes I felt certain that she must be dead; at others I was confident that she would recover. It may seem absurd to say that this poor creature caused a complete upheaval in my plans, but life is made up of these apparently trivial incidents. If I had not promised in the most emphatic manner to return and see how she was getting on, I would have made my journey south into Trans-Jordan over the desert road through El Sananein and Deraa, a road I badly wanted to travel. I felt, however, that it was impossible to compromise with my conscience.

So, to the bewilderment of my driver, I set off south along the ancient caravan road from Damascus to Galilee, and, branching to the west at Kuneitra, was in Banias before noon.

If the necessity of keeping my word had made me impatient and angry, as I confess it had, all such feelings were swept away as soon as I entered the ragged little village. I should have realised that I had been the sole topic of conversation in Cæsarea Philippi for a whole week! I should have known that those who were at work on the mountain-side were told about me when they came home; that some who had never seen me gave long and vivid accounts of the incredibly mad Englishman who had stayed to pick a dog out of the road. The result was that as soon as I appeared the whole village gathered round, but not with the grim, hard expression which terrifies nervous tourists: they were all laughing and smiling, and a cry went up "Abu kelb, Abu kelb!" which means "Father of the dog."

The Arab is a great hand-shaker. I went round the group shaking hands, telling the driver to ask them how the dog was.

"Come and see, O Abu Kelb!" was the reply.

And a crowd of bare-legged little children went running up between the mud walls announcing the great and spectacular news that "Abu kelb, the father of the dog," had returned.

I was led to the squalid little hovel behind the mud walls. The crowd was so great that we had to shut the gate, but the children climbed up on the wall to watch. A white mare was tethered in the yard. A *douanier*, whom I had not seen before, came out of the house, dressed in a pair of khaki breeches and a grey army shirt. He shook me warmly by the hand, explaining in French that he was a lodger in the house, but had unfortunately been out on duty when I had been there before. Now, however, how happy he was to make my acquaintance! How glad he was that I had come back. Two little boys brought wooden stools from a house and set them in the shade. The *douanier* sat on one and I sat on the other. The women and children grouped themselves round us. All the time the *douanier* bubbled with affability and I gazed round for the dog, but could not see her. My heart sank. So she was dead! Perhaps it was just as well. But I was too familiar with the habits of the Arabs to ask any questions. All would be known in time.

The *douanier*, it appeared, was an Armenian from Aleppo. He had a great affection for England. He had learnt English from a priest at a mission school in Aleppo. Ah, if some day he could go to London! He would like that very much. The English were a great nation. The last war was a sad affair. All wars are sad. All the English love dogs. The Arabs do not love dogs. But he, an Armenian from Aleppo, he loved dogs like the English. So he rattled on. Then the

crowd parted and the man who sweeps out the shrine of
El Kedir came up with the Saluki.

I could hardly believe my eyes. She could stand! Her
hind legs trembled woefully and her tail, bare and mangy,
was still well down. But her eyes had lost the fear of death,
although they were still full of pain.

The Arab had made her a little coat from a pair of khaki
trousers and he had bound up the wounds on her forelegs
with pieces of rag. The Armenian explained that he had
bathed her wounds with wine and oil—the remedy which
the Good Samaritan used on the wounded traveller.

The dog seemed to know in some way that I was the cause
of her present well-being and she did something which
completely finished me. She walked up to me and just rested
her bruised muzzle on my knee. I decided at that moment
that, grotesque and blown out with starvation as she was,
wounded, mangy and sore, I would somehow take her home
with me to England.

I thought how extraordinary it is that a show of interest
and a little money can make so much difference to any living
thing. The poor creature that a week ago had been stoned
and kicked about was now a feature of the village. She was
the protégé of the rich, mad, Englishman.

I asked the Armenian what would happen if I did not take
her away.

" This man," he replied, pointing to the Arab, " will look
after her as long as you pay, but when you stop paying he will
turn her loose, because he is too poor to buy food for her."

I told him of my intention of taking the dog to Jerusalem.
He shook his head. The Palestine Customs would not allow
her to enter in her present condition. But if I got an order
from the Government? I suggested. Yes, it might be
done.

So we agreed that they should continue the feeding and the
bathing of the dog, and I handed out some more baksheesh.

" That is the name of the dog," I explained. " I shall call
her ' Baksheesh.' "

This was a joke that everybody understood!

I went off, promising that I would either call again at Banias
or send someone in my name to take " Baksheesh " into

Palestine.   And as I went off I heard the children shouting
" Abu kelb! "

Weeks later I got a letter which read:

" My dear friend, Mr. Morton, I am verry glade I get a
great satisfaction by this relation which commenced with a
dog.   You can be able for its hospitality.   I brought a big
jar of sea water from Sidon by which I wash it evry day,
morning and evening.   Now it is better then bifore.   I
hope that we will not forget ourselves, and I am allways redy
to execute your commissions.   Excuse me for my mistakes,
because the last war of Turkey in 1920 wich resulted after two
years with all Christchen immegration has destroyed our
futur and high life.   God be with you till we meet.
                                                JOHN."

It was from the excellent Customs Officer at Banias.   So
he was bathing the dog with water from Sidon.

That sounded excellent.

In a few days I was able, through the kindness of the
Palestine Government, to get poor " Baksheesh " through the
Customs and into the kennels of the S.P.C.A. in Jerusalem,
an organisation that, although dying for lack of money, is
striving hard to make the Arab understand that animals can
feel and suffer.

The report was encouraging.   I saw myself taking " Baksheesh " for walks in Hyde Park and for long tramps over the
Sussex Downs.   Then one day I received a letter saying that
she was dead.   She was too weak to stand treatment.

" Knowing how much you cared," wrote Mrs. Reynolds, a
member of the Society, " I have buried her in my own garden,
where you can think of her sleeping among the rock flowers."

When I was near Banias again I made a détour to thank
John for all his kindness.   The Arabs and the children
crowded round my car with cries of " Abu kelb! " looking
and peering into the car for " Baksheesh."   I told them she
was dead.

" It is the will of Allah! " they said.

And they looked at me with the respectful sympathy due to any man who tries to defy the inscrutable will of God. Even John, the Good Samaritan, said it was a good thing, and that when I went to Aleppo he would give me two much finer dogs. Even he did not understand that the crucified eyes of poor "Baksheesh" had marked her out from all the other dogs upon this earth.

CHAPTER NINE

I go in search of the castle of Machærus where Salome danced before Antipas. In Trans-Jordan I walk the streets of a Roman city of the Decapolis, encounter the Arab Legion, and eventually ride into the hills and see all that is left of Machærus. I go to the crusading town of El Kerak and cross the desert to Petra.

§ 1

MOST travellers will agree that before setting out on a journey there are always one or two places that loom unreasonably large in the imagination. Sometimes they justify the hopes set upon them, often they woefully disappoint.

Long before I set foot in the Holy Land I was determined to visit Machærus. This is the name given to the fortress in Moab where Salome danced before Herod Antipas and in which St. John the Baptist was beheaded. When, however, I came to grips with the problem I discovered that few people had ever been to Machærus, and that in the writings of the last century the accounts of this ruin could be reckoned on the fingers of one hand. That, of course, made me more anxious to go there.

Machærus, or El Mashnaka, " the hanging-place," as the Arabs call it, lies on the top of one of the wildest mountains of Moab on the eastern side of the Dead Sea. No roads lead to it and the hills are full of armed nomads. They told me in Jerusalem that it would be impossible to go there without an escort of mounted police, and that the best thing I could do was to cross over into Trans-Jordan and consult the authorities at Amman.

Therefore I left Jerusalem by car early in the morning and ran down to Jericho. I saw the glorious sight of the sun coming up behind the savage Moab Hills, lighting the still waters of the Dead Sea and shining over the grotesque spectral hills of the Jordan Valley. Palestine ends and Trans-Jordan begins

at the bridge over the Jordan known as " Allenby Bridge."
It is an iron-clad, army bridge, and as you go over it the
loose planks rattle.

The road from Allenby Bridge runs up into a green and
lovely valley. Hiding in the oleanders and smothered with
brambles was a sight I had been told to look out for: an old
German howitzer crouching like a frog in the bushes. This
is the notorious " Jericho Jane," with whose assistance the
Turks could pitch a shell into Jericho during the War.

I saw a shepherd sitting beside the road with a rifle across
his knees. A little further along three Arabs passed with
long-barrelled muskets slung across their backs and their
chests covered with cartridge-belts. The Arabs in Palestine
and Syria are disarmed, or technically disarmed, but in
Trans-Jordan, where the national sport of raiding is still kept
up, it has been found that the best way to prevent casualties
is to let everybody carry a gun.

The exquisite valley ran into hills misty with almond blossom.
The sun shone through the reddish-brown leaves of the pomegranate trees and lit up the bright green of the fig trees, and
whenever there was room among the rocks little patches of
wheat and barley lay against the darkness of the soil.

The road climbed to a high tableland, an enormous
deserted plateau which in Roman times was one of the most
famous grain-growing districts in the East. Now the barren
hills lie against each other to the sky, and the road runs up
and down them and round the extreme edges of them, mile
after mile, with never a living soul in sight.

Once, beyond Es Salt and on the mountain road to Jerash,
a figure suddenly appeared against the sky. He was a
Bedouin mounted on a small bay horse. He held a rifle
across the saddle-bow. He sprang up from nowhere and
gazed down at us. Until I was quite sure that he did not
intend to take a pot shot, I am afraid I was rather blind to
the grace and beauty of his appearance. Turning a corner,
I saw the encampment to which this man evidently belonged:
fifteen or twenty low, black-brown tents pitched on the hill
slope with a few horses tethered near, the tent-flaps lifted so
that I could see inside where the clansmen were evidently in
conference.

Except in the Beersheba district of Palestine, you rarely see the genuine Bedouin until you enter Trans-Jordan. Here the tribes circulate slowly from grazing ground to grazing ground, perpetuating the earliest customs of the Children of Israel.

The district into which I was travelling is familiar to every reader of the Gospels as the Decapolis. You remember how on one occasion Jesus was followed by a great crowd from Galilee and from Decapolis. Again St. Mark tells us that when our Lord departed from the borders of Tyre and Sidon " he came unto the Sea of Galilee through the midst of the coasts of Decapolis." Also the man whose demons entered the herd of swine was a dweller in the Decapolis, and we learn that " he departed and began to publish in Decapolis how great things Jesus had done for him."

This Decapolis was a league of, at first, ten Greek cities. Some of them were perched high on the brown mountains that frown down on the Sea of Galilee from the east, others were placed to the south of the lake, near the Jordan, and some stood high on the eastern uplands, all ten arranged, however, with a strategical eye to the ancient trade routes commanding the way to the Mediterranean Sea across the Plain of Esdrælon and the caravan roads from Damascus to Petra. In the time of Christ they were brilliant, rich cities in constant touch with Greece and in daily contact with the varied foreign traffic that passed through them, coming north from Egypt through the gorge of Petra and flowing south from Damascus over the long brown desert road.

I have tried to show how Jesus when in Galilee was on one of the main roads of the ancient world; and the Decapolis was also a little archipelago of Greek culture set in a wide ocean of hills and desert.

I forget who said that civilisation is communication, but you realise how true this is as you travel the wastes of Trans-Jordan to visit the remains of a great city that is now stranded hopelessly in the hills. The roads that brought the life-blood to the cities of the Decapolis have vanished long ago. Sometimes you see a marble pillar standing bravely on a hill, or you see ancient paving running off at any angle into nowhere, and you realise that such are the last signs of the great roads which brought life to the old cities.

Nineteen centuries ago I would have been approaching Jerash over a paved military road that linked one city with another. I would have met bodies of troops on the march, merchants from Damascus, traders from the mysterious rock city of Petra far off to the south, rich travellers from Greece and Rome, trains of baggage-animals moving up into the hills with the European mails and—one can be perfectly certain—the latest feminine fashions from the West.

But now, as I looked, I saw the dangerous road slipping round the edge of mountains and, far off, a few pillars standing forlornly against the sky.

It was Jerash.

§ 2

This dead city will some day be as famous as Pompeii and Timgad. It has remained lost for centuries in an in-accessible part of the world, but to-day British archæologists are busy sorting out the confusion of its tumbled pillars. One comes upon Jerash delighted and astonished to find that while Gaza, Ascalon, Cæsarea Philippi, and other Roman cities have fallen into dust, this one at least remains with its pavements, its baths, the ruins of its temples, its theatres, its forum and its houses.

The human interest which is absent from Baalbec is present at Jerash. It is impossible to place oneself in the position of a worshipper at the shrine of Moloch, but it is easy in Jerash to know what it must have felt like to come into this lovely Greek city, with its luxury and its ordered European life, after days of wandering in the desert. How good it must have been to hear the chariot wheels on the paving-stones and to be told that *Medea* was to be performed that afternoon by a band of travelling players in the theatre behind the forum.

Just before I entered the main street of Jerash, I stopped to look at a huge pit in the earth to the left of the main road that leads through the south gate. Here were the remains of an immense circus for gladiatorial combats, and also a huge lake, now dry and grass-grown, in which mock naval battles were once staged, high up among the mountains, a

curious sidelight on the national character of the Decapolis:
a region of wave-born Greeks.

I went through what had once been the south gate into the
main street paved with blocks of stone, the grass sprouting
between them exactly as it does from the pavements of
Pompeii. It was quiet and still with the exaggerated stillness
of death. Groups of tall pillars stood at intervals on each
side of the road, and I noticed that there was a high side-
walk for foot-passengers. The heavy traffic over these roads
must have been tremendous, because the blocks of stone are
worn away in wheel-ruts. There was also an underground
drainage system. I noticed several of the man-holes still
lying in the road.

One of the chief buildings in the town is an exquisite Greek
theatre with the pillars and part of the post-scenium still
standing, the seats rising tier above tier in such perfect pre-
servation that you can read the numbered tiers—A B C and
so on. I climbed up to a back seat and looked out over the
ruined city. I could see the main road leading into a circular
forum, most of the pillars still standing, then running on,
with temples and great buildings on each side, to lose itself
towards the north among the grass and the thistles of the hill.

Near a beautiful fountain that once gushed water on its
four sides, I met a man who might have been a Scot. He had
red hair and a bristling reddish sergeant-major moustache.
I discovered that he was a Circassian, a member of one of the
colonies which Abdul Hamid settled on the edge of the
Bedouin country after the Russo-Turkish War of 1877. He
had the key of the museum and was the authorised caretaker
of Jerash; so we set off together.

My Armenian refused to leave his car, although there was
nobody in sight. He said that there would be nothing left of
it if he walked away from it for a minute. Therefore I was
forced to go without an interpreter, but the Circassian,
who was a most amusing and likeable fellow, talked to me
quite eloquently in sign language. He took me to a semi-
underground ruin and gave a vivid imitation of a man having
a Turkish bath. He panted as if the heat of it was too great
for him and mimicked the drinking of water. When, in order
to prove that I had understood that he was showing me the

Roman baths, I pretended to scrub and pummel him, his blue eyes lit up and he was over-joyed.

We then climbed up on a massive platform where the remains of a huge temple stand against the sky. I do not know whether this is a Temple of the Sun or a Temple to Artemis, who, I think, was the deity of Jerash. We crossed enormous desolate courts where lizards flashed away from our feet, we looked into dry temple fountains and upon the cold stones of altars.

Sitting on a high place near another theatre, we gazed round at the high smooth uplands, in shape very like the Cumberland fells, but harsher in colour and littered with stones.

It was ghostly to see the great Roman road, still so strong and paved in the city, slipping out of the north gate to vanish into the hillside. There are too many people always wandering about Pompeii, and making funny remarks to which one must listen, for that place to be very impressive, but Jerash, on its wild, bare hills, like a skeleton in a desert, lonely and silent on that bright morning, was something I shall never forget. I wondered, as I sat there, whether Christ ever visited the cities of the Decapolis. How impossible it is to say that He did not. The Gospels are concerned only with the last two or three years of His life. If it could be proved that during the unrecorded years of His life He journeyed over the sea to Rome, why should we be surprised? He was surrounded all His life in Galilee with travel and the news of travel. From the hills behind Nazareth He could see the blue sea and ships going out over the Roman world. The learned scholar will say, " Jews did not travel for pleasure "; but then Jesus did not always behave as a strict Jew : He made friends with Samaritans, He reinterpreted the Sabbath, His whole life was a revolt against the cold formalism of the Jew. Even though it may be clearly extravagant to imagine that He ever left the shores of Palestine, surely it is possible to believe that He did not on every occasion avoid the Gentile cities in His path.

I like to imagine that when Jesus " came through the midst of the coasts of the Decapolis " He entered these stately Greek cities, sought the shade of their lovely colonnades, listened to the talk in the forum and, with His kind, charitable eye, saw

K

something good there which had escaped the attention of his fanatical contemporaries.

We should not forget that it was one of these cities of the Decapolis, a city just like Jerash, which was destined to shield and shelter the living tradition of Christ. It was to Pella, a city of the Decapolis south of Galilee, that the Christians of Jerusalem fled when the armies of Titus camped on the Mount of Olives.

It was this Greek city that gave back in safety to the world eye-witnesses of the Faith. And in the course of time, when the story of the Christ came to travel over the world, it was the Greek language that carried it across the sea.

I retraced my steps over the wild road and came to an old mill that is worked by a stream. I saw an Arab with a sack of wheat slung on a donkey's back making his way to the mill. The driver came with me because I wanted to see inside the building. Crouched in the late afternoon sunlight on a stone near the door was a thin, rather elegant, but dirty Bedouin woman. She had two little beads let into her nostrils at each side, and there were tattoo marks on her face. Her bare feet were long and beautifully shaped. She was playing with a pretty little girl of about five, whose stomach, however, was monstrously swollen, a common deformity with Arab children, who have to eat what they can get.

As soon as she saw me, the woman crouched away with a savage expression and muttered something to the driver. I asked him what she had said.

" She thinks you are a Jew who have come to take away the land," he said.

" But why should she think so."

" Because you are wearing a hat," he replied. " The hat is the sign of the Yahudi. ' May God curse you with a hat,' say the Arabs."

I made him go back and explain to the woman that I was not a Jew, but that in my country everyone wore a hat. She became as affable as she had been unpleasant, and I shook hands with her, which I am sure was not the right thing to do. However, it pleased her, and she led the way into the mill.

I would never have believed it possible to see in this age
a Roman mill in going order. The stones were enormous
granite blocks of late Roman workmanship, and I suppose
they were grinding wheat when Jerash was alive.

The Arab and his donkey stood in the darkness of the mill
waiting for the sack of wheat to be ground. He was a fine-
looking fellow, and wore a large dagger stuck through his
belt. He began to talk to me, and the driver translated.

" How much do wives cost in your country? " was his
rather unexpected opening question.

" We don't buy wives in my country," I said.

The Arab gave me a piercing glance in which, I think, was
something like contempt.

" Tell him," I said, " that many fathers give their daughters
money when they get married."

The Arab seemed interested by this.

" He says," remarked the driver, " that such fathers must
be very big fools. There are none like that in Trans-Jordan."

I gathered that the price of wives had gone up in a scandal-
ous manner and the Arab was annoyed. He talked about it
with exactly the same expression, and in the same tone of
voice, that we discuss another sixpence on the income tax.
Then, slinging the sack over the back of the donkey, he made
the usual elaborate farewells, touching his forehead and his
breast, and went off into the sunlight up the hill path beside
the stream. . . .

It was almost dark when I got into Amman, the little
mountain capital of Trans-Jordan. There was not one hat
to be seen anywhere in the town and I determined to buy
myself a *keffiyeh* in the morning. Opposite the small stone hotel
rose a mighty Greek theatre with seats for seven thousand
people.

§ 3

I was awakened in the morning by the sound of a gun. It
was a small field-gun. It shook the windows slightly and went
barking over the hills. It fired at minute intervals. I looked
at my watch. It was fifteen minutes past four.

From my brief glimpse of Amman on the previous night,
it looked to me the kind of place in which anything might

happen, so I leapt out of bed and went to the window.   There was nothing to be seen but the enormous and attentive emptiness of the Greek theatre across the road.   The sun had not yet risen.   The shades of Sophocles and Æschylus seemed to be chasing one another over the empty tiers.   They turned out to be two Bedouin shepherd lads in their white shirts. Then the gun shuddered in the air again, and from somewhere in the hills at the back I heard a barbaric banging of drums and a squealing of fifes and—it seemed impossible!—bagpipes.

A man in the hall of the hotel told me that it was the beginning of a Moslem feast, and that the Amir Abdullah of Trans-Jordan was on his way to pray in the mosque.   I went out into the streets.   The sun was just rising.   People were all running in one direction, and I followed them.   I found myself on the fringe of an extraordinary crowd.   It was entirely Arab.   Sheikhs from the desert sat their horses and carried rifles slung at their backs.   A military brass band, the men in smart blue uniforms of European cut, marched past with the air of guardsmen.   Then came a detachment of Arab pipers in the same blue uniform, the pipes fluttering with Royal Stuart tartan.   Then the crowd became excited and a sheikh's horse began to prance and bucket, so that I have a confused impression of a troop of Circassian lancers coming down the hill at a gentle canter, tall caps of black astrachan on their heads, long black coats with scarlet facings, rows of cartridges over their chests, and from each lance a gay, dancing little flag.   The gun shuddered again and stopped.   The sun turned the dome of the distant mosque into a big white mushroom shining above the narrow streets.   There was silence.   And in the silence the Amir entered the mosque to pray.

I went into one of the shops, which were now opening their shutters, and with two or three words of Arabic bought myself, with the greatest ease, a Bedouin headdress, the *keffiyeh*, and an *agaal* of black twisted hair.   I tried it on in the hotel and was delighted: for sheer hard villainy I would have been difficult to beat, even in places known only to Lawrence and Doughty.

Great Britain has restored Amman to the dignity of a capital city, a position it has not held since Old Testament times, when it was the chief city of the Ammonites. It was here, as Moses says in *Deuteronomy*, that the huge " bedstead " of the giant Og, King of Bashan, was to be seen. This bedstead, by the way, is now supposed to be one in which Og slept not in life but in death, for several enormous sarcophagi have been discovered near Amman.

To-day the town, lying in a shallow valley and on the surrounding hills, is not very large to our eyes, but to the desert Bedouin it is a dazzling metropolis. A modest stone palace, which the British Government have built for the Amir, stands on the crest of a hill overlooking the town. The Royal Air Force have an aerodrome not far away. But the great feature of Amman is the headquarters of the Arab Legion.

This military police force is only a thousand strong, and it is estimated that there are ten thousand serviceable rifles among the surrounding tribes. The fact that law and order are so well observed throughout Trans-Jordan, that elderly ladies can motor across the desert to Petra without an armed escort and with nothing more to complain of afterwards than a severe jolting, speaks for the wonderful prestige of the Arab Legion.

The headquarters camp at Amman is a strange and, to an exiled Englishman, a touching sight. It looks at the first glimpse like a rather odd compromise between one of the lesser seaside resorts of the south coast and a section of a colonial exhibition. There are hundreds of fruit trees and a bandstand. Sometimes the band plays " Colonel Bogey " with a strong Arab accent. Across neat, ordered paths, from whose gravel a plentiful supply of convicts pick the smallest weed, stroll peacocks, turkeys, geese and guinea-fowl. There is a school for the children of the legionaries which might have been built in Aldershot, but next to it rises a white mosque, one of the few British-built mosques in the world. Within the camp is the central prison, which one might also call the University of Trans-Jordan! The prisoners (and the prison is nearly always full up) receive during their terms of imprisonment an excellent technical education. Prison carries with it no stigma in the desert; in fact, many a Bedouin does not feel that he has proclaimed his manhood until he has served a sentence.

I went through a heavily barred gate and saw a proportion of the three hundred and eighty inmates, including ninety murderers, busily and happily engaged in a laundry, a cook-house, a shoeing forge, a stone quarry, a mattress-making shop and a poultry farm.

Every building in the camp has been erected by the prisoners. It is an amusing fact that on release a large percentage of them wish to enlist in the Legion.

So great is the prestige of the Legion in Trans-Jordan that to have a son who is a policeman is regarded with the same pride that the peasantry of Ireland feel for a son in the priesthood.

The man who has turned the children of the desert into a battalion of guardsmen is known all over the country as Peake Pasha. He is a humorous, rather gentle-mannered, blue-eyed Englishman who was born in Melton Mowbray about forty years ago. He played a distinguished part in the Arab Revolt during the War. His name is a magic talisman in the country. It is spoken with respect and affection from the highest mountain in Trans-Jordan to the most desolate steppe. His achievement is one that could never have been accomplished by any man who did not know, understand, and like the Arab. He is assisted in command of the Arab Legion by two other British officers.

§ 4

I began to make inquiries about my journey to the ruins of Machærus.

"You cannot possibly go to El Mashnaka," I was told. "In the first place there are no roads to it and, secondly, you may be killed. The Bedouin in the hills are wild and poor and your body would probably be undiscovered for weeks, giving them the chance to slip off into Sinai or some-where else. It's impossible. . . ."

But I was determined to go to El Mashnaka—or Machærus —and I did the only thing: I went to Peake Pasha about it.

"You really want to go?" he said. "All right. You shall have a police escort."

I was told that a mounted escort and horses would meet me where the road gave up.

I rose at four a.m. and reported at the police station, as all travellers must in Trans-Jordan, giving my destination and probable time of return, and then I motored for three hours over the most terrifying road I have ever travelled. It is a road that loops its way in a series of spirals and hairpin bends over one of the appalling mountains on the east side of the Dead Sea.

This road had only just been completed, and so great an achievement was it considered that a toll of a few piastres was soon to be imposed. But it was not yet known whether certain stretches would resist the temptation of crashing down into the valley.

It had been made for the benefit of the thousands of Arabs from every part of the country who flock to the hot mineral springs at Zerka Ma'in, which are said to cure the most stubborn forms of rheumatism, neuritis and all the allied ills.

I have often been afraid in a car, but I have never been quite so frightened as I was when the double hairpins became so sharp that it was necessary to reverse with the rear wheels close to a drop of several hundred feet. One mistake and the car would have turned over three or four times in the air and have bumped from ledge to ledge in the valley below.

I was relieved to enter a deep gorge whose sides were stained green and rust-red with the hot mineral water that fell in clouds of steam down the rock. Here three mounted policemen were waiting for me with a spare horse.

When I asked them which direction we should take, one, who spoke a few words of English, pointed to the almost perpendicular side of the opposite mountain and said: " Over there."

Before setting off I examined the hot springs of Zerka Ma'in. There are about ten of them. They rise in a gorge that is too awful to be beautiful, a hot crack in the volcanic mountains, pervaded by the stench of sulphur and whose stones are stained and streaked with the mineral deposits of the springs.

It was in these springs, which have been credited with magical healing qualities, that the diseased body of Herod

the Great was bathed before his horrible death at Jericho.
The old name for them was the hot springs of Callirrhoë.

Few Europeans have ever visited these springs, but they
are famous among the Arabs, who trek from enormous distances on camel and horse-back to take the waters. They
have, I gathered, a regular season, like Harrogate or Bath.
They were just preparing for it, making rough shelters round
certain pools for the women and clearing a camping ground.
An Arab took me to a natural Turkish bath formed by the
rise of a hot spring in a cavern. The place was full of steam,
and the cave so hot that I could not bear the heat for more
than a minute.

He told me an extraordinary story about the hot springs:
that they were discovered by a black slave of King Solomon
and that mighty magic had been done there. But I could not
understand the point of it. Anything which is old and
unknown is attributed to King Solomon.

We mounted and set off. One policeman rode ahead with
his rifle at the ready. Fifty yards behind him rode the
second, then myself with the third. Our path lay steeply
upward over the course of a dry torrent. The horses picked
their way like mountain goats. An eagle with plenty of
white in its wing feathers circled in the sky above us and
flapped lazily away.

Our ascent took us into a land of desolate *wadis*, of bleak,
stone-littered desert over which it was possible now and then
to break into a short canter, and up slippery, dry stream-beds
where we let the horses pick their way. The mountains
appeared desolate, but the policeman told me that probably a
hundred pairs of eyes were watching us, and to each pair of
eyes would be a rifle.

" Do you often have trouble with the Bedouin? " I asked.

I knew that he was a Bedouin, but proud of his status as a
member of the Arab Legion and a representative of the
British Government.

" I would go," he said with a look of scorn, " alone and
empty-handed anywhere and arrest a whole village, and no
hand would be raised against me."

Suddenly the first policeman put his horse into a canter
across a fairly level stretch and drew up at a great pile of

stones. His quick eyes had seen a movement. Ten or fifteen Bedouin stood up at his approach. Each one of them had a rifle.

If I had been alone I suppose they might have robbed or shot me without a second thought. When I came up, the old sheikh advanced and grasped the rope that was my bridle. He gave me the customary greeting of peace and asked me to go over the hill, where his tents were pitched, to drink coffee. It is very difficult to refuse such invitations without giving bitter offence, but I begged the policeman to excuse me in any manner he thought fit.

We rode for three hours over the mountains, sometimes catching a glimpse far below us of the bright blue waters of the Dead Sea, sometimes dipping down into dreary clefts in the mountains or scrambling like goats up the sides of cliffs. The little Arab horses performed feats of agility which even an Exmoor pony would have found impossible.

At the end of three hours we came in sight of El Mashnaka —" the hanging place "—a name which surely perpetuates some ancient memory of Herod's terrible stronghold.

For a mile around on a neighbouring mountain top were the remains of an ancient city. There were tumbled walls and something that looked like the relic of a road. The ground became so rough that even the horses could take it no longer. We dismounted and, leaving them in charge of a trooper, began to scramble over the rocks.

We descended into a kind of gully between the two hills and came upon an ancient causeway of hewn stone. This led us to the foot of a tall, conical hill devoid of all vegetation, whose sides were slippery with small stones. This was the hill on whose crest once stood the mighty fortress of Machærus.

For the first time that day I felt a cool breeze. We were 3,700 feet above the Dead Sea. All round us rose the heads of the Moab Mountains, ridge beyond ridge folded against each other to the blue sky.

I have never, even on Ben Nevis or Snowdon, looked forward with greater excitement to the view that would open out before me when the hill was climbed. The two police scrambled up first, their rifles slung across their backs, grabbing for foothold on the loose shale with the stocks of their riding-whips.   Now and then a shower of stones would come flying past down the hill.

We reached the summit and looked down.   Below us lay a sheet of still, blue water—the Dead Sea.   From the opposite shores rose mountains, piled against each other in tortured confusion, brown, desert hills, rising and falling to the west, and far away on the very edge of the sky, crowning the highest ridge, a few pinheads of black—the buildings on the Mount of Olives.

To the right, where the Dead Sea ended in lines of salt hills, lay the bleached, stained salt heaps of the Jordan Valley, and in all those miles of white and khaki only one patch of green, Jericho, and through the brown flatness one thin silver thread, the River Jordan at the end of its journey from the Sea of Galilee.

I found nothing on the hill but a pit, the remains of what might once have been a vaulted well, and the relic of an old wall.

The ground was covered with small fragments of pottery. Lower down on the side of the hill is a dungeon.   This may have been the very dungeon in which John the Baptist spent his last days.

The three or four writers who have left brief accounts of this hill mention that it is possible to see the remains of the metal rings to which prisoners were chained, but I looked for them in vain.   If they were visible years ago I fear they must have vanished.   The dungeons are choked with rubbish, and the Bedouin who wander these hills use them as cattle shelters in the winter.

Climbing back again to the hill top, I saw that the tribes-men, who can appear with alarming speed out of apparent desolation, were standing about talking to the policemen.   The sheikh, a magnificent patriarch with the nose of a hawk and a thin grey beard, stood leaning on an ancient rifle.   His robes, blowing aside, revealed the fact that in addition to a scimitar and two curved daggers, he was padded with hundreds of brass cartridges.

He invited me to drink coffee with him, and looked as though he might shoot if I refused !   I asked him where his tents were pitched, and he pointed over two or three

mountains.   Again we made polite excuses, and after a good
deal of handshaking he cantered off.

I sat with my back against all that is left of the wall of the
castle of Machærus and tried to imagine what it must
have looked like to the Baptist and his contemporaries.   The
cone-shaped hill stands up isolated from the neighbouring
ridges, surrounded on three sides by precipices and linked to
the hills of Moab by the ruined causeway.

This isolated cone was fortified long before the Christian
era by the Jewish king Alexander Janneus.   Herod, who
had a passion for out-of-the-way fastnesses, must have seen
in Machærus an even more remote and invulnerable hill
than the Herodium, which rises almost opposite, among the
mountains that pile themselves behind the western shore of
the Dead Sea.   He therefore enlarged and re-fortified the
castle, and also built a town on the hills behind it.   These
were the ruins and the scattered stones that I had noticed
before coming to the causeway.   At the same time he built
for himself a magnificent palace.

Therefore, when John was taken prisoner and condemned to the dungeons of Machærus, he would have been
brought up from the hot springs over a Roman road that
twisted up and round to the hill-top town.   He would have
been taken through this town to the causeway that led to the
castle.   The walls and bastions of this awful stronghold
towered above a dead world.   The arsenals were piled with
all the latest weapons of defence and attack, as well as stores
of lead and bronze and iron.   The store-rooms and granaries
were full of wine, oil, dates, and enormous quantities of wheat
stacked ready for siege.   This was the horrible place in which
the Baptist found himself, cut off from the world and locked
away in the darkness of a prison on Moab's most terrible
summit.

Some critics have suggested that Salome danced before
Herod at Tiberias and that swift messengers were despatched
with orders to execute the Baptist and return with his head.
If this had happened, the going and returning would have
occupied at least four days.   It is impossible to do things
quickly in such a country as Moab.   Both St. Mark
and St. Matthew suggest that no sooner was Salome's

horrible request granted than the head of the Baptist was almost at once produced on a charger. The whole atmosphere of the Gospel account of this tragedy suggests in a definite manner that the dance and the murder occurred in the same locality. Dr. Moffatt's *New Translation of the Bible* even increases the pace of this narrative. Whereas the Authorised Version translates Salome's request as " I will that thou give me *by and by* in a charger the head of John the Baptist," Dr. Moffatt renders the lines as " I want you to give me *this very moment* John the Baptist's head on a dish." I am sure that anyone unbiassed by a cherished theory would say, after comparing the accounts of St. John's death as rendered in the Authorised Version, the Greek Testament and Dr. Moffatt's translation, that Herod, Salome, Herodias and the Baptist were all together in the same place on that tragic night. Even assuming that Josephus was in error, there is still one important historic fact that would point to the mountain fastness of Machærus as that spot.

In order to marry Herodias, Herod had been forced to put away his first wife. She was the daughter of the Nabatæan King, Aretas of Petra. His country lay far to the south of Machærus, between the Dead Sea and the Gulf of Akaba. Now, Herod's wife, swiftly hearing of her husband's intrigue with Herodias, fled to her father. She went first to Machærus —which was known as " the Watch-Tower of Arabia "—and from that place she was, as Josephus tells us, handed from general to general across the mountains and the desert until she reached her father's country. As soon as Aretas heard his daughter's story, he declared war upon Herod. The obvious movement of any Jewish commander threatened in those days by Petra was instantly to move up his forces and command the stronghold of Machærus, the most southerly castle on the Arabian side of the Dead Sea and the natural base for any warlike operations against the Nabatæans. And this, I believe, is exactly what Herod did. There even seems to be an echo of war in St. Mark's account of the guests at the banquet: " his lords, *high captains* and chief estates." It is significant in this argument that among those dining with Herod on the night of the Baptist's death were the chief officers of his army.

While I have no doubt that Machærus was the scene of Salome's dance and Herod's death, I am not so sure that the palace stood near the prison. After having looked carefully at the conical hill, I feel convinced that it held a fortified castle and nothing else, and that the luxurious palace of Herod lay on the ridge to the east, where the town once stood.

Calling to the police, I descended the hill and re-crossed the causeway. We rode to the ruins of the town on the hill. This is a flat, bare hill-top and a good building site. There are, I imagine, at least a square mile of ruins, or rather worked stones, lying in piles and scattered all over the ground.

We know that the town was surrounded by a fortified wall whose towers were one hundred and sixty cubits in height. Why should Herod have complicated the efficiency of his great fortress by planting a town near to it, and a town of such size, unless for a very definite object? I suggest that this town was built to minister to the great palace which must have stood somewhere in the centre of it. It is known that this palace was designed on a scale of great magnificence. Its colonnades were composed of pillars hewn from single stones, and its floors were made of pieces of coloured marbles. It had luxurious baths and a great banqueting-hall. There is clearly no room for such a building on the small conical hill of El Mashnaka. The palace must have stood on the now stone-strewn ridge. On this spot Salome danced before Herod Antipas.

It is possible, when one stands on this hill, to imagine with a fair degree of accuracy what happened on the night of the execution. Herod, his military staff and his court, and, of course, Herodias and her daughter, occupied the royal palace. All round them on the hills about shone the camp fires of the army. It was a night of festival. The Evangelists tell us that it was Herod's birthday. It was more probably—for the Greek word could have another meaning —the anniversary of his accession.

The men were alone in the great banqueting-hall, the Tetrarch, his captains, his nobles and his chief officers of state. The banquet was over. Slaves would be crossing the coloured marble pavements with the flasks of Greek wine. There was probably some music, and scent burning, and dark curtains moving as the slaves came in and out.

I do not believe that the dance of Salome was the climax to an orgy. I imagine it to have been a far more terrible thing. I think it was quite cold and deliberate. The men were alone. We know this because Salome had to " go forth " to whisper to her mother; and we can be certain that if Herodias was not at the feast she would not have permitted any other woman to be there. So the men were alone with their nervous, petulant ruler, drinking wine and probably listening to him as he told some old story.

It is a difficult thing to forget that you are feasting on the top of a savage mountain or in wild country. And I imagine that many of those at Herod's feast were thinking of the wilderness that lay about them and of the deep gorges that fell away into darkness. They would wish to be anywhere but on the fearful summit of Machærus, lifted towards the stars on the shoulders of a spectral world of hills. The happy, warm sounds of Tiberias were absent; the shouting of boatmen in moonlight on the lake, the cry of the birds. It was so quiet and chilly on Machærus. Even the banqueting-hall of Herod, with its coloured floor and its scented lamps, was like a warm, lit tomb on a hill top.

Suddenly the music grows louder and the curtains part. A woman comes into the light of the lamps and the braziers. And the men, who had been lying on their couches, with the wine moving drearily like a mist through their brains, are instantly awake, but not with lust or passion, but with astonishment and shame. For the woman is Salome, in whose veins runs the high blood of the Asmonæan princes.

Slowly she moves out into the open space. The music grows louder. The glasses are empty and are filled again. And the white body of Salome caricatures the movements of the Egyptian dancers and the slave-girls of Rome. The lords, high captains and chief estates watch a sight they never thought to see: an Asmonæan princess dancing; and their Jewish souls are ashamed. But Herod's ageing eyes light up with interest. Such abasement demands an extravagant reward. The music dies and there is a hush in which no one knows whether to applaud until the Tetrarch leads the way.

"Ask of me whatsoever thou wilt and I will give it thee."

The girl, whose beauty is famed as far away as Rome, glides like a ghost across the marble floor and out beyond to the hall where Herodias is waiting. She comes back and asks for the life of John the Baptist.

"And the king was exceeding sorry; yet for his oath's sake, and for their sakes which sat with him, he would not reject her."

A file of soldiers marches from the palace out over the high ridge towards the castle. Their iron-shod feet ring across the causeway and mount the hill to the guard-house. The stars are burning above them in the blue of the night, and they can see far below the shadow of the Dead Sea and the outline of Judæa. The executioner goes with his sword down to the dungeon. He returns with the head of the Baptist, still warm. And the night wind moves the hair.

They march back over the causeway towards the lights of the palace. The Jewish guards shrink from them in horror. A Greek smiles and polishes a silver plate with the sleeve of his coat. Into the blaze of the banqueting-hall, and across the broad marble pavement, they come right to the throne of Herod, holding before them the head of John the Baptist on a charger. And an old, old story, which no man can prove or disprove, says that Herodias leaned from her seat and thrust a bodkin through his tongue. . . .

It may, of course, have been quite different. But who can say? I can only put down the ideas that came into my mind among the ruins of Machærus.

Three hours later we dropped wearily down towards the hot springs at Zerqa Ma'in. The sun had left the gorge, which was now an even more threatening sulphurous gash in the earth's side. The police horses, which were familiar with the springs, walked unhesitatingly through the steaming water, but mine became temperamental and refused at first to enter it.

An Arab, who had erected a bell tent near one of the streams and proclaimed himself to be a health inspector from, I think, Amman, came forward to offer, with the usual fine manners of his race, the hospitality which I was only too thankful to accept. As he busied himself with the making of tea and the washing out of a tumbler and a cup, he told me that every year when the pilgrimage to the hot springs occurs he comes down and lives there to see that everything goes off as it should.

Crouched on the bed blankets in the bell tent, I drank the hot, sweet tea. My host sat opposite, surrounded by the paraphernalia of his exile—a rifle, a bandolier full of cartridges, a paraffin stove and a box full of oranges. He asked me to stay the night and I would dearly like to have done so, but I felt that it would have been unfair to those in Amman who had taken such pains for my safety and had made so many jokes about my possible failure to return.

It is not difficult to understand how men like Doughty and Lawrence developed an affection for the desert Arab. Although I become furious with myself for knowing no Arabic, finding myself always halted against the barrier of language, I can perceive, in a dim way, the bond of sympathy and mutual respect that could exist between Bedouin and Englishmen. The desert, I think, is an excellent school, and the Englishman instinctively comprehends its code of conduct. Aristocracy, and all the fine things that come with conscious pride of race, are slowly and surely dying from the world. But they are still alive in the desert.

I said good-bye to the health inspector and, after hideous hours on the sinuosities of the mountain road, came to the police station at Amman as the sun had set. A legionary came out, saluted, ticked me off on the chart of the day's travellers as " returned," and wished me good-night.

§ 5

What follows is, I fear, in the nature of self-indulgence, but I feel that the reader, if placed in my position, would have surrendered to the temptation and have gone, as I did, to Petra.

It seemed absurd to be on the eastern side of the Dead Sea for the first, and possibly the last, time in my life and to be only a day's journey from Petra without going there. It has no connection with Christian history except, as I have already said, that the war between Aretas, King of Petra, and Herod Antipas led to the gathering together at Machærus of those people who brought about the death of the Forerunner.

Petra, among the wild mountains between the Dead Sea and the Gulf of Akaba, has been until recently a difficult and dangerous place to visit. The ancient capital of Edom had been lost from crusading times until our own. It was discovered only a little over a century ago when Burckhardt, the traveller, disguised as a Moslem, managed to enter the gorge and gaze with astonishment at the amazing rock tombs on the pretext that he wished to sacrifice a goat at the neighbouring shrine of Aaron. This same inviolate shrine defeated the efforts of Robinson and Laborde. Irby and Mangles had to be content with a long-distance view through their telescopes, and even Dean Stanley, travelling with an escort as recently as 1853, approached the dead city among the rocks with the knowledge that he might be stopped by armed Bedouin and forced to turn back.

To-day, however, if you stand for a while in Cook's office in Jerusalem, you can hear elderly English women arranging to join a party for Petra, and reserving a tent in the camp which Cook's maintain there in the spring. If you have read the books of the men whose names I have mentioned, this would appear pure fantasy: it seems hardly possible that the ordinary tourist can venture into a place which hardened explorers entered at the peril of their lives only fifty or sixty years ago. During the Turkish régime I believe a few tourists went to Petra with an adequate armed guard, but in our time, thanks to the strength of the Arab Legion, the desert road from Amman to Maan and Elji is judged to be safe. And as the cars go bumping over it during the season, complacent elderly Englishwomen and their husbands gaze on the wilderness without the slightest idea that they are performing an act that would have made the hardy Burckhardt's blood run cold! I sometimes think that lack of imagination is the guardian angel of the English people.

I set off in the morning over the same road that I had taken to Machærus, for I wanted to ascend Mount Nebo, the mountain from whose summit Moses viewed the Promised Land and on whose flanks, it is believed, his body lies in a secret grave. I was armed with a letter to the police officer in Madeba.

He received me in his house and offered me lemonade. We sat there talking and smoking cigarettes while he showed me his little museum of Roman lamps and coins. I asked him if there were any Christian Bedouin. He told me that years ago there were a few, who used to have Mass celebrated in their tents, but they had nearly all died out or had settled in the villages. He mentioned an interesting nomad family called the Azizat, who camp round Madeba. They are Christians and came originally from the ancient Crusaders' town of El Kerak. It seems that during the Crusades this family heard of a plot to massacre the Moslems, among whom they had many friends. They warned the Moslems of their peril and from that time were exempt from all taxation. In 1912 there was, apparently, a readjustment of the tax situation in Moab and the privilege, which had lasted for so long, was abolished.

" But even to this day," said the officer, " a Moslem of El Kerak will stand in the presence of a member of the Azizat family."

We went out and took the steep and little travelled track to Mount Nebo. At times we were driving over ledges of bare rock, setting the car at the sides of hills and creeping gingerly over dry watercourses. At length the road expired and we got out and climbed the rest of the way.

Mount Nebo is nearly as high as Ben Nevis. It rises towards a cloudless sky and its summit, on which one could gather an army, collapses on the west into space. One looks down into horrible precipices and deep, khaki-coloured chasms where the foot of man has never rested. Below is the Dead Sea, calm and still like blue glass, and from its opposite shores the sterile mountains in humps and ridges lift themselves towards the long shoulder of Judæa where, outlined against the sky, are one or two small dots—Jerusalem, forty miles away.

It is literally true that from the summit of Mount Nebo you can see the whole of Palestine. You see the mountains above Hebron to the south, the highlands of Judæa and Samaria, and the Jordan Valley to Hermon. It is one of the finest views in the world. And there is no sound on Mount Nebo but the eerie sough of the west wind coming up over the edge of the mountain.

We examined the ruins of a Byzantine church which was built on the spot where, so tradition says, Moses stood when the Lord " shewed him all the land of Gilead unto Dan." There are a few columns, a few mosaics, and a stone which the monks of Roman times believed to be the stone on which Moses had stood.

While we were looking at the incredible relief map of the Holy Land, the Bedouin, who slip up like ghosts from no-where, gathered round, and one of them said that we were invited to the sheikh's tent. Leaving the windy summit of Nebo, we climbed down and came in time to the Bedouin encampment.

The sheikh, a middle-aged man with a dagger in his waist-band, advanced and offered us hospitality. As we went towards the black tents, the male members of his family ranged themselves in a line. I was introduced to each of them, passing down the line and shaking hands. We were shown into the sheikh's tent, where rugs were put down for us to sit on. A young boy entered with a pot of coffee, and a com-panion carried a tray with little cups. First the sheikh took a sip. Then the cup-bearer poured a teaspoonful into my cup. I drank it. He poured another teaspoonful into the cup. I drank that. He went on pouring it out in small medicine-like doses, which I drank with polite bows to my host. The Bedouin loves strong bitter coffee, which bears no resemblance to coffee as we know it. He pounds the berries in a mortar, and then adds a bitter herb. The sheikh made a polite speech which the police officer translated:

" He asks you to stay and eat with him," said the policeman.
I made my excuses.

" He says," continued the officer, " that it is a pity you are
in such a hurry because he is very anxious to kill a sheep for
you."

We extricated ourselves from the invitation with a torrent
of politeness, and the sheikh accompanied us some way over
the rocks and the fields until, coming, I suppose, to the confines
of his camp, he touched his head and his breast and bade us
good-bye.

The police officer, before we parted, offered to give me an
Arab horse. I wondered what would happen if one went
about accepting all the things one is offered so generously in
Arab countries.

The road towards El Kerak led for many miles over rough
hill country which sloped down and smoothed itself out into
land that was half desert and half steppe. It was a bare land,
with far horizons broken by slight hills and ridges. The only
living thing I saw for an hour was a dog fox with a beautiful red brush with a white tip to it. He gave one glance at
the unusual spectacle of a car lurching unsteadily in his
direction and then vanished among the sand-hills.

At this point we struck what is known as the main
road to Mecca, one of the loneliest railway lines on earth.
Once a week a train comes from Amman and goes south
to Maan. This was the line that Lawrence and his Arabs
were always blowing up with such gusto during the War.
We turned to the right and went south beside this line, which,
as mile stretched into mile and hour into hour, became almost
a friendly and companionable thing. It was with a thrill of
excitement that at one point I saw a rather dead-looking wagon
standing in a siding with " H.R." painted on it—Hedjaz
Railway.

In the afternoon we came to a station. It was called El
Katrani. There were three or four hovels, a police post, a
concrete station building, and a few telegraph poles, to one of
which a white horse was tied. We stopped to report to the
police. An Arab Legionary invited us to enter his station and

drink coffee, but we pointed to the sun and told him that we were going to El Kerak.

Turning to the west we climbed once more up into the hills, and from hills we climbed into mountains. All that afternoon we met only three mounted figures on the road: a man with a mail-bag escorted by two mounted police. As the sun was setting we came round the corner of a precipice and there before us, on a ridge three thousand feet above the sea, guarded on all sides by terrible gorges, defended by grey bastions and a tall crusading wall, stood El Kerak, the once famous city of Renault de Chatillon.

§ 6

Inside the wall are mud hovels, unmade roads, flocks of sheep, and Arabs who squat in the shade of walls and penthouses, instead of the knightly palaces and churches that one might expect to see.

Sometimes the silence is broken by the clatter of flying hoofs as two or three magnificently clothed horsemen ride through the town, leaping in and out of the saddle at a canter and exhorting each other to showy tricks of horsemanship with wild shouting and laughter.

Sheep graze on the mounds which cover one of the most enormous castles of the Middle Ages. In ruined halls, where the Crusaders once feasted, are herds of black goats, and the ruined chapels where the knights prayed are used as stables.

Everywhere I go in El Kerak I am escorted by a crowd of about thirty young Arabs. They hang curiously on my footsteps and watch me. If I look round suddenly they run away like shy animals. If they become noisy and I turn, there is an instant silence. Visitors rarely come to El Kerak.

From the ramparts of the castle I look down into deep ravines. Far off to the west I can see a blue slice of the Dead Sea lying in a cleft of the hills.

The magnificent castle is in incredible decay. It is almost frightening to explore the enormous vaulted halls which are filled with rubbish and débris half-way to the roof.

In Old Testament times El Kerak was "Kir of Moab," "Kir Haraseth," or "Hareseth." It is mentioned in the Bible as an impregnable fortress. The present town wall and the fortress are a relic of the Crusades, when the town was of supreme importance because it commanded the caravan routes from Egypt and Arabia to Syria.

At one time the Lord of Kerak was that remorseless Dick Turpin, Renault de Chatillon, who was in constant conflict with the courteous Saladin because of his frequent raids on Moslem caravans. This Crusader made continuous war on the pilgrims to Mecca, and swooped down from his stronghold to sack the rich caravans from Damascus.

Although Saladin besieged Kerak on and off for five years, the fortress was never taken by force of arms. Things were so bad during one siege that the Crusaders drove out their women and children, believing, apparently, that life in a harem was preferable to death from starvation. The story goes, however, that Saladin saved these women. It was not until 1183 that Kerak was forced to surrender.

I made the usual visit to the police station to register my name. I was the first visitor for several months. To-day, as in Turkish times, the town is a military depôt; but, instead of the Turks, one finds the charming and courteous members of the Arab Legion.

After I had registered, a policeman who spoke English said to me, as if he were showing off an art gallery:

"Would you like to see our jail?"

I looked through iron bars into a stone room which contained thirty-three prisoners, chiefly thieves and murderers. They gazed out smilingly and waved their hands.

The population of Kerak is Christian and Moslem. The Christians are divided between the Greek Orthodox and the Latin Churches.

The most interesting church is a small building dedicated to St. George. Like many another church of St. George in the East, it has a pillar with a chain firmly bolted into it, to which lunatics are attached. Why St. George should be the patron saint of lunatics I do not know, but there is a wide-spread belief in Palestine and Trans-Jordan that an insane person can be cured if he spends a night in a church of St. George.

" The mad people are brought here," I was told, " and chained to the pillar for a night. The church is locked up and, in the morning, perhaps St. George has taken away their devils."

I was astonished to hear that such notoriously pagan customs are still observed. These dream-cures used to be performed by Æsculapius, and were very common in ancient times. The sick person had to spend a night in the temple courts. When Christianity conquered the old gods, the dream-cures were transferred from temple to church. I remember reading somewhere of a temple of Isis so famous for its dream-cures that even Christians could not be prevented from going there. The local Patriarch solved the difficulty by expelling Isis and installing the bones of two martyrs from Alexandria; and the cures continued.

" Do many people spend a night in the church? " I asked.

" There was one last week," I was told.

I shall never forget that evening in El Kerak. The sun had set behind the hills of Judæa. A hot day was ended and a pink glow filled the sky. The town rode its hill crest like some battered old eagle. Brown bare feet suddenly pattered in the dust of the roads. People whispered. Astonishing news! Two other strangers had arrived. I found myself consumed by curiosity. Who could they be?

In the centre of Kerak, opposite the jail, is a little town garden composed of a few date palms and a handful of thirsty-looking shrubs enclosed by barbed wire. I was led to this and my guide, a small boy, parted the shrubs and pointed out the strangers to me: two young men in khaki shorts, who were sitting under the date-palms drinking coffee with the young chief of police.

I joined them in the little garden. A policeman brought out more sweet coffee in small cups. One stranger was an American, the other a Belgian; both of them were employed in their respective legations in Cairo. Having a week's leave, they had hit on the adventurous idea of motoring from Egypt through Trans-Jordan to Jerusalem. They had had a wonderful time and were full of admiration for the kindness and efficiency of the Arab Legion.

" Since we entered Trans-Jordan," said the young American, " we have lived with the Arab Legion, spending our nights at wayside police posts. You people in England must be very proud of them."

I was too ashamed to tell him that probably few people in England had ever heard of them.

" Things like the Arab Legion," said the Belgian, " justify your colonisation. . . ."

And while brown faces peeped at us through the screen of leaves, we sat talking of the desert and of the strange ideas that survive there untouched by the modern world.

The Crusades are the last great memory of Kerak. The common Arab term for all white-faced strangers in Kerak is still " Franks," just as it used to be with the troops of Saladin. And is it, after all, so remarkable that this should be? Locked away among the inaccessible mountains of Moab, Kerak has had little else to remember but the Crusaders, for nothing has happened since to compare with their downfall, no other memories have come between this ghostly town and its founders, and there are consequently no other stories to tell the children at bed-time.

The muezzin came out on the balcony of the minaret above the garden and called to prayer; and we sat on beneath a mulberry tree. The sun set and the bats came out, flickering.

" And when Saladin was besieging the town," said the chief of police, " they looked down from the wall over there and saw an army camped in the valley and on the hills. It was the marriage day of the lady of the castle. She begged Saladin to lift the siege for her wedding. And he did so. The next day, however, the war began again. . . . Then there was Renault de Chatillon. He was a bad man, but a brave one. Guy de Lusignan, who was King of Jerusalem, had made a pact with Saladin that the pilgrims should pass safely to Mecca. But Renault did not keep the peace. He attacked the pilgrims and killed them. But at the Battle of the Horns of Hattin both Guy and Renault found themselves prisoners of Saladin. It was a hot day, and the knights

CAUSEWAY TO MACHÆRUS

" Pharaoh's Treasury," Petra

were thirsty. As they stood in the tent of Saladin, water was brought and handed to Guy de Lusignan. He handed the glass to Renault. Saladin saw this and said: ' It is not I that give you this water but Guy de Lusignan.' And do you know why he said this to him? He said it because he was going to kill Renault and would not offer him even the hospitality of water; for with the Arab protection goes with hospitality. Saladin treated Guy with every honour of war, but he took a sword and with his own hands cut off Renault's arm. And the public executioner slew him in the tent of Saladin That was how the lord of Kerak died."

It was getting dark. The stars were out. Somebody said we ought to be moving. The young men were staying in an Arab house and I had a room in the little Latin monastery. We said good-night.

The Arab priest, whom I had first taken for a Frenchman, was waiting for me, a frail little man with a thin beard and large childish brown eyes.

" I feared that something had happened to you," he said, " until I heard that you were taking coffee with the captain. Dinner is ready."

We went down into a white-washed vault. There was an oil lamp on the table and a plate of dates. A young Arab dressed in a black cassock set before us macaroni soup, which he carried from the kitchen next door. While we ate this, we could see him roasting lamb cutlets on a wood fire.

We ate the meat and then peeled enormous Jaffa oranges, talking all the time of the inscrutability of God and the beauty and the ugliness of man. Then we talked of war. The priest's hands trembled as he stacked the thick orange peel on his plate and his big, innocent child's eyes seemed to grow larger.

" I was bastinadoed by the Turks during the War," he said quietly in his precise French. " I could not have endured it had I not remembered the scourging of Our Saviour. I was tied down like this, my arms out and my feet so, and they gave me three hundred strokes on the soles of the feet. My feet bled. God was kind to me. I fainted."

He sipped a little of the sour wine and smiled as if apologising for his confession.

" Why did they do this to me? They said that I had helped to conceal British spies."

" They might have killed you."

" God was merciful," smiled the little man. " I was exiled to Aleppo."

He took another sip of the wine and a light seemed to shine in his old face.

" And there," he said, " I had happiness. I saw the allied armies march in and I knew that Christians had captured the Holy Land."

Just as I was going to bed, the little priest came to me and whispered that the Commandant and his A.D.C. had come to bid me welcome to the town.

Five or six men in khaki, and several of the local sheikhs, were sitting silently in the little room that was decorated with pictures of the Crucifixion. They stood up to attention and bowed; and there was much ceremonial exchange of cigarettes. The little priest came in with a tray of coffee cups. Only the Commandant could speak English. His staff and the attendant sheikhs sat silently watching us as we talked side by side on a little sofa.

Our conversation was stiff and formal like a minuet. We paid one another compliments and talked of horses and hunting and manly things. The little priest in his worn soutane and his dusty biretta moved among us, silently filling the little coffee cups.

It was like a scene from the ancient world. In this way the wanderer was met—and his motives politely discovered—in the days of romance. I rose and excused myself, for it was late. The soldiers and the sheikhs rose and bowed, and we said good-night.

The music was the howling of dogs. I have never heard such howling, for a full moon was silvering the Mountains of Moab.

I lay awake for hours in my little white cell watching the moonlight fall through the bars of the window. The dogs of Kerak, and the dogs in all the mountain villages for miles around, were baying the moon. In the rare intervals when,

as if wearied out, they ceased to howl, far off would sound the
yapping of jackals; and that would start the whole chorus off
again.

I must have fallen asleep, for I awakened to find the cocks
crowing and the sun rising. I heard a voice crying in the
silence of the morning. It was the muezzin calling from the
mosque.

Then the bell of the monastery began to ring. I was just
in time to hear the little priest say Mass. A small Arab
boy assisted him. And every time the old man knelt before
the altar I looked at the soles of his feet and remembered the
three hundred strokes of the cane, which he had borne meekly
and with courage. . . .

We said good-bye that morning.

" God guard you," he said, " by day and by night. I will
pray for you."

He took out a piece of torn paper and, placing it against the
wall, carefully wrote my name on it.

" Perhaps you will come back some day," he said, with a
quiet smile and a complete disregard for the material difficulties and the claims of modern life.

" Who knows? " I said. " I will come back in thought.
Whenever I think of you saying Mass in the early morning I
shall be here."

" Thought and prayer," he said. " They are the same."

I walked on down the hill.

Often have I remembered him in the early morning as
he moves through the ancient ritual in the little chapel
on the crags of Moab. If the intercession of those who are
good and kind and simple and clean of heart can help one,
then I think the many sins I have committed may be a little
lighter on my shoulders.

§ 7

You travel for hours across the desert to the south of
El Katrani, meeting nothing all day except wandering
Bedouin with rifles slung across their shoulders, or a herd
of camels existing where any other creatures would die.

Then, far off over the burning flatness of the land, the sun shimmers over a small stone building. It is one of the police posts of the Arab Legion. You must again give your name, destination, the number of your car, or the colour of your horse or camel.

As you stop at the police post an incredible figure emerges, dressed in the uniform and spiked helmet of the Legion. He is incredible in the middle of the desert because he might be dressed for guard-mounting at Buckingham Palace. His buttons are small suns. His boots shine. His spurs are burnished.

He comes to attention, salutes like a guardsman, goes through his formalities, and then, even though he cannot speak English, he will make you understand that he wishes you to accept the hospitality of his lonely little station.

He gives you a seat of honour, makes for you either bitter Bedouin coffee or sweet mint tea and, if it is near sunset, he will always offer you a shake-down in the police station.

These unofficial hosts of Trans-Jordan hand you on to each other across the desert, smiling, charming, hospitable.

The long road to Petra runs due south over flat country where miles of glaring sand weary the eyes. Then come stretches of black basalt pebbles like the dry bed of an ocean. For a mile or two these stones are all of the same size, then they grow larger, and again larger, as if smoothed and shaped by primeval currents and deposited by long-vanished tides.

It is a wearying journey. In five hours I met only two cars lurching along in the opposite direction. The people inside them, sheikhs muffled up to the eyes in their white *keffiyehs*, gazed curiously at me. Terrible, cruel and monotonous as this road was, it was but the beginning of that trackless sand and rock and shingle which Charles Doughty has for ever captured within the covers of one of the great books of our time, *Arabia Deserta*.

We came to Maan in the afternoon, a small mud village with a few date palms round it. The landscape here became almost crowded. We saw a man on a trotting camel come in from the south, and we saw two mounted police riding out to visit a post to the north. We turned to the west and came into green land where hundreds of camels and their long-legged calves were grazing by the wayside.

In an hour or so we entered the fertile valley called Wadi Musa, " the Valley of Moses." The stream that enlivens it is said by popular legend to be that which sprang forth when Moses struck the rock. The more one sees of this strange country, the less one feels competent to say, as so many destructive critics of the Old Testament have no hesitation in saying, that this and that incident could not have happened. What they really mean is that certain events seem incredible to them because they are outside the range of personal experience. It would do such critics good to read the fascinating account of the Exodus and the Crossing of the Red Sea as reconstructed by a man who lives in the desert of the Wanderings. I refer to that excellent book *Yesterday and To-day in Sinai*, by the present Governor of Sinai, Major C. S. Jarvis. I have no doubt that many Old Testament critics have light-heartedly dismissed the striking of the rock by Moses as a picturesque fable, but hear what Major Jarvis says about it:

" The striking of the rock at Rephidim by Moses and the gushing forth of the water sounds like a veritable miracle, but the writer has actually seen it happen. Some of the Sinai Camel Corps had halted in a wadi and were digging in the loose gravel accumulated at one of the rocky sides to obtain water that was slowly trickling through the limestone rock. The men were working slowly, and the Bash Shawish, the Colour-Sergeant, said ' Give it to me,' and seizing a shovel from one of the men he began to dig with great vigour, which is the way with N.C.O.'s the world over when they wish to show their men what they can do, and have, incidentally, no intention of carrying on for more than two minutes. One of his lusty blows hit the rock, when the polished hard face that forms on weathered limestone cracked and fell away, exposing the soft porous rock beneath, and out of the porous rock came a great gush of water. It is regrettable that these Soudanese Camel Corps, who are well up in the doings of all the prophets and who are not particularly devout, hailed their N.C.O. with shouts of ' What ho, the Prophet Moses ! ' This is a very feasible explanation of what happened when Moses struck the rock at Rephidim, and, what is more, Moses—being an extraordinarily knowledgable man—had probably a very shrewd idea that something of the sort would happen."

We came, where the valley widened, to a village of stone and mud huts surrounded by a wall of baked mud, and there the road ended. Mounted police were waiting for me; but I was incapable of speech for a second or two because on the sky-line was standing something so grotesque, so unlike anything around it, so distinct and curious, that it might have fallen from another planet.

This was a range of fretted, jagged mountains, dark blue and purple in colour, so bare and so dead that they looked like the frontier of another world. Perhaps the mountains of the moon look like that. You realise at a glance that in remote times a volcanic eruption had flung out of the earth strange molten matter that had cooled into this incredible fretwork.

The surrounding landscape ends sharply at the foot of these hills. There is no gradual blending of one into the other. The green hill-slopes end suddenly and the gnome-like mountains begin, so split and cut by millions of crevices that the whole mass is always filled with small patches and pockets of shadow. In the heart of those grotesque mountains is the mysterious city of Petra.

My luggage was slung on the back of a donkey and I mounted a horse. With the police, one fore and the other aft, I clattered off through the mud village of Elji, and the road led over the white, dry boulders of a water-course.

I have often noticed that some mountains, although fantastic from a distance, are apt to become quite ordinary when you approach them. But that is not true of Petra. In fact the grotesque eruption becomes even more grotesque as you draw nearer to it. The Valley of the Dead at Luxor is a cheerful place in comparison with these mountains, which are like the blue, devil-haunted landscapes which early Italian painters have put behind their saints. They are so weird and ominous that I was grateful for the sound of the horses stumbling among the stones.

After three-quarters of an hour we turned suddenly to the right and rode straight into the face of the mountain.

Anyone watching from a distance might have believed that we had vanished like spirits into the rock, for the entrance to Petra is through a crack in the gigantic cliffs, so narrow in places that you can almost touch both sides with outstretched hands. It was dark and cool in this gorge and I was reminded of those caves in the cliffs round the Lizard in Cornwall. You squeeze your way into them and see dim cold walls of rock rising above, and the outside world is visible through a thin bright cleft cut by the sea in the rocks. The gorge, which is called El Sîk, is similar, only on a gigantic scale.

One of the police told me that no Arabs liked to pass through the Sîk alone after dark, and should it be necessary to make the journey after the sun has gone down, they would come through in companies, making a tremendous noise to scare away the evil spirits and to give themselves courage.

The Sîk winds in a curious fashion, now widening and now narrowing, and the ground underfoot is sometimes of smooth pebbles and sometimes of huge boulders. No city in the world has ever been protected by such a tunnel, and no city has ever possessed a more uncanny approach.

Framed in the end of the gorge, seen through the tall cleft of rock, is a red-brown temple. I know of nothing more surprising than this sudden, unexpected vision. It shines there through the thin crack in the rocks, so close that you cannot see the whole temple until you have emerged from the gorge. This, like most of the temples and the rock tombs of Petra, is not built but is carved from the face of the soft sandstone as a cameo is carved. This temple is called Pharaoh's Treasury by the Arabs, who believe that gold and jewels are hidden in the decorative Roman vase that surmounts the building. The vase is pitted by the rifle shots of those who, I suppose, hoped to see a shower of wealth descend on them.

We went on over a stony track with tall cliffs on each side; cliffs a little pinker than sandstone and honey-combed with black entrances to tombs, houses, and temples, some low down to which one could climb, others high up to which there was apparently no entrance. And each tomb and temple was faced with pillars and heavy Corinthian doorways. We passed the ruins of an amphitheatre, the rows of red sandstone seats much frayed by time, and emerged into the great arena between the hills on which the city of Petra once stood.

This arena, like the hills all round, is itself a curiosity. It might have been the crater of a volcano or the bed of some ancient lake. It is about two miles in length and is covered with the mounds of the old city. Enormous oleanders, wild figs, juniper trees, and tamarisk grow in great profusion. And the hush of death is over it. If I had to select one place among all the places I know in the world where the spirit of desolation might have its home, I would choose the dead city of Petra lying silent among the mountains of Arabia.

Our horses, having picked their way through the Sîk like goats, were now anxious to break into a trot, for the end of the journey was near. At the foot of a fretted mountain the blue-red colour of burnt clay, I saw five or six dots of white. This turned out to be the camp. There were a few bell tents and a marquee.

" Would you like to sleep in a tent or a tomb? " I was asked.

" I would prefer to sleep in a tomb," I said.

" Follow this man."

An Arab took my luggage as if he had been an hotel porter and set off up a steep track behind the camp. My tomb was cut in the face of a tremendous mountain known as the Acropolis. It was a large rock chamber with a square door and a roughly hacked window. Like all such places, it had at one time been used as a cattle shelter or something of the kind, and the roof was blackened by smoke. I could trace beneath the grime the fine chisel marks of the masons who had made the tomb thousands of years ago. There was a green canvas bed in a corner and the usual camp equipment.

" Are there any snakes? " I asked the Arab.

He searched thoughtfully for some English words:

" Snakes," he said, " not too much! But scorpions a little! "

Then he gave me a winning smile and went away. From the door of my tomb I saw across the broken ground the opposite mountain, el-Khoubta, whose lined, worn face was flushed to the topmost pinnacles with the pink of the setting sun.

§ 8

I was amused by the little company that sat down to dinner in the light of the marquee's paraffin lamp. There were three German professors in breeches and puttees, who talked loudly and made pencil notes as they ate. There were two young Englishmen in khaki shorts who were, I learnt, archæologists engaged on a " dig " at distant Beersheba. They had made the adventurous journey alone, motoring until the road gave out and then hiring a camel, which they had ridden in turn. I have no idea how many days they had been travelling, but the younger of the two lowered himself very tenderly into his camp chair!

Then there was a delightful middle-aged English couple who brought a strong atmosphere of Grosvenor Square into the marquee. The man had propitiated the gods of Old England by putting on a dark lounge suit, but there was an appalling hint of apostacy, I thought, in his white buckskin shoes. Most significant of all were four empty places. Our conversation was mainly about these absent and unknown companions. What could have happened to them? They were due to arrive before sunset. Could they have met with an accident? Could they have fallen into the hands of thieves? Although it was then too late for them to come through the Sîk, each time there was a sound outside the Arab servant went hopefully to the tent-flap and looked out; but there was nothing save the desolate ruins lying cold in a green wash of starlight.

Travel in Palestine must have been like this about fifty years ago, when lords and their retinues swept slowly over the ruins of the ancient world with a magnificent disregard for expense. I was interested to learn that the manager of the camp had learnt his trade during that opulent era which was brought to an end by the War. He took me into his private tent, which alone was almost worth going to Petra to see. Among ramparts of tinned food was a green camp bed with a rifle slung over it. There were huge sarcophagi lined with felt, his own invention, which, he told me, would keep beer cool in the hottest weather. There were barricades of potatoes and bastions of vegetables. Hens and chickens, unconscious of

L

their fate, walked in and out.   One had a vision of this prince
of comfort defending, if necessary, with the final drop of his
blood, the last tin of baked beans and tomato.

I sat in the dark watching the sky.   The great circle of blue
above Petra shimmered with stars.   Sometimes one or two
would drop into space and fall behind the shadowy hills.
Suddenly in the centre of the desolate arena where Petra's
streets, houses, and palaces once stood, a tongue of flame shot
up twelve feet into the night.   I could see wild figures piling
the dry stalks of oleander on it, and the fire roared up with
a loud crackling.   The cave-dwellers ran round it like witches.
A figure stepped out of the shadow.   It was one of the
police officers who had ridden with me through the Sîk.   He
told me that Peake Pasha had arranged for the Bedouin to
dance for me and had sent orders for a sheep and a goat to
be slain to make a feast.
I followed him in the direction of the fire.   The half-naked
Arabs who haunt the tombs of Petra had gathered round the
blaze.   There were blind old men tapping about with sticks,
naked children with deformed, distended stomachs, hag-like
women with wispy grey hair, and numbers of others whose rags
concealed their youth.   The flames lit up a group of four or
five crouched over the carcasses of a newly slain goat and a
sheep.   They were cutting up the meat and putting it in
cauldrons.   The flames leapt higher and higher.   They were
quiet folk.   They did not shout or sing but went about their
barbaric preparations in silence, although the fire shone on
white teeth and yellow fangs as they chattered together in
their excitement.   It is not often that a poor Bedoul tastes
meat.
As soon as the fire was going well, the men lined up and
began to stamp their feet, keeping up a rhythmic hand-
clapping.   Three awful crones strolled into the fire-light
grasping long knives.   They placed themselves opposite the
men, stamping and singing, at the same time flourishing their
knives in the faces of the men.   The same words were repeated
again and again.   The hand-clapping became louder and
maintained its rhythmic, almost hypnotic, beat.   The dust

rose in clouds, almost hiding the dancers, and the firelight exaggerated their grotesque movements. I looked round into the darkness and saw the shadow of the hills that hold all that is left of an ordered civilisation, and wondered whether anything like this dance would ever take place in Trafalgar Square or the Place de la Concorde. One has the feeling in Palestine that the civilisation that crashed into ruin was very like our own. One has more in common with the fallen pillars of Jerash than with the finest Moslem mosque. Our world, imperfect as it is, is still a Christian world and has its roots in Christianity. Everything that is against Christianity, no matter how trivial it may appear, is a spy from the forces of savagery which have always waited ready with drawn knives to dance among the ruins.

I turned to the firelight and saw the dancers whip themselves into a passion. The women crouched before the men, waving their knives, and the men advanced, clapping their hands. One old man, foaming with excitement, broke away and seized a hag round the waist. They fell to the earth together and rolled about in the dust, pretending to kill one another. But the knife flashed so dangerously near the old fellow's throat that a police officer ran up and separated them. The dance went on for nearly an hour until, in fact, the dancers were too tired and too parched to go on.

At this point men appeared in the circle of firelight bearing four cauldrons of boiled flesh. The Arabs took their places in relays round the food. The naked children with their spindle legs and blown-out stomachs ran about in great excitement, sometimes peeping over the shoulders of their parents to see if anything would be left. When the last relay had been satisfied, the children descended on the feast. They licked the cauldrons clean.

The fire died down and the Bedouin drifted away, drawing their torn rags round them, to melt into the mysterious shadows of the night.

I picked my way across the broken ground. The moon was up. I could see the hills all round and the square black openings of tombs and temples. In one of those same tombs I lay down to sleep, and through the opening I could see a silver-grey world wrapped in the silence of the grave.

§ 9

But I was unable to sleep. I lay watching the moonlight invade the tomb. The only sound in the vast silence outside was the yapping of jackals. Once a bat passed across the opening of my tomb, blotting out a thousand stars in its flight.

I began to think of John Lewis Burckhardt, the first modern European to gaze on Petra. He was a Swiss, born at Lausanne in 1784. I always think of Burckhardt as an old man because the only picture I know of him is an engraving showing him immensely bearded, and in Moslem clothes. But he was only twenty-eight when he discovered Petra, and only thirty-three when he died of fever in Egypt and was buried under a false name in a Moslem cemetery. He must have been an extraordinary young man, and his short but adventurous life awaits a biographer. Coming to England at the age of twenty-two, he appeared before the African Association and expressed himself anxious to devote his life to exploration. He learnt English and a little Arabic and, in order to accustom himself to hardship, slept on the hard ground, lived on vegetables and performed other austerities. He was sent East by the Association and in a few years spoke Arabic so perfectly that he was able to go anywhere as a Moslem, and was the first Christian to make the pilgrimage to Mecca.

The early death of Burckhardt was a tragedy. He was never able to do himself justice. His works are mostly brief observations which he scribbled down hastily under cover of a camel or in some dreary khan at night, and always with the fear of detection over him. In the calm language of a company report he tells us of his journey to Petra. He had heard stories of the mysterious city near Aaron's Tomb on Mount Hor, but the only way he could get there without exciting suspicion was by buying a goat and telling the people at Elji that he had made a vow to sacrifice it to Aaron. Only those who have been to Petra through the Sîk and have come, with a shock of surprise and delight, to the " Treasury of Pharaoh " shining in the crack at the end, can understand how Burckhardt's pulse must have quickened when his Arab guide turned aside by the oleanders and led him to the lost city.

He stayed there only for a few moments, but that time was enough to bring Petra for ever out of the unknown. He looked round him in astonishment, entering tombs and temples, until his guide's suspicions were aroused and he ventured to charge him with being an infidel in disguise. In order to save trouble, possibly to preserve his life, poor Burckhardt was forced there and then to sacrifice the goat in sight of Mount Hor and leave for ever the city he had found. How often must the tantalising memory of Petra have haunted Burckhardt's dreams; and how often must he have made plans to return some day. . . .

§ 10

When the sun comes up over Petra the arena holds the greyness of dawn for some time. The eastern screen of hills are dull and red, but those to the west are flushed with a brilliant terra-cotta light, so sharp and penetrating that the slightest cracks and fissures are visible, and the mighty screen stands up in the morning, a burning wall of light.

The mountains of Petra crumble like old Stilton. That description, homely as it is, really describes Petra far better than a more grandiloquent one. If you can imagine an ancient Stilton cheese stained red, with a great hollow scooped in the middle, you have, more or less, a little model of Petra. It is this crumbling away that one notices everywhere. The soft rock is gradually disintegrating in the wind and the sand storms. Some of the rock-cut temples are perfect, their pillars round and firm, their decoration clear-cut ; but a similar temple on the weathered side of the cliffs is melted away, its decoration smoothed almost to invisibility and its columns thin and eaten by the wind.

I spent two days wandering about Petra with an Arab guide. His great ambition was to kill a pigeon with a rifle bullet. He took several shots but never hit one. He was a coxcomb of a fellow who fancied himself tremendously and looked down with the utmost contempt on the wretched Bedoul who peered hungrily at us out of their caves. Hearing that these people were starving, I had taken thirty pounds of rice with me to Petra, a pitifully inadequate gift but better than nothing.

I made my Beau Brummell come with me into the filthy smoky caves in search of the hungriest and the oldest people. They were just like animals and would, I think, if capable of murder, have killed a traveller not for money, which is of little use to them, but for the food he might have on him. I was horrified to see the number of blind or semi-blind people among these cave-dwellers. Although in desperate poverty, they never begged. They were pitifully grateful when I told them to go to the camp and ask for rice, which all Arabs love. Some of them, I thought, looked very unlike Bedouin. They might have been Eastern Jews. Someone told me that the name Bedoul means " changers," which suggests that these people had at one time either changed their religion or their way of life. Is it possible that they are the relic of some civilised race that once inhabited Petra?

I heard that the sheikh of the Bedoul was fabulously rich. When I asked how much he possessed, I was told two hundred goats. He has evidently more than the average intelligence, because two archæologists had bought a twined serpent carved in black stone which they believed to be Nabatæan work until it transpired that the sheikh of the Bedoul had made it! Good luck to him. I saw this serpent and would most certainly have been deceived by it.

Petra appears in the Old Testament as the capital of the Land of Edom. In *Numbers* we are told how Moses, wishing to march through the Petræan territory, was refused admission, so that the Israelites were obliged to " compass the land of Edom." Throughout Old Testament history we find that Edom is sometimes on the side of Israel and sometimes on the side of her foes. During one of these periods the fierce wrath of Israel against Edom burst forth in prophesy, which every wanderer in ruined Petra to-day must feel has been literally fulfilled:

" O thou that dwellest in the clefts of the rock," cried Jeremiah, " that holdest the height of the hill: though thou shouldst make thy nest as high as the eagle, I will bring thee down from thence, saith the Lord. Also Edom shall be a desolation: everyone that goeth by it shall be astonished, and shall hiss at all the plagues thereof . . . no man shall abide there, neither shall a son of man dwell in it."

The most interesting features of Petra are not the rock tombs and the temples, but the " high places " on the tops of the mountains. I do not know how many of these there are, but in two days I climbed up to three of them and there must be many more. Every student of the Old Testament is familiar with " the high places of Baal," which roused the bitter wrath and called down the violent condemnation of the prophets. These are those same " high places." *Kings, Chronicles, Judges, Jeremiah,* and *Hosea* are full of the terrible clash between Jehovah and the Baalim. What happened, of course, was that when the Israelites, as desert Bedouin, invaded Palestine and became farmers, they began to take over the old Caananite gods with the land. Jehovah, the stern deity of the desert places, was forsaken for the gods of fertility, the local Baals, who made the sun shine and fattened the corn in the ear.

Every hill-top was sacred to some Baal and on these " high places," and among the pagan groves, the Israelites began to indulge in the gross sensualities of Nature worship. " The children of Israel turned again and went a-whoring after Baalim," we learn in *Judges.* " Hast thou seen what back-sliding Israel hath done," the Lord asked Jeremiah. " She is gone up on every high mountain and under every green tree and there hath played the harlot."

These Baalim were admirably described by Mr. Theodore Gaster in a lecture in London before the Society for Promoting the Study of Religions:

" The essential difference between an El and a Baal is, in few words, that the former represents the agent of a natural force, whilst the latter represents the ideal spirit of a society. There is an El of winds and of diseases, but there is a Baal of Bedford Square. If there were no men on earth there would still be Elim, but no Baalim. Baal partakes of the concept to-day represented by such ideas as Alma Mater, Mother England, and La France; he is the personification of a continuous spirit that both informs and is informed by successive generations. The El is what the Romans called Deus, the Baal what they called Genius."

Therefore the whole land was a confusion of Baalim. Wherever there was a village, there also was a local Baal on the hill-top who required the blood of men or animals and encouraged a licentiousness which is clearly described in the Old Testament. Elijah led a counter-revolution against Baal. Jehu locked up the priests of Baal and their worshippers and put them to the sword. But perhaps the most vivid account of an attack on Baal-worship is that in the *Second Book of Kings* which describes in detail how Josiah pulled down the temples throughout Judah, desecrated the altars with the bones of the dead and defiled the mysterious Topeth in the Valley of the Kedron at Jerusalem, where horrible child sacrifices were made to Molech, or Moloch. This was probably a huge pit over which a pyre was built for the burning of the victims. Late Rabbinic writers have imagined that this Semitic Moloch was a huge brazen statue with a hollow interior and arms on which the victims were placed. They appear to have confused this rite with that of the Carthaginian Moloch which, as Diodorus Siculus says, was a calf-headed idol filled with fire from whose arms the children rolled into a pit of flame while the worshippers danced to flutes and timbrels to drown their shrieks. The Israelite sacrifice was just as horrible, but it would seem that the children were first slain and then offered as burnt offerings. The reason for this was that blood was a necessary part of the sacrifice. " Also in thy skirts is found the blood of the innocent poor," cries Jeremiah to sinful Israel. " I have not found it at the place of breaking in, but *upon every oak*." Surely this refers to the custom of smearing the sacred tree with the blood of the sacrifice? Again Isaiah says: " Ye that inflame yourselves among the oaks, under every green tree; that slay the children in the valleys, under the clefts of the rocks."

It is interesting to note how Petra has affected different people. I think Charles Doughty is the only person who has ever called it " an eye-sore " and found its monuments

" horrible and barbaric." Most travellers are content to
repeat the words " a rose-red city half as old as Time," and
to discover romance and beauty everywhere. My own feeling
is that there is something vaguely sinister about Petra. One
comes across the ghosts of red staircases leading up into the
towering crags, stairs cut with infinite labour up the sides of
mountains, that disappear beneath a chaos of fallen rocks to
emerge again and lead up and ever upward, tracing a ghostly
red path to " the high places of Baal." It is, to me, extraordinary that anyone can look on Petra purely as a piece
of landscape or as a curiosity, for to my way of thinking
the whole place even now reeks of Baal. On the top of the
mountain above the Sîk I came to the chief " high place." The
summit had been hacked smooth. A pool for ablutions had
been cut in the rock. Two lonely and significant obelisks watch
over the well-preserved altars, one an altar of slaying and the
other an altar of burning. This " high place " is so well preserved, so clear in intention, that if the priests and priestesses
of Petra could come back they would be able to hold an orgy
under the moon without the knowledge that the shadow of
centuries has ever fallen on their altars.

Nearly everyone differs in his description of the colour of
Petra. That is because the colour varies with the light.
There are places where the cliff is deep red, others where it
is terra-cotta, and again others where the sandstone is variegated
and shows strips of red, blue, white, and green. These veins
of colour are sometimes worked by the Arabs, who extract
the various sandstones, one at a time, and fill bottles with
them which they sell to visitors. They blow a quantity of
powdered white sandstone into the bottle, follow it with red
and green and blue and yellow, taking care that the colours
remain in distinct stripes and never mix together; unfortunately the bottles are generally empty gin bottles and are so
ugly that few people would care to possess one.

After a tiring day spent in clambering up to the empty
rock tombs and temples and exploring the " high places of
Baal," it is good to sit in the valley and watch the last light
of the sun fade on the highest pinnacles of the eastern hills.
One can build up in the mind a picture of Petra as it appeared
in its glory, a large city with its paved roads set in its weird

amphitheatre of hills, the caravans from India and from Egypt coming slowly through the Sîk; but all the time the mind reverts to the key-note of the place: the ghostly red steps that lead up to the " high places."

§ 11

One morning I climbed the mountain known as Ed-Deir. On the summit, carved from the soft stone, is a Roman temple only eighty-three feet less in height than the west towers of St. Paul's Cathedral. This colossal building on a mountain nearly four thousand feet above sea-level, empty, desolate, with a few acres of wheat planted on the level space in front of it, fills one with astonishment. One feels that the people of Petra were not like ordinary people and could not have appeared so even to their contemporaries.

From the top of this mountain I had a wonderful view of Mount Hor, on the summit of which is a Moslem shrine built over Aaron's grave. None but Moslems are allowed to ascend Mount Hor. I was told that if I attempted to do so I would be either knifed or shot. Christians have, from time to time, by bribery or with a strong force of arms, climbed Mount Hor and entered the tomb, where there is nothing to see but a stone cenotaph draped with a dusty green flag.

While I was looking at Mount Hor, which is a long, jagged ridge against the sky surrounded by a number of lower cone-shaped summits, my sharp-shooter, the same pigeon-missing guide, pricked up his ears and crept like a cat to the edge of the rock with his rifle at the ready. I thought that he was about to miss another pigeon. But to my astonishment the khaki helmet of an Arab Legionary appeared from below, then a brown, sweating face, then the man's body. He climbed up, came towards me, breathing heavily, clicked his spurs together and, saluting, handed me—a telegram! The address was " Morton, Petra." I was completely taken aback. If there was one place in the world where I would have considered it impossible to be reached by telegram it was on the mountain overlooking Mount Hor. While I

tore open the envelope I thought in amazement of the journey
the man had made in order to deliver it to me. He had
ridden off from Elji early in the morning, had come through
the Sîk, had gone to the camp and, finding out my day's
climb (about which, as a matter of prudence, one always
informs the camp manager), had set off up the mountain-
side to trail me. The telegram, which was from the mighty
Peake Pasha, told me to return immediately, because I was
invited to an Arab feast at Amman. No one in Trans-
Jordan questions the commands of Peake Pasha, so I climbed
down the mountain and cut short my stay in Petra, which,
incidentally, no one should visit for less than a week or ten days.

The camp manager said that I could not cross the desert
before nightfall. I thought of the endless shattering road,
the wilderness of black basalt, the sandy horizon, and I
was inclined to agree with him. However, I took a horse
and was through the Sîk in less than an hour, and eight
hours later, half dead with fatigue and covered with dust, I
reached Amman in the first hour of darkness.

§ 12

I was glad to be back in time for the feast which had been
arranged in my honour. Not to have appeared would have
been an unforgivable breach of manners.

We found that the tribe was camped on a hill some little
distance from Amman. There were ten black goat-hair
tents. The sheikh and his two sons were waiting for us on
the edge of their territory. With charm and polish, for the
Bedouin have beautiful manners, the chief introduced his
two sons, who touched their foreheads and breasts in the
Arab greeting.

We then walked in procession to the sheikh's tent, which
was spread with gay rugs. We sat down cross-legged. All
the men of the tribe stood round the tent in the sunlight,
watching us. Only the sheikh and his two sons entered and
played the part of hosts.

I had been warned that the dish would be a communal
one and that I must only use my right hand, for the left is
considered unclean and to use it would be a terrible barbarism.

I was, however, totally unprepared for the size of the dish, an enormous copper cauldron, which was carried into the tent by ten men. It was bigger than an old-fashioned tin bath, and in this were the boiled carcasses of two sheep.

The animals had been slain that morning, cleaned, and cooked with rice. The top of the pyramid of hot flesh was decorated by the two heads with the jaws open to show the teeth and to prove, I suppose, that the animals were young and tender. Draped round the heads was the great delicacy, the fat of the tails.

Two men advanced to this alarming brew with large tins of hot, very yellow, melted butter. This they poured over the mess and the meal was ready.

I rolled up my right sleeve and, as the guest of honour, made the first dive. The hot butter burnt my fingers. I found that the only way of getting anything was to dig a finger into the mutton and tear downwards. A huge piece of meat came off. This I ate with ravenous haste, for it is not polite to eat a Bedouin meal slowly. You must pretend to be starving.

The meat was delicious, but the butter was sickly and rather strong. I watched the others and noticed that when they had eaten a piece of meat, they took a handful of rice and squeezed it into a ball which they flung quickly into their mouths.

I could not attempt the flinging action, but I grasped a handful of rice and squeezed until the melted butter ran out between my fingers and, conquering a strong feeling of nausea, ate it. The tail fat, which I attacked next, was delicious. It was not too rich, and tasted rather like marrow bones.

In a few minutes, for we had been eating at top speed like hungry wolves, the sign was given that we had had enough, and ten men came in and carried the cauldron of mutton outside.

The two sons of the sheikh brought us a long-necked pot full of water and a brass basin. We held our hands under a stream of water, washing off the butter and rice, and then we rose and dried our hands from a cloth hung for the purpose from the roof of the tent. Bitter Bedouin coffee was served in small cups like egg-cups; and the feast was over.

But outside a real feast was in progress! The whole tribe was lined up round the cauldron. Ten men crouched round it, tearing the mutton with their fingers, tossing the rice balls into their mouths and eating ravenously and in dead silence. As soon as they had finished they rose and gave way to ten more.

About fifteen half-naked little children sat watching the feast with longing eyes. They crept nearer and nearer. One, more daring than the others, peeped over the shoulder of an eating Bedouin, and the moment the last circle of grown-ups had left there was a wild rush of small brown bodies.

They did not sit round the cauldron like their brothers and fathers, but tore and scrambled like hungry puppies. They dived for bones and carried them off like animals, and sat gnawing them with intense enjoyment.

The extraordinary contrast between the barbaric character of the feast and the superb manners of our hosts is something I shall never forget. Our table manners had been, according to Western standards, terrible, but the compliments that flowed in a brilliant and formal stream would have put to shame the Court of Louis XIV.

The sheikh and his two sons gravely conducted us to the confines of the camp, where they bowed, called down blessings upon us and watched us depart.

Later the same day I dropped down into the Jordan valley from the heights of Trans-Jordan. I climbed the fierce gorge, passed the Inn of the Good Samaritan, and came into a Jerusalem that in my absence had changed. Its streets were full of pilgrims from East and West, for in a few days it would be Easter, the Passover, and the Feast of Nebi Musa.

CHAPTER TEN

The Passover, Easter, and the Feast of Nebi Musa occupy the attention of Jerusalem. The city begins to wear an expression that was familiar to Pontius Pilate. I attend the ceremony of the Holy Fire and watch the black monks " Search for the Body of Christ."

§ I

JERUSALEM was filled with the people of all nations. One heard French, German, Italian, English, Arabic, Yiddish and Hebrew in the course of one short walk through the streets. Droves of superior tourists who had come to gaze curiously on the rites of the Eastern Church were queerly mixed with humble Eastern Christians who firmly believed that the Holy Fire was soon to descend from heaven upon the Tomb of Christ. Opulent Jews from far away had come to eat the Passover in the City of David and Solomon. The Moslems were talking of the great pilgrimage to the tomb of Moses near Jericho.

The little booths near the Holy Sepulchre overflowed with incense and became festooned with the richest of candles. Large piles of shrouds appeared outside them on chairs. They were of the thinnest, cheapest linen and bore, printed in black, rough pictures of the Passion. I saw a peasant woman from, I think, Bulgaria, buy a shroud. Although they were all the same, she went from shop to shop examining them and fingering the miserable texture. It must have been force of habit.

In the dimness of Calvary a forest of candles burned; and all day long silent crowds knelt before the Tomb of Christ.

In the dark streets of the old city the Jews watched the moon of Nisan grow full, and went about their intricate preparations with an air of furtive secrecy. For the Passover was near.

A policeman, a young Scot, said to me: " I don't think we shall have any trouble this year." And he began to

speak about the annual contact of the three religions in terms
of trunchions and sword-sticks. I thought what an extraordinary thing it is that, although the last Paschal lamb was
slain on the altar of the Temple in 70 A.D. and the Temple
has not one stone upon another, yet the turbulent Passover
atmosphere which the Romans knew so well is still repeated
in Jerusalem every year. The young policeman might have
been one of Pilate's bodyguard.

§ 2

The Anglican Cathedral of St. George is distinguished in
Holy Week by the devotional walks which it organises, and by
the quiet dignity of its traditional ceremonies. An atmosphere
of England pervades the cathedral close with its flowers and
its quiet cloisters.

One of the first services I attended, and one that I shall
never forget, was the Anglican service in the British War
Cemetery in memory of the British troops who died during
the Palestine campaign.

The War cemetery stands on the northern end of the
Mount of Olives, to the east of Mount Scopus. Across the
valley that falls away from its gate rises the ridge on which
Jerusalem stands. The cross in the cemetery is faced by the
walls, the roofs, and the domes of the city, and rises over
the graves as the banner of St. George might have stood
above a company of Crusaders. All other war cemeteries
face the east, this one alone faces west. The Garden of
Gethsemane is only a little way from it in the hollow, and
from the cemetery you can see the site of Calvary.

There are 2,180 soldiers and airmen of the United Kingdom lying there, and 143 soldiers from Australia and 34
from New Zealand. There is one woman's grave in those
white ranks, that of Nurse Charlotte Berrie, of Neutral Bay,
Sydney, New South Wales.

There are always gardeners taking care of the flowers that
die so quickly in this fierce soil. Tall hedges of rosemary lie
between the graves, and someone with an English eye has
planted daffodils and marigolds, wallflowers and geraniums.
There are also wild red Flanders poppies growing there.

In the hush of afternoon English voices were lifted in
prayer and an English choir in white surplices shielded its
eyes from the sun which was sinking towards the western
hills. It was good to hear English prayers in a spot sacred
to the British race.

The clergy and the choir walked away between the graves
and the sun dipped down towards Jerusalem. I remembered the little priest of El Kerak who was so happy to have
lived to see Christian soldiers march into Aleppo. That his
feet will bear the scars of the Turkish rods until the day of
his death did not matter to him, for he had endured, he
believed, to some purpose.

§ 3

I had been invited to a house on the outskirts of Jerusalem
to eat the Passover with a Jewish family. I was late because
I had been given an insufficient address and wandered lost
for some time in a solitude like that of Christmas night. The
streets were deserted. I could hear cheerful festal sounds
from the front rooms of houses, and once, through a badly
drawn curtain, I saw a number of people sitting round a
brilliantly lit table, the men with their caps on.

The moonlight was a green rain falling on everything.
The shadows had a depth and softness that was exquisite to
see, and on a piece of broken ground where someone was
building a house I came across a solitary olive tree shining
in the moonlight among piles of bricks and stones, its little
leaves silvered all over as if covered with frost.

At last I found the house and was delighted to discover
that I had not kept my hosts waiting. I was given a skull-
cap and we went into the dining-room, where the grandfather of the assembly took his seat at the head of the table.
He explained the setting of the table to me: the shankbone
of lamb, the relic of the Paschal sacrifice, the roasted egg,
symbolic of the daily Temple offering, the plate of *haroseth*
made of apples, almonds, raisins, chopped cinnamon and
wine, said to represent the clay from which the children of
Israel made bricks, the bitter herbs and the dish of vinegar,
symbolic of the years of bondage in Egypt. An extra cup of

wine stood on the table. This was called " the cup of Elijah." In Jewish tradition the prophet is a wandering angel who may enter any house unbidden on the night of the Passover.

The head of the house, reclining easily against a great pile of cushions, looked round on his children and grandchildren and began the ceremony that celebrates the escape of Israel from Egypt. All over the world this strange race, which has retained its sense of difference throughout the centuries, was performing exactly the same ceremony.

The sanctification, or *Kiddush*, was pronounced, after which we solemnly drank a glass of red wine and water. A maid-servant came round with a bowl and a jug. She poured water over our hands. Parsley dipped in vinegar was distributed. The head of the household broke the middle *matzah* cake on the dish before him and concealed half of it, leaving the other half covered with a napkin.

These words came into my mind: " And as they did eat, Jesus took bread, and blessed, and brake it, and gave to them, and said, Take eat: this is my body."

Shining from the solemn ordinance of the Old Testament was the Holy Eucharist that on this night nineteen centuries ago, and within a mile of the place where we were sitting, had been instituted by the Priest who was also the Sacrifice.

The people at the table began to whisper together, asking who was the youngest. Presently a girl of about twenty stood up and asked her grandfather:

" Why is this night distinguished from all other nights? "

Then the old man repeated the ancient story of the Passover that has been kept green in the memory of Israel, and of the Jews, since Moses led the way out of Egypt. When he had ended, the first of the *Hallel* Psalms was sung:

" Blessed art Thou, O Eternal! who redeemeth Israel," chanted the master of the house. " Blessed art Thou, O Eternal, our God! King of the Universe, Creator of the fruit of the vine."

We lifted our glasses and drank the second cup of wine.

" Verily I say unto you," said Christ at the Last Supper, " I will drink no more of the fruit of the vine, until that day that I drink it new in the kingdom of God."

Once more water was poured over our hands and the host

gave to each of us a piece of the broken unleavened bread, which we ate with this blessing:

" Blessed art Thou, O Eternal, our God, King of the Universe, who bringeth forth bread from the earth. Blessed art Thou, O Eternal, our God, King of the Universe, who hath sanctified us with Thy commandments, and commanded us to eat unleavened bread."

The host next took the bitter herbs, the green tops of horse-radish, and after dipping them in the *haroseth* gave some to each guest.

Again we ate unleavened bread, but this time with bitter herbs. Then followed an excellent dinner. At the end of it the host took the broken *matzah* cake and handed a small portion—called the *aficoman*—to each guest. He said grace and we drank the third cup of wine. The door of the house was flung open with this defiant appeal to God:

" Pour out Thy wrath upon the heathen that know Thee not, and upon the kingdoms that call not upon Thy name. They have devoured Jacob and laid waste his dwelling-place. Pour out upon them Thine indignation and let Thy wrathful anger overtake them. Pursue them in anger, and destroy them from under the heavens of the Lord."

The fourth cup of wine was then filled and, after the singing of the *Hallel*, was emptied.

I said good-night to the kindly folk who had admitted me, a stranger and a Gentile, to this intimate glimpse of an ancient faith, and walked out again into the moonlit night. It was Dom Jean de Puniet who wrote in his book on the origin of the Mass that when Christ instituted the mystery of the Eucharist He was holding in one hand the chain of the old covenant which ended in Him, and in the other the first link of an unbroken chain reaching unto eternity.

§ 4

The Holy Week of the Eastern Church is marked by a number of ceremonies whose roots go back no man can say how far into the history of Christianity. They crowd one upon the other and are held all over Jerusalem in the churches of the various communities, so that it would be difficult to attend them all.

On the Saturday before Palm Sunday, Lazarus Saturday, the Greeks and the Armenians go in solemn procession to the Holy Sepulchre and the Russians hold an all-night service in their cathedral, where palms are blessed and distributed.

On Palm Sunday the most remarkable ceremonies to a Western Christian are those of the Armenians and the Syrians. The Armenians perform " the Ceremony of the Second Coming." Every picture and decoration in the church of St. James is covered with a veil, and the altar is concealed behind a tapestry. A bishop stands holding a key which symbolises the key of the church, while another bishop, invisible to the congregation, stands behind the tapestry, and there begins a dialogue between them, one asking for admittance and the other asking who it is that calls. Finally the Bishop outside chants: " Open unto me the gates of righteousness that I may enter into them and give thanks unto the Lord! " Slowly the curtain is withdrawn, and at the same moment the veils are drawn from the pictures, and the church, hitherto dark and shrouded, shines with candle-light.

The Syrian ceremony, which is almost the same and quite as protracted, is called " the Ceremony of the Bridegroom's Arrival." The altar of the church is concealed by draperies from the congregation. The Bishop and clergy go round the church in procession, halting before the curtain. *Kyrie eleison* is said forty times, ten times in Greek and thirty times in Syriac. Forty times the worshippers make a complete prostration. At length the Bishop cries, " O Lord, O Lord, O Lord, open unto us! " and at that moment the curtain is drawn, revealing the altar blazing with candles.

On Maundy Thursday the Greeks, Latins, Armenians, Syrians and Copts all observe the curious ceremony, rather like a miracle play, called " the Washing of the Feet." On Good Friday the Russians perform the touching " Ceremony of the Winding-Sheet." A shroud is placed on the altar, and after the service, while a choir sings " the Hymn of the Myrrh-bearers," the priests lift the winding-sheet, carry it three times round the altar and then to a sepulchre prepared in the church, where it is censed.

A curious and interesting service is the Good Friday " Entombment " of the Syrians. The Bishop, carrying a crucifix and followed by the clergy, marches round the church to commemorate the approach to Golgotha. Having reached a table that represents the place of Crucifixion, they place the crucifix on it, and put two candles, one on each side, to represent the crosses of the two thieves. The Bishop wraps a scarlet cloth round the crucifix to suggest the covering of our Lord before He was stripped of His garments. Then, as the service proceeds, the story of the Crucifixion is read from one of the Gospels. When they reach the incident of the two thieves, one of the candles, that representing the impenitent thief, is broken, and as the story of the death of Christ is read the crucifix is censed, lifted on high, and held to the four corners of the earth while a blessing is pronounced.

The crucifix is placed in a special coffin and carried to the altar. It is there washed in rose-water in which is a quantity of gall, and then it is tenderly wrapped in linen with powdered incense and replaced in the coffin. This touching and simple act of symbolism is concluded when the Bishop escorts the coffin to a place behind the altar where it is locked away and a seal placed on the door. A lamp is left burning in front of it all night and on Easter Eve the tomb is opened.

Saturday, Easter Eve, is the day for the ceremony of the Holy Fire, which I will describe in its place. On the same day, but late at night, the dark monks of the Abyssinia Church celebrate one of the most primitive of all the ceremonies: " Searching for the Body of Christ."

I was told to rise at five a.m. if I wanted to see anything of the Greek ceremony of the Washing of the Feet, which takes place at eight a.m. in the courtyard of the Holy Sepulchre. For all the ceremonies of Holy Week it is necessary to be in your place two or three hours before anything is timed to happen, and, as nearly everything begins late, you are often there for much longer. But the crowd is so varied and so interesting that the time passes swiftly.

I found myself perched above the wall of the Greek Chapel

of St. Mary Magdalene, from which I looked straight down
into the courtyard. Although it was not yet six o'clock, the
courtyard and the adjoining roofs were so crowded that it
did not seem possible that one more person could be admitted.
Yet when I looked towards the entrance to the courtyard
I saw a steady pressing forward, and realised that, impossible
as it seemed, a new stream of people was forcing its way into
the already overcrowded space. There is a mosque at the
back whose minaret overlooks the courtyard, and I was
amused to notice a veiled woman on the little railed-in gallery
where the muezzin calls to prayer, crouched with two or
three children and enjoying the best view of all.

The Christian crowd that comes to Jerusalem for Holy
Week is a puzzling one. It is dominated by excitable Copts
from Egypt, many of whom wear bright blue gowns and a
scarlet tarbush. There are also any number of Christian
Arabs who dress and look exactly like the Moslems. There
are also Christian *fellahin*. Added to these are numbers of
Greeks, Armenians, Syrians and, here and there, a dark-
skinned Ethiopian. Those are the Eastern pilgrims. The
Western pilgrims include Catholic monks, bands of pilgrims
from England, Italy and sometimes Spain, and crowds of
Europeans and Americans, touring either in droves or in
ones and twos, who are almost impossible to classify. Anyhow a gathering more oddly representative of the international character of Christianity could be seen nowhere
else.

In the centre of the courtyard a platform had been
erected. It was painted green, and there was an iron rail all
round it and two iron arches, one at each end, which held
old-fashioned candle lamps. There was a gilded chair at
one end of the platform and along each side, flanking it,
were seats for twelve priests.

This platform represented the Upper Room of the Last
Supper. While a Greek priest busied himself with a long-
necked ewer, a bowl and a towel, placing them carefully on
the platform, another priest lowered an olive branch on a rope
from a near-by wall. This branch symbolised the Garden of
Gethsemane.

The procession came slowly from the Church of the Holy

Sepulchre towards the platform, moving through a path made by the police. Earnest Copts and devout pilgrims, in their anxiety to touch him, nearly tore to pieces the old man who was acting Greek Patriarch (there has been no Greek Patriarch since August, 1931). He walked slowly behind his clergy, grasping his pastoral staff in one hand, while in the other he held a posy of flowers which now and again he dipped in holy water and sprinkled on the people. He wore a dome-shaped crown sparkling with precious stones. His staff was not the crozier of the Western Church, but a gold staff whose head was formed of two twined serpents: the rod of Aaron. Before him walked twelve elderly Greek priests in gorgeous copes of figured brocade.

They took places on the stage, the old Patriarch going to the chair at the head and the twelve priests seating themselves in two rows. The intention was clear. The Patriarch represented Jesus, and the twelve were His apostles.

After a short service the old man was undressed slowly and laboriously before the silent, wondering crowd. His great crown of jewels was removed, the pectoral decorations were taken from him, and then his heavy vestments were removed over his head and, behold, he stood revealed in a silk gown of pale lavender. I admired the simplicity with which he did all this, because there is something that can be so ridiculous about undressing, especially the undressing of someone as decorative as a Greek Patriarch. But very simply, as if he had been at home, he arranged his white beard and patted the soft white locks that blew about in the early wind of morning. I thought to myself that this is probably the only occasion when a crowd sees the Greek Patriarch, so to speak, *en déshabille*, because even in death the Orthodox Patriarchs, clothed in gorgeous vestments, are carried to the grave tied in their chairs and lowered into a vault where about twenty-four of their number sit clothed in the mouldering relics of their glory.

The old man girded himself with a towel, another was laid over his shoulder, and, with white hair blowing in the wind, he knelt slowly and heavily towards the feet of his clergy. Black lace-up boots and elastic-sided boots were shyly removed, so were white socks, and one by one the feet were washed in the water from the gold ewer and dried with the Patriarch's towel.

When he came to the priest who represented St. Peter, there was a piece of dumb show. " Thou shalt never wash my feet," says St. Peter. " If I wash thee not, thou hast no part with me," is the answer. Eventually the Apostle gives way and the Patriarch ministers to him.

When the feet-washing is over, the scene is changed to the Garden of Gethsemane. Three of the clergy, representing Peter, James and John, pretend to fall asleep on the steps of the platform. The Patriarch goes some distance off. He returns to tell them that Judas is at hand. The Patriarch is robed again in his splendid vestments and stands on the platform blessing the congregation. As the procession is re-formed, the gong of the Holy Sepulchre begins to ring a strange exciting rhythm:

> Dong-dong-dong
> a-dong-dong-dong
> dong-a-dong-dong
> dong-dong-dong.

It is a strange rhythm on one note. The deep-voiced gong seems to shake the very stones. The crowds press forward for the Patriarch's blessing. He holds the little posy of flowers in his hand, a tight little Victorian posy of small flowers, and, using it as an *aspergilum*, shakes holy water over the faces of the crowd.

§ 5

By courtesy of the Armenian Patriarch I was given a seat in the Armenian Gallery in the Church of the Holy Sepulchre, and was told to be in my place four hours before the ceremony of the Holy Fire would begin. The approaches to the church were full of excited people, and it was with some difficulty that I struggled through the crowds who had been waiting inside the church all night.

My seat looked directly down on the Tomb and gave a good view of the Rotunda, which was a tight press of people. The Eastern Christians, and many of them seemed to be Copts and Syrians, have little reverence in our sense of the word and therefore it is rather unkind to criticise them from our standpoint. They see nothing shocking in screaming, fighting and shouting round the Tomb of Christ, of trampling each other to the ground in a frenzied dash for the fire which they believe comes straight from heaven: but their belief in the sacredness of this fire is so great, so terrible in its stark, fierce faith, that one hesitates to write the usual disgrace-to-Christianity kind of tirade. So I will just describe what happened.

Hundreds of people had slept all night in the church. Between the pillars that support the central dome, wooden scaffolding had been erected which formed a series of little boxes, exactly like boxes at an opera-house; and in each one of these was displayed an intimate picture of domestic life. Most of the boxes seemed to have been rented by rich Copts. They sat cross-legged on cushions, surrounded by their families. Mothers, feeding their infants, sat on the bedding. The men sat in the front of the boxes, slowly telling rosaries of yellow amber or excitedly arranging to lower a bunch of candles on a string to be lit by someone in the crowd when the supreme moment should arrive.

The crowd moved like an uneasy beast. Something was always happening in it; either someone was fighting madly to escape from it or someone was struggling to enter the church. From the Coptic chapel came a tuneless Eastern chanting, and from the crowd came wild songs sung by Arabs mounted on the shoulders of their friends. These leaders, swaying perilously over the heads of the crowd, beat time with their hands or with sticks, and chanted in Arabic such verses as:

> The Fire has shone and we have feasted,*
> We have visited the Sepulchre of our Lord,
> Our Lord is Jesus Christ.
> Christ came to us, and with His blood He bought us.

And here is another one:

> We are rejoicing to-day,
> And the Jews are sad!
> O Jews, O Jews!
> Your feast is the feast of monkeys,
> Our feast is the feast of Christ!
> There is no religion but the religion of Christ!

---

* From *When We Lived in Jerusalem*, by Estelle Blyth (John Murray).

NEBI MUSA PROCESSION, JERUSALEM

Via Dolorosa

The songs went on, mingled with the chanting, working up a tense, excited atmosphere, so that I was reminded of the Bedouin of Petra, who clapped their hands as they danced. Once there was a serious dispute below me in one of the densest patches of the crowd. It appeared that some man, whether rightly or wrongly I cannot say, was believed to be a Jew. The police were quickly on the scene and the man was removed.

The crowds have been told time and again that the Holy Fire is a piece of symbolism, but nothing will shake their belief that on this day it descends from heaven into the Tomb of Christ. The ceremony is very old. I believe Bernard the monk mentioned it during his visit to Jerusalem in 870 A.D. In early times the Pope forbade it and, of course, only the Eastern Church now takes part in it. It is a thoroughly Eastern, and probably fundamentally pagan, ceremony. Dean Stanley, for instance, wondered whether the Arabs and Greeks who fight their way round and round the Sepulchre, attempting to make the circuit a certain number of times, are reproducing without knowing it a dim memory of the funeral games round the tomb of a king.

When the excitement had reached its height a number of banners were seen slanting perilously over the heads of the crowd. The police forced a way for the patriarchs and the clergy of the various communities.

On each side of the Tomb are two round openings set at a slant in the stone. The stone about them is blackened by the Holy Fire of other years, and at these holes stood runners, stripped for their ordeal, with bunches of candles shielded by caps of perforated tin. Instantly the fire springs from the openings in the Tomb these men have to fight their way outside, where others are waiting who leap into motor-cars and take the sacred flame to churches all over the country. In the old days a ship was always ready with steam up to take the Holy Fire to Russia.

In a noisy excitement greater than that of any crowd I have ever seen, the acting Greek Patriarch and the Armenian Patriarch were conducted to the entrance to the Tomb. On the steps, in full view of the shouting, gesticulating crowds,

the Greek Patriarch was divested of his cope and other
ornaments. His wrists were tied with linen bands. He
looked round, pitifully feeble to face such a howling mob.
I noticed that ten officers of the Seaforths surrounded him as
a kind of bodyguard. They all looked like Rugby forwards.
The old man then turned and entered the Tomb, while the
Armenian Patriarch waited in the vestibule.

There were three or four minutes in which nothing happened. The air was tight with suspense. Suddenly came a
burst of flame from each of the Tomb openings, one torch
being thrust out by the Greek Patriarch, and the other by
the Armenian. The next instant the church was a shrieking,
stamping madness. Tongues of flame swept over it. Men
fought to escape with the fire. The crowds lit candle from
candle, laughing with joy. Some moved the flames over
their faces. Women passed it under their chins and over
their breasts. The people in the galleries hauled up lit
candles on strings, and in the inconceivable pandemonium
the ancient figure of the Greek Patriarch emerged from the
Tomb, grasping a lighted candle in each hard, and was swept
onward like a piece of drift-wood on a flooded river, the
Seaforth officers fighting a way for him to the altar of the
Greek church.

While the crowds went mad with the fire, the bells of the
church began to ring and the strange wooden gongs of the
Armenians were beaten with strips of metal in the gallery.
The whole church was a chaos of sound and movement. In
the utter confusion of the moment all the lamps were re-
kindled in the Holy Sepulchre and hundreds of simple, but
apparently mad, Christians believed that God had sent fire
from heaven.

I sat there for an hour after the appearance of the fire,
watching the excitement of the crowds. The fire did not
appear to burn them as they licked the flames and ran them
over their faces, neither did it singe their hair. I thought
what an extraordinary thing it is that a frenzied ceremony
that might have occurred in a grove of Adonis should have
taken place at the Tomb of Christ.

§ 6

A friend who lives in Jerusalem offered to take me to the strangest of all the ceremonies of the Eastern Holy Week. It is held by the black monks of Abyssinia on the roof of the Holy Sepulchre.

As the moon was rising, a Greek monk let us into the church by a side door. It was pitch dark. We had to strike matches as we stumbled up over worn stairs to the roof of St. Helena's Chapel, where the black monks worship Christ under the stars. Long years ago, as I explained earlier in this book, the Abyssinians owned important shrines within the Sepulchre, but during centuries of struggle they were unable to hold out against more powerful Churches and so, bit by bit, they found themselves dislodged and driven from their sacred heritage. But, with a tenacity which has enabled these devout men to retain their faith since the fourth century, they sought refuge on the roof.

Lacking a church large enough to hold a big ceremony, they erect a tent in which once every year they celebrate a curious rite known as " Searching for the Body of Christ." This was the ceremony we had come to witness.

We found ourselves in bright starlight. The white domes gave to the roof the appropriate appearance of an African village. A long, brocade tent like a marquee had been set up in one corner, the flaps at one end looped up so that we could see inside, where, in a warm glow of candlelight, sat a barbaric assembly of Abyssinians dressed in gorgeous robes, with spiked gold crowns upon their heads. These were the cross-bearers.

A black monk led us to a row of cane-bottomed chairs at the end of the tent. Here we sat for a long time, watching the grave, dignified row of Abyssinians in their splendid vestments. They looked like pictures of the Magi.

After perhaps half an hour we heard the discordant African chanting and into the tent came the monks, leading the Abouna, or abbot, to his place.

On the ground in front of him sat two monks with large silver-rimmed drums which they played with a quick hand-slapping motion, while the others shook sistra, filling the tent with an extraordinary shivering sound like the noise of shaken coins.

The sistrum is a metal frame with horizontal rods placed through it; these jingle when the frame is shaken. It was used in ancient Egypt in the temples of Isis to attract the attention of the worshippers and also to banish evil spirits. I did not know that there was a religious community in the world which still uses the sistrum in its services, and the shape of the instrument used by the black monks was exactly the same as the sistra of antiquity, which are discovered in the tombs of ancient Egypt.

The tapping of the drums, the shivering note of the sistra, and the raucous chanting of the monks, made it difficult to believe that one was attending a Christian ceremony on the roof of the Holy Sepulchre.

There was something impressive in the sight of these black men worshipping Jesus Christ with a ritual so old that it has borrowed something from the ceremonies of ancient Israel and ancient Egypt.

Nothing could illustrate more vividly the many religious customs housed in the Holy Sepulchre. Beliefs and customs long obsolete in the Churches of the West persist round the Tomb of Christ. There is an echo of the language of the Pharaohs when the Copts say Mass, and the liturgical language of the Syrians is something like the Aramaic which Christ spoke: compared to these, the New Testament Greek used by the Orthodox Church is almost a modern tongue.

A plaintive note crept into the Abyssinian service. My friend whispered to me that the black monks were bewailing the death of Christ. The drum taps became slower and the notes of the sistra grew faint. The Gospels printed in the ancient Gheez, the literary language of Ethiopia, were brought to the abbot and, while the monks swung a cloud of incense towards him, he intoned the story of the Lord's Passion.

Then the tom-toms, which had formed a low, throbbing background to the service, became quicker and louder and, with the gorgeous crowned cross-bearers leading, we formed up two by two, and, candles in hand, went out into the light of the full moon to search for the Body of Christ.

This rite is really a simple dramatisation of the Resurrection. The abbot had read the Gospel story up to the point where the three Maries had gone to the rock-hewn tomb early in the morning with sweet spices to anoint the dead body of the Saviour. There they saw a young man sitting clothed in a white garment, and he told them that Christ was risen. . . .

And now the black monks took up the story and acted it. With a queer side-long, dancing shuffle they gyrated round the roof in the moonlight, crying that the tomb was empty, wailing because Jesus was dead, pretending to search for His Body in the dark shadows of the roof. Each monk held a lighted candle and the abbot walked under a green and gold umbrella.

The full moon was up, shining over Jerusalem, striking shivers of green and red light from the jewelled crowns of the cross-bearers. And so the fantastic assembly moved in a weird ritual dance to the sound of tom-toms and sistra.

Four times we circled the roof of St. Helena's Chapel. The plaintive chanting, dirge-like and inexpressibly mournful, went on, the African drums throbbed and the black abbot, surrounded by black monks, walked under his state umbrella making the sign of the cross in the moonlight.

When I looked behind me I saw the monks wailing in their sorrow, the moonlight turning them into grotesque figures from some savage African swamp, but in the nearer glow of the candles which they held, their mild black faces expressed every shade of devout emotion.

On the fourth time round the roof the tom-toms ceased, but the sistra continued to vibrate. The wailing went on and on. I remembered the words of the angels to Mary Magdalene:

"Woman, why weepest thou?

"She saith unto them, Because they have taken away my Lord, and I know not where they have laid Him."

These black men, performing their ancient rite on the roof of Christ's tomb, were expressing in their own outwardly barbaric way the sorrow of all Christianity in the death of Jesus Christ.

Suddenly the wailing stopped. In silence the black monks

re-entered the tent and grouped themselves round the abbot.
We slipped quietly away.

"They will remain sad until the morning," whispered my
friend. "Then they will celebrate the Resurrection and
will become as happy as they are now miserable."

We found the dark staircase and went through the silent
Church of the Holy Sepulchre out into the sleeping streets of
Jerusalem.

§ 7

I joined the crowds one morning near the Jaffa Gate to
watch the Hebron pilgrims march through Jerusalem during
the Feast of Nebi Musa. This Moslem festival always coin-
cides with the Holy Week of the Eastern Church. Devout
pilgrims, accompanied by a number of fanatical dervishes,
march through Jerusalem and, with sacred banners waving,
go down to the Dead Sea to pay homage at a white-domed
shrine which they believe to be the tomb of Moses. They
camp out there for a week and then return to their villages.
The history of this feast is curious.

The Moslems relate a legend that Moses, becoming lonely
in his grave, complained to God, who promised him an
annual pilgrimage. Another story is that, although Moses
was one hundred and twenty years old, God told him
that he should never die until he willingly stepped into the
grave. Whereupon Moses began to tread softly in case he
should step into a grave by mistake. One day, however,
tired and hot, he came over the Mountains of Moab, where
he saw four workmen who had made a deep cutting in the
rock. He asked what they were doing and they told him
that they had made a hiding-place for a king's treasure.
Moses, thinking that the cave looked cool and pleasant,
entered and lay down on a ledge of rock. The workmen
offered him a fruit of beautiful colour and of exquisite frag-
rance, but no sooner had he placed it to his lips than a deep
sleep came over him. The four workmen, who were angels
in disguise, then carried his soul into heaven.

The real history of the tomb of Moses is, I regret to say,
not so picturesque. It appears that long ago the Turkish

Government, alarmed by the enormous Christian crowds who flocked to the Holy Fire, determined to have an equal body of Moslems in the neighbourhood during the same period. Therefore the hitherto humble shrine of some obscure holy man near the Dead Sea was promoted into the tomb of Moses, and an annual pilgrimage organised to it.

The sun beat down on a crowd that pulsed and hummed with vitality. Hundreds of women, their faces hidden to the eyes in veils, lined the road and sat on walls, waiting. Peasants from all parts of the country wore vivid festival costumes. Lemonade sellers strolled through the crowd clapping their brass cups together and praising the coolness and the sweetness of the liquids. Men bearing trays of almond sweets, others with lettuces and some with coloured eggs, moved busily here and there; and from the distance came the throbbing of drums and beating of cymbals.

Slowly, and with but little organisation, the head of the procession came into sight. The leaders bore the sacred flags of silk, tasselled and embroidered and decorated with handkerchiefs tied to the poles, the votive-offering of village women. Each flag was carried by a member of a family whose cherished privilege it is to do so. Any attempt to interfere with this right would lead to instant bloodshed.

There was a flash of swords in the sunlight. The straggling procession halted. A ring was formed round two men armed with swords and bucklers. They executed a movement, half dance and half fight, hitting their bucklers by agreement, one-two, one-two, just like actors in a Shakespearean duel. The crowds applauded loudly.

Then came groups of wild haired fanatics who drugged their senses with a weird dance and a phrase known as the *Zikr*, or "the mentioning." It was a rhythmic repetition of the words " Lâ illálah ílla llâh . . . lâ illálah ílla llâh . . . lâ illálah ílla llâh . . ."—" there is no God but God." The effect of this repetition, and the shuffling dance that accompanied it, seemed to make them drunk. They sagged at the knees, wiped the sweat from their faces, tossed their wild hair, and all the time their lips moved in the " mentioning " and their eyes were vague and trance-like.

There were other bands intent on a different kind of excitement. They were mounted on the shoulders of their friends and were rushed rapidly up and down a clear space in the procession, beating time with their hands or with sticks like choir-masters, and chanting something to which the crowd responded with enthusiasm. I asked a man next to me what they were saying.

" They are cursing the Zionists," he replied. " They are singing: ' O Zionists what right have you in this country? What have you in common with us? If you stay in this country you will all find graves.' "

This gave me the clue to the whole procession. It was not an Arab procession at all! It was something from the Old Testament. This was the way the Hebrew fanatics danced and cried out against the Philistines and the Canaanites. The antics of dignified elderly Moslems, who came gyrating at the head of their villagers to the sound of timbrels and of hand-clapping, were surely those of David:

" And as the Ark of the Lord came into the city of David, Michal Saul's daughter looked through a window and saw King David leaping and dancing before the Lord; and she despised him in her heart."

It seemed to me that this procession of Nebi Musa preserved the atmosphere and the appearance of the crowds that came " singing unto Zion " for the great festivals of the year. It was a crowd like this, a crowd of excited, turbulent peasants, that congested the streets of Jerusalem when Christ joined the pilgrimage at Passover time. It was a mob like this that cried " Crucify Him ! "

My eyes happened to stray from the crowds to the tall brown ramparts of David's Tower. High up there I saw two Seaforth Highlanders. They wore shrapnel helmets and marching order. Quietly and unobtrusively the last relic of Herod's palace had been fortified, just in case the narrow boundary line between religion and politics should be crossed, as it is so easily crossed when three religions hold festivals together in the inflammable atmosphere of the Holy City. The sentries looked down, pink-faced lads from Scotland

with broad smiles on their faces, just as Pilate's troops must
have gazed down on the turbulent crowds of over nineteen
hundred years ago.

And, by a strange irony of time, the pilgrims who danced
and leapt like David and sang with the fury of the prophetic
bands of Bible times, passed through Jerusalem calling down
vengeance on the Zionists just as the ancestors of the Zionists
had called down vengeance on the invading Romans.

§ 8

I have discovered a place not far from the Garden of
Gethsemane, but higher up the Mount of Olives, where
no one ever comes. A few olive trees grow among the
rocks and the fiery earth is strewn with wild poppies. If
you sit without moving, lizards much brighter than those
which dart among the black basalt of Galilee will come and
play about your feet. I like to get away from the rising
excitement of Jerusalem, the babel of foreign tongues, the
eager marshalling of the heated guides and the superficial
judgment of the day tripper, and to walk down through
St. Stephen's Gate to the quiet open space opposite
Jerusalem.

Dean Stanley once said that travel in the Holy Land is
like travel in the dark. You traverse great tracts of country
with nothing to indicate any link with the past except that
you tread the same ground and breathe the same air. Then
suddenly a flash of lightning comes and for an instant tower,
tree and field are seen as distinctly as in the broad daylight.

Jerusalem in the throes of its religious and political enthusi-
asms is such a flash. In the strange agglomeration of ignor-
ance, cynicism, simple piety, sophistication, scholarship and
stupidity which fills Jerusalem at this time, I seem to see a
clear reflection of the Jerusalem of Christ.

If I could paint, I think that as I sit under the olives,
looking at Jerusalem, I could put down on canvas the very
city that Jesus saw when He came up to the Passover to be
crucified. It was filled with the same varied crowds: uncouth

M

provincials, simple Galileans, curious interested Greeks, prosperous Jews from Alexandria (just like the wealthy Zionists from London and New York), sight-seeing Romans, white-robed priests and Levites, smooth Sadducees, obvious Pharisees with broad fringes to their garments and large phylacteries on their brows, and Roman soldiers in their helmets and their chestnut-coloured tunics, spear in hand, aloof and alien as a Highland sentry.

It is not difficult to imagine the sights and sounds that surrounded Jesus as He came up for the great birthday feast of the Jews, the feast that commemorated the Exodus and drew all who could travel towards the Paschal communion at Jerusalem.

Its heralds were abroad in the land weeks beforehand. All the roads and bridges were repaired after the winter rains. Every sepulchre received its annual coat of whitening so that it shone in the sun, and thus lessened the risk of ceremonial defilement. Jesus, when He rebuked the scribes and Pharisees from the Temple mount, pointed to the rows upon rows of newly whitened sepulchres below Him on the slopes of the Mount of Olives and drew, as He so often did, a striking comparison with something visible going on around Him: " Ye are like unto whited sepulchres," He cried, drawing their attention to the shining tombs in their Passover whitewash, " which indeed appear beautiful outward, but are within full of dead men's bones, and of all uncleanliness." The sight of these whitened sepulchres was one of the characteristic signs that Passover was on the way.

Then in every little town and village throughout Judæa and Galilee appeared the *Shulchanim*, the money-changers, the collectors of the Temple tribute. They set up their booths and collected the half shekel (about one shilling and twopence) which every male Jew of religious age was forced to pay towards the upkeep of the Temple. They did very well for themselves because the tribute had to be paid in Sanctuary shekels, and the money in circulation included that of Tyre, Greece, Rome, Egypt and Persia. For every piece of foreign money changed by the *Shulchanim* a charge of a penny-halfpenny or twopence was made. The compulsory tribute was collected locally and sent up to the Treasury of the Temple. Anyone who refused to pay endangered his goods. And the annual sum collected for the Temple is said to have been about £75,000 of modern money. It went to defray the cost of the daily sacrifices offered on behalf of the nation (a cost which the Kings bore in times before the Exile in Babylon) and many other sacred observances.

When Jesus came through the excited countryside and climbed up to Jerusalem, we know that He went many times to the Mount of Olives to meditate and to mourn. He was mourning not for Jerusalem the city, but for Jerusalem the Sanctuary. He knew how debased and formalised the worship of God had become, how cynical and worldly were the priests, led by a High Priest who on great occasions officiated with silk gloves so that his hands should not be stained; men gorged with the riches of the world, in whose hearts observance had replaced faith.

What was this Temple like in the time of Christ? What happened there? What would we have seen above those white walls could we have gone with the Master in the dawn from the Garden of Gethsemane to the higher places of the Hill?

While it was still dark the Temple guards patrolled the gates and courts in twenty-four stations. Each station consisted of ten Levites, so that two hundred and forty watchers were on duty every night in the Temple of Herod. During the night the " Captain of the Temple " went his rounds and visited all the posts. The Romans divided the night into four watches, the Jews into three. Anyone standing on the Mount of Olives in the third Jewish watch would have seen the huge building wrapped in silence and darkness, the only light a red glow in the centre of the white terraces where the fire on the altar of burnt-offerings was kept alight day and night.

The priests who were selected to offer the daily morning sacrifice slept in a room in the inner court. In the third watch, while it was still dark, they would awaken and take a ceremonial bath to be in readiness for the casting of the lots. An official would come to them, still in the hours of darkness, and cast lots to decide on the priest who would remove the ash from the altar of burnt offering. This man, alone and with no light but that of the altar flames, would go out and wash his hands and feet in the brazen laver that stood before the altar. He did this by placing the right hand on the left foot and the left hand on the right foot. He then mounted the huge altar of unhewn stone with a silver chafing dish in his hand, into which he swept the ashes; and as he descended he would see in the renewed glow of firelight the other priests ascending with shovels and prongs to place fresh wood on the flames.

Then came the second casting. The president would range the priests before him and cast lots to decide:

who was to slaughter the victim;
who was to sprinkle blood on the altar;
who was to remove ashes from the altar of incense;
who was to trim the lamps on the seven-branched candle-
    stick;
who was to carry the head of the sacrifice and a hind leg;
who the two forelegs;
who the tail and the other hind leg;
who the breast and the neck;
who the two sides;
who the entrails;
who the offering of flour;
who the baked-meat offering of the High Priest;
who the wine and the drink offering.

When this had been decided the time had come to watch for the first hint of sunrise. One of the priests climbed to a pinnacle of the Temple and stood gazing towards the East in the greyness of the morning. The president and the priests waited below for his report. When his cry came down to them, " The morning shineth already," they would ask him, " Is the sky lit up as far as Hebron? " and not until he had agreed would the daily sacrifice begin.

The sacrificial lamb, that had lived for four days in a special room in the Temple and had already been examined for any of the numerous blemishes that would unfit it for death, was led out and again examined by the light of torches. It was given a drink from a golden bowl. Ninety-three

sacred utensils were brought from a room near by and the
lamb was led to the altar.   The forefeet and hindfeet of each
side were tied together and the head was placed through a
ring in the ground, the face turned to the west.

At this moment, as the first light of a new day began to
pulse upward from behind the Mount of Olives, the signal
was given to open the Temple gate.   As the gate moved
the priests lifted silver trumpets and uttered the three shrill
calls that announced every morning to Jerusalem that the
sacrifice was ready to be slain.

At the same moment, the two priests who had been
chosen to attend to the altar of incense and the lamps
ascended the steps of the Holy Place and entered to perform
their duty.   The opening of this gate was the signal for the
sacrifice.   One priest drew the lamb's gullet forward while
he thrust in the knife with an upward movement.   Another
priest caught the blood in a golden bowl and, standing at
the east of the altar, sprinkled the blood on the stones.   The
victim was then unbound and flayed.   The entrails were
washed on marble tables and the carcase was cut into pre-
scribed portions, each one carried by the priest to whose lot
it had fallen.   These portions were borne to the rise of the
altar, where they were salted.   The most solemn part of the
sacrifice was then ready to begin.

The priests gathered once more in the Hall of Polished
Stones to cast lots for the one who should officiate at the
altar of incense in the Holy Place.   He had to be a priest
who had never before performed this office, unless, of course,
everyone present had done so.   He then chose two assistants,
and while on his way to the Holy Place struck a great gong
called the Magrephah at whose sound the vast Temple
became alive with priests and Levites and ordinary worshippers gathering to pray.   Meanwhile the three incense
priests entered the Holy Place.   One spread the coals on the
golden altar.   The other made ready the incense.   They
then withdrew, leaving the officiating priest waiting for the
signal to burn the incense.   It was, no doubt, at this impressive moment that Zacharias, the father of John the
Baptist, received his vision.   " His lot was to burn incense
when he went into the temple of the Lord," says St. Luke.

" And the whole multitude of the people were praying without at the time of incense."

At this moment silence fell over the vast Temple. The worshippers " fell down before the Lord." Clouds of dense, sweet smoke rose from the Holy Place. Solemnly the priests gathered round the altar to place the portions of the burnt-offering in the flames. Then followed the two meat-offerings and the drink-offerings, and as the priest was bending forward to pour out the drink the Levites broke into the psalm of the day. At each pause in the music the priests blew twice on their silver trumpets and the worshippers prostrated themselves. As the flames licked the newly slain meat, burning brightly with the oil and the salt, the morning sacrifice in the Temple was over.

Day by day for centuries the same thing went on. Thousands of beasts and birds atoned for the sins of humanity at the altar of the Lord. Blood flowed in a never-ending stream, and the smell of the Temple was the stench of burning fat. In addition to the routine sacrifices, thousands of private individuals offered sheep, goats, and oxen. They brought forward their victims, placed their whole weight on them to symbolise the substitutive nature of the rite, and then slit their throats while the priests caught the blood. But that was all the Temple had to offer. It gave no spiritual direction. It was merely a sacred shambles. Isaiah sounded its death-knell centuries before the time of Christ: " For what purpose is the multitude of your sacrifices to me, saith the Lord," he cried. " I am full of burnt-offerings of rams and the fat of fed beasts; and I delight not in the blood of bullocks, or of lambs or of he-goats." From that time the spiritual history of the Jew was locked up not in the Temple but in the synagogue. The Roman who thought that in destroying the Temple he was destroying Judaism was wrong, because Judaism was no longer there.

Much has been written about the attitude of our Lord to the Temple. We cannot doubt that while He reverenced the thing it stood for, He condemned the thing it had become. " I will have mercy and not sacrifice," He said. His opinion

of the priesthood was well expressed in the Parable of the
Good Samaritan, and one might perhaps read into His
attack on the money-changers and the merchants in the
Temple a deeper meaning than a dislike for the carrying on
of business in a sacred place. Was it not also a protest
against the whole financial system of the Temple?

But what was this system? The priests literally raked in
the shekels and lived, quite as literally, on the fat of the land.
The Temple Tribute, or poll-tax, was only one of the imposts
levied on the Jews for the upkeep of the Temple. Offerings
of a different nature embraced every conceivable thing.

There were the first fruits, the so-called " seven kinds,"
which were wheat, barley, vines, figs, pomegranates, olives
and honey. Those near Jerusalem offered them fresh to
the Temple; those far away brought them dried. Philo
and the Mishna describe how the villagers assembled together
at the time of the offering of the first fruits and came up to
Jerusalem to the music of the pipes, the procession led by a
sacrificial ox with gilded horns garlanded with olive leaves.

In addition to the first fruits were the *terumah*, an offering
of wheat, wine, and oil; the *challah*, an offering of kneaded
dough; and the oppressive tithes which, says the Mishna,
covered " everything which may be used as food and is
cultivated, growing out of the earth." It was this rigorous
system of taxing the most humble crops, such as mint and
anise and cummin, that provoked Jesus to cry out: " but
woe unto you, Pharisees, for ye tithe mint and rue and all
manner of herbs, and pass over judgment and the love of
God."

Then there was the offering of all first-born sons and all
the male first-born of animals. The sons were ransomed on
payment of five shekels to the Temple Treasury, and a lesser
money payment was made for the first-born males among the
non-sacrificial animals, such as the ass, the horse, and the
camel. But the first-born of goats and sheep and oxen
belonged to the Temple.

In addition to all this the priests received incredible
quantities of meat. All kinds of sacrifices followed each
other at the altar: sin offerings, trespass offerings, meat
offerings, thank offerings, and burnt offerings. From all

except the last, which were entirely consumed on the altar, the priests received a good share of the meat for their private use. In sin offerings, for instance, only the fat was thrown on the altar, and the priests received a proportion of the carcass. In thank offerings they were entitled to the breast and right shoulder—and even in burnt offerings the skins fell to them, in which they did a profitable business.

Therefore the Temple must have been an enormous storehouse of every kind of food and produce. Its vaults were stacked with the very best that the country could grow. In them also were large gold deposits, for, like most temples in ancient times, it was a bank in the sense that it offered strong rooms and safe deposits for the wealthy.

It was this mighty institution which Christ entered with a whip in His hand. The market was a remarkable feature of the Temple. During the days before the Passover, it was at its busiest. It was a cattle market. It was a money market. It was also possible to buy the necessary food and drink offerings there. The market had no doubt grown up over a long period of time because of the demand for Levitically perfect animals, the need to change money into Sanctuary coin, and a hundred other material matters connected with the Temple worship. Instead of bringing his own lamb or goat to the Temple and risking its rejection by the *mumcheh*, or inspector, who passed all sacrifices for a fee, the worshipper could buy in the Temple market beasts which already had been examined by the authorities and were guaranteed Levitically pure. It is common knowledge that as soon as a few stalls are erected anywhere and an atmosphere of buying is created, all kinds of transactions begin to occur in the neighbourhood. Leather Lane, near Holborn, is a perfect example. Much the same thing must have occurred in the Temple precincts.

The market was held under the arcades in the great Court of the Gentiles. It must have been exactly like any market in Damascus or Jerusalem or Cairo to-day: a tense mass of arguing, bargaining people. Many a poor peasant was well fleeced there. We know that prices were artificially manœuvred and that on one occasion the cost of two pigeons was run up to the ridiculous price of a gold denar, or about fifteen shillings and threepence of modern money.

Before night it had fallen, through the intervention of an honest man, to the normal charge of a quarter of a silver denar, or about eightpence.

When Jesus entered the Temple Market it must have been loud with the bleating of the sacrificial sheep in their pens, the lowing of cattle and the cooing of doves. Men must have been arguing loudly, laughing, trying to get the better of each other, and gazing with contempt on the poor pilgrim who offered no man a profit.

There is an interesting point about this market. There is reason to think that it was the property of Annas, who had been High Priest for many years. Edersheim says that there can be no doubt that this was the place known as " the bazaars of the sons of Annas," and Josephus makes the significant remark that Annas, the son of the Annas of the New Testament, was " a great hoarder-up of money." If this was so, can we not see how Christ's attack was aimed not only at the prestige of the priests but at their pockets and the whole shabby financial system by which they had grown rich? One critic has even suggested that this was one of the main reasons for the arrest of Jesus.

It is, at any rate, certain that in cleansing the Temple Jesus delivered a blow at the vested interests of the aristocratic priesthood. His action was an invitation to all honest men; and the poor, patient multitudes, who were mercilessly squeezed to support one of the most numerous and best-nourished priesthoods in history, gave Him such support in his protest that even the Temple police, who usually corrected the slightest irregularity, did not dare to lay a finger on Him. " And he taught daily in the temple," says St. Luke. " But the chief priests and the scribes and the chief of the people sought to destroy him. And could not find what they might do : for all the people were very attentive to hear him."

So the Jewish authorities who had, before the Passover, already decided to arrest Him, put their heads together and instigated the plot that led to the Cross.

§ 9

In the early morning I have often walked over the
brook Kedron and up the slope of the Mount of Olives to
Bethphage, and over the ridge to Bethany. This is the road
that Jesus and the Twelve would have walked so often during
the last week.

Leaving the Temple, possibly by the Shushan Gate, they
would have crossed the great viaduct over the Kedron Valley
to the Mount of Olives—a roadway on double arches made to
prevent the defilement that might have been caused by a dead
body lying below. It was over this viaduct that the " red
heifer," the sin-offering for the nation, was led to death,
and it was also this way that the scapegoat—surely the most
pitiful symbol of a nation's transgressions—was taken on the
Day of Atonement and sent by relays of men into the wilderness, where he was cast from a rock. The Shushan Gate is
represented to-day by the blocked-up Golden Gate of the
Temple Area. It would have led down to the Garden of
Gethsemane, and then up over the Mount of Olives by
winding white paths, hot and glaring in the sun.

Just before He reached Bethphage, Jesus would look back
and see Jerusalem spread below: the marble mountain of
the Temple with its smoking altar, the brown, turreted walls,
the terraced streets, the flat roofs rising in tiers, the white
porticoes, the sudden flash of the sun from breastplates of
the Roman guard on the ramparts of Antonia, and the
blaze of light from the gold plates that sheeted the sanctuary
and from the gold spikes that rose above it to prevent defilement by birds. The next step, and Jerusalem would be
hidden. The road then went slightly downhill over rocky
ground planted with vineyards and olive trees. Wine-presses
were hewn in the rock, where their ruins can be seen to-day.
A few steps further and the roofs of little mud-brown Bethany
would be in view.

It is an even lovelier walk in the opposite direction, from
Bethany to Jerusalem, because, after the first climb up from
Bethany to the crest of the Mount of Olives, it is downhill

and you have the city in full view all the way. It was while on this path that Jesus " hungered " and approached the barren fig tree.

It seems to me that many commentators are wrong in the way they handle this incident. Even Dr. Edersheim, whose knowledge must induce feelings of the deepest reverence in all who attempt to write about the times of Jesus, seems to assume that Jesus was looking for figs on the fig tree. But He was not. The Passover month is too early for figs. " He found nothing but leaves," says St. Mark, " for it was not the season for figs." How unjust to curse a tree, some critics have said, because it did not produce figs out of season. This shows how difficult it is to comment on the Bible without some knowledge of the Bible country. What Jesus was looking for were not figs but green knobs about as big as an almond, which the Palestinian peasants eat to-day and call *tagsh*. These appear sometimes before the leaves, but always in the budding time, and, after growing to the size of nuts, fall off to make way for the real fruit. Therefore a tree without *tagsh* will have no figs later on. The Gospel accounts, although puzzling to anyone who does not know this, are always meticulously accurate.

Somewhere on the Mount of Olives Christ bade Peter and John go down into the city that lay below them and arrange the Upper Room for the Last Supper. At that time the large area to the south-west of Jerusalem was within the old wall. It was, in fact, the oldest part of Jerusalem, the original city of David, and the excavations which have been made on this ground reveal a mass of terraced steps and streets, house foundations, boundary walls, and one very perfect olive mill with a treading-place for a donkey and a little stable in which the animal was kept. All these remains prove that in the time of Jesus this waste and broken ground was a prosperous district with steep paved streets and houses on each side of them, many of them obviously the homes of wealthy Jews.

Now it seems to me a significant thing, and surely it must have been pointed out before, although I am not aware of it, that if the two disciples entered this part of the city they

would have done so by a gate, long vanished, called the
Water Gate. It received this name because it led straight
down to the Gihon, or the Virgin's Fountain as it is called
to-day, the only stream of living water round Jerusalem. It
would naturally be a gate used by all the water-carriers of
the district. Does this not seem to fit in with Christ's command: " Go ye into the city, and there shall meet you a
man bearing a pitcher of water: follow him." One can
never prove this in argument: it is just one of those prob-
abilities that spring to the mind and afford one a private
delight when reading the Gospels on the spot.

I imagine that the two disciples followed the servant with
the pitcher up the steep hill, ascending paved terraces just like
those in modern David Street, until they came to the house
which one of the strongest and most wonderful traditions in
the history of Christianity has associated with the Last Supper.
It stands to-day just a few paces outside the Zion Gate, and
was known from Roman times onwards as the Cœnaculum.
If this building is what tradition claims it to be, it is the
Mother of all Christian churches. And this tradition is
remarkable. Before the year 400 St. Epiphanius relates
that when Hadrian visited the ruins of Jerusalem in 135
A.D., " the Christians still possessed the little church . . . in
which the Apostles assembled after the Ascension of our
Lord. It stood in the quarter of Zion that was spared when
the city was destroyed."

From that moment onwards a steady tradition has claimed the
buildings that have risen, fallen and risen again on this spot as
those built on the site of the " upper church of the Apostles."
This building was the Upper Chamber of the Gospels in which
the Last Supper was held, and where Jesus appeared to His
followers. It was also the " upper room " of *Acts*, the house
to which St. Peter fled after his deliverance from prison and
the house in which the miracle of Pentecost occurred.

All the early pilgrims to Palestine mention the fine church
that had been built on this site. It was one of the holiest
places in the world. During the sixteenth century a report
was spread that the tomb of David, full of rich treasure, lay
beneath it, and the Franciscans, who had the guardianship,
were driven out by the Moslems. They seized the church

and turned it into a shrine. And it is still a Moslem shrine. It is called Nebi Daoud—the Tomb of David. I have seen it. The Upper Room is of crusading work. No Christian is allowed to kneel in it, and the Moslem guide hurries you through it as swiftly as possible. The ground floor, which is supposed to contain the tomb of David, is absolutely barred to Christians.

What, one wonders, was this house like when Peter and John were led to it by the man with a pitcher?

If it was the house of " Mary, mother of John, whose surname was Mark; where many were gathered together praying " when St. Peter fled to them from prison, we know from *Acts* that it must have been a large place capable of holding a good number of people. We know also that the servant girl who answered the door was called Rhoda. Perhaps the Upper Room of the Last Supper was the flat roof of Mary's house, which would have been covered with an awning, or temporary roof.

If this were so, we must imagine Peter and John ascending to the roof of the house of the Upper Chamber and, finding that everything was prepared, descending again to go and tell the Master.

§ 10

The Jewish Passover was a happy, tumultuous feast. The excitability of the crowds which thronged Jerusalem at this annual birthday of the nation is clearly visible in the Gospel narrative.

During the Roman administration of Judæa, Passover week was the time when the Government, fearing riots and disturbances, marched additional troops into Jerusalem. That was why Pontius Pilate, the Governor, was in Jerusalem at the time of the Crucifixion instead of his usual headquarters at Cæsarea. He had a two-fold duty to perform: he was there to take responsibility for military action, and his permission was necessary for the handing over of the vestments of the High Priest, which were kept under Roman lock and key in a stone room in the Castle of Antonia.

The feast drew enormous crowds to Jerusalem. Jews came

not only from every part of Palestine, but from the great
Jewish quarter of Alexandria, and even from Europe, to slay
the Paschal lamb in the only place where the sacrifice could
be offered: on the altar of the Temple of Herod. Gentiles
from all lands also flocked to Jerusalem out of curiosity,
because it was the great time to visit the city. Gabriel Miro,
in his brilliant piece of fiction *Figures of the Passion of our
Lord*, represents Pilate as the host of a globe-trotting house-
party of rich Romans who had come to observe the strange
habits of the Jews. The book is extraordinarily life-like and
probable.

In order to convince Nero of the importance of the Jewish
nation, Cestius Gallus, Governor of Syria, once counted the
sacrificial lambs during the Passover and the number was
256,500. Allowing for the minimum number of ten persons
for each lamb eaten at the feast, this gives us the enormous
total of 2,565,000. The city was naturally full, and the
pilgrims were also camped round the walls in tents. Jesus,
as we know, stayed at Bethany with His friends, and it is
interesting to learn from the Talmud that among the places
which were specially noted for their hospitality to pilgrims
were that village and its neighbour, Bethphage.

The gathering of such enormous crowds in one place, all
excited, all enjoying the great experience of the year, always
created an inflammable atmosphere in which wrongs and
grievances were easily fired. In fact, it would seem that the
annual pilgrimage, when Jewry was gathered as a nation
round the altar of the Lord, was a time deliberately chosen
by agitators to demonstrate against the hated Gentile rule.
The hideous instability of mind which the Passover mob
shared with all mobs in history is clearly seen in the Gospels
when the people one day cried " Hosannah! " and the next
" Crucify Him! "

The Passover lambs were slain on the afternoon of Nisan
14, the day of the first spring full moon. In order that the
thousands of animals might be slain, skinned, cleaned and
cooked for the table that same evening, the afternoon Temple
sacrifice was put forward an hour and the priests were free
to deal with the wholesale sacrifice of lambs at 1.30 p.m. of
our time.

Thousands of men, each leading a lamb, congested all the roads leading to the Temple. The lamb had to be without blemish, not under eight days old and not over twelve months. Each lamb had to be eaten by a company of no fewer than ten persons and not more than twenty.

The festal crowds were divided into three divisions, and each division was admitted in turn into the Temple. After the admission of a division the great gates were closed while the huge crowd and its animals were marshalled across the enormous Court of the Gentiles to the Court of the Priests. Two rows of bare-foot priests in white robes lined the path to the altar of burnt-offering, one row holding golden, and the other silver, bowls. Each member of the crowd slew his own lamb, and as he did so the nearest priest caught the blood in a bowl and passed it up the line, receiving an empty bowl in return. The priests at the head of the lines spilt the blood in jets at the base of the altar and the red stream ran away by underground channels into the brook Kedron. Trumpet notes rang out over the Temple to mark each sacrifice, and the Levites led the crowds in hymns of praise.

No sooner were the lambs slain than they were hung up on hooks along the Court, or suspended on staves between the shoulders of two men, and flayed. The inside fat was separated and offered with incense on the altar. The fleeces were left behind as the perquisite of the priests. Then the ceremony was repeated with the next division, and so on until hundreds of thousands of lambs had been slain.

After the great slaughter was over the priests washed the blood from the Court, while the crowds went to their homes, their lodgings, and their tents to make ready for the feast. A spit of pomegranate wood was passed through the lamb. Not one bone had to be broken, and the animal had to be roasted in an earthenware oven and carefully watched in order to prevent any part of it touching the oven. If this happened, the part touched had to be cut away and destroyed.

We can imagine how the tremendous activity, the bustle, and the excitement of the afternoon was succeeded by a Sabbath stillness as the sun fell and the pilgrims were busy with the preparation for their feast. The streets would be empty. Each householder would be at home arranging the final details. The smell of roasting meat would rise up over Jerusalem and spread even to the hills around. The last light of the sun would rest for a moment on the white marble of the Temple, touch the golden spikes on the Holy of Holies and vanish; and with darkness the oven fires on the Mount of Olives, where the Passover tents were pitched, would glow like rubies, a prophecy of the camp fires of Titus. Then, loud, imperious, and detached, the Roman trumpets from Antonia would ring across the silence to denote the changing of the guard. . . .

" And in the evening he cometh with the twelve. . . . "

§ 11

We can imagine, as darkness fell and before the large spring moon had lifted itself above the city, how Jesus and the Twelve came down from the Mount of Olives and entered Jerusalem by the Water Gate. They ascended the steep streets to the house of the Upper Room, and were shown up to the flat white roof where an awning, or a temporary roof, rose above them.

The greatest artists in the world have painted their conception of this scene. I suppose Leonardo da Vinci's fresco in Milan is the most famous. But no artist has been able to escape from his own time and show the Last Supper as it must have been in the Upper Chamber of Ophel by the light of the Paschal moon. I remember a Titian, I think in the Escorial, in which the Last Supper is set in a palace, and another, a Tintoretto somewhere in Venice, where the surroundings are those of an Italian inn. The truth is, of course, that the scene was a simple Eastern meal. There would have been a low table with cushions round it in a U-shape, in order that the table could at a point in the Paschal meal be removed without disturbing the guests, and replaced at another point in the meal. In the old days it had been customary to eat the Passover staff in hand and dressed for a journey, symbolic of the flight from Egypt. In the time of Christ the Jews attended the feast in festal garments and ate lounging on a divan in a free position, leaning on the left side, in order to symbolise freedom after bondage.

That Jesus and the Twelve reclined on cushions in this way is proved by the fact that John, who sat next to our Lord, was "leaning on Jesus' bosom." This would have been an ill-mannered and clumsy attitude if table and chairs had been used, but, if you have ever eaten an Eastern meal, you will know that it is quite usual to lean back towards one's neighbour to put a question.

The hush of a moonlit night wrapped itself about the House of the Last Supper. As the full moon rose, the light would have slanted in under the awning in green angles on the white stone. There would have been a lamp burning, a bright spark floating in olive oil, and beyond the stillness of the Upper Room the pinnacles and towers of Jerusalem would be seen lying against the stars like the city of a dream. And Jesus said: "Take eat: this is my body . . . this is my blood of the new testament which is shed for many."

"And when they had sung an hymn they went out into the Mount of Olives."

Is there in all literature a greater feeling of stillness than in this chapter of the Gospels? The last week in the life of Jesus is, so it seems to me, an extraordinary contrast of noise and peace. At one moment the shouting of a crowd comes to us over nineteen centuries, loud, violent and terrible; and at the next a hush has fallen and Christ is walking with the Twelve over the Mount of Olives. There is something awesome in the description of Jesus before the Crucifixion. The evangelists did not strive after any effect. They were interested only in setting down the most important happenings in their lives in a few simple words, yet through the stark economy of their writing shines something beyond the power of words to describe. We get the impression, Dr. Sanday has said, "that there is always a vaster consciousness waiting to break through." Nowhere in the Gospels is this "vaster consciousness" so evident as it is when Jesus Christ moves through hate and treachery and all the baser things and, founding His Church in gentleness and in love, walks in a ghostly calm through moonlight to the Garden of Gethsemane.

N

§ 12

One night, when the full moon burned above Jerusalem, I went down past the Zion Gate and stood at the angle of the Temple wall, looking towards the Garden of Gethsemane. Every limestone path was clear and white on the dark mass of the hill. The thousands of whited sepulchres that lie in the heights and in the hollows gleamed in the moonlight like companies of sheeted ghosts. The lamps that sometimes shine amid the hovels of Siloam were all extinguished, and the whole Mount slept in the green downpour of the moon.

In ancient times the Jews called it the "Mount of three lights," because the altar flames in the Temple lit it up at night, the first light of the sun appeared from its summit, and the olives that grew there made oil for the Temple lamps. To the Christian it suggests only one Light: "Then spake Jesus again unto them saying, I am the light of the world: he that followeth me shall not walk in darkness, but shall have the light of life."

I noticed that low down on the slopes, just above the dark cleft of the brook Kedron, a shadow marked the place where the moonlight was falling through the olive trees in the Garden of Gethsemane. The little garden of the Franciscans looked inexpressibly lonely, a patch of shadow on the bare rocks. The moonlight was so bright that I could see the boundary wall round the trees.

It was on the night of the Passover long ago that our Lord said, "Sit ye here while I go and pray," and, taking Peter, James and John, He went a little way off in the shadow out of the brightness of the moon.

"My soul is exceeding sorrowful," He said, "even unto death; tarry ye here and watch with me."

And He went still deeper into the shadow.

When He came back the three Apostles had fallen asleep:

"Peter," He said. "What, could ye not watch with me one hour? Watch and pray, that ye enter not into temptation: the spirit indeed is willing, but the flesh is weak."

He went into the shadow for a second time and prayed:

" If this cup may not pass away from me, except I drink it, thy will be done."

And when He came back the second time the three were again asleep. Jesus went for a third time into the shadow, but when He came back this last time He looked down on the sleeping men and said:

" Sleep on now and take your rest."

For His hour had come, and He stood waiting in the light.

The eight disciples who had been left near the entrance to the garden had seen lamps mounted on staves swinging against the darkness of the Temple mount. These lanterns descended into the valley of the Kedron and then advanced up the slight hill towards the garden. They recognised the tramp of the Roman soldiers, who wore sandals studded with nails. They heard the excited whispering of the Jews. Although the moon was full, the approaching men came swinging their lights so that they could see into all the caves and dark places.

Judas, after he had slipped away from the Upper Room, had gone to the priests and called for a guard. The priests must have approached Pilate, for at the head of the troops came the *chiliarch* of the Twelfth Legion, the officer commanding the Jerusalem cohort. The soldiers must have first gone to the house of the Last Supper and, finding that Jesus had left, had descended the steep streets of Ophel and crossed the Kedron, taking the same road that Jesus had taken a few hours before.

How else can one explain that strange and vivid incident in the Gospel of St. Mark, the incident of the young man who fled naked? Surely this could be no other than St. Mark himself, a young boy at the time. We can imagine how interested he would have been in the great Rabbi who had come to the Upper Room in his mother's house; how, when he was fast asleep that night, the tramp of the soldiers and the knocking on the door would have awakened him, filling him with curiosity and fear. Slipping a linen cloth about him, he would have crept from the house and followed the bobbing lanterns down the hill. Perhaps his eager young mind was bent on giving an alarm, on telling Jesus that men with swords and staves had been asking for Him; or possibly he was merely filled with the normal curiosity of a boy. His young figure in its linen cloth shadowed Judas and the band, sometimes stepping out of the moonlight as they paused, sometimes running on clinging to the shadows. Unknown to anyone, he would have been watching outside the garden when Judas stepped forward and betrayed Christ. He would have seen and heard everything. He heard Judas say:

" Hail, Master."

He heard Jesus reply:

" Judas, betrayest thou the son of man with a kiss? "

He heard the sudden tumult and saw the flash of steel in the moonlight as Peter struck at Malchus, the servant of the High Priest. He heard Jesus ask:

" Whom seek ye? "

" Jesus of Nazareth," they said.

" I am he."

And when the disciples, except Peter and John, had fled, the young man, leaving his hiding-place, would have followed Jesus and His captors as they went from the garden towards the dark ravine of the Kedron. It was then that the young eavesdropper was noticed by one of the soldiers, and St. Mark says:

" And a certain young man followed with him, having a linen cloth cast about him, over his naked body; and they lay hold on him; but he left the linen cloth and fled naked."

Who would have noticed this triviality during the arrest of Jesus except the man to whom it had happened?

It was perhaps three o'clock in the morning when the guards with their Prisoner arrived at the palace of the High Priest, which stood on the slopes of the southern hill not far from the house of the Last Supper. As the gates were unlocked the Roman legionaries marched away towards their barracks in the Castle of Antonia, leaving Jesus in the hands of the High Priest's men. They passed through an outer court-yard and through a door into an inner court with a gallery round it leading to the main apartments.

On the high hills of Judæa it is always chilly at night in the month of Nisan, and the flames of a charcoal fire glowing in a brazier shone redly on the gallery. The servants who had been awakened, and those who had returned from the Garden of Gethsemane, discussed the arrest as they held their hands out and thrust their faces into the light.

The two disciples who followed the Master had become separated. John, who knew the servants of the house, had pressed his way with the guard into the inner court and, as he stood there among those round the fire, he looked for Peter but could not find him. He went to the locked outer gate and saw him " standing at the door without." He asked the maid-servant to let him in and Peter came silently into the courtyard, where the light of the fire was flickering round the gallery. He was cold, and he moved to the brazier.

The night was fading. The sky began to lose its deep blue, and already the first uneasy stirrings of dawn moved over the Mount of Olives.

In the audience chamber of the palace Jesus was standing before Caiaphas and a few members of the Sanhedrin who had been drawn from their beds to attend the private inquiry. There were false witnesses, spies who had been following the Master in the Temple, whispering with Judas, listening at keyholes. But even these wretches could not agree in infamy. Jesus stood in silence watching His foes.

" Answerest Thou nothing? " cried Caiaphas.

And Jesus held His peace.

Then Caiaphas saw the way to trap Him, and administered the solemn oath:

" I adjure Thee by the living God, that Thou tell us whether Thou be the Christ, the Son of God! "

It was a command that no Jew could disobey:

" Thou hast said," replied Jesus.

Then the High Priest, rising as ordained by the Law whenever blasphemy was uttered, took his priestly garments at the neck and rent inner and outer garment so that they could never be mended. The silence of death was over the room.

" Behold, now ye have heard his blasphemy: What think ye? "

From the circle of faces came the answer:

" He is guilty of death."

Downstairs in the courtyard Peter was warming his hands at the brazier. It was now almost day. It was that grey time, the colour of a dove's wing, when there are no shadows. It was the time the stars die one by one. As Peter bent over the fire, the maid-servant who had let him in and the others who were warming their hands nudged each other and whispered:

" Thou also wast with Jesus of Galilee! "

And Peter drew back and said quickly:

" I know not what thou sayest! "

Uneasily, angrily, he left the fire and moved away to the porch, but there another maid saw him:

" This fellow was also with Jesus of Nazareth," she said.

" I do not know the man," cried Peter.

" Surely thou also art one of them," persisted those round the fire, " for thy speech bewrayeth thee? "

" I know not the man! " he cried angrily a third time.

And immediately the cock crew. It was the only sound in the stillness of the dawn. It came from the gardens on the Mount of Olives. The sharp sound was like a knife in Peter's heart. As he turned in the agony of his self-abasement, his eyes were drawn upward to the gallery where a figure in the white festal garments of the Last Supper was standing, His wrists bound with cord. Our Lord turned and looked down at Peter. And Peter went out in the cold wind that blows before the morning, and saw the colour stealing back into the world and the sky behind the Mount of Olives pulsing with the promise of a new day. And Peter wept.

§ 13

When Pontius Pilate came up to Jerusalem from Cæsarea on official visits it is almost certain that he did not live in the garrison quarters of the Castle of Antonia, but in the magnificent palace of Herod the Great. This palace, after the banishment of Herod's worthless heir, Archelaus, had become the property of the Roman State. In the same way the Roman Governors had at Cæsarea transformed the great Herodian palace fronting the sea into Government House.

Pilate was a privileged person. He was the nominee of Sejanus, the man behind the throne of Tiberius, and he was the husband of a member of the ruling house, Claudia Procula, who is said to have been a grand-daughter of Augustus. It was probably this friendship with the imperial household which enabled him to set aside the rule which forbade Governors to take their wives with them into their provinces. The social life of Pilate was, therefore, not that of an ordinary Governor; and his wife, who had been brought up in the luxury of the Imperial Court, probably enjoyed the privilege of entertaining guests in the huge palaces which were at her disposal in Cæsarea, Jerusalem, and Samaria.

In his chief palace at Jerusalem Herod had indulged his passion for magnificence and his love of building. It was constructed in two colossal marble wings which stood among gardens high above the city. The great hall contained one hundred dining-couches, and the rooms, pavements and colonnades shone with the rarest marbles in the world. The old trees which stand to-day in the gardens of the palace of the Armenian Patriarch are believed to be the descendants of those trees which grew around the fountains and the canals in the pleasure-gardens of Herod. It was probably in this palace that Pilate and his wife Claudia were living when the Sanhedrin arrested our Lord.

Tradition says that Jesus was brought before Pilate in the prætorium of the Castle of Antonia, where the *Via Dolorosa* begins. And this is no doubt so. Pilate would have administered the Roman law in a judgment hall in the garrison buildings, although he and his wife were staying in the neighbouring palace.

When we read with care the four accounts of the Trial of Jesus, certain things are terribly clear and others are shadowy and uncertain. From a word here and a sentence there they challenge our intelligence and compel us to try to fit them together as the archæologist attempts to reconstruct the fragments of an inscription. One of the mysteries is the message which Claudia sent to Pilate early in the morning, begging her husband to save Jesus.

One must imagine that Pilate and his wife talked about Jesus on the night of the Agony in the Garden. Mr. Frank Morison has developed this theory with great plausibility in his remarkable book *Who Moved the Stone?* He believes that Caiaphas, the only man in Jerusalem who could have demanded a sudden interview with the Roman Governor, presented himself at the palace, acquainted Pilate with the intentions of the Sanhedrin, and asked him if he would be willing to try the case early in the morning in order that the execution might be effected before the Sabbath, which began at sunset on the day following.

" Does anyone with personal knowledge of the immemorial characteristics of women suppose for a moment that an incident like this would pass without Claudia wanting to know something about it? " asked Mr. Morison.

There is another reason, confirmed by one word in the Gospel of St. John, why Pilate and Claudia must have discussed Jesus on the night before the Crucifixion. In the Greek Testament the word used by St. John to describe the officer who came with the " band " to arrest our Lord is *chiliarch*. Now, a *chiliarch* is the Greek equivalent to the *tribunus militum*, the commander of a cohort, and unless St. John uses the term in a general sense it means that Annas and Caiaphas were so afraid of the power of Christ, fearing either that He might escape by miraculous means or that the crowds would defend Him, that they persuaded the commanding officer in Jerusalem to go in person with his men to the Mount of Olives. If that really did happen, it opens up an interesting train of thought.

The *chiliarch*, or tribune, of the cohort of the Twelfth Legion which garrisoned Jerusalem at that time was the only resident Roman of Pilate's class in the city. He was, in fact, Pilate's deputy. He must have been well known to both Pilate and Claudia. It is reasonable to suppose that he would have discussed the plot of the Sanhedrin with the Governor and his wife and would have told them not only of the Triumphal Entry and the Cleansing of the Temple, but many other things concerning the Man who " went about doing good."

It is useless but fascinating to speculate what effect this may have had on the mind of the woman who tried to save the life of Jesus. She may already have heard of Him. Stories from Galilee may have come to her ears, perhaps she had known some who believed in His Divinity. Perhaps she herself believed. But whatever occurred on that night in the palace of Herod, the attitude of Pilate on the day following, and the message which Claudia sent post-haste to the prætorium, cause us to think that in the lonely halls of Herod's palace Pilate and his wife talked together of Jesus of Nazareth. We do know that Claudia dreamed of Him and, awakening, found to her alarm that Pilate had already left for the prætorium. She called for a messenger and wrote: " Have thou nothing to do with that just Man."

And Pilate read it as he sat on the judgment seat.

§ 14

" Crucify Him! "

" Why? " asked Pilate. " What evil hath He done? I have found no cause of death in Him."

Pilate looked at the violent crowd below him, a crowd of fanatics who would not enter the prætorium in case they would contract ceremonial defilement; and he loathed them. He had seen the same crowds before and had worked off his disgust by ordering his guards to charge. He hated their capacity for intrigue, their casuistry, their internal hatreds, their sectarian feuds, and their genius for shifting on to others the responsibility for their deeds, as they were now attempting to do.

He knew that Jesus Christ was innocent of the crime they had invented. He saw how subtly the priests had twisted it into a political offence. Our Lord's silence startled him.

" Answerest Thou nothing? " he had asked in amazement. " Behold how many things they witness against Thee."

" And He answered him to never a word; insomuch that the Governor marvelled greatly." Who was this Man who could be so calm in the face of death?

Pilate, whose record was that of a stubborn, arrogant, and impatient tyrant, the man who had marched the legionary standards into Jerusalem, who had appropriated the Corban, who had trampled on the most tender susceptibilities of the people and had lashed crowds who came to beg for mercy, was now, St. John tells us, moved by a strange awe.

He stood on the steps of the prætorium, under the marble colonnade, and faced those who stood below; then, turning, he entered the judgment hall.

Jesus was standing beyond the portico, in the shade of the hall. A guard of the Twelfth Legion stood leaning on its spears. Jesus was robed in the rich mantle which Antipas had cast on Him in jest. Pilate saw it with a sense of frustration. Eagerly he had caught at the word " Galilean " and had sent Him to Antipas in the belief that the Tetrarch of Galilee would have defended one of His own subjects against the wrath of the Judæans. But that ruse had failed. Jesus had been sent back from the Asmonæan Palace in the cast-off garment of a prince. The crafty Herod, " that fox," was far too sly to involve himself in any charge of *majestas*. And Pilate's second attempt had also failed. He had offered to scourge Jesus and let Him go, but the mob had refused the offer with shouts of rage. In the silence of the hall he asked:

" Art Thou the King of the Jews? "

The formality of the trial, the attitude of judge to prisoner, had broken down. The awe and the curiosity which this silent Man created stirred uneasily in Pilate's mind.

" My kingdom is not of this world," said Christ to Pilate.

" Art Thou a king, then? " asked Pilate.

" To this end was I born, and for this cause came I into the world, that I should bear witness unto the truth. Everyone that is of the truth heareth My voice."

Pilate looked into the eyes of Christ and expressed in three words the hunger of the pagan world:

" What is truth? "

Then Pilate, turning, went towards the crowd in the sunlight beyond the portico. He stood there, a white figure, on the steps. When the shouting had died down, he said:

" I find in Him no fault at all."

The hatred of the crowd beat up against him like fire. He looked into faces twisted with rage. Then a third attempt to appease them came into his mind. It was his duty to

release a Passover prisoner. He offered them the choice
between Jesus of Nazareth and Barabbas, a zealot who had
committed murder, never doubting that they would prefer
Jesus.

"But the chief priests moved the people that he should
rather release Barabbas unto them."

"What will ye then that I shall do unto Him whom ye
call the King of the Jews?" asked Pilate.

It was an ironic request. Up to that moment he had no
intention of taking the advice of the ugly crowd.

"Crucify Him!" they shouted.

Pilate turned away and gave orders for the scourging—
"the intermediate death." The punishment was either delivered by lictors with thin elm rods, or by soldiers with the
horrible *flagellum*, a short whip whose leather thongs were
weighted with rough fragments of metal. Pilate had no lictors.

In a short while the waiting crowds saw two figures on the
steps beneath the portico. Christ stood there, a crown of
thorns on His head and over His bleeding shoulders a red
military cloak. Beside Him stood Pilate:

"Ecce homo . . . behold the Man," said Pilate.

There was no contempt in his voice. They were the
words of a weak but fair-minded man who hoped that
the piteous spectacle of the scourged Christ would soften the
savage hearts of His enemies. "Ecce Homo!" The sight
is one that has roused the pity and the love of the Christian
world; but to the Jews who fought and screamed that morning in Jerusalem it meant nothing. The cries "Crucify
Him!" rose up louder than ever. The suffering Christ was
led away into the darkness of the prætorium and Pilate faced
the crowd alone:

"Take *ye* Him and crucify Him!" he cried, "for I find
no fault in Him!"

Once again he wasted his bitter irony on them. He knew
how they were trying to burden him with the penalty of
their hate, and he told them to do the impossible. Only he
could crucify, and in those words he refused. Once again
the awe which the silent, suffering Christ had awakened in
his heart returned and, leaving the Jews shouting for the
blood of Christ, he went again into the prætorium, and once

again judge and Prisoner spoke together, and it was the judge who was frightened. Pilate looked into the suffering eyes beneath the crown of thorns:

" Whence art Thou? " he asked.

He seemed to be thinking: " I know that this is no ordinary man. There is something about Him that I do not understand. He is outside my experience of men. It is my duty to save Him from the howling savages outside. Who is He? What is His mystery? "

" Whence art Thou? " he asked.

The only answer was a glance from the eyes of the Lonely Man:

" Speakest Thou not unto me? " pleaded Pilate. " Knowest Thou not that I have power to crucify Thee, and—have power to release Thee? "

In the silence of the judgment hall, with the guard standing round, Jesus spoke to Pilate at last:

" Thou couldst have no power at all against Me, except it were given thee from above: therefore he that delivered Me unto thee hath the greater sin."

Pilate looked at Christ. He turned again to the portico and stood on the steps facing the Jews. " Pilate sought to release Him," says St. John. Then a new sound came from the crowd. No longer did they shriek " Crucify Him! " They threatened Pilate.

" If thou let this Man go, thou art not Cæsar's friend!

" Whosoever maketh himself a king speaketh against Cæsar! "

Then for the first time Pilate knew that the Jews had beaten him. He was not a great enough man to stand up against blackmail. Nearly a hundred years before, Cicero, defending Flaccus against a charge of injustice to the Jews, had been forced to lower his voice in the Forum in case the Jews rioted. " You know how numerous these gentry are," he had said, " how they cling together and what pressure they can bring to bear in assemblies. I shall lower my voice when pleading, speaking just loud enough that the judges can hear me."

Perhaps Pilate, when he was threatened with disloyalty to the Emperor, remembered the words of Cicero. Perhaps

also he remembered Strabo's comment on the influence of
the Alexandrian Jews in his time: "These Jews," said
Strabo, "have penetrated in every country, and it would be
hard to find anywhere in the whole world a single place that
has not had to put up with this race, and in which it did
not obtain the mastery."

Now a crowd, headed by the rulers and chief men of the
Jewish nation, was threatening Pilate. It was no trivial
taunt. Pilate did not under-estimate the underground influence of the Jews, and there was probably much in his record
that he wished to hide. His resistance collapsed, broken
down by self-interest and fear.

He ascended the judgment seat, which was set on the
pavement.

"Behold your King!" he said.

Jesus stood before them with blood on His brow and the
stripes of the *flagellum* staining His body.

"Shall I crucify your King?" asked Pilate.

It was his last futile plea. The sight of Jesus must have
wrung it from him.

"We have no king but Cæsar!" came the hypocritical cry
from Annas and Caiaphas and the chief men. They had
twisted a charge of blasphemy into one of politics and, having
failed to win their point, they had probed round to the self-
interest of the judge and had turned events so that the judge
now stood in the dock with the Prisoner.

Pilate stands condemned before history for his weakness.
He could have saved Jesus. But the accusers were too
cunning for him and he gave way. He called for a bowl of
water and, before them all, he washed his hands so that his
action could be seen even if his words were not heard in the
tumult of the crowd:

"I am innocent of the blood of this just Person: see ye
to it."

"Then answered all the people and said, His blood be on
us and on our children."

Pilate solemnly pronounced the horrible words:

"Ibis ad crucem."

"Then the soldiers of the Governor took Jesus into the
common hall."

§ 15

Four forms of capital punishment were recognised by the Jews: stoning, burning, beheading, and strangling. Stoning was the most usual. The victim was flung from a high place and, if still alive, was stoned until dead. The Jews never crucified living persons. There is evidence, however, that they crucified the corpses of blasphemers and idolators. The men were exhibited with their faces to the people, women with their faces to the cross, or " tree."

Death by crucifixion was originally an Eastern punishment. It was practised by the Persians, the Egyptians, and the Phœnicians. With them also it was the custom to crucify dead bodies as a mark of contempt, as Polycrates was crucified after suffering a death too terrible for Herodotus to describe.

It is believed that the Romans adopted crucifixion from the Carthaginians, who were among the most cruel of all the ancient peoples. When Pompey put down the revolt under Spartacus, six thousand prisoners were crucified and hanged along the Via Appia. It was a death from which Roman citizens were exempt, although rare instances are recorded in Sicily and Spain in which Romans were condemned to the cross. Cicero said that no word was too terrible to describe a man who had condemned a Roman citizen to such an end. Crucifixion was, therefore, a punishment reserved for slaves and for provincial malefactors.

The terrible punishment became more frequent as the slave population increased under the later Empire, and the crosses that stood outside the city were a perpetual warning to those slaves who contemplated revolt. In the provinces of the Roman Empire crucifixion could be inflicted on those guilty of murder, brigandage, piracy, revolt or conspiracy. Judæa was familiar with the sight of the cross before and after the time of our Lord. Varrus, Prefect of Syria, crucified two thousand rioters after the death of Herod the Great, and the obstinacy of the Jewish nationalists, whose heroism reached a climax with the Maccabees, was often paid for on the cross.

When Titus besieged Jerusalem, the hills all round the city were covered with a forest of crosses. Josephus tells us that the soldiers became weary of inventing new tortures and the crucifixions were stopped from lack of wood, which Titus needed for his siege engines. It was on this occasion, in 70 A.D., that every tree on the Mount of Olives was hewn down to make crosses and assault-ladders. Later, when the Jews opposed Hadrian, the Emperor authorised five hundred crucifixions a day.

There were three kinds of crosses: the *crux decussata* shaped like an X, also called the *crux Andreana*, because it was on this form of cross that St. Andrew was crucified at Patræ; the *crux commissa*, or St. Anthony's Cross, which was shaped like the letter T; and the *crux immissa* of Christian tradition, which had a head-piece projecting above the cross-bar.

Half-way up the upright wood of the cross was a slight projection known as the *sedile*, or seat, or as the *cornu*, or horn. This took part of the victim's weight, which would otherwise have been too great to have depended entirely on the out-stretched hands. It is not known whether there was a foot-rest. Sometimes, it appears, the victim's feet were nailed to the cross, at others it seems they were merely bound with cords. Death was always a lingering doom. The victim was left to sob the days away, exposed to the sun, torn by pain, hunger, and thirst, until his executioners, becoming weary of his agony, despatched him with the *crurifragium*, or the breaking of the legs.

Crucifixions were always executed outside city gates and in prominent places near high roads in order that publicity might be given to the agony of the condemned and to the crime for which he had been sentenced. It was quite usual to leave the main upright of the cross in position on a recog-nised place of execution and the only other portion necessary, the cross-beam, was carried by the victim on his shoulders to the place of death. Artists are wrong in picturing our Lord bowed beneath the weight of the entire cross.

Most modern artists err also in giving too great a height to the cross. It was considered sufficient if the victim's feet just cleared the ground. If the cross on which our Lord suffered had been as high as most artists imagine, it would not have been possible for the soldier to have offered the sponge of vinegar on a short reed.

In Jerusalem a society of charitable women provided a merciful drug for those about to be crucified. It was administered just before the victim, stretched on the ground, was nailed to the cross-beam. The inspiration for this act of compassion was the ordinance in *Proverbs*, chapter thirty-one, verse six: " Give strong drink unto him that is ready to perish."

It is believed that the potion offered by these women was a mixture of wine and drugs, including frankincense, laudanum, myrrh, resin, saffron and mastich. This is " the wine mingled with myrrh " mentioned by St. Mark. It was offered to Jesus before the Crucifixion, but " he received it not."

In Judæa the usual practice of crucifixion was modified in deference to the Jewish law, which forbade a victim to hang on the cross all night. The bodies had, therefore, to be taken down before evening in order that the ground might not suffer pollution, because everyone who suffered death on " the tree " was, according to *Deuteronomy*, accursed. This explains the haste in which Jesus was condemned and executed, the early trial before Pilate, and the breaking of the thieves' legs in the early afternoon. Additional urgency was felt on this occasion because at six p.m. on the evening of the Crucifixion the Sabbath of Paschal week began.

The most shameful symbol of the ancient world has become the sacred emblem of the Christian Faith. In the days of the early Church the first Christians defended the cross from the sneers of the pagan by pointing out its universal presence in Nature and in everyday life: the wings of a flying bird, the branches of trees, the projecting oars of galleys, the ship's mast and yard, the yoke of a plough, the handle of a spade, the nose and eyebrows of the human face, and so on.

" If any man will come after me, let him deny himself and take up his cross and follow me."

With these words the cross took on a new and glorious meaning. The symbol of Death became the symbol of Life.

The *Via Dolorosa* was mercifully short—scarcely a thousand paces. It lay from the Prætorium to the Gate Genath. Out-

side this gate, and a few yards from the city wall beside the
main road into Jerusalem from the north, stood a place called
Golgotha, the Place of a Skull.   There is nothing in any of
the four Gospels to suggest that Golgotha was a hill, but it
has been assumed that it must have been so.   The first person
to call it a hill was the Bordeaux Pilgrim, who visited Jerusalem in 333 A.D., when the Church of the Holy Sepulchre was
being built.   He mentioned " the little hill of Golgotha
(*monticulus Golgotha*) where the Lord was crucified."

For hundreds of years after Latin writers continued to refer
to Golgotha as " the rock of the cross " or " the rock of
Golgotha," and it was not until the sixth century that again
the idea of elevation was associated with it, and we read of
" Mount Calvary."   By this time, of course, the original
elevation had long been disguised by architects.

Those who thronged the streets near the Prætorium would
have seen the terrible, but familiar, procession of death.   A
centurion in charge of a half maniple of the Twelfth Legion
came first, riding on horseback and clearing a path through
the narrow streets.   Behind him walked a legionary bearing a
notice board on a pole.   Written in red on a background of
white gypsum was a brief account of the crimes committed
by those about to die.

Jesus followed, bearing His cross-beam, clothed no longer
in the scarlet gown of the mockery but, as St. Matthew tells
us, in his own raiment.   There is an old tradition that He
wore a black robe girded at the waist with a leather belt and
that under it was the rich vestment given to Him in derision
by Herod.   He did not wear the crown of thorns, which was
carried by one of the executioners in order that He might be
crowned again on the cross.   Worn out with suffering and with
emotion, our Lord was unable to keep pace with the procession, and it seems that in the pressing into service of Simon,
the Cyrenian, we may detect a touch of kindness on the part
of the centurion, Longinus, who was soon to testify to the
Divinity of his Prisoner and to embrace the Christian faith.

The two thieves followed, bearing the cross-beams;   and
behind them, marching six to the rank, came the remainder
of the half maniple, spear on shoulder.   The Sanhedrists,
who wished no doubt to enjoy their triumph, followed at the

end of the procession, but, when they came to the Gate Genath, kicked their white mules into a canter and went on ahead to Golgotha.

In the sunlight of a spring morning, when the swifts were flying above the walls of Jerusalem as they do to this day in the month of Nisan, three crosses were set up outside the city gate. Those who were " looking on afar off " covered their eyes and stood with breaking hearts. And the hours wore on. The soldiers beneath the Cross shook dice in a helmet for the seamless coat. They lay down on Golgotha in the heat of the day to eat bread and cheese and to drink their sour wine. They heard the Divine words of compassion break from the lips of the Lonely Man :

" Father, forgive them; for they know not what they do."

At three o'clock in the afternoon the Sanhedrists went to Pilate to demand the *crurifragium* in order that the bodies might not hang on the cross until the evening, which also was—how little they knew it—the beginning of a new day. And the soldiers hastened the death of the two thieves, " but when they came to Jesus, and saw that he was dead already, they brake not his legs."

.   .   .   .

The night before I left Jerusalem I went out into the streets of the old city. It was a lovely night and the moon was rising. Behind the Damascus Gate a flight of steps goes up to the city wall. Mounting the ramparts, I walked in the direction of Herod's Gate along the narrow path made for the bowmen of the Middle Ages.

The moon rose, steeping the city in a fall of green light. A breathless silence lay over Jerusalem. Each dome, tower and minaret was clearly etched against the sky; each tree stood in its own small pool of moonlight. Sometimes the sentry walk descended by steps to a lower level and mounted again; sometimes I entered guard houses set at intervals on the wall,

small stone chambers through whose bow-slits I saw a narrow
vision of the moonlit roads beyond the city.   Crossing Herod's
Gate, I came at length to the corner tower and, turning to
the south, walked along the east wall that overlooks the
Mount of Olives.

The moon hung above the Mount, touching the ridge with
a gold haze, washing every white track in light, painting each
olive tree in shadow against the rocks.   How hushed it was
in the light of the moon.   Not a footstep rang in the streets
below me; no one moved in the silence beyond the wall.
Above the black shadow of the Kedron Valley I could see
the moonlight silvering the trees in the Garden of Gethsemane. . . .

Upon the third day, early in the morning, Mary Magdalene
hastened to the Tomb, and when she saw that it was empty
sorrow filled her heart, so that, St. John tells us, she wept.
As she turned to go, Someone stood before her, and she heard
a Voice asking:

" Woman, why weepest thou? whom seekest thou? "

" Sir, if thou have borne him hence," she begged, " tell me
where thou hast laid him, and I will take him away."

" Mary."

" Master! "

Jesus instantly exhibited the strange difference that is
noticeable in all his subsequent contact with the Apostles:

" Touch me not," He said gently, " for I am not yet ascended
to my Father."

One imagines that Mary in her joy had flung herself at the
feet of Christ and had tried to touch Him.

" Go to my brethren," He commanded, " and say unto
them I ascend unto my Father, and your Father; and to my
God and your God."

In the greyness of the morning the woman ran back with the
message that Christ had Risen.

BIBLIOGRAPHY

Arendzen, Dr. J. P. *Men and Manners in the Days of Christ.* (Sheed and Ward, 1928.)

Bentwich, Norman. *A Wanderer in the Promised Land.* (Soncino Press, 1932.)

„ „ *England in Palestine.* (Kegan Paul, 1932.)

„ „ *Palestine.* (Benn's "Modern World" Series, 1934.)

Besant, Walter, and E. H. Palmer. *Jerusalem.* (Chatto and Windus.)

Bolitho, Hector. *Beside Galilee.* (Cobden-Sanderson, 1933.)

Bridgeman, Charles Thorley. *Jerusalem at Worship.* (Jerusalem, 1932.)

Burckhardt, John Lewis. *Travels in Syria and the Holy Land.* (John Murray, 1822.)

Clarke, Dr. W. K. Lowther. *New Testament Problems.* (S.P.C.K., 1929.)

Combes, Louis de. *The Finding of the Cross.* (Kegan Paul, 1907.)

Conder, C. R. *Heth and Moab.* (Richard Bentley, 1883.)

Crowfoot and Baldensperger. *From Cedar to Hyssop.* (The Sheldon Press, 1932.)

Crusades, Chronicles of the. (Bohn Library, 1843.)

Deissmann, Adolf. *Light from the Ancient East.* (Hodder and Stoughton, 1910.)

Didon, Rev. Father. *Jesus Christ.* (Kegan Paul, 1895.)

Dobson, Rev. C. C. *The Empty Tomb and the Risen Lord.* (Martin and Parnham.)

Dollinger, Dr. John, J.I. *The First Age of Christianity and the Church.* (Gibbings and Co., 1906.)

„ „ *The Gentile and the Jew.* (Gibbings and Co., 1906.)

Duckworth, H. T. F. *The Church of the Holy Sepulchre.* (Hodder and Stoughton, 1922.)

Edersheim, Rev. Dr. *Jewish Social Life in the Days of Christ.* (R.T.C., 1876.)

„ „ *The Temple and its Services.* (R.T.C., 1874.)

„ „ *The Life and Times of Jesus the Messiah.* (Longmans, Green and Co., 1891.)

Emmerich, Anne Catherine. *The Dolorous Passion of Our Lord, Jesus Christ.* (Burns, Oates and Washbourne, Ltd.)

Farrar, Dr. F. W. *The Herods.* (Service and Paton, 1898.)

Forder, A. *Petra, Perea, Phœnicia.* (Marshall Bros., 1923.)

Fosdick, Dr. Henry Emerson. *A Pilgrimage to Palestine.* (Student Christian Movement, 1928.)

Glover, T. R. *The World of the New Testament.* (Cambridge, 1933.)

Goodrich-Freer, A. *Things Seen in Palestine.* (Seeley Service, 1927.)

Gore, Bishop Charles. *Belief in God* (John Murray, 1921.)

„ „ „ *Belief in Christ.* (John Murray, 1922.)

Hanauer, Rev. J. E. *Walks In and Around Jerusalem.* (London Society for Promoting Christianity amongst the Jews, 1926.)

Hastings, Dr. James. *Dictionary of the Bible.* (T. and T. Clark, 1905.)

„ „ *Dictionary of Christ and the Gospels.* (T. and T. Clark, 1906.)

Israel, The Legacy of. (Clarendon Press, Oxford, 1928.)

Jarvis, Major C. S. *Yesterday and To-day in Sinai.* (Blackwood and Sons, 1933.)

Jeffery, George. *The Holy Sepulchre.* (Cambridge University Press, 1919.)

Josephus, *Antiquities.*

„ *Wars of the Jews.*

Keim, Dr. Theodor. *The History of Jesus of Nazara.* (Williams and Norgate, 1876.)

Lake, Kirsopp. *The Historical Evidence for the Resurrection of Jesus Christ.* (Williams and Norgate, 1907.)

Latham, Rev. Henry. *Pastor Pastorum.* (Deighton, Bell and Co., 1894.)

„ „ *The Risen Master.* (Deighton, Bell and Co., 1901.)

Malden, Rev. R. H. *Problems of the New Testament To-Day.* (University Press, Oxford, 1923.)

Masterman, Ernest W. Gurney. *Studies in Galilee.* (University Press, Chicago, 1909.)

Moffatt, Dr. James. *The Historical New Testament.* (T. and T. Clark, 1901.)

„ „ *Introduction to the Literature of the New Testament.* (T. and T. Clark, 1920.)

„ „ *A New Translation of the Bible.* (Hodder and Stoughton.)

Morison, Frank. *Who Moved the Stone?* (Faber and Faber, 1930.)

Neil, James. *Palestine Explored.* (James Nisbet, 1907.)

Palestine, Early Travels in. (Bohn Library, 1848.)

Petrie, Sir W. M. Flinders. *The Growth of the Gospels.* (John Murray, 1911.)

„ „ *Egypt and Israel.* (S.P.C.K., 1912.)

„ „ *The Status of the Jews in Egypt.* (Allen and Unwin, 1912.)

Ramsay, Professor W. M. *Was Christ Born at Bethlehem?* (Hodder and Stoughton, 1898.)

„ „ *The Church in the Roman Empire before A.D. 170.* (Hodder and Stoughton 1893.)

„ „ *Luke the Physician and other Studies.* (Hodder and Stoughton, 1908.)

Sanday, Dr. W.   *The Authorship and Historical Character of the Fourth Gospel.*   (Macmillan, 1872.)
,,   ,,   *Sacred Sites of the Gospels.*   (Clarendon Press, 1903.)
,,   ,,   *Outlines of the Life of Christ.*   (T. and T. Clark, 1906.)
,,   ,,   *The Life of Christ in Recent Research.*   (Clarendon Press, 1907.)
Schofield, A. T.   *The Journeys of Jesus Christ.*   (University Press, Oxford, 1913.)
Schweitzer, Albert.   *The Quest of the Historical Jesus.*   (A. and C. Black, 1910.)
Smith, Dr. George Adam.   *Jerusalem,* 2 vols.   (Hodder and Stoughton, 1908.)
,,   ,,   ,,   *The Historical Geography of the Holy Land.*   (Hodder and Stoughton.)
Stanley, Dr. Arthur Penrhyn.   *Lectures on the History of the Jewish Church.*   (John Murray, 1863.)
,,   ,,   ,,   *Sinai and Palestine.*   (Murray, 1864.)
Stanton, Dr. Henry Vincent.   *The Gospels as Historical Documents.*   (Cambridge, 1903.)
Stapfer, Dr. Edmond.   *Palestine in the Time of Christ.*   (Hodder and Stoughton, 1886.)
Swete, Dr. Henry Barclay.   *The Appearances of Our Lord after the Passion.*   (Macmillan, 1922.)
Thomson, Dr. W. M.   *The Land and the Book.*   (Nelson and Sons, 1913.)
Torrey, Charles Cutler.   *The Four Gospels.*   (Hodder and Stoughton, 1934.)
Tristram, H. B.   *The Land of Moab.*   (John Murray, 1873.)
Warren, Charles.   *Underground Jerusalem.*   (Richard Bentley, 1876.)
Warschauer, J.   *The Historical Life of Christ.*   (T. Fisher Unwin, 1927.)
Watson, Sir C. M.   *Golgotha and the Holy Sepulchre.*   (Palestine Exploration Fund, 1906.)

GUIDE BOOKS

The Handbook of Palestine and Trans-Jordan, by Harry Charles Luke and Edward Keith-Roach.   (Macmillan, 1930.)
Guide to the Holy Land, by Father Barnabas Meistermann.   (Burns, Oates and Washbourne, Ltd., 1923.)
Baedeker's Palestine and Syria.   (Out of date but indispensable.)
La Palestine, par les Professeurs de Notre-Dame de France à Jerusalem.   (Maison de la Bonne Presse, Paris, 1932.)

INDEX

INDEX OF SCRIPTURE REFERENCES
Compiled by Mr. G. Vanner Rowe.